# It's (not) shite being Scottish

DUNCAN SPENCE

Copyright © Duncan Spence 2022

All rights reserved. No part of this publication may be reproduced, distributed, stored, or transmitted in any form or by any means, including recording, photocopying, or other electronic or mechanical methods, without the prior written permission of the author, except in the case of brief quotations embodied in critical reviews and certain other non-commercial uses permitted by copyright law.

"Cancer was the best thing that ever happened to me."

"Those should be the first words of your book ..."

"... there are already far too many books about living with cancer, it has already become a genre."

"But yours will not be about cancer."

This book is dedicated to the memory of
Eleanor Anne Duncan, née Spence,
14th August 1931 – 23rd April 2016.

# CONTENTS

**Preface** ..................................................................................1

**2014 prologue** ......................................................................11
   Ben Alder .............................................................................13

**2015 remembering** .............................................................21
   Ben Chonzie .........................................................................23
   Atholl to Deeside and back ..................................................27
   Beinn a' Ghlo ........................................................................35
   Glas Tulachain .....................................................................39
   Glen Lyon Horseshoe ..........................................................43
   Bynack More ........................................................................49
   Sutherland ............................................................................53
   Lochnagar ............................................................................71
   The Ben Lawers Squiggle ....................................................75
   Meall nan Tarmachan ..........................................................81

**2016 learning** ......................................................................89
   Ben Vorlich Loch Earn .........................................................91
   Meall Glas ............................................................................95
   Gleann Calliche .................................................................101
   Glen Clova .........................................................................107
   Balquhidder .......................................................................115
   Creag Meagaidh ................................................................121
   Mullardoch and Strathfarrar ...............................................125
   Schiehallion .......................................................................133
   Stob Binnein ......................................................................137
   Derry Cairngorms ..............................................................141
   Buachaille Etive Mor .........................................................147
   Ben More Dochart .............................................................151
   Ben Avon ...........................................................................153

**2017 ignorance** .................................................................. 159
    Meall Ghaordie .................................................................. 161
    Sgiath Chuil ....................................................................... 163
    Glen Shee ........................................................................... 169
    Ben Dorian ......................................................................... 175
    The first Geal Charn ........................................................ 179
    Stùc a' Chroin .................................................................... 185
    Glen Lyon .......................................................................... 187
    The Great Moss ................................................................ 189
    Glen Shiel .......................................................................... 197
    The Mounth ...................................................................... 203
    Bidean nam Bian .............................................................. 209
    Loch Treig ......................................................................... 215
    Bare Mountains ................................................................ 221
    Exposure ............................................................................ 227
    A tale of midges and tourists .......................................... 231
    High Laggans ................................................................... 235
    Killing Fields ..................................................................... 245
    The Buddha of Braeriach ................................................ 253
    Ben Cruachan ................................................................... 259
    Ben Challum ..................................................................... 263
    Mount Keen ...................................................................... 269
    An Socach ......................................................................... 273
    Beinn an Dothaidh ........................................................... 281
    The Bochel: New Year and the magic between-us ...... 285

**Epilogue** ............................................................................... 291

**Bibliography** ........................................................................ 299

# Preface

In March 2020 the world changed, never to be the same again.

At the particular moment when the population of Scotland was called upon to return home and to stay put until further notice, my wife and I were parked up in our little campervan (not a motorhome) at a place called Corriechoille, which lies at the end of the back road out of Spean Bridge, on the south of the River Spean, with the Nevis Ranges dominating the skyline. The previous day we had taken a walk south from here up the track through forest, past a wooden sculpture known as the Wee Minister, now engulfed by trees, upwards steeply past access paths to the Grey Corries Range and onto the open moor in the direction of *Lairig Leacach*.

Our plan was to get to the bothy at the base of **Stob Ban** and to find out if I were fit enough to get back out into the mountains again after a prolonged period of medical intervention. There was an intense perishing wind against us all the way; it was exhilarating, the muscles in my legs were working well. We stopped for a snack not far from the summit of the pass, with a sublime view of **Stob Ban** baked solid with ice, then decided to return to the cosiness of the campervan. After all, we had not started our walk until nearly lunchtime. The magnificence of the mountain, clothed thick in deep frozen snow, illuminated by early spring sunshine tempted me intensely. I had not seriously expected to climb it today, although I did have spikes with me; in these conditions at the start of the year, it would have been wise to take along an experienced companion in any case. Although my wife enjoys long walks, she does not climb mountains. The walk to this point had nevertheless shown us both that there was strength again in my legs and that it was set to become an excellent season in the mountains.

Back at the van we heard the announcement on the radio that from the next day, a strict lockdown would be in force, that there would not be any *season in the mountains* for anybody who had none in their back garden. A car arrived and parked next to us. A man got out and we struck up a conversation. He said that he had decided to come to live in his house in Lochaber rather than stay at home near Cambridge, because he could carry on with his work online, while having all this in his back garden, within his permitted zone of daily exercise. He indicated with a sweep of his arm, the shimmering snows of the Grey Corries and Aonachs, miles of undulating forest from here to *An Gearasdan*, the Garrison town, also known as Fort William, nestling beneath the highest mountain in the land. He pulled out a very expensive, old school mountain bike

1

from the boot of his car, declared that he knew nothing about it when I tried to engage him in nerdy bike talk, that he had been given it by his brother-in-law who did not need it anymore, then cranked towards the forest on the low ground to the west. He had no idea at all that he was sitting on over five grand's worth of bike.

As we drove back along the back road to Spean Bridge, angry young men in white vans gestured aggressively, curtains twitched and no expertise in lipreading was necessary to understand that it was us in our campervan who were the greatest danger to the locals, that we should fuck off back home forthwith. Which was in fact what we were doing in response to the First Minister's request; despite having provisions in the van for at least another week, extra petrol in a jerrycan and intimate knowledge of every nook and cranny, every back road and hidden track in the central and northern highlands. We decided to take responsibility by returning home, which because we only have one house, meant a journey from this intense beauty and these mountains to the Howe of Fife, with its own secret beauties, little hills and surrounding long wide beaches.

For the previous months I had been working on converting my blog about climbing mountains into a book and I was getting along quite nicely. But something about the Covid pandemic immediately blocked the writer in me. For a while I followed the news avidly and learned all there was to know about viruses, viral load, and pandemics, thinking this might clear space in my head. Meanwhile I embarked upon a task I had been putting off for a long time; clearing out our rat-infested back garden and creating a space where we could sit in the sun and enjoy growing things. At the end of the first lockdown in July 2020, the garden looked much better; I continued climbing mountains and blogging about it, but my motivation to write the book had changed. There was something about the voice of what I had already written that did not chime well with the changed circumstances of the world.

My working outline divided the book into eight larger sections, one for each year of my adventures from 2014 until 2021, within which there was a chapter for each visit I made to the mountains. The names of each of the larger sections were supposed to represent the general tone and character of the year in question: *2014 prologue, 2015 remembering, 2016 learning, 2017 ignorance, 2018 deterioration, 2019 determination, 2020 acceptance* and *2021 epilogue*. There was an implicit arched structure to this division; that it was uphill to the end of *2017 ignorance*, and then downhill from *2018 deterioration*.

At the end of 2020, on the same day that Donald Trump's expulsion from the White House was officially decided, I climbed the most westerly pair of the Mamores in sublime autumn sunshine, gazing over shimmering squiggly coastlines backed by enormous mountains, with my friend Martyn, his friend Gwynneth and their dogs Coll and Poppy. This took my total to an impressively large and nicely round number, so I decided to call it a day. About two weeks previously I had achieved a personal ambition when I reached the summit of ***Sgùrr Mhor*** in the Fannaichs, the last of the top fifty, all those summits above 1100 metres or about 3609 feet; even if I were never to get to the summit of every Munro, I had now reached the summits of the top fifty and achieved my minor, doable ambition. It is my experience that there is a definite change in topography and climate round about this altitude, give or take, that these higher peaks create more challenging conditions for a being eking out a living here, the weather is more severe, they are rockier and more barren underfoot and there is much less vegetation, demanding special adaptations, like being able to change the colour of feathers or fur to white in the winter, or to find sturdy boots, spikes and layers of quality technical clothing made from down, fleece, Goretex and Windstopper. I am proud to have made it to the summits of all these big mountains, many in the most spectacular weather. I felt then that with this achievement and the nice round total number, the book would end positively.

I was in any case, not yet dead, though now no longer in denial that it might not be long. Nobody knows when they are going to die. Least of all those of us with a terminal illness. We only know that until death every breath we take is precious and that it may be the last. Amidst all the insecurity of writer's block, I realised that the arched structure of the outline would also make it possible to split the work in two, to make of it two books rather than one. For there was indeed a natural break at the end of the section called *2017 Ignorance*.

I decided therefore to concentrate on completing the first half and to leave the rest until I could work out how I was going to do it. The second half was in any case more or less extant, still available along with a lot more besides, at the blog on my website. This did not take away the writer's block, but it relieved me of a degree of pressure, because I was more than halfway through what would now become the final section of the first book, where I could continue using the same voice and style. I imagined that the style and form of the second book, if it ever saw the light of day, would be very different from the first. So, I picked up work again and found the voice to complete the book you are now holding.

Stories about climbing mountains inevitably take the form: we did or did not make it to the summit and did or did not return safely to the nether worlds of ordinary life, while on the way enjoying conversations, adventures and experiences worth sharing. There is nothing more at the top of the mountain than the top of the mountain; what you take with you, the ground beneath your feet and what you see around you, which in bad weather is only the ground beneath your feet, and which in good weather can be the most sublime panorama you have ever seen, until next you are privileged to stand atop of one of this country's magnificent little peaks, surveying again the most sublime panorama you have ever seen.

The challenge of writing about climbing mountains is finding something to say other than the above. The challenge of writing a collection about climbing mountains is not to say the above over and over again. We climbed a mountain and then one up the road the next day. Two weeks later we climbed some more mountains, and then another we could see in the distance from the first. And so forth. Unless it is to become a simple guidebook, a compilation of tales of climbing mountains must include the effects they have on the lives of the climbers, their stories, the reasons why they have left the netherworlds of normality, even if only briefly, to breathe the pure clear air of the heights and to walk along ridges looking down on the lumpy surface of the planet while standing firmly on solid ground.

With each new summit new perspectives emerge, new views of old territory and prospects of future journeys, new plans and adventures. Routes up new mountains present themselves; old friends smile along the horizon. Each of us who goes into the mountains does so for different reasons, mine are what this book is about, what the mountains mean to me, how they saved my life.

The short version of my story is that at the beginning of October in 2012, while I was living in The Netherlands with established work as a bicycle messenger and bicycle mechanic, it was confirmed that I had aggressive malignant prostate cancer, which I was told would likely *kill me within three years*. Since this prognosis, I changed my life and took control of my health. I left behind my life in The Netherlands and returned to live in Scotland, because if I was going to die, I wanted to be in my home country. In my younger days I spent most of my holiday time on walking or cycling expeditions through mountains and sometimes I visited summits; after returning home to Scotland, I took up ticking off Munros as part of my healing, as a way of coming to terms with the prognosis, exercising my heart, mind, body and spirit and connecting with the earth. The rest of this book is the first half of the long version of my story.

A blog is a kind of public diary. Each entry or post is written in a temporary, transient space, the ever-living, impermanent present, and describes a particular recent event, experience, encounter or burning issue. All references to other events and places are related back to the events described in the post. There is no necessary continuity between posts, these are rather implied by the advertised content of the blog, and in the writing, using *hyperlinks* to external sites or other posts within the blog.

A blogger hopes for a readership or following to develop, for readers to learn the continuity of the story and for interesting discussions to take place in the comments sections at the end of each post. Each post must be assumed however to be written for a new audience of readers who have not read previous posts. Only after a certain following builds up does it become possible to refer to previous posts on the assumption that readers will know or might be able to remember their content.

To this extent also, blogging becomes a kind of duty; a blogger has a responsibility of sorts towards readers, to keep them in the loop of the story, to share the latest news or to account for periods of silence. The first page of a blog is usually either a pinned post, explaining the basic topography of the place, where to start reading, the different sections and so forth, or it is the most recent post, so that newcomers must work backwards, or dip in randomly, or decide to find the very first post and work forward in time, to follow the story in catchup.

It is easy for a writer under these circumstances to develop an alter ego or persona; the writing becomes then another of the masks worn during the ordinary course of a life, failing thus at some level to reveal the truth of the one behind the mask, the writer, alive in the dirty empirical mess of actual existence; in my case, sharing intimate details of what it is like to have been given a death sentence by prostate cancer, while conquering demons by bagging Munros.

Each new blogpost is fed into the newsfeed, using the ordinary networking tools to which we have now all become accustomed, seeking an audience, likes, comments, feedback, some evidence that here is something readable and interesting, so algorithms will be able to sort it, attach it to an advertising stream or data gathering scam, or let it drop back into the infinite, exponentially accumulating archive of digital detritus, through which data miners rummage, upon which policy farmers guzzle and future historians might one day feast.

The point of a blogpost about a life is very different from the point of a chapter of a book about a life, even if they are describing the same journey, referring to the same events, expressing the same emotions and ideas, articulating the same truths.

Each chapter of this book is an episode in the continuous narrative of my life, a new step on a journey, written from the position of that journey now being at an end. The job of writing is to tell the long story with the big picture hanging on the wall behind, to introduce themes and events that will become more relevant as the narrative proceeds, to develop these and weave them together in such a way that expresses the truth of the journey.

About half of the following chapters were written anew, in the sense that there never was any blog about the ascents or expeditions in question; every chapter in sections *2014 prologue* and *2015 remembering* is entirely new. This gave me a blank slate from which to begin and sufficient momentum to have already laid down themes, tropes and important issues by the time I was confronted with the task of converting texts of existing blogposts into chapters of a book. These are in sections called *2016 learning* and *2017 ignorance*. The way that tenses swim around in English must be a terror to users of more grammatically formal languages. Converting even the simplest description of an experience from the present indicative of the blogger's alter ego to the past historical of the narrator is a fascinating technical puzzle requiring advanced skills in wordsmithery. It was fun work, but there are places still where I might have got it wrong. This is for the reader to decide. There are chapters about ascents that have been completely rewritten, others that are much the same as the relevant blogpost; at the very least, all have had their tenses tweaked.

Readers may find it useful to consult a map during these descriptions of mountain journeys.

My own maps of choice are the Ordnance Survey (OS) 1:25,000 *Explorer* series; when writing I have referred to these for the names of places and geographical features. Not all of these coincide with names on other maps, in particular with the OS 1:50,000 *Landranger* series. The *Landranger* maps are favoured by many walkers because they cover a greater area, their broad topography is easier to read and the cartography less busy; others feel the fine detail of the *Explorer* maps makes navigation easier in complex terrain, while adding both to the verisimilitude and aesthetic experience of the representation, or the truth and beauty of the map.

Digital access to the OS database allows for zooming in and out on screen, which flips between these two depictions, and which therefore affords a substantial resource. A great deal of preparation for every journey involves precisely this zooming in and out, in addition to laying out paper maps on the floor. Google Earth in 3D too offers an excellent tool in preparation, particularly when visualising relative sizes and gradients and locating places to park a car.

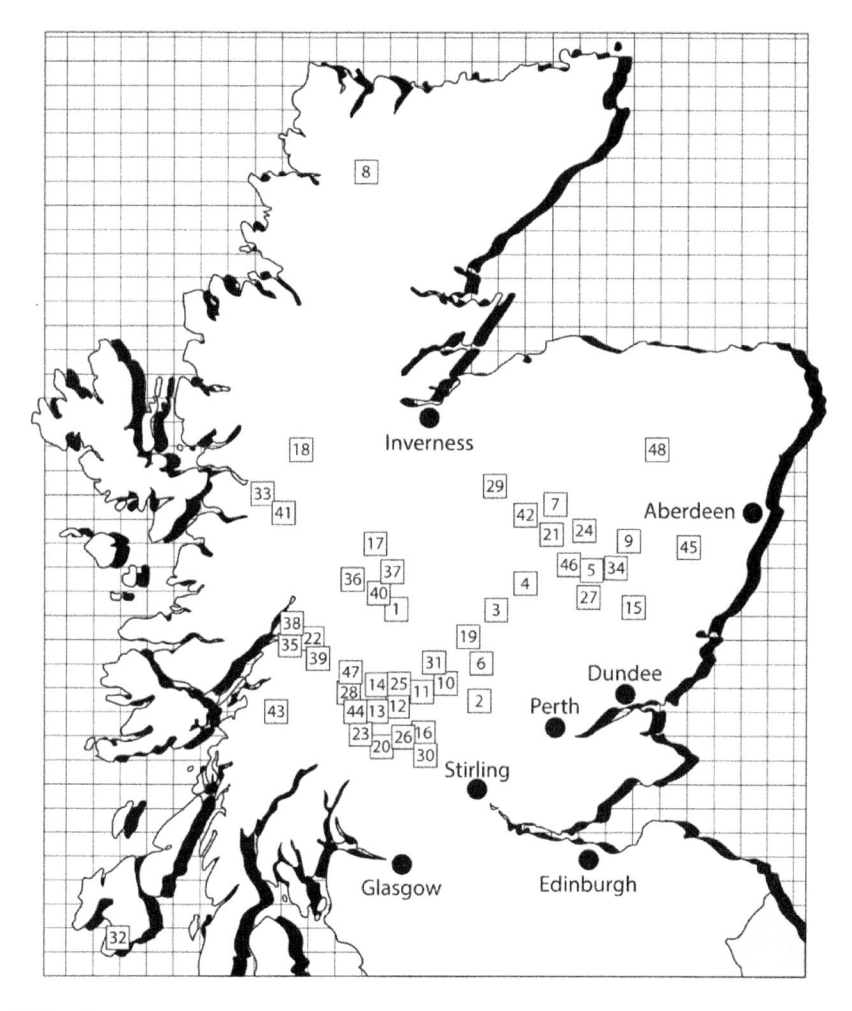

**2014 prologue**
1. Ben Alder

**2015 remembering**
2. Ben Chonzie
3. Atholl to Deeside
4. Beinn a' Ghlo
5. Glas Tulachain
6. Glen Lyon Horseshoe
7. Bynack More
8. Sutherland
9. Lochnagar
10. The Ben Lawers Squiggle
11. Meall nan Tarmachan

**2016 learning**
12. Ben Vorlich Loch Earn
13. Meall Glas
14. Gleann Calliche
15. Glen Clova
16. Balquhidder
17. Creag Meagaidh
18. Mullardoch and Strathfarrar
19. Schiehallion
20. Stob Binnein
21. Derry Cairngorms
22. Buachaille Etive Mor
23. Ben More Dochart
24. Ben Avon

**2017 ignorance**
25. Meall Ghaordie
26. Sgiath Chuil
27. Glen Shee
28. Ben Dorian
29. The first Geal Charn
30. Stùc a' Chroin
31. Glen Lyon
32. The Great Moss
33. Glen Shiel
34. The Mounth
35. Bidean nam Bian
36. Loch Treig
37. Bare Mountains
38. Exposure
39. A tale of midges and tourists
40. High Laggans
41. Killing Fields
42. Braeriach
43. Ben Cruachan
44. Ben Challum
45. Mount Keen
46. An Socach
47. Beinn an Dothaidh
48. The Bochel.

There is vigorous discussion about which maps are best for hill walking and mountain climbing, but at the end of the day it is a matter of personal choice. With increased use of digital maps and navigational devices, paper maps seem to be becoming a bit old fashioned; people appear sometimes to be exclusively reliant on power packs, devices and signals, while more established methods fall by the wayside. Being able to read a map, both while spread out on the floor and bracing against a gale at the top of a hill, and using this to navigate with a magnetic compass, *are absolutely essential skills.*

There are many good reasons for using powered navigation devices, they are often quite precise and they fit into a pocket very well; the OS provides several excellent apps. But there are *no good reasons at all* for not learning the principles of map reading, nor knowing how to use a compass, or learning that the energy to which a compass is sensitive arises in the depths of the planet, from the continuous swirling of molten iron at the core, that the *magnetic field* this swirling generates not only allows us to locate ourselves and to navigate with a degree of precision, but also protects us from the damaging effects of cosmic rays, thereby helping to preserve the fragile layer of breathable gases clinging to the surface, and upon which all of life depends.

These are the beginnings of a vital relationship with the land. Being without map and compass in the mountains, not being able to know or to find out where I am when the mist comes down or if I stumble, lose the way or fall does not make me feel good. Being without map and compass and my knowledge of how to use them to locate my position, is like being naked, unprotected, and unsafe, vulnerable to turning weather or questionable navigational decisions, ungrounded and lost.

The names of Munro summits are indicated with **bold text**. All Gaelic names are *italicised;* if they are also Munros then they are ***in bold italics***. Hence, English or Anglicised Munro names are **bold only**. I also use italics for the names of products and brands, and, according to the usual conventions, for emphasis and words or phrases in non-English languages, except for the word *bealach*, which signifies the lowest point between two peaks, because it has become so common in the language of hill walking that it is now thoroughly Anglicised.

Although ticking boxes is the basic point of bagging Munros, it is really only the means to another higher end. Being able to survey the earth from above while never taking feet from the ground; sitting behind cairns or outcrops munching on lunch in the sunshine at three and a half thousand feet, watching clouds billow and dissolve, the rays of the sun filtering through layers of cloud to create more colours than were thought possible, watching landscapes become more finely detailed from each new perspective, finding routes that stay up high for longer, following the lie of the land, wandering plateaux, shoulders and ridges, after which each time it becomes more difficult to come down again.

Apart from my wife Shona and her family, my brother Colin and his, in alphabetical order, this book would not have been possible without input from: Sanne Bergenhenegouwen, Ellie and Martyn Breeze, Lorna Campbell, Ron Culley, Jackie le Brocq, Deb Brown, Martha Duncan, Jane Kellock, Deirdre Levinson, Guilia Liberatore, Ian Malcolm, John and Maggie Mathews, Angus and Janine Meiklejohn, Michael O'Flòinn, Ruth Russell, Brion Sweeney, Trish Swift, Rita Wall and Pam Wardell.

# 2014 prologue

## Ben Alder

### 3rd to 6th July 2014

It was raining gently when I parked my old Dutch Volvo at Rannoch Station. It rained as I walked back along the road to where the path to Corrour Old Lodge slants gently northwest into the wilderness. It rained all along the path, and it was raining when I pitched my tent on the grass in front of the ruined buildings of the lodge. There were midges too, in great abundance. It was about four in the afternoon. I was tired and a bit low, having discovered along the way that my old rain jacket was not as waterproof as it once was. So I climbed into my sleeping bag and dozed off.

A few hours later I awoke to the heat of the sun on the tent, opened the flysheet and looked out onto the northern reaches of Rannoch Moor. The Blackwater Reservoir was shimmering, backdropped by pointy peaks, flanked to the north by *Leum Uilleim*, a hill familiar to anybody who has seen the film *Trainspotting*. A tiny train rattled along the track towards Corrour Station, apart from this ruined lodge and the denatured landscape, the only other sign of human presence.

I laid out my wet things in the sun to dry and set about cooking supper. Behind me, above the old lodge buildings, was a gentle climb of little more than four hundred metres along the course of a burn onto a bealach, just to the south of what was going to be my first Munro after returning to live in Scotland with aggressive, incurable prostate cancer, and since surviving an intense course of focused radiotherapy. No longer was it necessary for me always to have immediate access to toilet facilities, the scarring of the organs and tissues surrounding my prostate was healing and excretory functions had returned to something akin to normal. The blood marker had dropped to next to zero. My fitness level was reasonable; I was keeping myself healthy with good food and exercise, and my confidence was returning. My core strength had not been much affected, either by the disease or by the radiotherapy.

Specific planning for this trip had been vague; until this sunshine I was not sure what my route was going to be. It was depressing enough trudging in the wet over heather and bog, along this ancient, badly maintained path, and I had no desire to ascend into cloud to the ridge to the east to get wetter still just so I could get to the top of a mountain. Which, under more clement circumstances, might have been a plan. Had I not come upon this grass by this ruined lodge I would have carried on to the shore of Loch Ossian for the night, and then walked northeast towards the turn on the path southeast to Alder Bay, where I was aiming to camp so I could ascend the mountain above without a heavy pack. I had food enough for three nights out, maybe four.

**Ben Alder** was my only real goal. I wanted to come at it from a new direction, having many years previously walked through from Dalwhinnie to Fort William past its precipitous northern buttresses. With this disease, I had become accustomed to making choices about what to do with the rest of my time, and **Ben Alder** had been on my wishlist ever since I can remember. Always I wanted one day to climb it, even before I knew that the enormous lump of snow-filled corries west of Loch Ericht, clearly visible from the A9 corridor north of Dalwhinnie was called **Ben Alder**. Reports I had read described grassy pastures at three and a half thousand feet, impenetrable corries and steep access paths. A worthy focus for my initial ambition simply to get out again into the hills, while I still could.

For the rest of the evening and into the night I reacquainted myself with tent life; the little rituals and ordinary chores made necessary by lying on the ground insulated from the elements by technical equipment, aluminium tentpoles, *goretex*, down and *windstopper*. It had been many years since I had camped out in Scotland; in more recent years this little tent, or one very like it, had been pitched all over northwest Europe, and once on a cycle trip from Calgary through The Rockies to Seattle and Vancouver.

This particular tent was nevertheless reaching the end of its usefulness. Its low-profile design made it impossible to sit up at the front and to look out; it was only possible to lean on an elbow and squint backwards, which was not what my body wanted to do as it approached the second half of its fifties. This was the most strangely shaped tent I have ever slept in, utterly asymmetrical, but oddly spacious and very light, useful on mammoth journeys by bike, but after the waterproof jacket, it was next on the list of new things I would need for any future expeditions into the mountains. At this particular moment, I was still under the impression that my death was imminent, my mental life was still scarred from radiotherapy, my spirit weakened by a year or so of inactivity and recovery, not to mention the disease. I was unsure whether or not I would continue to pursue this outdoor thing, and had invested only in what was absolutely necessary, a new rucksack and a new pair of boots. For the rest, I was relying on stuff left over from travelling by bike in Europe, and stuff stored in the attic at my mother's house.

I slept well that night, excited from time to time by looking out into starry summer skies and arose early. I had forgotten about the ferocity of midges until that moment. This was the most glorious morning of sunshine, burgeoning heat and wispy clouds. Insects and flowers, twittering birds, this grassy knoll, where burns from the ridge behind the lodge gurgle over rocks in little gullies through a slight pasture before spreading out into a morass downhill, a vast expanse of hags reaching into the headwaters of the Blackwater Reservoir. These fascinating ruins of a once well-appointed lodge with outhouses, stables and walled gardens, and this view of pointy peaks. I had forgotten how much more beautiful this country is on the inside, beyond the end of the road. At this moment though, I was entirely focused on moving about so as to create drafts sufficient to fend off midges, all the while eating muesli with almond milk and packing for the ascent.

It was hard work, through rough heather, following the burn. The sweat felt good though. I emerged smiling onto a rocky ridge from which it was a straightforward plod north to the summit of **Carn Dearg**, my first Munro with cancer. I sat for a while, took a couple photos and turned northeast towards Munro number two, **Sgor Gaibhre**, following an easy path through outcrops and over a minor boulder field to peaty pastures in a shallow bealach, followed by a long slow grassy trudge to the summit. Halfway up I was overtaken by a group of six, firstly three young men and a few minutes later, three young women. When I arrived at the summit, they were all sunning themselves and admiring the views. Somebody offered to take my photo, so I stood earnestly with my arms folded in front of one of the few mountains I recognised, **Ben Nevis**. On the way to the next top, *Sgòr Choinnich*, I met a couple of ladies of my own generation, one of whom suggested that bridges be built across such chasms as this to aid more mature walkers. It was a steep descent indeed, followed by a steep climb. From which there was another steep descent, all of which following the northern lip of a corrie, surrounded by dark crags and brutal cliffs, concealing a shallow lochan, dazzling in the summer sun.

At the next bealach, I decided I was fed up with all this up and down, that it was time to traverse the steep edge of *Meall a' Bhealaich* towards *Bac na Craoibhe*, a shoulder that would lead gently east and down to my destination on the grassy shore of Loch Ericht by Benalder Cottage. It was not long before I remembered that traversing is not always as straightforward as might appear, particularly where there is deep heather growing through loose scree and boulders. The flatter route out along the floor of the corrie from the lochan was a mess of peat hags and squiggly rivers, totally out of the question, so I persevered until I found the flat of the shoulder, and also its boggy hags and mossy pools. Eventually there were also outcrops of rock where I could sit, rest and look out at my goal for the day. I tarried and snacked in the sunshine gazing down on my campsite, reluctant to leave to pitch my tent quite yet. I had no idea what time it was. There was not a cloud in the sky. It was warm.

Benalder Cottage nestles under the southeast corner of the Ben Alder massif, beside burns flowing into Loch Ericht; two coming off the bealach between **Ben Alder** and **Beinn Bheòil**, another flowing beside the stalker's path that connects with the path to Corrour. There is a bit of ancient enclosed pasture garnished with tussocks of reed, a few straggly alder trees and evidence on the ground of more ancient habitation. The cottage has a reputation as one of the most haunted in the Highlands, and has been turned now into an open bothy for walkers. Many years previously on an overnight visit to an allegedly haunted bothy in Sutherland, I was aware immediately upon entering that I did not want to sleep in the room to the right, but found the room to the left most welcoming. So I was keen now to visit Benalder Cottage to see if there was any obvious odour of ghosts.

Hauntings are social phenomena, entirely reliant on stories. The most popular explanation for a ghostly presence at Benalder Cottage recalls the last permanent resident who is said to have hanged himself in the lobby. The truth is that the last resident had an attack of pneumonia and went to live in the lodge further up the loch, after which he retired and moved into a cottage in Dalwhinnie, where he died at a ripe old age. The story of the last resident's suicide was no doubt made up by somebody at the estate to discourage poachers, or by poachers to frighten off others, and despite being debunked it has percolated into the climbing fraternity. Which does not of course mean that nobody ever hanged themselves in the lobby.

This is a location with a long history, lying at the intersection of important paths through the glens. Stories persist of strange things happening in the night, music playing, doors banging, of visitors being so scared out of their wits they preferred to leave, even in the dead of night at the height of violent storms to pitch tents outside, rather than endure a moment longer inside. There are many tales purporting to explain the unhappy presence and maintain the reputation of the place.

Of a woman, destitute, derelict and trapped in the bothy by a storm, who felt she had no choice but to kill and eat her own baby, and whose bitter, wailing grief is said at certain times of the year to reverberate still. Several unidentified or unidentifiable corpses have been discovered over the years on the mountain above. Assorted navvies, employed during the construction of the great hydro projects of the last century and billeted round the loch, succumbed to the weather, or were killed in accidents, or just drank themselves to death. In the century before, there were clearances involving the usual brutality and indifference, and before that, the flight from Culloden, the first purges by British imperialism against highland culture.

I stopped more than once at rocky outcrops on the way to my intended campground. Eventually I crossed a burn and followed the path to the bothy, which I decided to investigate before making camp. A little nervously I set down my pack and opened the door of the outside lobby, a wooden attachment to the old stone building, and pushed open the double doors to the inner lobby. I did not like it in there, not one bit, it was pitch dark and claustrophobic, immediately I felt very uneasy. In the room to the left, a work party had stowed inflatable kayaks and assorted kit; the bunks in the middle room appeared to have been reserved with sleeping bags and thermal mats; in the main room to the right there was some scattered equipment, but it was devoid of furniture and lacked several wall and ceiling panels, rubbish had been piled badly in the hearth. In general the place was a mess, it stank of wet decay and sweaty human.

I was very glad I would be sleeping in my own stench, in my little tent outside, well ventilated. I winced, shivered and closed the doors to the rooms, before standing again briefly in the inside lobby, soaking up the atmosphere, which remained unsavoury. Backing out into the outside lobby, I stood reading a notice pinned to the wall about how sporting estates cooperate with each other to ensure that the surrounding ecology is managed, that the deer population is regulated and employment provided for local people. There was also a note, handwritten and attached to the panel wall with a wooden handled vegetable knife, warning visitors that unless they took their rubbish away with them and disposed of their excrement responsibly using the spade provided, far away from the bothy and nowhere near any water courses, the owner would withdraw permission for its public use. Two sheds attached to either end of the building were already in use exclusively by the estate, secured against entry by padlocks and sturdy metal shutters. It would no doubt take little more than an afternoon's labour to fit similar security measures to the public section of the building.

Scathingly I moved outside into the fresh summer air and crossed the burn to pitch my tent with the entry facing away from the bothy. After which I did a bit of a recce of the environs, then cooked and ate supper and sat on a rock gazing over the loch, allowing my mind to absorb the sparse events of the place, overwhelming my senses with not very much at all. I sat like this for hours, feeling the privilege of being alive, gazing in awe at the far shore of Loch Ericht, where native trees cling inconceivably to screes, only punctuating the stillness with cups of tea, urination and visits to the burn to replenish my water. Here I met some of the people from the bothy. None had heard stories of hauntings.

At length it got darker and I went to sleep with the tent front open to the night. There were surprisingly few midges. In the morning it was misty. I waited as I prepared for the climb up **Ben Alder**, hoping the sky would open. The bothy was empty when I passed it by, but there was plenty stuff still lying about. On the way up, the path passes a hole in a crag described optimistically on the map as a cave, one of Prince Charlie's many hideouts as he was pursued by government forces after the slaughter at Culloden. It is a steep unmanaged walker's path, both boggy and rocky. It had a familiar feel under my feet, but it was hard work.

When the path became less steep, I was able to pick out a route up the side of Ben Alder. Cloud still hung round the plateau, wisps dangling down, torn off by crags. There was a route following a branch of the burn to a outcrop in front of what appeared to be a grassy slope all the way to the round stump of the southeast shoulder and onto the plateau. But there was no real path. Complex terrain. Large rocks. Tussocky grass. Water flowing from every pore in the ground, gathering into burns and dispersing again, cascading beside the path to the bothy and into Loch Ericht. As I climbed, a fine drizzle melded into thick fog hanging in the air, then more general cloud moving along in the morning wind, although tantalising glimpses of light seemed to promise more than this gloom.

I passed by a couple of dark pools nestling inside a claw of crags, and found a slight gully slanting past more rocky stuff, dark and imposing in the swirling cloud. I was a bit trepidatious; the ground was rougher underfoot than can be detailed on maps, steep and always upwards into thicker cloud. From time to time I paused to pick a route over or past scree, snowbanks, boulder fields and outcrops. Somewhere near the end of the climb, as the gradient became more forgiving, I disturbed a fluster of ptarmigan. Then navigation became a bit easier, the clouds were now lighter, the sun palpable above, but it was still monochrome. Following a spur to the plateau, I found a path hugging precipitous corries, rambling through rocks and boulder fields and over a slab or two of snow, one of which obscures the allegedly highest body of standing water in Scotland. And then towards the summit, a massive cairn atop this enormous mountain, at the very edge of a vast expanse of grassland sloping gently down to the west, with deep cliffs to the east. Mist blew past, thinner, but still no sunshine. I wandered about the plateau near the summit, trying to persuade myself that it was not so important that at the top of the mountain there was no view beyond the mountain top.

I sat for a while eating oatcakes, then took many selfies with every possible angle of the grassy plateau in the background. Proving to myself beyond any doubt that I have definitely been here, utterly in awe of my achievements, and grateful. I hung about for a while before deciding that the cloud would never lift, then headed west to what appeared from the map to be a relatively less steep descent. As is the way of these things, the cloud began now genuinely to disperse, so I returned immediately to the summit, to admire the view north up Loch Ericht into Speyside and to gaze down on remnants of mist still swirling in corries, scraping past crags and pinnacles.

The long walk down became exponentially steeper as I approached the stalker's path round the mountain and back to Alder Bay. It turned out to be a glorious day. On the way I stopped several times just to sit in the summer air, to breathe in the odours of peat, cascading waters and flowers, to watch the diversity of plants growing amongst the rocks and take in the view towards Loch Rannoch and the hills behind - of which **Schiehallion** and **Ben Lawyers** were the only ones I recognised.

Back at the tent, I pottered about the bay and extended my recce to the remnants of a path round the corner and north up the loch. Then I made supper and again sat on my rock facing the opposite bank of Loch Ericht, observing the occupants of the bothy returning from their days out to make food, prepare for the night or for the next stage of their journeys. Presently, the work party inflated their boats and launched them into the loch, full of black bin liners, and rowed north round the corner. I began to see the people in much the same way as the fox I saw sniffing about under the roots of an old pine by the shore, or as the snorting young stag blundering by, apparently oblivious to my presence.

At about seven in the evening, a middle-aged couple arrived from the northwest down the stalker's path on top-of-the-range mountain bikes, wearing only light cycling gear and shoes with cleats. Clearly they had a bit of a communication issue going on. He looked in at the bothy, portly, supping at his bottle, while she persevered along what she thought might be a path behind it, until coming to grief, then carried on, pushing. Even from a distance, the body language between them was unmistakable. I watched as they sought paths round the loch to the north, she through tussocks and he over the rocky beach.

Loch Ericht forms part of the extensive hydro system contained by the catchment of the River Tay. Its outflow at the south is dammed and water piped to turbines on the shore of Loch Rannoch below. At its north end there is also a barrier and extra water is added via channels taken from burns that would otherwise drain eventually into the Spey. Consequently its shoreline is not stable, no longer created by natural water cycles, but managed according to demand on the national grid. Over the years, the consequent rising and falling of the water level has left a bald, three metre vertical scar of white rock all along the loch's edge, which unlike the seashore, is inert and barren. Such a moonlike shoreline is a defining feature of all lochs that are dammed, whether as reservoirs of drinking water or of power. Where the shore is flat, for example at Alder Bay, there is a bit of a beach of stones where rocky skeletons of former land features, gullies and outcrops can clearly be discerned; where it is steep north of the bay, the remaining shoreline of dense peat, heather and scrub hangs over the bleached rocks, demonstrating both the tenacity and fragility of life. The path along the western shore on this precipitous section weaves through a mix of bracken, alder, rowan, birch and heather, hanging precariously above the peaty depths of the loch, very often undercut.

At the corner of the bay, there is a large rock that forms a cliff into the loch. Here is also an iron fence descending from the mountain above, enclosing the entirety of the promontory. There is a swivel gate in the fence where the fragile path from the north merges with paths to the bothy. I watched from my tent as the couple struggled to pass their bikes over the top of the fence; the width of their handlebars would never fit through the swivel gate, the portly man seemed also to be having difficulties fitting his person through the gap. At length, they disappeared round the corner, bikes and all.

After a few minutes, they had not returned. I began to invent all sorts of stories about what might befall them, mainly involving collapsing ground, cold deep water and tired bodies. I was quite sure they would never be able even to carry their bikes along the path. After a few more minutes I booted up and decided I wanted to know if they were alright. I was genuinely concerned for their safety, but also just plain curious. It was already late, they were equipped with nothing but bikes and they were at least twelve miles from the public road at the north of the loch, and seven from the estate lodge.

I found them not far from the gate in the fence. She was not at all happy; he was trying to look on the bright side. They had cycled from Dalwhinnie via Loch Pattack and round the mountain following excellent paths and tracks. Now this. They asked my advice. I suggested cycling back the way they came, for at least there was a path that was suitable for bikes. Or staying overnight in the bothy first to recuperate a little. But they had absolutely nothing with them. He said that he had been here once before many years previously when it looked different. Then he wandered up the path to investigate the route ahead while she waited. She had to be at work in Inverness in the morning and had not expected the trip to turn out this way. He returned with the hopeful suggestion that they could probably walk up the path but that they would have to leave their bikes and come back for them another time. I pointed out that they were wearing cycling shoes, which are not designed for walking, and suggested they would be lucky to get to Dalwhinnie before midnight, adding that I had food at the tent if they wanted something. They declined and I left them to their plight.

On the way back, I popped into the bothy to discover that all visitors had now departed. The rubbish had gone too, but it still stank of mildew and sweaty human, and I still did not like what was hanging about in the inside lobby. Back at the tent, I continued gazing at the opposite shore of the loch, this evening garnished with rainbows and intense orange light from the setting sun. At last, I climbed into my sleeping bag for the final night out. In the morning, before packing for the walk out, I returned to the path round the loch. A little way ahead I saw two mountain bikes nestling in the heather. I could only assume that their owners had not fallen into the loch, but had made it safely back to Dalwhinnie.

It was gloomy. Thick high cloud, with the threat of rain in the air, and a little colder. I packed and found a path south over a wooden bridge to the remnants of a regenerating pine forest, bits now enclosed against grazing animals. I should have found a way through to the shore of the loch before I did, for I am sure the going would have been easier. I found myself trapped by an impenetrable deer fence, ploughtering through bog and peat. Eventually I found a gate into the plantation and then another in a muddy corner out again to an estate track that would take me back to the road. Towards the south end of the loch there was a large well-appointed wooden building with a marvellous prospect and a gruesome function, combining a veranda and lounge with a substantial barn, the former for the pleasure of those who pay money to kill red deer, the latter for preparing gathered carcasses. It was at this moment that my bowels decided to move. For the first time since leaving home. Urgent and persistent. Briskly, I repaired to the rocky edge of the loch, where just under the grassy bank high above the water level, I found a hollow to deposit my waste, after which I piled it high with stones.

The journey to the road from here was long and stony. After two miles plodding along the track I branched off on an old walker's path, mainly to avoid following the track through a monoculture plantation and also to give my feet a feel again of softer ground. The path was boggy, but my new boots were working well and my feet remained dry. It hugged the edge of the plantation until on the other side of a stile it joined the estate track again, now through mixed woodland towards the western end of the road along Loch Rannoch, where I turned right and stuck up my thumb to passing vehicles. Within five minutes I got a lift from a French couple who were driving, as many do, to the end of the road at Rannoch Station just to see what is there. My old Dutch Volvo was exactly where I left it. I dumped my pack in the back, changed my shoes and drove home.

## 2015 remembering

## Ben Chonzie

19th April 2015

**Ben Chonzie** was the first real mountain I ever climbed, my first Munro, when I was just fifteen, during a school orienteering expedition. The head of the maths department sat all day at the summit, sheltering behind the cairn with flasks of tea, encouragement and a rubber stamp, while scores of teenagers flocked past on their way to finding other members of staff and other rubber stamps at assorted locations around the upper reaches of Glen Almond. Buses dropped us off at *Coishvachan*, at the end of the road up Glen Lednock from Comrie, quite a feat of driving, and then picked us up again in the Sma' Glen at Newton Bridge. I took part in two more orienteering expeditions before leaving school, although the summit of **Ben Chonzie** was never again a checkpoint. I almost climbed the mountain again with a girlfriend in my early twenties, but we gave up because the weather was horrible.

Much had changed since my expedition to **Ben Alder**. Apart from ongoing political upheavals in the aftermath of the Scottish independence referendum, I had returned my Dutch Volvo and acquired another, with a more appropriately positioned steering column, from an old school friend for a very good price. I was working again in the city, delivering stuff on my bike and also sometimes in a van when the regular driver was away. It was part time, freelance and irregular, but it was what I did. From late 1997, I worked as a cycle messenger in Utrecht and also from time to time in Rotterdam, Den Haag and Amsterdam. I was the founding member of a collective messenger company in Utrecht. My new work in Edinburgh was at a high-end digital printer, waiting for jobs to come off the production line, so they could then be taken immediately to clients. Although different from traditional messenger work, which involves being constantly on the move through a city under the guidance of a dispatcher, picking up and dropping off along the way, I still enjoyed the many pleasures of cycling through the city, picking jobs up from clients and dropping off completed work. Every day was still an adventure and never the same as the last. In the van I discovered new disciplines and challenges, always enjoying the puzzles of navigation through the barely restrained chaos of city traffic.

Despite all appearances, the blood marker of the disease was also rising again. It was not much higher than normal, but it was rising, exponentially, with a doubling time of about six weeks, so I had to keep an eye on it. I was being encouraged by my oncologist to begin again with hormone medication, which I had stopped taking at the time of the radiotherapy because it turned me into a menopausal wreck, chemically castrated, demotivated, depressed, bereft of libido and impotent, breaking out every two hours in a hot flush lasting anything up to five minutes, an unfamiliar prickly heat shimmering behind my eyes, spreading round my head and neck, to my torso and down my limbs, pushing out a thin layer of cold sweat, cocooning my body in a clammy shroud, diverting all attention to the search for cool air, a draft, any kind of relief from this strange personal hell. Not a condition I was willing to repeat unless it was absolutely necessary.

I still had no systematic desire to reach summits. And I had no plans to bag this one. I just wanted to experience the great outdoors with my partner Shona, to go for a walk during a period of uncharacteristically warm spring weather. We drove through Glen Lednock in bright sunshine, new growth beginning to burst through the flattened winter ground, the odour of earth swelling up into warming air. We parked at *Coishvachan* and followed a track past cottages to the hill. Already Shona was not enjoying the gradient. It has to be said that this is not the prettiest of mountain ascents. At an intake for the hydro dam round the hill at Loch Lednock, a rough estate track crosses a burn and gouges the hillside to afford access to grouse butts and killing fields on the plateau. In places it is very stony and steep. Although the views over the mountains were excellent, with many snowbanks still garnishing the landscape, the gradient and ugliness of the path did not contribute positively to Shona's mood.

With some encouragement we reached the point where a walker's path branches off from the track to cross a fresh burn bubbling down the mountain, after which Shona's attitude happily changed. She was still a bit grumpy and the path still steep, but at least we were walking now over real ground, a surface of peat, grass and heather. Many hare were running about, partially clothed in winter livery. Plovers and ptarmigan too, gurgling as they flew from our approach. Where the ground levels out, we could see the summit ahead of us, along a round shoulder of moss, stones and snowbanks. Shona asked, now much less grumpy, how long it would take to get there, to which I replied with a deliberately vague and conservative estimate of there and back in maybe half an hour, adding that since I had been there before, I had no particular desire to get to the summit and was happy, if that were what she wanted, to hang out here and soak up the surroundings for a while. She was determined though; having got this far, she was not about to turn back. She had never been to the summit of a Munro before. She strode off and I followed. About fifteen minutes later there we were, admiring views of snowclad peaks to the north and west, and of greening spring valleys to the south and east. I was proud of her for making the effort, and she was clearly happy to be here.

We dawdled on the way back over the plateau, enjoying the antics of hare and the gurgling of ptarmigan and later, lower down in the heather, the croaking of grouse and tweeting wheatears. At the estate track, Shona's mood changed again. Descending over such stony ground is no easier than ascending, and in fact in some respects it is much more difficult. Climbing against gravity is controlled and steady, while resisting its downward force always endangers tumbling uncontrollably. Neither do stubbed toes and wobbly knees make progress any easier. Nevertheless, we made it back to the car intact and content. It was my fourth Munro since the diagnosis and Shona's first ever.

## *Atholl to Deeside and back*

### 21st to 25th April 2015

I began planning this expedition through Atholl to Deeside before our walk up **Ben Chonzie**. Having arranged time off work while the glorious period of unseasonably warm weather continued, I was looking forward to travelling again into the heart of the Cairngorms, my favourite mountains. When I was younger, inspired by the experience of orienteering, I made many expeditions from all points on the roads enclosing these mountains in the direction of the plateaux above Speyside. Mostly I concentrated simply on finding interesting ways of getting from one side of the wilderness to the other, but sometimes also, when the weather permitted, I visited summits. This expedition would be a chance for high level navigation in fine spring weather, towards two Cairngorm summits I had never before visited, on the way taking in three others.

    I arrived by train in Blair Atholl before lunch then followed the left bank of the River Tilt through woods until the track angles above the perimeter of a firing range and onto the moor. A gentle climb, uneventful except for a woodpecker pecking at a dead old pine by the Tilt and a little yellow brown lizard darting across my path further up. It was hot. Snowbanks dribbled and grouse gurgled. At a gash in the hillside where a burn plunges from the plateau to the bothy at *Allt Schiecheachan* and into the Bruar Water, the path steepens as it traverses, then climbs zigzagging onto the start of the round red top of **Beinn Dearg**.

    At the summit I sat for a while, pleased with myself, admiring views through hazy air to mountains all around, then followed a bit of a path north off the summit. It petered out at a shallow bealach, after which I slid down snowbanks and soggy grasses, flattened and blackened by months under snow, towards the watershed of the Tarf Water and a tributary of the Bruar, which from the map looked like it would afford campground between squiggles in the river. About half way down I sat on a rock contemplating the way forward. I could now see yellowed winter grass as expected, contrasting with deep browns of heather and peat, and giant patches of old snow. I trudged on with tired legs and a joyful spirit. Here was freedom *and* security. I felt safer here in the middle of nowhere than anywhere.

    Where the ground levelled out there was a complex mass of peat hags and tiny streams, swollen by the day's thawing and partially obscured by deep banks of snow. Emerging over the lip of a peat hag, I saw before me exactly what I had hoped for. On the other side of the young River Tarf, the perfect spot for my tent on a grassy bank by a loop in the flow, although getting there did not look so easy. I hurried forward with a dance in my step. As I was contemplating the best way to cross the water, I lost my footing in the squelchy ooze and fell over backwards, and in the effort of balancing myself, succeeded only in slithering further into the mire, landing on my right side with my pack on top of me with my head pointing downwards into a pool of muck. Uncomfortably wet, I picked myself up with some difficulty and carried on more carefully. The river was narrow and deep, emerging at one point from under a tunnel of snow, there did not seem to be any obvious way across that did not involve leaping or wading. A little further upstream there were more crossing opportunities, but getting there required traversing a patch of snow that bridged a feeder burn. Inevitably I put a foot through an unseen weak point and sank up to my crotch into a cold wet hole, leaving an uncomfortable asymmetry. I was tired, hungry and now wet, becoming cold.

This was indeed a marvellous spot for a tent. At the very edge of the burn on soft, well drained, albeit lumpy ground, with a low horizon to the east to ensure the rising sun warmed the tent as soon as it could. I went about my chores, cooked and ate supper, washed up my pots and fell asleep to the soothing chatter of running water. The stars in the night were dense. In the morning, the level of the stream had dropped by a foot at least, there was new ice at the water's edge. The rising sun was still inadequate to the task of warming the tent, there was no wind and not a cloud in the sky, nor any wisp of mist. I could already tell it was going to be hot. Suddenly, my bowels signalled they were about to move, uncharacteristically for a first night out. So I found a hollow in the heather, after which I gathered dead twigs and parched grass to set a fire above my waste, warming myself in the flames. Before I struck camp, I doused all embers and covered the stain with rocks. Looking back there was no discernible trace of my camp, no evidence of my presence here.

Immediately I climbed up the round flank of the small hill behind the camp, which connects to a series of shoulders and tops leading to the day's summits. These two Munros are extremely isolated, the nearest approach is from the Linn of Dee at more than ten miles; from Blair Atholl it is over fifteen. It was a bit of a plod to the first top, but I was glad to be doing this now before the heat of the day. Another twelve feet and *Beinn Bhreac* would also make it into Munro's Tables, for it is a prominent peak. It is classified as a Corbett and affords splendid views of smiling mountains in all directions.

From *Beinn Bhreac*, I travelled predominately northeast in a big squiggle over or past a number of minor tops to **Carn an Fidhlier**, also known as **Carn Ealar**, the first Munro of the day. The sun shone, the walking was excellent, I lost track of time. Surrounded by snowbanks and spring mountains, with the Cairngorm plateaux now clearly visible to the north, I was overwhelmed by familiarity, utterly bewitched by my surroundings. To borrow a phrase from Neil Gunn, I came upon myself. It was becoming almost laughable that despite being told I would live no more than three years, even if I took the medication, here I was in the middle of nowhere two and a half years later, having initially rejected both medication and prognoses and gone my own way, living life under my own steam, very far from impending death, celebrating this precious gift of life with every step. Munro number six with cancer was in the bag.

Between *Carn an Fidhlier* and *An Sgarsoch* there is a bealach at an altitude of about seven hundred metres, a steep northeast facing drop still packed deep with snow, topped by a marvellous cornice, the frozen form of the wind through this gap, piled up from below as it whips through the space between the mountains, and pressed down from above as it hammers over the plateau, coming to a point, like the photo of a breaking wave. Although not hanging above anything cliff like, there was nevertheless an overhang through which I did not want to plunge; I did not know what sort of ground it concealed, nor how deep or stable it might be. Approaching from the top, looking for a way down, it was a sheer drop into a white void with only a vaguely defined edge. I sought a way past. At a point where the traces of other human legs were visible in the snow, I decided it would be safe to descend. As I crashed through the cornice it became quickly clear that this old snow was thick and stable, making the descent easy. At its edge, water seeped out, flowed into little burns, starting its journey into either Deeside or Tayside, wetting the ground and bringing life to the planet.

Before ascending to the next summit, I rested awhile at some rocks, looking back at the vast bank of thick snow plastered against the slope opposite, transfixed by the life bursting through the ground on the sunny side of this deep soggy gap between two stony mountains. All day and all of yesterday until I descended to pitch my tent, the ground beneath my feet had been hard, mostly rocky and predominately dry. Here spring waters made the ground squashy and they were visibly working their natural magic. I saw lizards, or maybe they were newts or salamanders, frogs and toads fucking promiscuously, mayflies and little moths, twittering larks and pipits, grouse, wheatears. It was a good place to prepare for the ascent, three hundred metres up in less than fifteen hundred, a gradient of twenty percent.

I climbed, steadily but now tired, less from exertion than the sheer exposure of walking at above two and half thousand feet all day in the blazing sun. More lizards, newts or salamanders darted away, too fast again properly to identify. I had never seen so many such creatures in the same place, what with the little lizard yesterday, and these specimens today, apparently different. Is this bealach perhaps a particularly fecund location for amphibians and reptiles; or maybe I just happened along at exactly the right moment. Who knows? At the top, the ground again becomes stony, garnished with moss and sparse grass, with the buds of tiny flowers now too beginning to look out from beneath their rocks. It is a broad flat lump with several descending shoulders and a big cairn of flat stones at the very top, the highest point between **Beinn Bhrotain** in the north, and *Beinn à Ghlo* to the East, with **Beinn Dearg** about the same height to the southwest. I sat awhile in the sun.

Presently it was time to make tracks in search of a flat bit of ground next to water. The haze of the day was beginning to boil up a bit into clouds, hanging high and taking the heat off the sun. Tired and hungry, but not wet and cold. I took the north shoulder off the mountain, aiming for a path to the left of

*Scarsoch Bheag*, marked on the map as coming up from the ruin of Geldie Lodge in the broad strath of the Geldie Burn. On the way along the path I met a young man from Spain, lightly packed and heading for the two peaks I had just visited. Although it was late, he was not bothered that he would be walking back to Linn of Dee in the dark. It is after all a good track, with these open skies the light will fade slowly and most beautifully.

In the distance, the familiar profile of the high Cairngorm plateaux, great corridors of snow filling northeast facing slopes. In front of which, a path I have often followed, along the Geldie Burn from Deeside to Speyside via the watershed with the River Feshie, past its confluence with the River Eidart, then down into a remnant of Caledonian forest clinging to screes and dense with juniper. I wanted not to go down yet to the burn, but to camp as high as I could, preferably somewhere like the previous night, with fast flowing water and firm ground. Although I knew I would find this among the squiggles by the Geldie Burn, it was getting late and I took the first opportunity I came upon, in a hollow beside a dribbling snowbank and a bubbling spring, with an excellent prospect of the rising sun.

I slept well enough, but it was damp in the night with condensation. Not enough wind. Definitely need a new tent. Again the stars were dense, but hazed away as the night progressed. The dawn was nevertheless quick, with warmth immediately on the tent as the sun came up at the lowest point on the horizon, just above Deeside. Not long after I struck camp, clouds began to accumulate, and the wind got up. The forecast was for this period of unseasonable heat to break at some point within the next few days. Although there was nothing ominous on any horizon, nor sign of approaching fronts, I was wary.

I took a straight line towards the path on the other side of the Geldie Burn, intending to follow it west to the River Eidart and follow this north to swing west again and up onto the side of **Monadh Mor**. On the way I passed over a substantial forest of bogwood, the roots of ancient trees, long felled or fallen, preserved in peat and bleached by weather. Excellent firewood, but not easy to harvest without a saw. When I arrived at the path I saw that the ground north from the path would make for easy going. Already six hundred metres up and windswept, the heather is stunted. Patches had also suffered muirburn, exposing thinning peat and gravelly ground. Ahead, the southern shoulder of **Monadh Mor**. Although I wanted to visit *Gleann Eidart* again on the way up the mountain, for it is long, flat and beautifully isolated, a more direct route lay beneath my feet.

On the way I met many ptarmigan in various stages of changing from white to mottled brown, making them almost invisible amongst shiny stones, old brown heather and patches of snow. Also black corkscrew shits, evidence of foxes. I plodded up the interminable shoulder, stopping at a knoll on the way, then up again above a vast corniced snowbank plastered against the eastern slope of the shoulder. Snow partially filled the corrie under the bealach between **Monadh Mor** and **Beinn Bhrotain**, completely covering the exit into the narrow outflow towards the Geldie Burn. Just before the first top of this nondescript pile of rocks I met a group of three on their way from *Achlean* in

Glen Feshie to ***Beinn Bhrotain***. A long day out, I thought to myself, not quite realising that it had taken me nearly three to get here. I was at the summit at about two in the afternoon, surrounded by familiar summits from a new perspective. It was colder up here. In places rock hard puddles of ice.

I pressed on, returning south to find a way through the upper end of the same corniced snowbank I had followed on the way up, seeking a way through to the bealach and up ***Beinn Bhrotain***. Others had gone before and there was an easy path to follow past banks of hard snow, on grinding red gravel and round half-buried stones. At the snowbank, there was an easy way past. The lowest point on the bealach is the same altitude as ***Stuc a Chroin***, a prominent mountain visible from the central belt, situated above Callander in the Trossachs, higher than nearly a hundred Munros. I sat here at the edge of a precipitous cliff, where the massive snowbank filling the northeast corrie was palpably sliding into *Gleann Geusachan* to feed the River Dee. Possibly the nearest thing to a glacier in Scotland, an almost Himalayan experience, looking upwards to the giants of ***Cairn Toul***, ***Braeriach*** and ***Bheinn Macduibh***, and backwards to my route over the Atholl Hills to get here. I checked back into the photos in my camera and saw the view of where I was from where I had been, able to fill in the fine details of the horizon. This seemed suddenly to have been the reason for the expedition, this perspective, sitting among mountainous old friends, reflecting on the journey so far.

The way up ***Beinn Bhrotain*** is badly defined, or at least, I did not find much of a path through the pile of enormous red boulders pouring down from the summit, ranging in size from an armchair to a small vehicle. The group of three I had met earlier passed by at a distance on the way back to Achlean, waving, as if they were following an actual path. Circumnavigating these boulders was hard work, but sometimes I came across sections where the rock was made shiny by passing boots or scraped by crampons, reassuring me that I was on the right track. At length the gradient eased and I emerged onto the round flat summit of the nineteenth highest Munro, my ninth since the diagnosis. It was getting cloudy now and on the western horizon there was sign that the front was on its way. But there were still patches of blue and the view extended as far south as the Lomond Hills in Fife.

My task now complete, the expedition suddenly became only a matter of getting home, which could mean another two nights out. I headed due south off the summit, to where the ground plunges steeply, and waited, looking out over the broad strath of the Geldie, deciding how best to descend. To my right was a long steep bank of snow extending to the edge of the strath, obscuring a burn, sagging in the middle. To my left, a very steep scree slope, partially grown through by heather; before me, a plausible descent over mixed rocks, squidgy moss, deep heather and water bubbling out of the ground. After all I had been through these last three days, this prospect stopped me in my tracks, for a moment I was genuinely scared that I might lose my footing on the descent and fall down the hill. The air beneath my feet seemed to suck me forward. But the feeling passed as I sat with it and I descended to meet the burn downstream from where it emerged from under the snow. On the bank, the skeleton of a deer, picked clean by scavengers, scraped by fox teeth, bleached by weather.

It was early evening when I pitched my tent by the Geldie, with the entrance facing west. As supper cooked, I found a hollow in the ground, surrounded it with stones from the river and built a fire with last year's grass and heather twigs. It was a bit smoky but it warmed my spirit as the cold of the night gathered. The sky was open again, all clouds dispersed and the approaching front held at bay. Smoke rose thin and vertical. I slept well under starry skies.

In the morning, I packed carefully for the day's journey. First along the track to the ford of the Geldie Burn at its confluence with the Bynack Burn and then south past the ruin of Bynack Lodge over the flat watershed of Dee and Tilt towards the first V of Glen Tilt. I have camped on these rutting grounds often, which at night when sounds appear to come from anywhere, surrounded by grunting stags and clattering antlers, can be quite alarming. It was a long thoughtful day through familiar country. My first ever trip into these mountains with a tent began after the General Election of 1979 with a walk up Glen Tilt from Blair Atholl, when naively I believed I would be able to walk all the way through the *Lairig Ghru* to Aviemore, but was stopped in my tracks after a challenging night under a blizzard, beside a mountain properly called **Bod an Daemhain** by deep snow, inadequate equipment, arrogance and inexperience.

I stopped as I always do, at the Falls of Tarf, where the water I slept beside nearly three days earlier came crashing over a series of terraces through a gorge into a big black pool of gravel, merging with the infant Tilt. There was just enough sun to sit for lunch and to recall other journeys passing this place. I could not remember how often from which direction, though once was from the east, on a walk from Straloch in Strathardle to Speyside, otherwise always up or down. It is a place people stop. Very peaceful, with positive energy hanging in the air; upstream, no more than a few hundred metres, the burn I followed from the watershed merges with a substantial flow, fed by burns with sources far to the east, a stone's throw from Glen Shee; downstream no more than a few hundred metres, water coming out of Glen Loch to the east of **Beinn à Ghlo** joins the river. There is a lawn by the shore on the north side of the pool of the Tarf, beside an iron suspension bridge, built by the army in memory of one who drowned trying to cross near here. There are scorched patches on the grass where fires have warmed tired bodies, space enough for small tents. I have camped here myself, and also a bit further downstream, in a howling northern blizzard, almost freezing overnight.

A little to north of the Forest Lodge in Glen Tilt, it was time to decide where to put up my tent. I did not want to be too far away from the road in the morning, for the weather was undoubtedly closing in, but equally I did not want to make camp in farmland, which is what the ground was becoming, at least on this side of the river. Rain had begun spattering from above and the wind was up. I rejected many good camping possibilities believing there would be a place at the end of a shoulder of a mountain further down, where the river makes a kink. I met an elderly couple, lodging in a cottage nearby, who happily confirmed my suspicion. They told me it was a place where many people camp.

The fire is probably still burning, the man joked. Which was not far from the truth. There was a neat firepit carefully surrounded by rocks, with a bed of recently doused embers, though not soaked, and half burnt sticks beside an unruly stack of kindling and a fallen birch bough. I found a place for my tent at the edge of a nice piece of grass, under some trees on the bank above a scramble to the river, backed by a slope of dead bracken to the track up the glen, from which this place was only partially visible.

As my food bubbled in the stove, I built a fire, gathered wood, snapped it into fire-sized chunks and sat on a rock warming myself against increasingly inclement weather. Snowflakes mingled wetly with the drizzle, the cloud blew down obscuring all views of mountainsides. In the declining light the colours intensified, winter birches, impossible to place, somewhere between orange and purple, or both at the same time, even the meagre green of the grass, wet and vibrant. I ate, washed up and returned to my tent, then fell asleep. In the morning there was a covering of wet snow. The shoulders of *Beinn a' Ghlo* high up on the other side of the river were sporting a fresh new coat.

After breakfast, I packed quickly and plodded down the track in intermittent lumpy rain. Two hours later, I was waiting at the station in Blair Atholl for a train back to the city.

## Beinn a' Ghlo

23rd and 24th May 2015

Access to **Beinn a' Ghlò** begins from Loch Moraig, at the end of the road up the hill from Bridge of Tilt just outside Blair Atholl. It being a Saturday and the middle of the day, there was very little space. Packed for a night out, I intended after climbing the mountains, to find a place for the tent in Glen Loch, at their back. Despite seeing all these vehicles parked for the day and despite having done so once or twice myself, I had still not got used to the idea that it is possible to climb a cluster of mountains in a day, without all the bother of carrying a tent, sleeping bag and cooking gear. I was still living in my past, turning trips to the hills into epic adventures, heroic journeys to overcome adversity, existential struggles of man against geography. There was always something much more satisfying about travelling with no deadlines, equipped with everything necessary for survival and no aims in particular, than bagging summits and carrying only what might be needed for a day out, not dependent on car parking or public transport. I believed this was a more authentic way of experiencing the great outdoors, for it meant living through the cycles of the day, meeting the indigenous inhabitants of the land, feeling the ground not only as challenging path, but as mattress, pillow and shelter, as the very source of life.

From the place where vehicles are left, *carpark* would be to exaggerate its status, there is a plod along a farm track before a walker's path turns uphill over rough pasture. There are some fences and a section of gloopy peat before the gradient steepens, after which it is an inexorable slog all the way to the first summit, **Carn Liath**. I climbed this little mountain once before in the middle of winter. It has splendid views into Killiecrankie and Glen Garry with **Schiehallion**, **Ben Lawers** and the Glen Lyon hills behind. The best view though is north to where the round top blends into a sublimely curved ridge, snaking down into a cleft, topped perfectly by a well-trodden path, which can be clearly seen again, on the other side of the cleft slanting round to the summit of the first and most unpronounceable of *Beinn a' Ghlo's* two Munros.

Then, with so few hours of light, this tempting traverse was beyond the possibilities of the day. Though I always remembered the view, the image of the route before me, snowclad, coloured by layers of cloud and low sunlight; now here again unchanged, similar low hanging cloud and struggling sunshine, but warmer, higher light, windier, only old persistent snowbanks remaining, many more hours of daylight before me, no need to get back to the car, packed for an expedition. The most common way of climbing this cluster is to follow a clockwise route from here along the path to the summits of **Beinn à Ghlo** and back to a path down the shoulder of a subsidiary top to join the farm track from which the upward path initially turns. It was late in the day. I met only two other human beings, near the bottom of the first hill, going up and back down again, after that I was alone on the mountain with the hare, ptarmigan, plovers, ravens, peregrine and eagles. Many human beings pass along this path no doubt, but they do so at more or less the same times of the day, determined by the number of daylight hours remaining. For the rest of the time the local inhabitants go about their lives undisturbed.

I reached the summit of **Braigh Coire Chruinn-bhalgain** (Upland of the Corrie of the Round Blisters) at about four thirty, two hours after leaving the summit of **Carn Liath**. What a wonderful walk this was; all the way watched by birds and hare, following a clear path over easy ground, earthy in the cleft, above which I stopped before the ascent for a bite to eat by a sheltered hollow under an overhanging slab, designed and dug out for and by sheep. I gazed down on empty glens, high pasture and grouse butts as the sun began at last to penetrate thinning cloud. The ascent was wonderful, slanting out of the cleft to another sublimely squiggling ridge, on one side a cavernous corrie and on the other a round slope steepening into the void of Glen Tilt. It was cold here at more than three and a half thousand feet, and windy. To the west, I could see my April journey through Atholl to the Cairngorms, naming the peaks along the horizon, new friends; **Beinn Dearg, Carn an Fidhlier, An Sgarsoch, Monadh Mor** and **Beinn Bhrotain**. Immediately off the summit to the west and north, above the sharp gash made by the Tilt through these round hills, the sides of the mountain are graced by a number of shoulders between which inaccessibly steep valleys hang, partially carpeted by aging snowbanks, dirtied by fallout from frost shattered crags, thawing wet as they seep into the scree, their waters filtered clean and gathering again in precipitous V shaped chasms, within which tiny forests flourish.

I pressed on to the dip to the less unpronounceable of *Beinn à Ghlo's* Munros, **Carn nan Gabhar** (The Hill of the Goats). The drop is less than two hundred metres and the climb less than three hundred. The path is easy to follow and never steep. I decided not to visit the subsidiary top of *Airgold Beinn* because the day was getting on and clouds, which only a few hours earlier thinned sufficiently for the sun to penetrate, were now thickening again, threatening rain, and I did not want to be up so high and exposed if any deluge began. I had still not got myself a new waterproof jacket. I paused at the summit only for a selfie, still believing that I needed independent evidence of some sort to demonstrate I had been here. From the summit I moved north, looking for a way down to the east into Glen Loch, a place I had always wanted to visit. The ground is stony and was now pathless; to the left crags and corries garnished with grubby snowbanks plunging into Glen Tilt, to the right a wall of sheer cliffs and crags above Glen Loch. At a shallow bealach of just over seven hundred metres I found the start of a slanting gully of grass following a couple of burns to the banks of the outflow from the loch, where spoilt for choice, I pitched my tent.

During the night in the mountains there are often noises, local fauna rummaging and calling, usually only birds or rodents, but during the rutting season also grunting stags and clattering antlers, most memorably at the watershed of Dee and Tilt. Tonight, the unmistakable call of a loon, or great northern diver, a spooky cross between a hoot and a wail. Maybe this was why I had always wanted to come to this secluded little glen that stretches from the Tilt at the Falls of Tarf to the pastures of Glean Fearnach and Strathardle. To hear the loon and maybe even see it. A great northern diver is not a common bird.

In the morning the weather was much better and I packed lazily for the walk round the mountain back to the car. At the first opportunity, I sat at the shore of Loch Loch, looking out over the water, waiting. I was not disappointed, for within only a few minutes I saw a bird with a heavy dark head and low flat body, semi-submerged on the water, intermittently disappearing and resurfacing several minutes later at random locations far from the point it dived. Presently I noticed another. Here was a pair. I could not see whether they had any young; probably still too early in the year in any case. Eventually the birds moved off out of sight and I dragged myself back to the path home, content. Reflecting upon this encounter later, I realised that if these were great northern divers at this location and this time of year, it was a very rare sighting indeed, and thought perhaps that it might have been the slightly less rare black throated or the more common red throated diver. Possibly the former, but the latter is slighter with a less bulky head and has a different call. At the time, it seemed obvious what the birds were.

This is a glen that has suffered much clearance. The map marks the locations of many sheilings, with several sizeable communities perched along its edge, now on the ground only outlines of foundations, piles of stones where people once lived. The usual ghosts. South of the loch is a flat grassy watershed, with squiggly rivers meandering and gurgling through holes and channels. I walked happily over the deserted landscape, avoiding paths and deliberately not aiming for the end of a track, increasingly disturbed by noises of construction. Bearing right and up another valley to the pass back to the car, climbing slightly, I looked back at the track down towards Glean Fearnach to see a JCB toiling with boulders repairing (or improving) the track, although presumably not because ruined communities are in line for reinvigoration.

There was a bit of a climb to the next glen, along which there is both a broad estate track and an older stalker's path; though I chose instead to follow the river between them and pick out a route over unimproved ground. Soon enough I would be back at civilisation, tramping along pavements and driving metalled roads, for the moment I was happy with the naked surface of the planet. At the level of a line of grouse butts spreading north up the mountainside, there was another watershed, where the peat hags briefly challenged, but soon I was walking again down a flat, beautifully secluded valley, scattered with the outlines of shielings. Hundreds of people evidently frequented these interconnected glens, now there is just a noisy JCB moving rocks on a track used only privately to gain access to killing fields, which under some loophole in legislation are considered to have the same status as agricultural land, and over which access tracks may legitimately be constructed, despite leaving ugly scars or obliterating older, more topographically responsible paths.

It was a longer walk than I had anticipated, not that this bothered me. In fact I regretted not having time to stay out longer, having to get back to life in the city, to the responsibilities of work and the realities of the disease. The blood marker was rising and had reached a level beyond what is normal for a man of my age. I was under pressure from oncologists to accept medication that would suppress production of testosterone and so deprive malignant prostate cells of the hormone they require to function. Every step towards the car was a brutal reminder of what I am able to forget for as long as I am in the heart of the mountains, living with their cycles, sharing the space with wild animals and contemplating the existence of the people who once lived here.

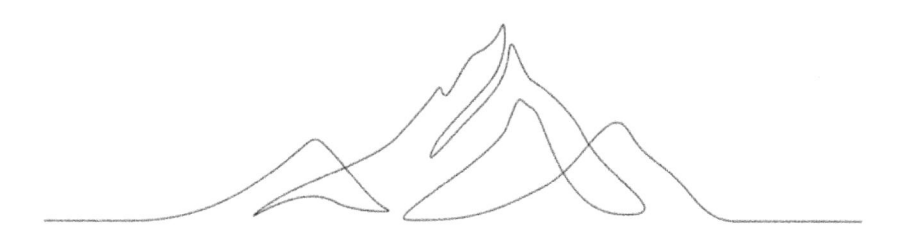

## *Glas Tulachain*

### 6th and 7th June 2015

After my night out with loons, I decided that nights out would be something I would be doing as often as possible from now on, so I bought a new tent. Same manufacturer, North Face, but different model, symmetrical this time with space enough at the front to sit up and look out, and a stable geodesic frame of three interlocking poles, allowing it to stand freely without pegs, which is very useful for positioning on lumpy ground and restricted space.

The weather was not however offering much in the way of opportunity. Since the heat of Atholl in April, there had been a return to more wintery conditions and despite the date, summer had not begun. I was also committed to work during most of the week and my trips restricted to weekends. Again I had a cluster in mind, with just one night out, starting during the day and walking in, climbing the next day and walking back to the start. Still my aspirations were dominated by expeditions, still the idea of bagging summits in a day seemed inauthentic, not quite conferring the correct measure of respect on the land, not allowing the elements enough time to impinge on the experience of being there, seeing instead these denatured mountains only as boxes to tick on a list of arbitrarily selected high points, and the landscape as an obstacle course.

I left the city at three in the afternoon, prepared for one night, knowing there was daylight still for many hours. Although the weather was not promising, I was bursting to try out my new tent. I parked at Spittal of Glenshee, on the north side of the old bridge at a place where cars often park and grit is piled in preparation for winter. There was plenty space. It was wet, windy and gloomy. The mountain tops were shrouded in rain clouds. Not a good day to be outside. I walked west through pasture, gradually rising past isolated barns, sheepfolds and dipping cages, then turned right up the flat glen of the *Allt Ghlinn Thaitneich*. It was a long walk, but it was never more than a walk along a farm track, until the end of the strath, where two burns cascade down steepening valleys and come together. An eagle soared into the cloud and a massive herd of deer gathered on the far side of the glen.

I took the left fork following a rough track that petered out into a faint walker's path. Although it was not yet properly raining, the ground was sodden and the river high, in some places overflowing its banks and scattering gravelly detritus over flattened summer grass. These were places where normally I would think about finding space for a tent. For a while I had been following a pair of human beings about a mile ahead; at length I passed them by, putting up their tent on a damp piece of ground that seemed to me far too close to a creeping patch of damp emerging from some moss round a boulder. I wished them well and persevered.

There was a wind now too howling down the valley, which narrowed ahead, steepening into a V and culminating in a wall over which water poured. I saw from the map that immediately on the far side of the lip, there was a lochan with flat ground at the outflow, nestling between two of the three mountains I intended to climb the next day. But I did not know what the flat of the map meant, whether or not it signified camp ground. A scale of twenty-five thousand to one is not quite enough detail to mark the difference between flat bog, flat tussocks, flat rock, grassland. I have been caught out before, notably on a journey from Glen Carron to Torridon in changeable weather, where at the height of the pass on my old fifty thousand map there was plenty flat to be seen, but on the ground this flat was naked rock, slabs devoid of any vegetation and deep lochans surrounded by cliffs. I could have slept out in some crevice perhaps, but the threat of rain encouraged me to persevere. Looking out below for flat ground on the way down, aiming for meandering burns with high grassy banks, everything I came across that had appeared from above to be a plausible place for a tent, turned out to be utterly impossible, all the flat ground on the way down was simply too rough and lumpy. Eventually I camped on the bank of the River Torridon under a row of red pines that has been a place people have camped ever since people have camped, next to the road back east and a mile from the village shop.

I have learned never to expect to find secure camp ground anywhere and with the wind like this, I did not want to get up too high, so adopted a strategy of *the next opportunity is the best opportunity*. Not far beyond where the couple were putting up their tent, I found what seemed to be a reasonable place, then rejected it and walked on, regretting the decision as nothing more presented itself. Only rough ground. If only it were not so wet, there would have been more opportunities, but water was pouring down the sides of the mountains, the ground universally sodden. It was getting dark by the time I found a place by the path, surprisingly well drained between two soggy watercourses, far enough from the burn to avoid overflows or floods. I was able to place the tent perfectly on exactly the right bit of ground.

The new sleeping space was luxurious in comparison to the old, there was room for all my stuff, for me to move about without coming against the inner tent, to sit up and look out on a view. Not that there was much to see back down the valley but wet hills and low cloud. It rained a lot in the night and the wind blew continuously. I felt secure and slept well. In the morning there was a bit of blue sky behind lighter clouds, still hammering past on a fierce wind. The tent dried as I packed, when I discovered that it packed larger than my last little tent and took up more space, suggesting I might need a larger rucksack for future expeditions.

The rest of the day was a struggle against wind. Hard and unrelenting. Infuriating. At the top of the glen, the path clambered up beside a gushing waterfall to the flat ground at the edge of the lochan, which was indeed good campground, with a patch where fires are made, but the wind was merciless, hammering over the top, pushing water out of the loch. A path circumnavigated the left bank towards routes up and round the mountains. There was an old snowbank still dangling over the edge, above which I passed by over squelchy, flattened grass following other boots. I was aiming for the far side of the loch where there is a shallow gully in the side of *Beinn Iutharn Beag*. It was a short clamber through tall heather and rock, opening out into boulder fields and screes. From here I found a clear path towards a shoulder of **Beinn Iutharn Mor**, which I gladly followed. The wind was intense, sapping away all energy with the effort of remaining upright, though gradients were now not steep.

The summit of **Beinn Iutharn Mor** is an undistinguished pile of rocks. Perhaps on a beautiful spring day, surrounded by snowfields, this might be a remarkable summit, but today it was part of an excuse to get out to play with my new tent. *Beinn à Ghlò* and **Carn na Righ** dominated the view south and west; to the north and east, the Cairngorms and Glen Shee. On the way off the summit, the path up **Carn na Righ** was clear and visible. On a good day I would have left my pack at the base and climbed it before heading back to the car via **Glas Tulaichean**. But the wind had drained my resources, dampened my spirit; better to wait for a better reason to climb it, better to use the energy I have left to get back to the car.

The only sensible route back from here, apart from the route in, was to climb the gentle northern slope to the summit of **Glas Tulaichean** and then follow a track off the summit in the direction of Glen Shee. It was a relatively easy plod, with the wind at my back, more or less, to a round flat summit serrated on the east by deep corries. From the summit cairn a track descends and splits into four others, each following one of the mountain's shoulders, but only one finds a route all the way down. I did not stop much at the top more than to admire the impressive drop into the eastern corries, before checking I was following the right track to descend.

The wind was still fierce, but the sky was clearing and the views splendid. I was accompanied all along the way by many mountain hare, bouncing over this mottled ground, stopping suddenly, coming to a complete standstill and becoming hereby utterly invisible. At the end of the track, in the cleft of Glen Lochsie there is a ruined lodge, from which a dismantled railway traverses the steep side of the hill to Glenlochsie Farm, part of the infrastructure of a previous time when massive numbers of animals and birds were regularly slaughtered and had to be removed from the hill. From above, the two-storey building appeared to be in reasonable condition, but coming round to the front revealed a gaping hole in the wall, now connecting together two windows and providing no support for roof beams. I looked inside from a distance to see assorted rubbish and detritus scattered on the earth floor, and then walked on towards the dismantled railway, expecting this to be a path down. I was disappointed, but there was no other way. The rails were long gone, leaving only concrete plinths embedded into the ground upon which sleepers once lay. Although spaced regularly, these are in assorted conditions of decay and have eroded the surrounding ground randomly, making walking between them more challenging than regular ground. At last I was out of the wind, but the going was harder work.

At the end of the dismantled railway there are remnants of loading platforms. A grass track continues over pasture through Glenlochsie Farm. As I closed the gate behind me on the way out, I saw a notice kindly requesting hillwalkers to follow a detour path round the farm, which of course I would have done had I not approached from the hill side. I walked on down past a hotel, on the opposite side of the river I could see my car parked where I had left it. The weather was definitely easing, with blue skies beginning to dominate. I looked forward to returning one day to climb *Carn na Righ*, and to taking my new tent on further adventures. I was hatching many plans.

## *Glen Lyon Horseshoe*

**11th June 2015**

The day after my foul weather tent testing expedition in Glen Shee, summer arrived. Heat, balmy wind, tourists crawling all over the city. I also got the result of another blood test. The news was not good. On the spur of the moment, I decided to climb some mountains.

A couple of weeks earlier I saw a headline on the internet about a circular walk from Invervar in Glen Lyon, and so I scrutinised the map, although stubborn as I am, I did not consult the article under the headline. It would be an easy day, I thought, and the route would only take a few hours, for the distance was not great. With all this daylight and such glorious weather, I could linger. There was something especially attractive about the prospect of climbing up high only once, then without losing much altitude, following a route past no fewer than six separate peaks, of which four are Munros.

The blood marker for prostate cancer is a protein called *prostate specific antigen*, or PSA, the level of which under normal circumstances remains stable at about 4 ng/ml or less. Although PSA is not diagnostic, in the sense that a high value only indicates increased prostate activity, if prostate cancer has already been diagnosed, levels of PSA are a good indication of the state of the disease. For the previous year or so, since a month of focused radiotherapy in April 2014 and after my first experience of chemical castration, my PSA level had been low, and for a while within normal margins, but recently it was rising again, oncologists were getting very twitchy and had almost persuaded me once again to endure hormone suppressing medication. Almost, but not quite.

Glen Lyon is one of the most beautiful in Scotland and it is said to be the longest, although how such things are measured is probably a matter of dispute. It is one of a number of parallel glens that drain east into the Tay river system, it is sandwiched between Loch Rannoch to the north and Lochs Tay and Earn to the south. Along its length it is surrounded by Munros, about twenty, depending on how they are counted. The entrance is at Fortingall, reputedly the birthplace of Pontius Pilate, where the River Lyon passes through a narrow gorge, after which, the glen opens out into farmland and plantation, then further up into remnants of Caledonian forest and the usual combination of high pasture, killing fields and dammed lochs. About half way along, at the hamlet of Bridge of Balgie, there is a junction with a road south over a high pass to the trunk road along the north shore of Loch Tay. The road up the glen is hereafter marked as a *cul-de-sac*; it does not however come to an end at the last dam some twelve miles further up the glen, but south on the other side of a high pass towards Glen Lochay, where there are gates into pasture. Not long after returning from The Netherlands, I drove over the pass in my old Dutch Volvo and then all the way down into Glen Lochay to meet the road back to Killin. Many years before this I climbed *Beinn Heasgarnaich* from the highest point on the road with colleagues, having driven up from Glen Lochay in a university minibus. The most difficult section of the road is here, behind farm gates, zigzagging through churned up cattle pasture, badly eroded and unmaintained. It is the only section not part of the public road network, the reason why there is a *cul-de-sac* sign twenty miles away in Glen Lyon.

Invervar however nestles only a few miles from the entrance to Glen Lyon in a little deciduous woodland where a burn flows from corries to the north and down a hanging valley surrounded by plantations, which when I visited were in the process of being harvested. There was also a new track under construction to accommodate heavy plant and give access to a micro-hydro turbine further up the valley. Invervar is only a few houses by a bridge, a red phone-box and a place where walkers park. I arrived late in the morning and squeezed into the last plausible space. After a false start into somebody's garden, I found the right path, through a dense green woodland busy with chattering birds.

Leaving the woodland, the path was immediately obliterated by the newly constructed track, scraped out of the ground for use by caterpillar tracked and large wheeled vehicles of many horsepower, not feet in boots. A little more than a few hundred metres of steep ugly ascent later, I spotted a path flanking east through a meadow of new bracken, unfolding, the harbinger of summer. About half a mile further, a beautifully maintained stalkers' path traverses steadily up from the bracken of this steep pasture into heather under the first crags and outcrops of the plateau. Views opened up along Glen Lyon and towards **Ben Lawers** on the other side; summer in full bloom along the floor of the glen, while substantial snowbanks still lay thick in northeast facing slopes above.

The path wends its way past crags into moorland and upwards to a mix of stones and earth. I arrived atop *Meall na Aighean* just before two in the afternoon. The only mountains I recognised on the north side were *Schiehallion*, the Cairngorm plateaux, **Ben Alder** and **Ben Nevis**. The rest I had to guess, or accept that I simply did not know. The route for the rest of the day beckoned, over a flat earthy bealach towards the snowclad crags of the next peak. During the course of the next hours, I would descend no more than a hundred and forty metres below this altitude, and rise little more than sixty. I followed a well-worn path through many configurations of rock, crag and earthy ground, from time to time passing pools and lochans fed by melting snowbanks. The sky was blue, the sun warm, the air still. The snowclad horizon shimmered in the heat.

Clearly it had been a severe winter with much snow; not only were the snowbanks numerous, they were also very thick, the remnants of drifts plastered against the sides of the mountains by wind, then rained upon and frozen, immune to this summer heat. In the distance in the shadow of a cornice on a vast snowbank reaching far into the corrie, a herd of deer cooling off their feet. Around the edges of the plateau and below in the corrie, flattened grasses and blackened ground where until recently snow lay. Despite the greening of the glen below, winter was still up here, melting away, but not yet absent.

Gradually I was coming to realise what was happening. After reaching the summits of **Càrn Marig** and then **Meall Garbh**, I rested in the dip before the final climb to **Càrn Gorm**, looking east. I could do this any time I fancied. And there are hundreds more mountains out there. In fact I could turn it into a challenge to myself, a motivating drive, something to which I might strive, to climb as many Munros as I can before this allegedly malignant, aggressive disease takes me. With the deadline now approaching, the third anniversary of being told I would live no longer than three years, what better way of proving them wrong, of living beyond these three years despite the disease, subverting the deterministic logic of progression with my very life? My strategy of refusal had taken me this far, why not further?

It was after five in the afternoon before I arrived at the grassy summit of **Càrn Gorm**, the final of the day's four Munros. I sat at the top chomping on nuts and raisins and admiring the incredible views. All this is freely available to anybody with the resources and wherewithal to get here. And as I experienced the previous weekend, even though the weather is rarely as spectacular as this, there are always beauties, challenges and now, here, epiphanies. These mountains will surely provide for a number of vital needs, spiritually and physically, intellectually and emotionally too, as places of reflection where I might achieve perspective amongst the complex realities of civilised existence and the sicknesses it unleashes. A kind of mindfulness combining physical exertion with mental discipline, and satisfying the most fundamental urge, the desire simply *to be alive*. When first I started working as a bike messenger, nearly twenty years earlier in The Netherlands, my dispatcher told me I had a natural talent for finding the right address in whatever weather no matter what the time of day. The dogged persistence and determination to get the job done, this self-reliance and preparedness for any eventuality, this cavalier attitude to weather, were all formed in my youth as I wandered through mountains. Time to return to these roots, and doggedly to persist *being alive*.

When I was told about the severity of the disease, it was immediately obvious from the demeanour of the urologist charged with conveying the news that it was not going to be good. I was told later by friends working in health services and related professions that the fashion of the moment in relation to bad news was to make it short and sharp, without any sugar coating. And so it was, when presented with the question of how long I might be expected to live, he answered with the brutal truth as far as he saw it, that unless I took the medication he was offering I would be dead within a year, and that even if I took it, I would likely live no longer than three. Short and sharp, without any sugar coating.

This was the culminating conversation with a team of urologists, each of whom had endeavoured to persuade me without delay to accept the medication, to endure the chemical suppression of the testosterone production required by my malignantly proliferating prostate cells and thereby hold at bay the inevitable progression of the disease. I was reluctant immediately to do this; I wanted to investigate alternatives, and revisit stuff I had learned from my mother about the power of nature to heal a body when it is cared for and lives simply, in a condition of health, eating a low-protein diet almost entirely of fresh fruit and vegetables, avoiding the poisons offered in these societies in the name of medicine and food, while eschewing the toxins of the mental environment.

I presented the matter to the urologists as entirely my own choice. From their point of view I was not only being utterly irrational, I was challenging their institutional values and status, their clinical expertise and also their egos. But only this one man, the one who delivered the bad news, could not keep his ego in his trousers. During previous conversations, this particular urologist was most disparaging, contemptuous of my opinions, dismissive of everything but the well-established protocols of prostate cancer management. His answer to the question was loaded, infused with a kind of resentment, motivated to blackmail me emotionally into taking the medication, finding some way of ensuring I realised just how serious this was, treating me like an unruly adolescent, telling me off for not doing what I was told. Whether this insensitivity was deliberate or an unconscious effect of institutionalised procedures, just a bad habit, is less important than the logic of the message and its effects.

At the start of October 2012 my future was reduced to this: I had a disease that would progress predictably until it killed me; if I carried on doing what I was doing I would be dead within a year, the only hope was an injection of hormone suppressing medication that would work for only two years more. It was simply a matter of time. It did not matter what I ate or how much I exercised, nor whether the knowledge upon which these prognoses are based can be seriously doubted from many points of view, that there are different ways both of thinking about and treating disease. The protocol was as it was, deployed in the management of prostate cancer by the assemblage of state subsidy and insurance capital that has inherited the Dutch system of health care, and which paid the medical bills.

It has never mattered that no other doctor was prepared so precisely to offer such a prognosis, nor to do so with such binary certainty. This is how the disease exists in my head. Its conceptual shape is as diseased as the disease itself, malignant and aggressive, affecting every aspect of my mental life, overwriting what I used to think of as *my* future with crushing logic, peppering the past with intense regrets and stupidity, making the present the only sensible place in which to exist, endangering thus the irresponsibility of hedonism, opportunism and cynicism, none of which were unfamiliar territory. Fortunately however making it possible also for all residual nihilism to become the beginnings of wisdom.

So I walked away from the medical model, accepting neither option. Instead I decided to return to a simpler way of life, to return to my mother's ideas, to cut out poisons and to take important decisions about what to do with whatever remained of my time here. The first move was to clean up my diet; within a week I had cut out all processed foods, all meat and dairy products, alcohol, caffeine and sugar, and was living exclusively on predominantly raw organic fruit and vegetables, nuts, crackers and bread. This was the start of the current journey, my determination to overcome the determinism of medical prognostication. Within a week of cleaning up my diet I felt the benefits, and after six months the PSA had risen only very slightly, within the margin of statistical insignificance, vindicating my decision from the very start and already subverting the notion of *doubling time*, by which the rate of progression is measured. And yet the mental consequences always lingered. Once you have been told you are going to die within a certain timeframe, and you give the matter serious thought, no amount of contrary evidence is going to undo the effects of being told.

A great deal had changed in less than three years. Perhaps now I was prepared to die, sitting on top of this mountain in the evening sunshine. I had left behind my previous life, said my final farewells to good friends, human, feline and canine, endured the anguish of divorce, had written a little book of aphorisms expressing my final message to the world, sold my wee bike shop to a friend, given away a lot of stuff, left a collective messenger company I helped establish. Now here I was with a brand new life. Living with the love of my life, my beautiful Shona, again delivering stuff in a city, with permanent access to these hills. It seemed miraculous.

Although of course, access is granted only under certain conditions, with rights come responsibilities; walkers must always defer to instructions from estate employees, especially during killing seasons, and should avoid areas where game is stalked, where animals shelter or breed. If it were up to some landowners, walkers would be confined to specific paths and denied access to open country. This corrie is perhaps a case in point, for it is requested, on a notice that I read upon my return to the car, that walkers keep to the path on the tops and not stray into the bowl of corries and hanging valleys between, lest they worry the deer. It also seemed that I had walked round the horseshoe in the wrong direction, anti-clockwise rather than the recommended clockwise, although apart from getting a different view, quite what difference it would make to which direction a person walks round these hills remains unclear.

At some point in the not too distant future I would be taking the medication again. It would begin with a daily pill of *Bicalutamide*, a female analogue of testosterone that blocks testosterone from its usual receptors, to be followed two to three weeks later by an intramuscular injection of *Decapeptyl*, which works for three months to shut down the entire hormone production system deep inside the brain. This is the treatment I rejected immediately after I was diagnosed. Although, after six months on my new diet when the PSA was unchanged at around 140, which is still very high, I was persuaded to take an increased dose of *Bicalutamide*, which dropped the PSA to the much less alarming level of 25, while feminising my body quite intriguingly. I continued with this until arriving back in Scotland, when the PSA rose again.

According to the Dutch protocol, the *Decapeptyl* injection was to be repeated every three months and continued until my demise. In general, this drug will suppress the disease for a while, but eventually it will stop working, depending on how malignant and aggressive it is. In my case, extremely aggressive, meaning that it replicates very quickly and easily invades surrounding tissue; and very malignant, meaning that it is able quickly to adapt to a lack of testosterone and replicate nevertheless. Hence the bleak prognosis. If immediately I had taken the injection at the time of diagnosis, it was expected that it would work for less than two years, after which there would be a year of metastatic decline.

The oncologists in Scotland had a less formulaic response to my condition. In order to spread out the time during which the disease was expected to develop resistance to the drugs, they suggested an intermittent schedule, by which I would be medicated for six months, and after which I could allow my body to recuperate from the side effects while monitoring the rise of PSA, until such time that it rose again to levels that alarmed the oncologists. This was where I was, on the verge of starting a second period of hormone suppressing medication. Putting it off for as long as possible; the first time I had accepted the treatment, I did not know what to expect, now I did, and it horrified me.

The descent from the mountain was uneventful, beginning over a large snowbank under a crag where a ring ouzel flew by, peeping distinctively, then through grass, heather and bracken overlooking a heart-shaped mossy pool, a source of the burn through Invervar. The ugly new track turned out to be the only way down, which did not raise my mood, for it was steep and the surface loose, challenging my knees and toes. I was glad to return into the little woodland on the way back to the road, still busy with birds. The complete circuit had taken rather longer than I had anticipated, reminding me that even on a good day, with very little climbing over easy terrain, mountain miles are much longer than regular miles. I arrived back at the car just after seven, rejuvenated and inspired, working on my plans with new determination, still not quite ready to take the medication.

## Bynack More

12th July 2015

While staying at a cottage in Speyside, Shona and I took a walk from Glenmore Lodge past the Green Lochan towards Ryvoan Pass and then round to the path to **Bynack More**. Shona wanted to get up another Munro and I assured her that save for taking the funicular up **Cairngorm**, this one would be the easiest in the area and would probably not present too many challenges, for although it was quite a long walk, it was not steep, until perhaps the final summit cone.

The cottage is leased from Rothiemurchus Estate by friends; it is situated at the edge of the forest and is invisible from the road. This cottage is a place dear to our hearts, for it is where first Shona brought me on holiday in the summer of 2013, just before I packed up all my stuff and left my continental life behind. Shona and I were friends at school and apart from a couple of random encounters, we had not seen each other since, aged eighteen, we went off to have lives. We connected again on the dreaded Facebook, and not long before my diagnosis in the summer of 2012, some thirty-five years after we had last bumped into each other, we met up for real when I was visiting Edinburgh. Over the next year we messaged regularly; slowly and very carefully we unleashed a passion that as children we did not understand, and that blossomed for the first time in this little house.

The cottage has a conservatory looking over Rothiemurchus Forest to the twin plateaux of the high Cairngorms, held apart by the dark gash of the *Lairig Ghru*. Shona says that I sat here when I first visited the place, gazing at **Braeriach**, my favourite mountain, crying out all the stuff that comes with being diagnosed so far from home and so brutally with such a voracious disease, letting go of many years of untold emotion in the safety of a love that had lain dormant nearly forty years. Apart from being madly in love, we were in awe that after all this time, we were together, still best friends and now also lovers. Perhaps we needed the experience of life to be able to know how to take responsibility for the love that always existed between us. Love is such an intimate mystery, so fragile, so easily diverted by emotional fashion and subverted by desire. That somehow the universe brought us together again remains the most beautiful mystery of this life.

We return to the cottage as often as we can. This visit was almost exactly a year after we entertained a dozen or more friends from The Netherlands at the beginning of the summer of 2014, not long before my trip to **Ben Alder**. Shona and my dearest Dutch friends were determined that I would once again climb a mountain, specifically **Braeriach**, the large hump behind the three snow filled corries to the right of the *Lairig Ghru*. Several large Dutch messengers were equally determined that if I were not able to get to the summit under my own steam, they would carry me. As it happened, the weather was not as clement as it might have been. The party was large and it began to spread out just at the moment when the rain came down seriously for the first time, after the ascent of *Sron na Lairige*, the most northerly shoulder of the mountain that forms the western side of the *Lairig Ghru*. There is precious little shelter at this altitude, well actually, there is none at all, but for crouching in the lee of the largest boulder or lump available, and just waiting it out until the fury passes over, or until good sense suggests it would be better to return, which is not always a very good plan either, particularly in whiteout conditions when it is easy to get utterly lost or walk off a cliff.

Five made it to the summit that day, the fittest and most adventurous, while the rest turned back down along an older path following a burn bubbling out of a large patch of snow. It was a reminder of what these mountains mean, for as we descended, heat returned to the air, clouds now only briefly blocked out the sun, not swirling with needles of frozen drizzle, nor throwing down torrents of cold lumpy water. From below it appears simply that the mountain is enveloped in dark cloud. The ones who made it to the summit experienced more of it that the rest and arrived back just before an almighty storm drenched Speyside, taking away all the heat that had accumulated during what turned out to be quite a nice day. These mountains have their own climate, they thrust upwards into the Arctic and catch a more turbulent kind of air, something quite rare. Apart from the lump of Ben Nevis and its three nearest neighbours to the west and Norway to the east there is nothing higher; to the south it is somewhere in central France, and in a great circle through the north pole nothing higher until Antarctica. If the weather can turn so nasty at midsummer in this broad valley of woodland trails, tourist attractions and discrete forestry, what carnage is it unleashing on the plateaux above.

Apart from having a special place in the story of my life, there is a natural homeliness about the cottage that intersects with my strong sense of belonging to these mountains. The Cairngorms are the mountains through which I have wandered most intensively, their peaks were the most common goal of my youthful expeditions. Before the diagnosis I had reached the summits of all six of the four-thousand-foot peaks, five of which are Munros, several times, and three of the other eleven. Bynack More sits almost on its own to the northeast of the main group, sticking out from a vast plain of low brown hills fissured by narrow valleys that stretches into the rich pastures of Aberdeenshire.

The walk in to the mountain follows a well-known path towards the forest of Strathnethy and the pass of Ryvoan, past the much-admired green lochan. Before the highest point it swings right towards the valley of the young River Nethy. Here there is a bridge to a slowly rising path up a long shoulder to a low plateau. The ground is about the same altitude as the *Lairig Ghru*, but has a completely different character. Very gradually the terrain changes as the vegetation thins, opening out into stony ground clumped with mosses and grasses. The path is long but not challenging. Shona's understanding of steep is however different from mine and she was already feeling uncomfortable. At the point where she was no longer able to lift her legs high enough to deal with the gradient of the summit cone, she had to admit defeat.

Not so far away there was a lump of rock about the size of a small building furnished with a cave like cleft where she could shelter. These tors are common to the high ground on this side of the Cairngorms, remnants of the last ice age when the ground was covered in slowly moving ice dragging along boulders beneath. At least two of the major summits are atop such a boulder. I left Shona somewhat reluctantly, but she found shelter and I followed the path to the top, by this time now covered in cloud. It was only the initial section that was steep. Soon the path skirted along the edge of a narrow ridge, which it sometimes crested to reveal a fainter path on the other side. Presumably with winds coming from either side of the hill, sheltered walking has been sought on both sides of the mountain, creating two routes up.

As I climbed the weather deteriorated and the cloud thickened. On the way I was surveyed by many ptarmigan, and it became progressively wetter. I had by now bought myself a new rain jacket, which was doing sterling work keeping my inside dry and warm. The top of the mountain is relatively flat, but there is a jumble of red boulders and rocks, which in the thick cloud confused navigation. It took a while to work out the position of the actual summit, though when I saw it, it was obvious what it was. I did not hang around and returned quickly to find Shona chattering in the big rock. Another reminder that in the middle of summer the weather at these altitudes in the Cairngorms is often very far from summery. I was wet and she was cold, but we dried off and warmed up quickly as we continued back down. Clouds parted and blue skies again emerged. Looking back, we saw the summit of the mountain still engulfed in cloud.

Dry warmth returned as we descended; by the time we were at the bridge back over the Nethy, it was positively hot. We dawdled down the path taking photographs and admiring the landscape. At the green lochan we stopped for a while to rest in the sun and gaze into the deep clear water, in awe of ancient trees growing through screes behind the water and sliding slowly down the hill. In the depths of the lochan, centuries of waterlogged tree carcasses, preserved in this crystal-clear aspic as densely green as tarnished copper.

Shona was disappointed not to have reached the summit of another Munro, but I was proud of her for getting as far as she did, to add to the heights she reached on **Braeriach** a year before and **Ben Chonzie** earlier in the year, grateful once more for the reminder of how extreme the weather can become within the climates these mountains create.

We had to decide when I was going to start taking the medication again. We were putting it off because we knew how seriously it would affect our relationship. The first time we experienced this we were presented with the greatest challenge we had hitherto encountered. Almost exactly a month after the first hormone suppressing injection was administered, its most profound effect kicked in. What had worked the previous night, stopped. I changed from a confidently sexual red-blooded male into a menopausal eunuch. This change continued to affect both of us very deeply, cumulatively and in very different ways.

## *Sutherland*

17th to 27th **July 2015**

In 1987, I bought a used mountain bike from a friend, one of the first in the country. This was the beginning of adventures among local hills and expeditions into the Highlands and Islands, and the start of my fascination with bicycle mechanics. Every year until I left to live in The Netherlands, I took cycling holidays up and down the west coast of Scotland. During this period I fell in love with Sutherland, the most north westerly region of the mainland, the most sparsely populated and geographically interesting. Twenty-eight years later, I was determined once again to visit by bicycle before I died, now with the added incentive of along the way climbing the five most northerly Munros, of which four are in Sutherland.

Preparations for this expedition had been ongoing for a month or so and had to be more precise than for regular excursions, anticipating over a week of every possible eventuality. Much the same as with other cycle journeys. Although the only extra stuff I needed to carry were my boots, a daysack and a few more clothes, I realised after planning a route that I would need to carry quite a lot of food, for I wanted to avoid main roads as much as possible and to find routes I had not before followed. I would not be passing by very many places where there are still shops.

When I lived in Utrecht, I took many backroads journeys. Apart from thousands of miles within the borders of The Netherlands itself, I travelled into the German Eifel and back, to Basel, to Copenhagen and back following only tiny country roads and forest tracks. I cycled twice to Berlin, and the second time onward to Warsaw. On the northern European plain oak and pine forests mingle with maize, mixed arable and pasture, becoming progressively less managed travelling east, the only visible borders now massive meandering rivers held at bay by levees, and changes in styles of architecture and street furniture, until in Poland hedgerows and sheaves of grain drying in stooks, reminiscent of my childhood in rural Perthshire. Cycle touring remains the most intimate way of experiencing the fine details of the landscape, passing through ways of life invisible from the velocity of arterial routes, watching subtle changes to the land as it rolls past beneath wheels, powered by continuously revolving legs as a mind is free to reflect in its own space.

My trips to Warsaw and Berlin were on a fixie pulling a trailer, to Copenhagen on a racing bike pulling a different make of trailer. In Scotland, I returned to a more conventional arrangement with racks and panniers on a mountain bike frame; the same as for my trips to the Eifel, to Basel and through the Canadian Rockies and Washington Cascades. For the geeks: Ritchey 26" steel mountain bike frame; rigid steel high clearance fork and Cane Creek headset; Shimano XT eight-speed derailleurs, chain, square tapered bottom bracket, crank set with 46/36/24 Black Spire chainrings, and hubs with a custom 11/12/13/14/16/18/21/24 cassette; Shimano XT nine-speed parallel push v-brakes; Ritchey drop bars with Shimano STI shifters and *frog-leg* brake levers; DT spokes and Mavic rims; Time pedals, Thomson seatpost, Ritchey stem and Flite saddle; Schwalbe tyres and wide mudguards; Tubus racks, Ortlieb front and rear panniers, saddlebag, handlebar bag and stuff sack.

Packing was more straightforward than I had expected. All cycling and camping gear, all food and domestic necessities fitted easily into the panniers, with the bulk of the weight in lowriders on either side of the front hub, while the rear bags took all the bulky stuff, with a down sleeping bag pressed into a large waterproof stuff sack attached above by bungees. This turned out to be a useful flexible space, for although the sleeping bag puffed out to fit happily inside the whole size of the sack, it could be pushed down to accommodate whatever I might need to pick up along the way. It served too as a minor back support, for when I leaned back I could feel it there, almost as if the bike had become an easy chair. And it prevented the toolkit secured under the saddle from flapping about. Finally, all my personal stuff, camera, wallet, phone and charger, maps, reading, writing material and so forth fitted into the handlebar bag, on top of which was attached a waterproof map case.

I left Haymarket on the morning train with a return ticket to Dingwall, whence I planned to take the old road over Struie Hill and to stay the night with a friend who lives at the very edge of Sutherland in Ardgay. Leaving Dingwall, I followed the cycle route north up a steep hill, a sudden reminder of the effort required to carry such weight, how the heart beats faster and sweat seeps insistently from every pore. Muscle groups adapted quickly as I selected the most sensible gear and settled into the rhythm. Near the top, Shona phoned to wish me *bon voyage*, whereupon I remembered that talking on top of all this work uses too much oxygen. We made it nevertheless to the top still in conversation, where the road turned right out of the town along a minor road parallel to the trunk road below, rising slowly through farmland banked by thickets of heavy green trees and hedgerows, with views over the Cromarty Firth and Nigg Bay.

The road rose to a high point at about a hundred metres and undulated down to Evanton. Through the town at the industrial estate I turned north towards Struie onto what is now a minor road serving only the communities along its length. This was once the trunk road north, but since the opening of the bridge over the Dornoch Firth at Tain, traffic is directed there along the coast from Evanton, rather than over the hill to the older crossing of the narrows at Bonar Bridge. What a difference from the days when these gradients were clogged with heavy vehicles and traffic was continuous. Once, when the new bridge was constructed but not yet open, I followed the low road, on the off chance I might get to sneak my bike across, but also to avoid the chaos over Struie. Needless to say, I found no way over the bridge and had to cycle the perimeter of the Dornoch Firth, which turned out to be only a little longer and to involve the treat of cycling through the forest of Spinnigdale between Bonar Bridge and Dornoch, the most northerly remaining patch of indigenous oak forest in the country. This is a road that now too takes only local traffic.

The road rises slowly out of Evanton before plunging steeply into the gorge of the River Averon, after which it climbs and climbs past a derelict petrol station and café, and a few isolated houses until it levels out at about two hundred metres. The road drops very slightly at Strathrory then reaches its highest point before traversing a flat moorland once used for peat extraction, now flourishing with young indigenous trees and shrubs, fenced in against grazing. The road leaves the north edge of the moor following a tiny stream gathering in flat marshy ground between two steep sided low hills. The watershed is barely noticeable and after a bend to the right and a turn to the left, the road descends quickly to reach sea-level a few miles east of Ardgay. On the way down, I stopped at a viewpoint with tourists in motorhomes and leather clad Germans on BMWs. It was a fine day with blue sky, warm sun and slowly moving high cloud. The Dornoch Firth below, deep blue and sparkling, rimmed by verdant growth and yellow beaches. To the northwest Bonar Bridge and the Kyle of Sutherland, where waters from the rivers Carron, Shin and Oykel gather into a slender tidal finger reaching twenty-five miles inland from the Bridge at Tain, which at its most westerly point is not much further away from the sea at Loch Broom at the edge of the Atlantic Ocean, making this possibly the narrowest point of mainland Scotland.

After a most enjoyable stay with my friend, let's call him Malcolm, I headed off hopeful that the gentle weather of the previous day would persist and the cloud that had gathered in the night would be thin enough to burn off. I followed a marked cycle route along the west side of the Kyle to Carbisdale Castle where it follows the railway line towards a bridge. Instead of continuing to follow the railway over the bridge, the path hangs beneath it, at the bottom of two flights of metal stairs. That this is regarded as appropriate for bikes is a consequence of guidelines by which pedestrian and cycle paths are constructed according to the same engineering criteria, very different from the design requirements of cycle infrastructures in The Netherlands to which I had become accustomed. It irritated me slightly, but I accepted that this is how things are done here. I went about the task of unhooking all the bags and panniers from my bike, carrying them one by one down to the bridge and putting them all together again at the bottom, to repeat the procedure on the other side where there was another flight of stairs down to the level of the road.

I was now on the way to Lairg, which is where I would have got off the train had I not wanted to visit Malcolm in Ardgay, nor enjoy the pleasures of Struie. Only a few hundred metres further, I turned left at the junction with the road to Strath Oykel, then crossed the River Shinn and followed it on the west side through dense mixed forests, passing Shinn Falls where salmon leap and anglers pay a fortune for the privilege of trying to catch them. At Lairg I stopped to snack and to put on my wet weather gear, for as I rose inland from sea-level the mist became thicker, blending into cloud and then into fine drizzle. It was not cold, but it was a bit miserable, with views restricted by a ceiling of cloud hanging at about fifteen hundred feet. I was very glad to have brought along neoprene overshoes, for when unprotected from the chill of fast-moving air, wet feet become cold feet very quickly.

Although a more direct route to the first Munro of the journey runs north from Lairg, I took the road east to Rogart because I had never cycled this road before and it would lead to a new route north; there was one road in particular I wanted to travel again and several I wanted to investigate for the first time. I almost missed the turn at Rogart and had to turn back to find the back road to Brora, up a gentle hill past lush thickets, rich pasture and many farms. At the highest point it seemed that the sun might come out, tantalising flashes of light garnished the forests and pastures of Strath Brora below. The cloud lifted a little as I ate lunch before the descent. I bypassed the town of Brora to the north and had no choice but briefly to follow the trunk road hugging the sea towards Thurso and Wick. After only five miles I turned north up Glen Loth along a tiny single-track road, at the start of which signposts warn users that there are only limited passing places, and that it would really not be a good idea to attempt it in winter. The initial climb from the main road was very steep indeed, but it settled into a slowly rising plod, first through meadows of bracken along the edge of a narrow V shaped valley, then over a massive desolate corrie, with signs on the ground of many deserted settlements, enclosed on the east by low hills and on the west by imposing cliffs thrusting into the cloud. On the way up I noticed absolutely no passing places. Just beyond the highest point as the road begins to slant down into Strath Kildonan, I met a chap wearing tweed breeches leaning against a long pickup, surveying the surroundings through binoculars, parked and taking up the whole road, pointing in the direction I had come. It was a bit of a tight squeeze, but I managed to get my bike past. What happens when vehicles meet each other on this road the man was reluctant to share, saying only that it hardly ever happens since so few tourists ever think to come this way and he is one of only a small number who ever use it.

The descent to Kildonan was initially steep and the road a bit broken up with much grass growing through the asphalt, but there were one or two places where vehicles could pass each other. It was a marvellous run down through open sheep country flanked occasionally by red pine woods. At the bottom, the road follows the railway line on the south of the River Helmsdale for a few miles before joining the road to Kinbrace at Kildonan Station. This is a most beautiful glen; had I not wanted to investigate Glen Loth I would have continued from Brora up the coast to Helmsdale and followed Strath Kildonan all the way from the sea as it rises imperceptibly towards the boggy expanses of the flow country through native forests, dense patches of gorse, flower filled pastures and smallholdings. It was now getting on in the day, and I had travelled more than ninety kilometres, nothing in comparison to the distances I consumed on the northern European plain, but respectable enough. It was time to find space for a tent on the banks of the river.

Midges are a well-known challenge for all mammals in the Scottish highlands at any time from May to September. I have a great deal of experience keeping these invisible dragons at bay and I was carrying a full complement of protection and discouragement, the most potent of which being incense-like coils, which produce a smoke from which all insects are visibly repulsed. I found a lovely patch of grass for my tent on the bank of the river under some trees next to a path used by anglers. The cloud was down again and the air still. Although it was damp it was not raining. Within seconds of stopping I was overwhelmed. It is difficult adequately to describe to anybody who has never experienced midges just how violent and insistent their presence can be. There are salves and unguents that can be smeared on skin to discourage them alighting and biting, but these are not always effective nor very pleasant on the skin and the tiny monsters usually find a way through clothing. Some people react very badly to midge bites; I only experience brief albeit intense itchiness, but the greater challenge is their crawling and swarming. And so I pitched my tent on the north bank of the River Helmsdale just before Kildonan Lodge, dancing about and running up and down like a thing possessed in order to create as much moving air as possible, in the vain hope the midges might disperse.

I can honestly say that of all the places I have pitched a tent, this was the most midge infested. Secure inside, I was reluctant to venture out at all and lit coils under the flysheet at the front. Fumes filled up the space. Outside I could see them in their billions, obscuring the view downstream, lusting after my blood but maintaining a distance from the smoky tent entrance. I ate, closed up the front of the tent and fell asleep. Just after midnight I awoke in urgent need of answering nature's call, a necessity the prospect of which I did not relish. Urination is never straightforward with prostate cancer, but doing so in the dark, swarmed by imperceptible blood sucking insects, inexorably attracted to exposed mammalian flesh does not make it any easier. In the morning I fired up the coils again and smeared myself with a mixture of olive, lavender and citronella oils, especially prepared by Shona, which I hoped would fend off the insects for long enough to pack up and get back on the road.

Not far beyond where I camped, the woods thin out and the road rises into open sheep pasture then moorland. Kinbrace junction is a clump of trees, a few houses, a primary school and a railway halt. The main road carries on north through the flat expanse of the flow country and then into the agriculture of Caithness. The other turns west, rising slowly through sheep country and enclosures of grazing deer, then more steeply to an immense shallow corrie of dense bogland, desolate and isolated, passing odd shaped lochs and bridging squiggly black trout streams, gushing deep through the peat, the only habitations a settlement not far out of Kinbrace and an hotel about ten miles further on, claiming to be the most isolated in Scotland. After this, nothing but random and incongruous monoculture plantations until the hamlet of Syre at the bottom of a steep hill in Strathnaver.

The first time I passed through Strathnaver, there was a huge brown road sign pointing in the direction of a "heritage site" on the east side of the river. On the map it is still marked as a tourist attraction and is described as a "clearance village" where visitors are invited to survey the remnants and foundations of the houses of Rossal, razed to the ground in the nineteenth century by factors employed by the Duke of Sutherland. The people who had hitherto eked out a precarious existence at the pleasure of his Lordship, in the fertile valley of the River Naver, on the banks of Loch Naver and in the gently wooded northern slopes of **Ben Klibreck**, were in possession now only of their labour power. Alienated from any connection with the land, they were forced to find work elsewhere, in the fishing villages on the north coast, in the factories of Glasgow or far off in the colonies. Two thousand people lived along this glen once, now there are no more than a few dozen, if that.

It enraged me then and it enrages me still that the word "heritage" could be used in relation to these events. That people were burned out of their houses is an indisputable fact of history, but that this might be described as "heritage" sends my mind into paroxysms of confused fury. "Heritage" signifies valued tradition, a past of which those who share it can be proud, something to show off and celebrate. I simply cannot understand how the entitled privilege of landowners deliberately burning people out of their homes, can be seen as "heritage", least of all when the current landowners are direct descendants of the ones responsible, and who perforce continue to profit from the conduct of their ancestors. Unless of course we believe it is a good thing that they did so, that these were, according to the prevailing mythology, improvements to the land, ways of encouraging the people to better themselves by seeking gainful employment elsewhere, never doubting the absolute right of landowners to use and dispose of this property as they see fit, amongst whom were the people and creatures who live on it. A degree of sense has now prevailed on signage; brown coloured signs are much smaller, referring only to "Rossal Forest Walk", and there is a discrete wooden notice at the end of the access track pointing simply to Rossal Township. On the opposite side of the river, there is a stopping place with a more tasteful memorial, one of many along the length of the glen, where information boards recount the experiences of those burned out of their homes. I stopped here on the way up the hill to Loch Naver to pay my respects and reflect on my country's heritage.

The weather was not looking promising for my ascent of **Ben Klibreck**, which would have been visible for the last twenty miles or so and now dominating the view on the other side of Loch Naver, had the cloud not been hanging only fifty feet above my head since Kinbrace. Cycling beside Loch Naver was nevertheless excellent, this is a quiet road rolling along the north shore through sparse native woodland, short cropped grass, gorse and bracken, busy with birds. On a previous journey along this road I was followed for a while by a falcon whose apparent interest in my trajectory had no doubt more to do with the little birds startled in my wake. It was a grey day then too. At the junction north of Altnaharra, where the roads to Tongue and Hope cross, there was a notice declaring the latter to be closed, which rather spoiled my plans for the next day. On the way through the village, I stopped at the hotel to ask the barman what the sign meant, who without going into details assured me I would have no problem getting past with my bike. Encouraged by this, I stomped up the hill side in search of a place for my tent in the vicinity of **Ben Klibreck**, still obscured by dense cloud.

At the point where the road bridges the burn, not far from where people park to climb the mountain, I found an adequate piece of grassy bank beside a clump of gorse at the bottom of an embankment. Despite being more or less next to the road, it was peaceful enough inside the tent. I was tired and beginning now mentally to prepare for the ascent in the morning. Gurgling water and a slight breeze held the midges at bay, but cloud still hung over the mountain. I ate, washed up, prepared my boots and went to sleep. I awoke again at about four in the morning and could not get back to sleep, so slowly I got myself together. Cloud still hung over the mountain. After much vacillation, impatience got the better of me and at about six I headed off towards the only visible shoulder of the mountain, about a quarter of a mile away over lush moorland garnished with cotton grass and bog myrtle.

Peat lies thick and squidgy over quite a lot of Sutherland, with huge areas of blanket bog and occasional islands of mossy vegetation wobbling atop unknown depths of watery mire. There are also places that can suck a body down without warning. Where the ground is more solid, it is lumpy and covered in tussocks, which often conceal holes of black gloop. Grass grows thick during summer, further obscuring slithery dangers beneath. At the same time, greater warmth and more hours of daylight dry it all out a bit. I bounced over the ground towards the hill, dodging gullies in the peat and trying to follow a bit of a path, still hopeful that as the sun rose, cloud would burn off. Once on top of the shoulder I was inside the white gloom, only able to see about twenty metres ahead. Luckily there was a path along the spine of the mountain and I had my map at hand to check the geography as I walked past. The ascent was straightforward and pleasant, and the path reasonable. The ground remained peaty, with enormous cracked hags hanging at the edge of steep slopes of scree, as if the entire mountain had been smothered in thick chocolate sauce, which was now sliding off very, very slowly.

The last I saw of any sunshine was at a low bealach between the first top and the rest of the mountain, where I stood just below cloud level looking north towards Altnaharra and a patchwork of little puddles of light. Thereafter the weather became progressively worse. Far from dispersing or blowing off, the cloud seemed to be thickening, more densely enveloping the mountain. The ground gradually became rockier, the rain moved a few notches above drizzle. From where I emerged onto the first crest, the route goes a bit north of east for slightly more than a mile, before climbing another crest to turn north along a narrow ridge for about the same distance, then culminates with a steep short plod east again to the summit. By this time the weather was nasty. At the top, I took a selfie beside the ruins of a trig point, rent asunder by what forces I do not know, lying in pieces on the ground. I returned hurriedly down the way I came, confident that I would be able to follow memory back along the ridge.

All was going well until I decided, for reasons I am still unable to fathom, to descend to the east of the narrow part of the ridge, while believing that I was actually descending west back along the spine of the mountain. The ground became steeper and piled high with enormous rocks and boulders. When it flattened out, I saw the silhouettes of a stag and hind at the edge of the grey void, into which they silently merged, then noticed water glistening black under steep screes to my right. Still believing I would be now approaching a lochan on the west side of the mountain, I became utterly confused. The orientation was all wrong. I circumnavigated the lochan and crossed over its outflow before I realised where I was. Looking at the map, I knew that the only options now were either to climb back onto the ridge and more carefully return by the route I had taken, or to continue down into the glen below and follow an old drover's path that runs southeast of the mountain from Kinbrace to the Crask Inn, only a mile or so from my tent.

Suddenly almost beneath my feet, a baby deer curled up under the heather, dappled and motionless, one eye open and focused intently upon me. I was thrilled, but sensitive to the fawn's vulnerability, moving gently to take out a camera and record the moment. The little one's parents were undoubtedly not far off, eyeing me carefully, ready to respond in some way were I to pose any threat. This is a moment I will always cherish. Although I was not quick enough to catch a photo of the two adult deer before they slid into the mist, it is an image burned deeply into my mind's eye. Standing here, high up on the wrong side of an isolated mountain in the middle of the most sparsely populated wilderness in Scotland, knowing this was not my world, that I had stumbled into a private moment in another way of life, I was humbled and disarmed. I could smell the parents' musk hanging in the dank air, feel their presence somewhere nearby and imagine their watchful eyes. I imagined their concern for their infant, their knowledge that I am one of the kind who kill them, their mistrust of my stumbling, their ability to wait it out, almost as if they were giving me the benefit of the doubt.

I backed away from the fawn and moved off towards the outflow of the lochan, to follow the water down into the glen, knowing that I would be adding at least two hours to the journey, but glowing with the magic of the moment. From here, the descent was initially gentle, but the ground was rough, with thickening heather and stunted shrubs filling gaps between enormous rocks strewn over the ground, fallen from crags and screes above. Presently the flank of the mountain steepened dramatically and I found myself descending very carefully through increasingly large boulders and dense undergrowth. At the bottom at last I found the path, well maintained by stalkers and no doubt used also by long distance walkers, it would certainly be a fantastic day out walking all the way through in either direction. Above, the cliffs and crags of the mountain tumbled into a forest of giant boulders, birch, rowan and gorse, creating many hollows and crannies. On the opposite side, something similar, with a much denser woodland, grassier slopes and a tall waterfall cascading into a secret corrie from cloud-soaked hills.

I marched forward happily on solid flat ground to the end of the glen, where there is a steep wall to a bealach, towards which the path slants gently along the flank of the mountain. Looking back down the glen, monochrome in the gloom, the subtle beauties of Loch Choire quietly smiling in the mist, solitary trees at the edge of the water proud of the land, forests almost green, watching. After the top of the path there is hardly any descent and the thick peaty moorland returns, with cracked hags apparently pouring slowly over the edge into the glen below. The path hugs the flank of **Ben Klibreck** beneath crags and cliffs at the very edge of the morass, at which point I found a rock and sat down for a breather.

I became aware of birds, flying at great speed between perches on the cliffs, screeching at each other. Their size, shape and velocity could only mean peregrines, playing in the air, maybe showing young ones how. Another secret moment in the life of the mountain, another treat I would have missed had I not come off the wrong side. Sometimes the reasons we do things become clear only after their consequences have played out. I was disappointed that the gloomy conditions made it less than easy to pick out and watch predominantly grey birds flying about in swirling grey mist or sitting on dark grey rocks, and I was not sure if there were three of them or four. But again I have a strongly burnished image of their spectacular flight, and my ears still ring with their joyous squawking.

With this encounter, my day was made. But it was a long walk back. I was a bit anxious about having left all my stuff beside a main road for longer than I had anticipated. My bike was locked to itself and my tent zipped up, but the whole lot could be easily picked up and carried off in the back of a pickup. It can happen. I followed the path as best I could until I saw a good line over the moor to a stone on top of a slight rise in the ground, on the far side of which I reckoned I would find my camp. After a long straight plod through squelchy tussocks, I was back at the tent at about twelve thirty. No pickups had taken my stuff. I ate lunch, packed and hit the road again, down the hill to Altnaharra.

As I passed the sign at the start of the road to Hope telling users it was closed, I felt a kind of freedom I had never before met; for the next fifteen miles or so I would be the only vehicle on the road and I could take up all of it by myself. There is a small estate farm at Mudale, a few miles from the junction, but nothing after that but access points to fishing breaks and killing fields. I had no idea why traffic was being diverted, but I was happy to be alone on the road in the middle of this vast tundra bordered by rocky mountains, hoping that the barman at the Altnahara Hotel had not been winding me up. The road passes lochans and little plantations following the burn to its source at Loch Meadie, then over the watershed where there is a track to Gobernuisgach Lodge, which also leads further south to Merkland on the main road connecting Lairg to Laxford. After a few miles of gentle descent, the road plunges into Strath More through bracken and gorse meadows.

The first (or last) building by the road in Strath More is a ruined broch, then there is a whitewashed one-storey lodge with some outbuildings, beside a gap in the road where once a burn flowed through culverts beneath. Here was the reason for the road closure, it had quite simply been washed away. Fording places had been constructed through piles of gravel and broken bits of culvert. Getting my bike over was indeed no problem. On the other side, the road was intermittently scattered with gravel and much detritus, with evidence on the hillside above of a great deal of water having flowed down every tiny gully, turning them all into furious torrents. In several places the road surface had been badly eroded. At Muiseal, where the path up **Ben Hope** begins, more shattered road, rocky detritus, culvert parts and temporary fords. Up the hill too, signs that the burn had been pushed beyond its capacity by terrifying quantities of water and tumbling boulders. Although the damage here was more extensive, repairs were more advanced, with shiny new culvert tubes waiting in a pile and a shallow ford to allow access from the north to visitors to **Ben Hope**.

The grassy riverbanks upon which I had expected to be able to pitch my tent had been obliterated. The weather was not wonderful and it had been a long day. I stood for a while in the lee of a cattle shed contemplating my condition and waiting for a sudden shower to pass. I was a bit low. At length I plumped for the pasture at the start of the path up **Ben Hope**, sharing the grass with several highland cattle who regarded me with complete indifference. After which, the sun looked as if it might come out, but it was windy, and the top of the mountain was still covered in cloud. I went about making supper and settled in for the night, undisturbed by passing vehicles.

I kick myself that I climbed **Ben Hope** when I did. The best time would have been the evening I arrived, for the sun did indeed come out for a while and cloud dispersed; or at the end of the next day, which turned out to be glorious; but certainly not the next morning, when I did actually climb it. It is a short sharp yomp to the summit and back that took me little over three hours, but the weather was absolutely appalling. After a reasonable night's sleep, I was awakened early by my bowels for the first time on the journey, and had to obey their insistent call, among a pile of rocks brought down by the floods nestling in a dense crop of gorse. After breakfast, I lay in my tent, watching cattle graze, reflecting on the journey so far and waiting for the right moment. Light rain dusted the tent, midges were kept at bay by breezes and chemical attrition, cattle munched mindfully, enigmatically looking upon their landscape from behind thick ginger fronds.

At about nine-thirty, vehicles began parking behind me and people walking past, some passing the time of day, others clearly ill-equipped to be going up a mountain in such weather. There was a couple of couples, then a church group, one of those passing announced, eighteen in total and a wee dog. When I observed conversationally that some appeared ill-equipped for bad weather, he said that not all were aiming for the summit and asked if I was also going up. I told him I had not yet made up my mind. I watched people spread out along the path up the hill, their unnaturally coloured clothing contrasting with intense wet browns and greens of the land. I really should have sat it out some more, waiting for the weather to improve, but I was bored and my ego got the better of me; if this ill-equipped crocodile of Christians could climb the mountain, then so could I. So I booted up.

It is a rough path over rough ground made more difficult by recent erosions. It follows the course of one of only two burns that take water from the west and south slopes of the mountain, the other further back at the broken road near the broch. Looking at the map to see how the contours work, it was no surprise at all that the road had been washed away at these two places. It seemed also quite strange that it does not happen more often, for a very large area of mountainside drains into burns that have only two channels available to flow over a cliff, which runs for several miles along the west of the mountain, all the way to its summit, in addition to which all the water that bounces off the northern summit precipice joins the flow into the burn I was now following, its banks expanded and broken, littered with stones and gravel. Above, I could see places where new channels over the cliff had been created, adding to the carnage.

Quickly, I caught up with one of the couples, who were clearly not going any further, were not enjoying the terrain and did not speak a great deal of English. Further up I met three of the eighteen church group with the wee dog, now separate and contemplating returning. The path slithers over peat before finding a way through a gully onto the gentle south flank of the mountain, after which the ground was solid and easy and the path well-trodden. Now in the midst of thick cloud, with rain driving heavily into my side on a stiff south westerly, I met another ten of the eighteen, who were still not sure if they would be going to the summit. I asked if they all knew how many were in each group and told them I had already passed by three. They said that there was a group of five up ahead, equipped for the conditions and determined to get to the summit. I carried on, wishing them well.

In good weather, this would be a marvellous ascent, the path is well defined and not steep, and there would be spectacular views of both the flow country to the east and Sutherland's stony mountains to the south and west. But alas, all I saw was the ground beneath my feet, and water. The second couple passed by on the way back down, and a little later the last five Christians. All had just touched the summit and immediately turned round. I did the same, deciding that I would have to return on a better day. Back at my tent, as I was packing up, more vehicles arrived full of eager walkers, the wind died down and the sun came out. I almost climbed back up the hill, but I decided instead just to let it go, and to use this lovely weather to enjoy cycling for the rest of the day, past Loch Hope and round the coast to Durness.

The road north from here is wonderful. Before it reaches Loch Hope it is straight and flat, then it winds and undulates through a dense native woodland, predominantly birch, but also rowan, alder and sporadic oak, undergrown with bracken and gorse, alive with little birds. The road is very narrow and the trees sometimes overhang to create verdant tunnels; there are grassy picnic places, paths to fishing breaks and boathouses. Rowing boats moored among fluffy green reedbeds on the loch echo the forms of the mountains in the background, which were for the first time visible in all their glory. **Ben Hope** too, northern buttresses resplendent, pointy summit standing higher than the rest, reminding me one day to return. At Hope there is a junction, a lodge, a few cottages, and a bridge over the almost shortest river in Scotland, all nestled in lush deciduous woodland reaching down the edge of a geo, almost to the sea. I turned left up a familiar hill, a pleasant plod of about three miles at the top of which views open out over Loch Eribol.

Prevailing winds blow northeast along Loch Eribol, although winds from the northeast are not uncommon; there will always be both following and headwinds going round it. On the east side there is a substantial climb and a long descent; on the west it is predominately flat. I have cycled both ways round the loch in fierce winds, on the east side unable to freewheel on the descent and on the west struggling to maintain a speed much more than walking, while conversely being blown up the same hill on the east and hitting forty on the west. Today the air was calm. Intermittent summer showers intensified the light over the deep blue of Loch Eribol, wetting slabs and cliffs on surrounding mountains, creating sparkling jewels and mirrors for the sun. Rainbows came and went and came again. From the first sight of Loch Eribol at the top of the hill, until I stopped for a seat by the first beach on the north coast at Rispond, I was entirely in the moment. I circumnavigated the loch at a leisurely pace, enjoying the space and the clean fresh air. Despite the showers, all traces of the previous day's damp and gloom had vanished. The air was warm and dry. I was on the road to the northern ocean, to the most isolated community in the country, one of my favourite places.

From Rispond the road rises and falls for only a few miles, clinging to the northern ocean past cliffs, coves and crystal blue waves crashing up sandy beaches, before it passes by the cave at Smoo and arrives at Durness. I checked in to the campsite and pitched my tent on firm turf at the edge of the cliff, looking over open sea. Apart from Iceland and the Faroes, there is no land north of here until the coast of Russia at the other side of the pole. The Orkney Islands are clearly visible to the northeast. On the afternoon of my arrival, as I explored clifftops, beaches and verdant dunes, the wind got up. In the evening I treated myself to a meal at the splendid Sango Sands Oasis. During the night a storm arrived, and in the morning it persuaded me to stay for another night, rather than attempt a journey south into its teeth. I lay in my tent all day resting and reading, battered by wind and rain. The storm blew itself out towards the end of the day, the next morning was calm and clear, perfect cycling weather. I stocked up with fresh vegetables at Mackay's general store and set off towards the next Munros on my list.

Leaving Durness is always a return. There is only one road through the village, one way in and another out. They both eventually return to the start of the journey. The road south follows the shore of the Kyle of Durness then gradually rises along the flank of a hill with views over *Strath Dionard* to impressive peaks, several of which only just fail to reach the magic three thousand feet for inclusion in Munro's tables. About half way up the hill, I had to wait by the roadside as a large flock of sheep was shepherded off the moor to be sheared and dipped. Dogs ran about fastidiously obeying whistles and calls, men on quads bounced over the ground while a fleet of pickups took up the rear. An odour of sheep shit and lanolin hung in the air long after the throng had passed.

The road reaches a high point at Gualin House, after which the geography changes again; the architecture of rivers carving glens north between stony mountains from blanket bog to the open ocean is replaced by the chaos of fjords, islands and peninsulas of the west coast. The road now weaves a way through tiny lochans full of lilies, short rivers and lumpy ground, reaching sea level again at Riconich at the end of Loch Inchard, where the road turns off to Kinlochbervie, still one of the busiest fishing ports on the Atlantic coast. When I first came along this road, it was unimproved and followed the contours of the land. It has since been rebuilt and widened to accommodate lorries taking the catch from Kinlochbervie to markets in the south, cutting straight through or bridging obstacles rather than finding ways round or past, which although creating more space for cyclists and other vehicles, channels the wind in ways that do not always make progress on a bike very easy. The road rises south again until the top of Laxford Brae, a short steep decent back to sea level on the shore of Loch Laxford, like Loch Inchard another fjord filled with tiny islands and lined with thick kelp, gravelly beaches and chained up little boats.

At Laxford Bridge, I turned right towards Scourie, *Scobhairigh*, along the south shore of Loch Laxford, gradually climbing inland. From the highest point looking back over the loch, the multitude of tiny islands scattered over the sea mirroring the myriad tiny lochans garnishing the land. A few miles out of *Scobhairigh* there is a steep descent followed by a challenging plod by the side of a loch, in a narrow cleft that always has a fierce wind blowing through it. I carried on through the village without stopping, on one side there is a small harbour and a large camp site, and on the other the bowl of rich pasture protected by rocky outcrops and dense underbrush, from which the village gets the name, *a sheltered grassy bowl*. The climb out of Scourie is long and gradually reveals the beauties of Eradichils Bay, another fjord filled with many islands shimmering under the low summer sun. The following miles are a series of ascents and descents cutting direct lines from one squiggly inlet of the Atlantic to the next, with no flat sections at all until the bridge at Kylesku, after which there is a mammoth ascent past the multiple peaks of the Quinag, another Sutherland mountain that fails by not that much to reach Munro's magic altitude. And then a long peaceful descent to the road along Loch Assynt that connects to Lochinver. Here the geography changes again. The influence of the sea is gone, the banks of the loch are grassy pasture and there is much less peat. On the far side of the loch there is plantation; behind this, the first view of the best known and most photographed mountains of Assynt, *Suilven* and *Canisp*, protruding strangely from the surrounding moorland.

At the Inchnadamph Hotel there is a track east through pastures clustered with clumps of gorse and bracken, leading towards paths to limestone caves and to the next Munros on my list, **Ben More Assynt** and ***Conival***. The change from tarmac to gravel took my legs by surprise, after so many miles smooth turning, suddenly there were lumps and bumps and very good reason always to look very carefully ahead and choose the right line. I dropped the chain onto the smallest ring; for petrol heads, a bit like using the low gear set in a Land rover, the same rear cluster now being driven by the smallest chainring. What a pleasure it was again to feel legs doing what they do to clamber over rough ground with a fully packed ATB. One or two technical sections only encouraged them further. After little more than a kilometre, I came upon a narrow bridge, on the other side of which was a respectable spot for a tent. A little further away from the burn, traces of old buildings with rowans growing from the ruins. I took my bike down a slope of boggy bracken to the bridge, unpacked it and took it over piece by piece. There was a bit of a wind to keep off the midges and a blue sky with fluffy white clouds flitting by at about Munro height. I pitched my tent, made supper and settled in. I felt this immediately to be a comfortable place. I was relaxed and ready for the challenge of the next day.

In the morning the weather was much the same, warm blue sky with clouds blowing gently over from the ocean and gathering around the tops of the mountains. Maybe today would be the day I sit on a summit with a view of more than the wet ground beneath me. I set off through meadows of bracken, gorse and short cropped grass. After passing by an old farm building and through a gate, the ground changed to deep heather and thickening peat, randomly protruded by sharp rocks of many sizes. The path became more challenging as it rose; although there were views opening up towards the Assynt peaks and the coastline beyond, my eyes were focused entirely on ensuring that forthcoming footfalls would be safe. About half way up, in the middle of the path, a great big lump of white quartzite, emblazoned with the unmistakeable outline of a fish skeleton. There was no doubt it was a fossil and I really wanted to take it with me, but it was far too big and heavy so I took photos and walked on.

The path becomes progressively rockier as it rises. Near the top there is a slight scramble up a little cliff after which a small corrie strewn with fallen boulders and scattered with pools of clear water. The path becomes more difficult to find but there is only one way onto the ridge, which soon leads to the summit of *Conival*. Here clouds were moving slowly past about ten metres above my head, so I did get a view of more than wet ground, but the underside of the cloud, as well as lower clouds in the distance obscured any panoramas. The ridge to Ben More Assynt beckoned, very rocky and flanked by precipitous scree slopes. The path, such as I could discern it, looked challenging. Initially there was a difficult drop over a tumble of sharp boulders to a flatter section, where the going did not get easier. Although it took me only three quarters of an hour to reach the summit of **Ben More Assynt**, it felt like much longer; at no point was I able to walk without concentrating on every step and balancing carefully between a plethora of sharp randomly sized rocks, so despite not being in cloud I did not enjoy any views, unless I stopped, and even then I could only see downwards over cliffs and screes to flourishing green moorland studded with shiny rocks and lochans. Throughout the traverse, the final ten metres of **Ben More Assynt's** highest crags stubbornly held onto a clump of cloud, and so no views were available when I arrived at the summit.

Disappointed again to have been standing on a Munro without a view, but nevertheless pleased with myself to have ticked off another, I returned back along the ridge to *Conival*, which was no less challenging in this direction. The summit of *Conival* was still free of cloud, while the summit of **Ben More Assynt** still held onto its little bit of weather. On the way down, I was not able to find the fossil fish again; I wanted to convince myself that it really would be too heavy to take away and to take a photo of it with some familiar object beside it as reference.

As the path flattened out I met two students of geology from a London university who were surveying the rocks. This little valley is much visited by geologists, for it forms part of a fissure of limestone that runs from a little further south at Knockan to Smoo Cave by Durness. I told one about the fossil fish and he became quite animated, asking for specific directions to its location. I was able to provide him with only a vague description; smack bang in the middle of the path towards **Conival**, at an altitude of maybe five hundred metres. I also mentioned that he would probably need some sort of barrow to transport it off the mountain, and crowbars to prise it from the pile of boulders that surrounded it. I thought that if ever I were to return here one day in order to get a better view from the tops of the mountains, I would also be interested to discover if the fossil is still there, although if it were not to be found, it would be impossible to know whether this was because inundations had tumbled it further down the path and covered it over, or because geology students from a London university had taken it away. One seemed very keen to try.

Back at the tent I ate and packed. I was on the road again before four, turning left at Inchnadamph towards Ledmore Junction and then straight on, back inland, or at least to where the sea encroaches again on the east of these islands. The road flows first over a flat watershed of marshes, where I stopped only to admire the rear view of *Suilven*, resembling from this angle an enormous receding lizard, lumbering back to the sea, pinnacles for a tail. Apart from the views, this is a wonderful road for cycling, in either direction, the gradient is gentle, dropping from less than seven hundred feet, undulating through forests along the upper edges of Strath Oykel to sea level in a bit less than twenty miles. At Oykel Bridge, I turned right into the village in search of the entrance to Strath Mulzie. At the start of a gravel track into a dense woodland I paused to consult the map and confirm that this was the road to where I was heading. The midges were suddenly voracious, spurring me forward.

A kilometre further on, the track crosses a bridge, out of Sutherland and into Ross, then flanks the southern edge of Glen Einig to Duag Bridge. I stopped here briefly at the old Schoolhouse, now used as an open bothy, before following the track left, steeply up and south into high pasture and sporadic birches, firstly above the narrow gully of the Duag Water then along the banks of the Corriemulzie River. At a plantation there is a sign indicating the end of the public road, beyond which only authorised vehicles may proceed. A little further on I proceeded through the yard of Corriemulzie Lodge, believing that I was not a vehicle and that my passage would not be affected by authorisation. Less than a kilometre further I found the perfect spot for my tent, high on the bank of the river at a bend where floods have piled up gravel, at the edge of a well-drained meadow of thistles and tiny yellow flowers. I felt that this was now the whole point of the journey. To get to this place. It was about seven, the sky was clearing, opening out into pure blue; there was a gentle breeze, the sun was dipping down, painting orange shadows. The ground was flat and comfortable, the tent pitched well. I settled into a familiar routine, laid out all my stuff, fluffed up my sleeping bag on top of its self-inflating mat. I prepared and ate supper, looking through my portable window on the world; a drystane sheepfold on the other side of the river, with steps of moraine further upstream, the lowest end of a narrow plantation of pine, behind which one of the most remote mountains in the country, the enigmatic **Seana Bhraigh**.

In most guides to climbing Munros, **Seana Bhraigh** is included in the **Beinn Dearg** cluster, which is approached from Inverlael on the shore of Loch Broom, from which the mountain appears as high points on a row of round hills fronted by shallow boggy corries. From the boat between Ullapool and Stornoway it is the last high point on the north edge of the hills round Loch Broom. This is a classic escarpment. Looking at the map it becomes fairly obvious that the line of craggy cliffs on the far side of these round hills would be completely invisible from the **Beinn Dearg** side. From the upper reaches of Strath Mulzie on the other hand, where I had pitched my tent, the mountain is magnificent. Two peaks are visible at the top of a line of precipitous cliffs and deep corries; the lower and most prominent *Creag an Duine*, a sharp tooth protruding from the main line of cliffs, with many crags and slabs on the way to its top; and **Seana Bhraigh**, rounder with a gentle route to the summit. The obvious way of climbing these would be to clamber up the pointy one, the SMC guidebook mentions a path requiring only basic clambering skills, then to skirt round the horseshoe above the cliffs while looking south over round boggy hills towards **Beinn Dearg**, eventually to reach the summit and the final Munro of the expedition.

The morning was cloudless. I ate my usual breakfast: hot turmeric, lemon and honey; prunes, apricots, raisins and goji berries soaked overnight; and porridge sweetened slightly with agave syrup. Mist poured over the escarpment, tinted pink by the rising sun, gathering in the lee of *Creag an Duine*. This is one of those moments that will last forever. Mist continued pouring, evidently produced by a temperature inversion at the west coast, boiling clouds slowly burning off into puffs of white nothing, hanging over the summits as the sun rose to warm the day. I booted up and was on my way at about eight. Even from this advanced basecamp in Strath Mulzie it is a long walk to the first slopes. The route described by the SMC guide up the front of *Creag an Duine* was not making itself evident, even as I climbed the path into *Coire Mhor*, where there is a very well-maintained bothy, which I investigated briefly on the way past. Round the end of the loch, having rejected any effort to find the alleged path up the front of the mountain, I ploughtered over some peat hags, then through an ancient forest of bogwood towards what looked like the start of a grassy ascent to the left of the crags and all the way up. It was long and steep, but it took me up to the end of the ridge.

When I reached the top, I freaked out completely. Lost the place in a fit of terror. Suddenly I was standing on a series of flat slabs with a great deal of air underneath. There was a bit of a path coming up from the void behind the crag to the right, presumably the one mentioned in guidebooks; in front of me was a bench of flat rock, on the other side of which was a sheer precipice of about a thousand feet to a mess of broken boulders in a corrie below. The path to the main plateau of the mountain was blocked by an enormous blunt pinnacle with no way round on either side, and no way over the top that made me feel comfortable. Perhaps if I had stopped to take stock properly of the situation, I might have plucked up the courage to traverse the pinnacle, for there were shiny places on the rock where boots had gone before, but at that moment I could not even contemplate such a thing. Motivated entirely by panic, I retraced my route down the grassy slope and then round the underside of the summit pinnacle looking for a way to traverse an increasingly complex arrangement of cliffs, badly angled slabs and outcrops, until I found a gravelly gully up and onto the plateau. I do not remember much of this, except for moments when I thought I was stuck, with no way forward and no way back. Evidently though I overcame them.

I walked back towards the pinnacle of *Creag an Duine* for a quick look at what I had missed by not coming over the top, and was glad I had missed it. I had not yet found my ridge walking legs. Hereafter the day was nevertheless easy, with lovely soft flat ground all the way round a perfect corrie to the summit of **Seana Bhraigh**, and panoramic views to Assynt, **Beinn Dearg**, the Fannichs, Fisherfield and beyond. North too over the reaches of Sutherland. I sat at the summit for a while, eating and soaking up the heat of the sun, contemplating the landscape, my eyes drawn inevitably to the sheer cliffs, crags and pinnacles of *Creag an Duine* at the other side of the corrie, trying not to beat myself up for wimping out.

The descent to the track was over easy ground, but it was a long way back. I was very glad of my comfortable camping place, where immediately I could rest, then eat and get a good night's sleep in preparation for the journey home. I did not know whether this would be the last place I would pitch my tent with a bike, but I was happy that if this indeed turned out to be the case, it was here among these summer flowers by this mountain, near the end of this journey.

The morning was grey. I was expected again at Ardgay later in the afternoon. From here it would be a journey of no more than two hours, downhill for most of the way. So I decided to extend it a bit by meandering along the south shore of the Kyle of Sutherland from Inveroykel, the highest reach of tidal waters, and investigating the roads at the end of Glen Carron, places where there are tracks into the hills as good as the road to Strath Mulzie, routes west with access to the rear of the **Beinn Dearg** cluster. Maybe in the next life.

After another enjoyable visit with Malcolm in Ardgay, I cycled back over Struie, stopping once or twice along the way to shelter from increasingly inclement weather. By the time I got to Dingwall, rain was falling heavily. At Inverness, I had to wait for several hours for a train that would accept my bike, so I found a sheltered place in the park by the River Ness, my head still on the road, in the vast reaches of Sutherland, walking along beaches at Durness, sitting in the sun on **Seana Bhraigh**, meeting a fawn in the mist on **Ben Klibreck**, clambering over broken rocks between **Conival** and **Ben More Assynt**, cycling round Loch Eribol, along Loch Naver, Strath Kildonan, Glen Loth. All these beautiful places holding back the reality of the future, of what was going to happen when I got off the train.

At the beginning of the journey the blood marker for the disease had risen quite quickly to a level considered by oncologists to be a cause for great concern. After not much more than a year, the effect of the radiotherapy had worn off. Rogue prostate cells were proliferating again. I was also beginning to feel slightly cancerous; a sickly feeling of unwellness like the edge of flu, a diffuse sense of discomfort that flips into acute foreboding, an emptiness deep in the pit of the stomach, an inexplicable and insatiable hunger. After which realisation and consciousness, the awareness of its significance, of what the disease means, the terrors of metastasis and fears of dying, the regrets of a life squandered, the desperate hope that medication will assuage some of it.

For the duration of the journey, I had been swallowing a pill every morning, a drug called *Bicalutamide* containing a female hormone analogue of testosterone designed to slot into testosterone receptors, thereby neutralising all cells dependent on testosterone, in particular rapidly proliferating prostate cells and testicular cells responsible for producing testosterone. This was in preparation for the injection of an artificial hormone designed to shut down the regulation of all hormone production, deep inside my brain. Stark reality was impending again; I had an incurably aggressive, exponentially malignant cancer and I was returning home to be chemically castrated.

It is hardly surprising really that I wanted to show myself what I could still do, despite the disease and this imminent treatment. Over five hundred cycling kilometres, five Munros, eight nights sleeping on the ground. Now approaching the third anniversary of being told I would live no longer than three years, still unwilling to believe in my imminent death, stubbornly alive. Yet still, by accepting the medication, deferring always to the deterministic logic used by medical science to conceptualise both disease in general and this disease in particular, believing still that no matter what, it would one day kill me, that the only hope was to slow it down for a while.

The day after I arrived home, I visited the surgery for the injection of *Decapeptyl*, in my backside. For another two weeks I continued with the daily *Bicalutamide* tablets, at the end of which I had developed little breasts. Two weeks after that I was neutered; all masculine bodily functions now switched off, my libido died and I became impotent, my beard stopped growing and my body hair began to fall out, my emotions became volatile and my motivation harder to engage, I broke out every two hours in hot flushes and cold prickly sweats, my muscle to fat ratio altered in favour of fat, I became weaker, more quickly fatigued and irritable, permanently deprived of sleep.

## Lochnagar

### 5th and 6th September 2015

The side effects of chemical castration can be listed without difficulty; their combined consequences are however complex. After a while these conditions become the new normality, which because they are not by any means normal, create new perspectives from which to view what is generally assumed to be normal. It becomes depressingly obvious, for example, after only a few weeks living without testosterone, the extent to which normal social life is an expression of testosterone motivated desire, and that power defers always to a kind of toxic masculinity, which *will always* get its way or it will eject toys from the pram, or break stuff, or beat the living shit out of somebody, or project its emotional insecurities onto the nearest woman and hold forth in *ad hominem* tirades against imaginary enemies without letting any other word in edgeways. After a single hot flush, I understand quite intimately the silent torment of the menopause; after months of hot flushes, I understand why there needs to be political discussion about their absence from public discourse. Severing motivation from the drive of testosterone means that it must now be manufactured. It becomes perforce entirely mental, from which it is not difficult to conclude that quite a lot of what is normally regarded as freely willed conduct is nothing of the sort, that the predominant condition of (male) consciousness is a variety of habitual mindlessness. Having been feminised, having experienced the budding of breast development and felt the agony of bumping tender young tissue into doorframes or open cupboards, which is certainly as painful as a good wallop in the bollocks, I have developed deeper bonds with many women friends, become able to share something utterly beyond the experience of normal men, something like a nonbinary, or much better *un-binary*, way of being.

The neutering happened as predicted, during preparations for another expedition, with my brother Colin and his fifteen-year-old son Fergus. I had by now bought myself a 75-litre rucksack (65 litres is not quite enough for longer trips), I still had a large two-person tunnel tent, another larger stove and two of quite of lot of other stuff. I packed two rucksacks with what we would all need collectively and Colin packed one for him and Fergus. We just had to wait for a weather window, the next weekend with open skies. I had a plan to climb one of the country's favourite mountains, starting from a place we knew as children more than fifty years in the past. On the way we would reach the summits of four others and spend a night out under the stars, maybe see the Milky Way. I wanted to share something of the joy I experience in these mountains, impart my mountain craft and maybe encourage my nephew to get out here for himself one day. If I had a son I would certainly be doing much the same.

My first memories of Glen Clova are from the early 1960s, when we visited for family picnics. My uncle was sometimes there too with his wind-up cine camera, and my Grannie, sedately sunning herself on a Royal Stewart tartan rug, looking like a film star with her headscarf and dark glasses. In those days the road stopped before the bridge, where there was space for only a few cars to park and a gate to a track through thick pastures. On the other side of the bridge was a Scout camp and the path to Glen Doll. There were only a few trees, sporadic alders and rowans on the banks of the river, but the land was already being parcelled up, prepared for plantation. Further up the glen we could see the first young patches, although it was too far away for our young legs to investigate. In the years that followed, every time I have visited Glen Clova, the forest has been thicker and more extensive than before.

At a brute physical level, this chemical neutering boils down to sleep deprivation. *Decapeptyl* flushes happen about every two hours. Sleep cycles normally divide into two periods of three to four hours every night. Flushes disturb this randomly, interfering with the numerous physiological and neurological processes that take place while asleep. It is possible that a body adapts to the disturbance, that sleep cycles find ways of compensating for depletions in the neurotransmitters and other chemicals that are replicated during particular segments of the cycle, but the overall effect remains a kind of grumpy listlessness, a yawny feeling of never having had a good night's sleep, with regular life brutally interrupted every two hours with a hot flush or cold sweat or both, all of which are a permanent reminder of the condition. Without medication I had the luxury of forgetting, particularly in the mountains, of temporarily not knowing about the disease. Now I carried it with me all the time in the palpable side effects of the medication used to control it.

The right weekend arrived at the start of September, forecast to be warm and cloudless, with a slight north wind. I had not yet become used to the fact of my flushes and was still experimenting with clothes best suited to sudden profuse sweating and changes in body temperature. We left the city sharp on Saturday morning, arriving before lunch at the improved parking facilities on the other side of the bridge, where there is space enough for countless vehicles. We booted up and followed the path through what is now a lush forest on the west of the River South Esk in the company of a ranger, who had heard of people camping among the trees and building a fire. He was planning to explain to them where they could camp and why they should not light fires. At the place he expected to find the illicit campers, there was no sign of anybody. We crossed a footbridge to a track along the east of the glen, along which he returned to other duties.

It is a fine path, slowly rising through plantations and open grazing past a couple of decaying farms, crossing the river again and into the narrows of Glen Clova, where it becomes steeper and more rocky as it climbs to the last patch of trees. Here we stopped to rest and munch on muesli bars, although we did not linger, for there were feasting midges, focusing their assaults primarily on the others. Perhaps another side effect of the medication. Are these insects less attracted to me than I remember? Have the others become decoys? Routes split here; to the left a path winds up onto the moor to meet Jock's Road and the route to Deeside; straight ahead there is a stalker's path into killing fields; and to the right on other side of a footbridge, a zigzag path onto the high plateau of the White Mounth, where two of the highest of its eight protruding piles of stones are classified as Munros. There is also easy access to three higher peaks and ample camp ground next to good water.

In contrast to the last time I came this way, when I had to find my way with map and compass in thick hill fog on one of my excursions towards the Cairngorms, it was a beautiful day with cloudless sky and clear air. Apart from one or two slightly steeper sections, it was a gentle walk all the way up. We were presented with no difficulties, the mountain tops are simply pimples on a vast plateau of round lumps; solid ground of grasses and mosses scraped clean by winds exposing rocks at the tops, teeming with mountain hare, babies too. We reached the summit of **Broad Cairn** just after three, and **Cairn Bannoch** just before four. At about five we found a place to camp, slightly above three thousand feet by some pools gathering waters from a shallow corrie before plunging over the precipitous edge of the plateau to feed Loch Muick.

I acted as guide. Pitched the tents, made food and let the others explore. I enjoyed watching them run about over the mossy plateau, being hares, or sit watching colours change in the sky as the sun lowered through wispy high clouds that had billowed up from the shadows of surrounding glens. They were evidently a little overwhelmed. We ate well, washed up and prepared for the night as the sky cleared and stars began to pierce the pastel autumn hues. During the night, the Milky Way was clearly visible and we saw shooting stars. Although my sleep was disturbed, the cooling air helped attenuate the flushes; the others said they had slept as well as they expected and were refreshed, ready for the day. I made porridge and boiled water for hot drinks. There was not a cloud in the sky, a slight north wind, the temperature had dropped. In fact it was cold. We left the tents just after eight. Half an hour later we were standing on the round flat summit of *Càrn an t-Sagairt Mòr*. From here we dropped to a path round *Càrn an t-Sagairt Beag* where we pottered awhile amongst the remaining wreckage of a jet aircraft, before proceeding towards the second nondescript lump of the morning. From a distance we could see on the lowest point on the ridge ahead of us, at least two figures, silhouetted against the bright morning sky.

When presently we met the figures, two men, they explained they had wanted a good view to sleep out with for the night. Looking towards the Cairngorm plateaux from here I could understand their decision. But seeing how cold they were, supping hot tea round their tentless encampment, waiting for the sun to rise high enough to warm them into action, I felt the benefit of layers of insulated air held still by technical fabric stretched over geodesic aluminium, warmed from within by a body. It was certainly cold enough for a touch of frost early this morning, but where we camped was sheltered in a shallow corrie; up here at eleven hundred metres, under an open sky with a north wind, the windchill would have been bitter. We wished them well and turned right towards *Carn a' Choire Boidheach*, even flatter than *Càrn an t-Sagairt Mòr*, the precise summit of which would be complete guesswork without the cairn in the middle. It was about half past nine. The only remarkable feature of this summit is the views it affords, not only to the surrounding mountains, the Mounth, Atholl and the Cairngorms, but to the Lomond Hills, far away in Fife, clear as a bell.

From here we turned towards the highest point of **Lochnagar** and walked in a line. The summit gravel and tussocks beneath our feet changed to grass and then dipped into a bit of peat hag and over a gathering burn before we joined rutted paths along the edge of a mighty precipice, a bite shaped corrie linking the minor peaks of *Càrn an t-Sagairt Beag* and *Stuic* with the bulk of **Lochnagar**, offering splendid views over Balmoral Estate and Breamar to the Cairngorms and upper Deeside. Crystal clear. We reached the summit before ten thirty and hung out for a while in amongst big red boulders, gazing out at mountains, reflecting on things, taking photos of cliffs and pinnacles. At length we returned, once again stopping at the wrecked aircraft in search of fragments for my brother's substantial collection of detritus, from which he makes interesting jewellery and other *objets d'art*. Back at the tents, we ate lunch and prepared for the walk out.

We were on the move by one, not heading back the way we came, but following another shoulder off the plateau towards Jock's Road and Glen Doll, from the top of Fafernie due south. Many hare were bouncing about, visible only in their movements, camouflaged immediately by stopping suddenly and standing stock still. After coming off the Shank of Fafernie we missed the path and foutered around on the wrong side of Crow Cragies, eventually finding a route along a thick grassy hillside following the upper reaches of the White Water. My nephew appeared to be not entirely happy about this, having been promised a path. On the way, we met a couple of ladies who had lost the way going in the other direction. Upon reaching the path at last, his disappointment was only exacerbated. For this is unimproved, a route created only by feet following the best line possible round rocks and boggy holes, over heather and grass, bypassing oozing springs of moss and feeder burns. At an emergency shelter, a dark hole with a door, built under a pile of stones in the lee of a crag, the path does not improve much as it plunges into a lumpy gully, then flanks the hill as rivers and burns cascade over slabs and complex outcrops, gathering into a V and flattening out into a boulder strewn strath, ringed by cliffs and crags, garnished with tiny birches and rowans, beyond the reach of grazing teeth. The going became easier, the ground eventually flattened out and Fergus' pace and mood improved.

At a gate, we entered mature forest, after which there was nothing to see but the track beneath our feet and trees. Having been ahead of the others for a lot of the time on the way down, they now left me for standing, keen to find toilet facilities. I was tired. Sunshine striped through tress and smiled on mountains. Back at the car, Colin wasted no time, he and Fergus both having made good use of the facilities. On the way home, we stopped for fish suppers at Kirriemuir.

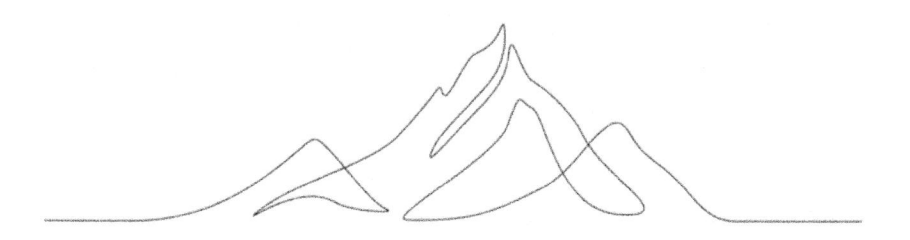

## *The Ben Lawers Squiggle*

### 19th and 20th September 2015

As a child I was timid of animals that jumped up, and downright terrified of anything bigger than sheep, which I regarded as thoroughly benign from an early age, having fed orphaned lambs on my grandfather's farm and known households where sheep were kept as companions. In particular, I was always wary of cattle. They look at you and form into a phalanx before slowly advancing, and they can buck, suddenly break into a run, or even charge. My parents were always very patient during family walks through farmland, indulging my need to bypass cattle by whatever means my childish imagination deemed necessary. Despite much adult experience of the docility of these beasts, particularly the highland variety, and confidence now to be able if necessary to shoo them off, I have also encountered cattle who have not helped dispel my fears. A bit like my little panic on the pointy mountain at the end of my trip to Sutherland, from time to time it happens, I get myself into a fankle because cattle are looking at me.

So it began, when I emerged round the corner to Dericambus. From the moment I came through the gate onto a track over pasture to the farm, the small herd of cattle at the other end were already looking at me and adjusting their postures to create a solid bovine wall. Behind them was a little cluster of farm buildings and the beginning of an elderly stalker's path zigzagging up the mountain. Not only marked on the map, but clearly visible on the ground. The start of another expedition to bag multiple Munros. Except that cattle were looking at me, from the other side of a field more than two hundred metres away, slowly gathering together and focusing on my presence, blocking the way.

There was only one thing to do. Take a wide berth. So I turned right towards the edge of the field, where I was able to climb a fence into open hillside, which I then traversed, expending rather more energy than had I walked through a field of cattle. I passed by several plantations and climbed another fence or two before crossing a burn in a little a gully to meet the first zig in the path at the top of a steep bank. From here I looked down on the route I could have followed through the farm. Cattle remained gathered round the only access to the beginning of the path. I sat down on a rock to prepare for the climb.

I was back again in Glen Lyon, now heading south for the start of a longer circuit than the Horseshoe to the north. These mountains had been visible in my mind's eye since they were emblazoned at the start of June from the summits of the Horseshoe. Massive grassy lumps, gashed by crags and impenetrable cliffs, steep flanked with no straightforward access from this side, still holding large quantities of snow. Behind the farm on the other side of the river from Invervar, I could see a zigzag path leading to a shoulder at the east end of a ridge of seven Munros, tempting me from the moment I first saw it.

Younger legs than mine bag all of these summits in a day, the usual approach is from the village of Lawers on the shore of Loch Tay, or from the visitor car park by the high road to Glen Lyon. I decided to enjoy it over two days, starting from Invervar, a route which I was surprised to discover is not mentioned much. Apart from time added by avoiding cattle and negotiating more than a few miles of squiggly single-track road to arrive at Invervar, it is logistically sensible to start here, the distance is less and it is certainly a more aesthetically pleasing circuit, well actually it is more of a squiggle than a circuit, joining the dots of summits on a map draws the mirror image of a fallen over question mark. A squiggle.

It was a fine day. Blue sky and cloud competing for control, still warm enough for sporadic midges, and humid. The path zigzagged up through steep pasture and bracken. On the other side of a fence the heather grew deeper, the ground became rockier and the path more difficult to find. After the zigzags, it follows a burn through a gully to a patch of boggy grass at about five hundred metres, on the other side of which is a fence, which crests a shoulder all the way to the start of the ridge. It was a slow plod, following the fence as far as possible over lumpy ground, dense with heather, scattered with rocky outcrops and boggy pools, making straight lines difficult to find. Higher up, the heather becomes stunted and the going less lumpy. At a slight bealach, I dumped my pack behind a prominent rock and headed east over easy ground to the first Munro of the day.

I reached the summit of **Meall Greigh** at about two in the afternoon. To the north Glen Lyon, resplendent, lush and green. Glittering in the low autumn sunshine, to the west, south and east, the enormous squiggle of Loch Tay. Looking west, the route for the rest of the day, three more Munros under an open sky, with others behind. It all looked perfect. I wandered back to my pack and carried on. As I picked a way through very pleasant country of grassy hollows and blunt outcrops, clouds began rolling in, scraping past the summits and lingering, spoiling the perfection. Climbing to the next summit, **Meall Garbh**, I was enveloped in swirly mist. I scanned through my camera for photos I had taken not an hour earlier of these very mountains under an open sky, trying to find a reason why this might have happened, where all these clouds came from. Not that it mattered. It was in any case a fine climb to the long flat summit of **Meall Garbh**, which I reached about three, but I saw little more than cloud and the albeit interesting ground beneath my feet. At least there was no rain. Descending again, I emerged from the cloud and could see down into deep green glens, pocked with traces of shielings. At the bealach I stopped for a breather in preparation for what lay ahead.

The third Munro of the day, **An Stùc**, appears from a certain angle to be only the highest point at the end of a subsidiary shoulder of **Ben Lawers**, from other angles it is much more prominent. The mountain was not included in early editions of Munro's Tables and has only in recent years been admitted. It remains however somewhat anomalous, particularly since (at the time of writing) there is disagreement about its altitude between the Scottish Mountaineering Club (SMC), which keeps Munro's Tables up to date, and the Ordnance Survey (OS), which surveys the ground. On OS maps, **Meall Garbh** and ***An Stùc*** are marked respectively as 1123 and 1117 metres, while on the SMC list and all others derived from it, both are recorded at 1118 metres. All of which raises many issues; what should be the proper criteria for Munro classification, why does the SMC apparently ignore the conclusions of OS surveyors, and how can there be any doubt at all about the height of a mountain? Surely it is a persistent stable physical thing, with stable dimensions that can be accurately measured and objectively recorded?

According to the purists, the most important criterion for being a Munro, apart from having a summit more than three thousand feet above sea level, is entirely qualitative, that a mountain has a *distinct character*. I was about to discover precisely the characteristic of ***An Stùc*** that distinguished it from the bulk of **Ben Lawers**. As I sat, two others passed me by heading up the mountain, mentioning the difficulty ahead and asking if I had ever experienced it. They seemed to be seeking reassurance of some kind. I replied that I had heard of it but that this was my first ascent. They looked at my large pack in a way that did not seem significant until I was almost at the top. The path rose steeply from the bealach, zigzagging and circumnavigating crags and rough ground, following gravelly gullies, becoming narrower and much steeper until it is but a shallow cleft in a rockface, with protruding lumps of turf and shiny holds for clambering hands and feet, upwards for about three metres into the unknown.

Near the top of the scramble, I discovered why my pack was given such a look. Swinging up and left towards what appeared to be the only way forward, my pack scraped against the side of the cleft, which knocked me off balance, disturbing the rhythm of the ascent, causing me to look down, to check for footholds where I could support myself, turn without hindrance and climb on. A lot happens in such a moment. It was a long way down. My heart was racing. Sweat dripped off my nose. Fear taunted my consciousness, filling my mind's eye with other terrifying heights of air that sucked me down, remembering in particular the terrors on *Creag an Duine*. I was aware suddenly that it was only my momentum that kept me from falling. I found a foothold, turned safely and climbed on. At the top there was a good path, skirting the mountain and already becoming much less steep. I looked back to see that I had effectively climbed over the lip of a sheer cliff.

The summit was not far off. I was elated, but again there was nothing to see but the ground beneath my feet and cloud round my head, so I was also disappointed. From here the path follows a sharpish ridge down to a shallow bealach, where again there were views through sunshine into glens, lochans and corries. After this, it is a slow gentle plod for a bit less than a mile along a blunt ridge to the summit of **Ben Lawers**, sixteen feet short of four thousand and the tenth highest Munro. I reached the summit at about five, in cloud, lingered briefly and turned towards the final summit of the day, ***Beinn Ghlas***. The descent to the bealach between the two mountains is a bit scrambly and requires care and concentration, especially with a big pack. At the bealach the path opens out again for a gentle stroll all the way to the summit, which I reached at about six, now clear of cloud, but still gloomy and threatening rain. From here I dropped to the pass to the east of the mountain to find a flat piece of ground for the night.

There was not a lot of choice at the lowest point, where there is an elderly path up the glen from the visitor centre, which then zigzags down and peters out under the shadow of the curve in the squiggle from ***An Stùc*** past **Ben Lawers** to ***Beinn Ghlas***, the strath below dense at its head with signs of ancient habitation. I followed the dribble of a tiny burn towards the approach to the last two Munros of the squiggle, where I found a place for my tent looking down on the strath to the north. Quickly I got myself together, ate and prepared for the night. It was getting dark already, the weather was deteriorating and I was tired.

Camping on the White Mounth with Colin and Fergus even a few weeks earlier, I was able to attenuate the flushes by having the tent front open to the cool of the night. Now with blustery winds and sporadic rain, this would not be such a good idea, and yet it was easier here than inside a building to awaken from a flush and find refreshing air. Something about the smell of peaty ground, the noises of moving air and occasional spatters of rain. Sleeping well for a change pulled my consciousness away from a series of strange dreams that had been haunting me ever since the side effects of the medication kicked in properly, about three weeks earlier, every night being brought back to the same unspecifiable historical space where similar events play out, wobbling in and out of an actual lucidity between real sleep and drowsiness, blurring reality and challenging my perception of events.

The morning was cooler, with a stronger wind coming through the pass from the southwest, cloud still hugging the summits above about three and half thousand feet. I took my time. I was in no hurry. All I had to do was climb a little less than two hundred metres along the line of an old fence cresting the eastern shoulder to reach the summit of ***Meall Corranaich***, then to follow a ridge north to ***Meall a' Coire Lèith***, thereby completing the squiggle. About half way up I entered cloud again, the summit was much stonier and rounder than previous peaks. Old iron fenceposts, flapping gently with Tibetan prayer flags led the way to a pile of stones, scattered with rusting fenceposts also decorated with Tibetan prayer flags. A lovely greeting. I took photos and walked on north.

After the long narrow summit, there is a narrower ridge along which the path is well defined, but after a subsidiary top it disappears into thick mossy grassland. In good visibility there would be absolutely no problem finding the way, but the cloud was still down and I did not properly look at the map to get my bearings before flanking the wrong ridge north. When the ground beneath my feet did not match what I had seen on the map, I realised what I had done. Instead of returning to find the missed path, I carried on until I came out from under the cloud to see a narrow corrie below and the path on the other side, running along the edge of a grassy ridge. Descending in search of a place for late elevenses, I found a lovely spot where a large boulder was lodged in a crevice next to the burn, creating a little waterfall, some pools and a stretch of grassy bank. There was little sun but I was at last out of the cloud and sheltered.

On top of the boulder there was a tiny forest of mosses, heather and lichens, which appeared even from quite close by to be a distant ridge of trees, scrub and undergrowth. I drifted in and out of sleep for a while, sheltered from the weather, securely protected from the elements by clever clothing, content with being exactly where I was. Meditating upon this and developing more general strategies that will make it possible to be content exactly where I am, back in the reality of life in the city, or anywhere else, is a different matter. It is easy, at least it is for me, to be utterly content, without a care or worry in the world, sitting beside a gurgling mountain burn contemplating the ease with which it is possible to flip perspective, to see growth on a nearby rock as a verdant mountain far away. It is less easy to be as fascinated by the moment-to-moment duplicity of perspective while getting on with regular life. I sat for a while, flipping the view, seeing a nearby boulder or a mountain far away, then clambered up a slope to the path.

On the other side of the ridge there is precipitous series of corries, which peters out into the steep round east flank of **Meall a' Coire Lèith**, the seventh Munro of the squiggle. The path skirts the edge, affording excellent views of the hugeness of **Ben Lawers**, *Meall Garbh* and *An Stùc*. Again, the summit was shrouded in cloud, so I came off quickly, carefully consulting the map beforehand and skirting a sheer corrie bitten into the north side of the mountain, down a grassy ridge to the east strewn with boulders, towards a gathering of ruined shielings in the strath, not far from the end of a track into Glen Lyon. At the bottom I rested again, preparing myself for a long walk back to the car, probably about five miles. It was still only two in the afternoon.

I was tired and in no hurry. The track down from this high glen cuts into the edge of a steep V shaped valley, almost all the way down into farmland. I bypassed the first farm through a field of sheep and found myself on the wrong side of a dense barbed wire fence, my passage to the farm road on the other side blocked. I walked on through the field, traversing several sheepy ditches and boggy puddles until I found a gate, over which I could easily climb. After this the road passes by several farms, where people passed the time of day, and then passes through a gate into woodland, past a house guarded by a pack of random barking dogs, who were a lot less intimidating than they thought they were, and occupied by a friendly German woman, happy now to call this country home after several decades. I told her she was welcome, as well as fortunate to live in such a beautiful, peaceful place as this.

I sauntered on through the trees, beginning to sense autumn in the air, leaves less green, some now yellowing at the edges, some already turned completely. Fly Agaric and other fungi bursting through mossy ground under birches, swaying thoughtfully in the breeze. The River Lyon meandering steadily, frothy bubbles swirling on its surface making shapes as if in some alien script. Clouds continued to dominate, although there was sometimes sunshine, and out of the wind it was still warm. I reached the car at about four thirty, changed my shoes and made myself a cup of tea before driving back to the city.

Two days later Shona and I flew to New York to celebrate the fact that exactly three years previously I was told my life would last no longer than this.

# Meall nan Tarmachan

### 31st October and 1st November 2015

No account of this life would be complete without describing the journey Shona and I took at the end of September 2015 to New York and Toronto, in particular our visit with an old schoolfriend of my father's and her husband in their 13th floor apartment looking over Broadway at 96th street in Manhattan. I had met them twice before, once in 2005, while my father was still alive, when I was in New York for the annual Cycle Messenger World Championships (CMWC), and then again in 2008 when I was travelling to Toronto for the CMWC there. My parents had visited several times before this and I had an open invitation to visit whenever I got to New York.

From the first moment I met her, I knew we would be firm friends, just as she and my father had been sixty years earlier. She surveyed me sometimes with a penetrating gaze, as if looking at, or for, my father, while resecting traces of my mother from what she saw. Small of stature, fierce of intellect and scarily perceptive, she always wanted to know about what I was working on and challenged my ideas in a most refreshing manner, forcing me to think very carefully about my language and helping me to understand what writing is for. We talked about the politics of the times, philosophy, the meaning of life and everything else. She was most passionate about what used to be called rhetoric, having taught English for many years at New York University, during which time she said she had witnessed a general decline in standards of public discourse and language use. She was on the whole positive about my writing and encouraged me to keep practising, but she was less than enthusiastic about my philosophical musings; nobody is interested in abstract concepts and relations strung together on a washing line, she scoffed, no matter how perfectly arranged. She was not a fan of modern literary criticism, and claimed not to understand Derrida and his ilk, while quite accurately articulating the point of deconstruction. The most important thing about writing, she said, is not to become infinitely self-reflective, but to be able to use the subtle differences of meaning and context embedded in every word that is placed, in order to clarify thinking and to express precisely what is at issue at that exact moment, to depict an event, tell a story, recount a conversation, describe the weather, paint a landscape, present an argument, express an emotion, and so forth, all very concrete. She became particularly exercised by slovenly word choices that elided meanings, neologisms that obfuscated experience and incorrect use of prepositions, which she felt led to systemic failure to understand the diversity of relations between things in the world and the actual stuff of creation. I learned a great deal from our meetings. I also enjoyed conversations with her husband, a Freudian psychoanalyst to trade, whose gaze was, if anything, more penetrating and whose questions more challenging, one of the sharpest minds I have ever known and one of the kindest, most compassionate human beings. They felt like long lost relatives, living on this *Island at the Centre of the World*, as Russell Shorto calls Manhattan in the book of the same name, one of the spiritual homes of my profession, a place of great significance in the international messenger community.

For nearly a week we stayed in a room walled with books, high above the Upper West Side. Every day we went out into the city to explore and soak up the atmosphere. We went on a boat trip, got stuck in traffic on an open topped bus, strolled in Central Park, ate pizza in Greenwich Village, visited the MET, the MOMA and the Guggenheim, and wandered like awestruck tourists under mountainous buildings along cavernous avenues. On the evening before our departure, Shona was entertaining our hosts' grandchildren in the study while I stood in the kitchen chatting to our hostess about the events that had brought us here to this place.

"Cancer was the best thing that ever happened to me," I told her after a slight hiatus in our conversation.

She responded without pause, "those should be the first words of your book ... or should I say, your *next* book."

I cannot remember if she was actually wagging her finger as she said this and her smile was palpable, at least in her eyes, but she could have been admonishing me. The first book to which she was referring was the book of aphorisms I had produced in the immediate aftermath of the diagnosis. Inspired by Twitter, which at that time limited the size of each tweet to one hundred and forty characters, I assembled my thoughts into one hundred and forty aphorisms each of which contained exactly one hundred and forty characters. This was genuinely my last statement to the world. Having spent most of my life reading philosophy, carefully observing how ideas come and go during the course of history and how they move and mutate through discourses in the service of particular interests and powers, having failed in my academic aspirations and having never published anything but minor articles in obscure pamphlets, I was damned if I was going to go to the grave with nothing to show for my philosophical labour but piles of notebooks full of illegible scribbles, a random collection of rants and diatribes on my hard drive and whatever remains of the hundreds of thousands of contributions I have made over the years to online debates. Nevertheless, no publisher I approached would touch the book and a literary agent with whom I was put into contact did not even know how to classify it. So I published it digitally and distributed a few hard copies to interested friends. It remains as a sort of ethereal historical document, a snapshot of what I thought the world should know as I left it.

"Ach," I said, almost but not quite scathingly, remembering that the labour of writing is complex and time-consuming, time better spent being alive. I had not anticipated this life now and the future felt like such a precipice. So little time, so much life to live, so many places to go, things to do, people to see, "there are already far too many books about living with cancer," I continued, "it has already become a *genre*."

Her response was curt; "but yours will not be about cancer."

I was brought up short. I had no answer. This exchange has animated my efforts to produce a book ever since.

I have tried on many occasions to describe the thought processes and emotions to which I was immediately subject, but these were so *cascade-like* that no single line can be drawn through them. The immediate consequence of all this introspection was however more prosaic; I had forgotten why I said that cancer was the best thing ever to happen to me. And then suddenly two small children ran giggling into the kitchen pursued by my lovely Shona, making silly faces and tickly fingers, bringing joy and light to sweep away the dust left by our cogitations. If I had not been diagnosed with cancer, Shona and I would not have re-ignited our old friendship to discover the passion it concealed. From which so much more followed, most notably that I would probably not now be alive, that I would likely have been unable to escape the negativity that had brought about the cancer, continued with my bad habits and followed the prognosis according to medical expectation. But it was not so, perhaps it was always meant to be, which is why cancer was probably the best thing that ever happened to me.

The next day, we picked up a rental car from a few blocks south of our hosts' apartment, said our farewells and drove out of the city on the first leg our journey to Toronto. In spite of meticulous planning, hours poring over images of the Henry Hudson Parkway on Google Maps and plans of the relevant interchanges and slip roads, I missed the exit and found myself in Harlem. Immediately I recognised where I was from the first time I was in New York, ten years earlier at the CMWC. It was at the end of the day of the final race, when hundreds of messengers cycled together from downtown Jersey City where the competition had taken place, all the way up the western shore of the Hudson River, across the George Washington Bridge into Harlem and back down Broadway to the start of an alleycat, a sort of treasure hunt, in Riverside Park. Although then I was on my bike coming off the bridge and now in a rental coming off the Parkway, the road into Harlem was the same. I followed my intuition through familiar projects back to Broadway and then to the next exit right, back onto the Parkway, which I followed until this time taking the correct exit onto the lower layer of the Washington Bridge. This took us effortlessly onto State Highway 4, which we followed until the interchange with State 17, where we turned north and then west along the interstate to all points in the direction Cleveland, Buffalo, Rochester and Syracuse, under the southern edge of the Catskills, past forests of autumnal trees, provincial cities and rural USA. We drove all day, breaking off where the freeway swings north, cross country to meet State 20, which we followed due west under an enormous sky, layered with cloud and backlit by deep orange, through farmland, past farmsteads and tiny junction hamlets, then suburbia, railroad yards and vacant lots, straight into downtown Buffalo where we checked into our hotel and deposited the keys of the rental.

The next day we took a bus over the border into Canada where we met Shona's son and his girlfriend. We took in the sights round Niagara Falls, visited Niagara on the Lake and a busy winery before driving back round Lake Ontario to the eastern suburb of Toronto where the couple lived. Another city dear to my heart, with many friends from the messenger community. We stayed here for a little over a week and made a trip to Lake Skugog a few hours north of the city, to Shona's son's girlfriend's family farm for Canadian Thanksgiving.

Throughout this trip I was learning to become accustomed again to the side effects of the medication. My life was once more dominated by hot flushes and disturbed nights, odd dreams that merge into reality, inhabit another level of perception, confuse memory of events and disrupt the discipline of mental life. Every two or three hours, irrespective of ambient temperature, prickly heat erupting behind my eyes, pushing out through my forehead, spreading over my whole body until I was dripping with sweat and utterly distracted. At night, the flushes interrupted natural cycles, randomly pulling me in and out of strange dreams, or preventing me from dreaming at all and sending me into another kind of consciousness, a sort of unfamiliar delirium. Sometimes I awoke from some other place, completely disorientated, unaware of where I had just been, where I was now, not knowing whether this was sleep or wakefulness, my life or somebody else's, what language I should be using here. I always knew something was happening, but not necessarily to whom. My dreams were often vivid, like memories of past lives, premonitions of lives to come or flashbacks from this one in anticipation of death.

Although usually it was the beginning of one of the flushes that awoke me, sometimes it was just the terror of the disease, the brute fact of its existence, its presence in my body and the ever-present spectre of its meaning. Sometimes I would not awaken until the flush was fully underway, which was always especially disturbing and most likely to leave me not knowing what was going on. Usually I stumbled out of bed to look for a place where it was cool or for something to drink. On the way I would often knock things over, blunder into inappropriate rooms and bump into furniture.

One night in Toronto, I dreamed I was Shona, in conversation with our hostess in Manhattan. Only one fragment of this has left any trace in my memory.

"His mother was damaged, you know," said our hostess tentatively after a pregnant pause while I listened attentively, as Shona. The apprehensive assertion seemed out of the context of the immediate conversation, but our hostess's expression revealed she was talking predominately about the son, not the mother, alluding to the transmission of stuff from one generation to the next, rather than to the characteristics of either.

And then another hot flush awakened me into a state of panicked delirium, repeating the words over and over, "his mother was damaged, you know, his mother was damaged," until Shona woke up beside me, comforting, taking me away from these terrors of the night. Sometime later, she told me that after I had gone to bed on our final evening in Manhattan, she and our hostess had been lounging in the big sitting room, talking about stuff, about me, my mother and our diseases. I had stumbled into the room briefly on my way to the kitchen at about the same time that she had said something a bit like this. They did not know if I had been aware of what I was doing or what was going on around me. They had made sure I returned safely to bed and then said their goodnights.

After this, something changed. The linearity of things seemed always on the verge of dissolution. Reflection became messier, more infused with old emotions I believed I had already located in the past. It became more difficult to pull a single narrative through my life, more and more ridiculous, absurd even, to think of myself as any variety of persisting something. The comfortable fiction of the liberal individual facing the external world collapsed, forcing me once again to find ways of living in a world where such things are taken for granted. And to reassess my past, to confront the damage.

After our return from the other side of The Atlantic, we settled back into ordinary life. The day after receiving the second and final injection on this six-month *Decapeptyl* cycle and having my blood tested again to make sure the stuff was still working, at about three in the afternoon, I parked at the Ben Lawers visitor centre carpark beside the high road from Loch Tay into Glen Lyon, booted up and took to the path towards **Meall nan Tarmachan**, my thirty-seventh Munro since being diagnosed. It is possible to include this mountain on the same squiggly ridge as **Ben Lawers**, but it is detached somewhat, separated by a much lower pass at the high point on the road to Glen Lyon, and it has a very different character. It is sometimes climbed in marathon circuits with the other seven by those seeking a serious challenge, but mainly it is climbed for its own sake.

**Meall nan Tarmachan** will be immediately familiar to anybody who travels regularly on the road north from Lochearnhead. After the pass into Glen Dochart, it can be seen clearly as the gnarly, four-peaked, ridge towering over the town of Killin. Despite the prominence of three lumpy tops from this distance, the highest summit is set back from the others, rather dull in comparison and hardly prominent, nor very gnarly. The appeal of the mountain is to traverse the gnarls, although I had a different plan.

As I walked away from the car to a path through moorland of orange grass and dying heather, which appeared to lead quite quickly towards the face of a cliff, people were now on their way down, having enjoyed a glorious day traversing gnarls. My full pack turned one or two heads and when asked, I said I was going to camp out for the night at the top of the mountain. It took me less than two hours to reach the summit along a well-used path, which turns out to be a lot less precipitous than appears from the start, suggesting that anybody thinking of climbing all eight Munros on the squiggle might be advised to begin with a warmup yomp up and down this one. The ground was every hue of ochre, intensely autumn with hardly any remaining green. Clouds hung in the air in layers, sometimes scraping over the summits. The sun shone low, reflecting in the still waters of Loch Tay. I climbed higher as flurries of rain swept like curtains over the horizon, with only rainbows adding colour to the complexity of cloud in every shade of grey from off-white to deep anthracite.

At the steepest point, just beneath the last crag, the path follows a slanting gully, earthy underfoot and grassy, invisible from below. Near the top it turns back on itself towards the summit and briefly becomes quite steep. Up ahead, carefully walking over the ground in search of morsels among the stunted vegetation, a congregation of ptarmigan, now partially liveried in winter white. I waited while they went about their lives, perfectly aware of my presence and yet unbothered. I took the opportunity to snap some photos and to rest a little from the climb. The birds sauntered off. The summit is little more than fifty metres beyond where the ptarmigan were grazing, a tiny pile of stones on top of a pointy rock protruding from flat grass and gravel at the edge of a cliff. By the time I got there cloud was swirling about my head and obscuring views. I stopped only briefly. It was after five, not far off getting dark, so I carried on towards the start of the gnarls in search of a flat piece of ground near water for my tent.

Light fades quickly at this end of the year; cloud also obscured perspective. I found a promontory looking down on the flickering lights of Killin and I pitched my tent, gathered water from a nearby spring and prepared for a long night. I had reached the summit and could conceivably have returned to the car and driven home with another box ticked. But I was not finished. I wanted to investigate some of the gnarls, to reflect on the previous year and prepare for the next, although most of all I wanted to sleep out under the stars and wake up in the morning surrounded by a sea of cloud. Despite thickening around me as I made camp, I was sure this weekend would as predicted provide the right weather conditions and that at dawn all cloud would be in the glens below.

I was not disappointed. From the first glimmers of light, I could see that the sky above was open. It was cold too, but not quite frosty. Clouds in the distance were gathering just below or at the same height as the tops of the hills, swirling around the higher peaks. **Ben Vorlich** and *Stuc a Chroin* seemed to be holding back a sea of pink, hanging over the lowlands to the south. Below, above the surface of Loch Tay, mists formed and dispersed, rising into layers of ethereal white, contrasting with the dark shadowy land beneath, reflecting in the flat water, confusing perspective. The morning sun dazzled low against the cliffs opposite my tent, fluffy clouds tinted pink as they danced about in infant thermals. The familiar caw of a raven echoed in the corrie. Occasionally a ptarmigan gurgled in the distance, content with this new day.

Presently I was no longer able to slumber. Leisurely breakfast, looking down on the slight Sunday movements of Killin, reading yesterday's paper, doing the puzzles, watching the planet, breathing in this cold clear air. After breakfast I booted up and went for a walk, carrying no more than my walking stick and a camera. Ptarmigan sunned themselves, ignoring me. The previous evening in the low light and mist I had decided to go no further in search of campground than a gnarl that appeared to require some scrambling to get past. I was disappointed after coming through without any scrambling at all, to discover a better place for my tent on a grassy ledge beside a deep clear pool, looking southeast towards the low hills of Perthshire, still holding back a sea of pink cloud. I noted this place carefully and walked on to the summit of *Meall Garbh*, the most prominent of the mountain's gnarls and its second highest top, then found a place to sit against a rock and look out over the world.

Despite this year of expeditions, my confidence in my own capacities and experience did not yet extend to going into the mountains alone during winter weather. I knew therefore that this was going be the last expedition of the year and also the last Munro until spring. Being in the mountains in winter is a completely different discipline, requiring at the very least, certain specific skills and quite a lot of special equipment. It is also a good idea to have companions. Apart from having none, I still harboured the notion that trips into the mountains, in order to be properly authentic, must involve sleeping out, which, I knew from bitter experience in the teeth of a blizzard battering down Glen Tilt near the Falls of Tarf, is a very different prospect in winter. I was also being genuinely careful; although I had in the past almost as much winter as summer experience, I was not yet ready to dig out my crampons and ice axe. I still felt I needed to reacquaint myself with mountain craft before venturing out in the depths of winter. At the beginning of next year though, in the slow transition to spring, I was planning to maintain the momentum of this year and gradually to remember the special skills and challenges of a Scottish winter.

It was now more than three years since being told I would live no longer than this, but I was still very much alive, albeit temporarily neutered, still not used to the side effects of hormone suppression, becoming now systemically weaker, less muscular and more lethargic. Always on the edge of grumpiness and tears, disturbed every two hours by hot flushes, sleep deprived, continuously reminded of the disease and the prognosis, and thus determined to subvert the deterministic logic by which it was first presented to me. Even though it was not yet nine in the morning and even though I was leaning against a rock at the top of one of **_Meall nan Tarmachan's_** gnarls looking south to **Ben Vorlich** and **_Stùc a' Chroin_** protruding through a pink sea of cloud, even although this still being very much alive really was so very much being alive, I was brought down by a new fear. Now that this deadline had passed, it must mean that death could come now at any time. By busting the prognosis, my death was not suddenly indefinitely kicked down the road; on the contrary, in my mind it became more imminent and the time I had left more pressing.

For the moment though, the medication was doing what it was supposed to do. At the start of next year when its effects wore off as I entered the *off* phase of the *on-off* medication cycle, I would begin again, return to these mountains to learn, having during the last year remembered, and take myself away from these familiar comfort zones, travel beyond Perthshire, the Cairngorms and Sutherland, take more daytrips to places I have only passed through, seen from a distance or examined on maps. In the meantime I was going to sit, soaking up the warmth of the morning sun, watching it burn off the mists in the glens below. I still did not know the names of very many mountains to the north and west, except **Ben Nevis** and the pointy giants of **Ben More** and **_Stob Binnein_** above Crianlarich, which are a lot higher than everything else. But I looked forward to getting to know them all.

I hung out for a long time at the top of this little mountain just watching the world. When people started arriving from both directions along the ridge, I became a bit self-conscious and decided I should get back. At about one, I packed up and struck camp then sauntered back to the car, returning on the way to the summit of the mountain. The views I did not properly see the previous evening were resplendent all the way down. The giants of **Ben Lawers** and ***Beinn Ghlas*** smiled at me, waiting for the first snows of winter.

Returning to the city with Sunday afternoon traffic, I saw my life as it is, and I looked forward to more of it, in particular to the end of next January when the effects of the *Decapeptyl* would begin to wear off and I would be able to get a good night's sleep.

# 2016 learning

## Ben Vorlich Loch Earn

### 20th March 2016

It had been a long winter, and it was by no means over. The effects of the *Decapeptyl* wore off as expected and gradually I was getting some strength back. My attention was not however focused on mountains, but on my mother, who was in need of being looked after.

Shona and I had spent New Year on the Holy Isle, at Lamlash Bay off the east of Arran on a brief retreat. A week learning about meditation on an island of only a few miles long and hardly a mile wide, with a little mountain in the middle, populated by feral goats, otters, small brown sheep and two separate herds of wild ponies. Holy Isle is owned by the Scottish Buddhist community and is part of a protected area. There are retreat centres and refuge houses at either end of the sheltered western side. Day visitors are welcome and overnight stays can be arranged with the island's caretakers. Along the path on the east of the island, between buildings at the north and south ends, there are caves and hollows where early Christian monks took up lives of secluded contemplation. Hence the name.

When we returned from our retreat, we discovered that my mother had quickly declined and was not managing to look after herself very well. Having lost her best friend suddenly to a stroke the previous autumn, she had become progressively more despondent and housebound, debilitated also by osteoporosis, stooped and unsteady on her feet, not to mention in great pain. She had always been quite an anxious person, she confessed to being more than slightly neurotic, and her decline exasperated this, but she remained as sharp as a pin, intellectually as lucid as always, which did not always make life easy for her.

Hereafter Shona and I, my brother Colin and his wife Jo, took it in turns to make sure she was never alone in the house, traveling back and forth from the city to the family home. With some persuasion, she accepted Shona's offer of help with personal care. From time to time, she was also taken into respite at a friendly care home in a nearby seaside town, giving her a change of scene and the family a break. Caring for my mother like this was not easy, for she was clearly suffering and frankly stated that the experience of bodily deterioration meant she no longer wanted to be alive. She had, she said, had a good life and just wanted to get it over with, a sentiment I could perhaps understand a little more crisply than those who do not know what it is like to be still alive beyond the expectations of terminal prognosis. Although my mother's decline put me in mind of my own, I kept it to myself, scrupulously refusing to tell her anything about my condition. It was difficult enough knowing she knew my life might not extend much beyond hers, if at all, and I did not want to make it any worse. There was nothing visible about my disease; as far as she was concerned I was doing very well, living according to the principles of health and nutrition by which she had raised me, more or less, following my passion by climbing mountains.

It was deeply upsetting to watch this magnificent woman collapse before my eyes; it was however a privilege to share this time with her, listening to her recollections, trying to focus her mind towards places where she was content and peaceful. I was getting to know the young woman who was yet to give birth to me, rather than the married woman who under complex circumstances looked after me as a child. During the course of our conversations she described her life before my arrival in ways different from before, less matter of fact, more thoughtfully, as if lifting the veil on the narrative of motherhood; the same stories she had told me from an early age about her life were no longer those told to her growing son, but reflections on past events shared with another adult, imbued with a degree of emotion I had never witnessed in her, which revealed what an extraordinary life of physical hardship, emotional terrorism and social privilege she had endured, and why she was considered by all who knew her to be such an inspiration.

With all the toing and froing I had allowed my level of fitness to drop, although I did not properly realise this until my first trip out of the year, a beautiful Sunday climbing **Ben Vorlich** with clear skies, still air and dry ground, a day that dared not believe spring might be not far off. I chose this mountain on a Sunday with open skies and warming sunshine because I did not have a companion and knew it would be busy, so that in the unlikely event of an emergency I could blow my whistle and expect to be heard. I parked at the end of a row of vehicles on the south bank of Loch Earn near the entrance to Ardvorlich Farm under leafless birches dripping with lichen. From here the path rises continuously without much flattening out all the way to the summit of the mountain, an unremitting slog from start to finish.

It really was a glorious day, but my body was not coping well with the exertion, so I took it slowly. At first the track passes through the farm, then steeply from pasture to scrubby woodland, where it rises more gently along the flank of a sharp ravine. At a water intake, the track culminates and the way up the mountain continues along a well-trodden walker's path, initially over a moor, measured with grouse butts, then along the edge of a sharp ridge all the way to the summit. I stopped regularly along the way to catch my breath and look out over snowy peaks in all directions, smiling in the late winter sunshine. My heart pounded and my legs felt like lead, which worried me a bit until I remembered that apart from sitting in front of the television with mother, I had spent the previous several weeks delivering stuff from the van rather than on my bike, and concluded on this basis that my condition was bound to be a bit meagre. Mentally reassuring perhaps, but my body was still struggling. At a large solid snowbank blocking the path and seemingly leading all the way up to the summit, I decided it was time to put on my crampons; the first time used in anger for many years, having carefully adjusted them to fit the new boots.

After crunching insecurely through lower snowbanks and slithering on hardened pools of meltwater, my feet were now fastened to the ground by hardened spikes of steel. This is one of the most reassuring experiences I know. Though icy solid, the snowbank turned out to be much shorter than appeared, and the summit closer by. There was also an easy way round for those without crampons. I felt a bit self-conscious at the top, with all the others out for a walk on this beautiful spring day, having spent so much care ensuring the crampons were strapped safely to my boots and having used them for no more than a hundred metres or so to the summit, but I was glad to reacquaint myself with the feeling of security crampons provide. It takes a bit of getting used to on mixed ground of rock and ice, and care has to be taken not to pierce clothing and stumble, but it is worth learning the techniques required to traverse iced-up snowbanks without any risk of sliding off.

I sat at the eastern summit of the mountain resting, eating lunch and looking over to the precipitous northern buttress of **Stuc a Chroin**, searching for a path. I had been hoping to be able to climb both peaks today, but it was already obvious that my body was not willing. The route from here appeared challenging, so I decided to wait for another day. After lunch, I followed the western shoulder off the mountain and took off my crampons at a stony path heading towards **Stuc a Chroin**, at which point I almost changed my mind, but turned northwest towards a flat bealach on the northern shoulder of the mountain. This, and the ridge I had followed on the way up enclose a deep corrie with a long-corniced snowbank spread along its eastern edge all the way back to the summit. At the lowest point I found a safe way of crashing through the snow and down into the corrie below.

My knees were aching and my chest was as tight as a drum. I shared the route for a while with a lady a little older than me who noticed my discomfort and suggested that walking poles would relieve the strain on my knees. I explained that this was my first day out of the season after a fairly sedentary winter, that I was thus a bit out of condition, but I thanked her for the tip. I could see exactly how walking poles would cushion and support every descending step, taking pressure from knees and spreading load to upper body muscles. I was convinced and resolved to get a pair. In the meantime I had to get down the mountain. Eventually I found the flat floor of the corrie where I followed a lovely burn gurgling through awakening vegetation, tumbling between rocky pools, warm in the afternoon sun. The tightness in my chest had turned to pain, my knees felt as if they might explode. I was getting a bit stressed out, worried that this chest pain might mean something else.

With heavy legs, I reached the water intake again and the beginning of the track back down to the farm. The going became easier, but my body hardly noticed. I distracted myself by admiring the spectacular colours of the ground, reflecting that each season paints the mountains with a distinctive palate, here again the mysterious hue made by birches as they turn from winter, standing high on the other side of the glen, casting feathery shadows on dark orange bracken straw, reminiscent of the maroon and saffron of Buddhist robes. I plodded on, breathing gently to avoid exacerbating the chest pain, stopping from time to time to rest and take snapshots of scenery. Towards the end of the descent, at the steepest point above the farm, my knees were screaming at me to get them walking poles.

Back at the road, many others were returning stiffly to their vehicles with glowing faces. Evidently, mine was not today's only first trip out of the year. I drove back along the south side of Loch Earn, past many happy campers and picnickers, settling into views of lowering light, pottering at the shore. Campfire smoke rose vertically into pastel skies. There was an air of peace. At Perth I popped into a well-known outdoor equipment shop to buy myself a pair of basic walking poles. By the time I was driving south again, the pain in my chest had subsided, from which I concluded it was nothing more sinister than exertion. And the usual hypochondria engendered by the deterministic logic of disease progression.

## Meall Glas

### 2nd to 4th April 2016

Often in good weather my mother would say to me that I should be away in the hills rather than watching television with a decrepit old lady. I replied that I was happy to spend time in her company, that the mountains are not going anywhere, and that anticipating periods of good weather this winter had not been easy. She was however nothing if not insistent, so there was always a plan at the back of my mind. I had a notion to camp out for the first time this year on the plateau of **Beinn Heasgarnich** or the bealach to **Creag Mhor**. Opportunities were now dependent both on work and on others being able to look after mother. When one opened, I prepared everything, but then the weather turned nasty. Though disappointed, I knew I had simply to accept that the weather is the absolute limiting factor when climbing Scottish mountains, and to make alternative plans. I did not however unpack my rucksack.

The previous week, a young woman wearing only shorts, a tee shirt and track shoes had been assisted from high on the **Ben Nevis** snowfield in a state of advanced hypothermia by a group of climbers. She believed she would be able to walk up the so-called tourist path to the summit with no equipment except a selfie-stick. Having been soundly ticked off by *Lochaber Mountain Rescue* for her irresponsible stupidity, she apologised, which did not much endear her to users of social media, where her antics were the subject of heated discussion. The level of her antisocial, irresponsible stupidity precipitated a serious pile on and opened up the usual cans of worms, for she did not only not understand that the weather at the top of the mountain might be too much for her attire, she did not even understand to wonder whether it might be, *even after she had passed the snowline*. That she climbed the mountain to where the snow begins and then waded through it wearing only running shoes without thinking that this might not be such a good idea, was regarded as a special kind of stupid.

Compassionate commentators forgave her, pointing out that we all make mistakes. More extreme opinion tried to attach her naïve hubris to the fact she was from England, a reaction that was always going to be as moronic as it is prejudiced and illogical. It is perhaps true that those who travel to Scotland from other countries have less flexibility with time than those of us lucky enough to have mountains in the back garden, and that they might push themselves a bit more than sensible to get to a summit because returning another day is logistically more complex, not to mention expensive, but this is hardly an ethnic trait, just an accident of geography.

This was by no means an isolated event. People are often assisted from popular mountains like **Ben Nevis** and the Cairngorms because they have not adequately equipped themselves against what the mountains can become. Not only is this landscape staggeringly beautiful, it is deadly. Even those highly experienced in all the right techniques and in possession of the best quality gear can die in the mountains. At about the same time as the woman with the selfie stick was being castigated on social media, the bodies of a young couple emerged from melting snow in the northern corrie of **Ben Nevis**. They had been missing, presumed lost, for a number of weeks. They were experienced climbers who knew the risks and died doing what they loved. Many would much rather end their lives like this than rot away in a hospice, demented, dribbling and incontinent. Everybody with any common sense should know what the mountains mean and acquit themselves appropriately. That there are those who do not, seems almost an affront to reason; there must surely be something wrong with our societies if they offer individuals so much freedom of choice that they are unable to perceive that the actual circumstances, their actual present experience, might be perilous and therefore circumscribe any choice.

Of course, we all must learn. On my first expedition into the mountains in 1979, I was poorly equipped and believed I could do anything. However, when I became overwhelmed by a blizzard, I knew the basics. If I had belligerently followed my plan to walk north through the *Lairig Ghru*, I may have come to grief along the way. I did not however succumb, either to the weather or my arrogance. I had the wherewithal to change my plan and to protect myself, I had enough stuff with me to survive, enough food to eat, an ex-army sleeping-bag and a *Force Ten* tent. I looked after myself without inconveniencing or alarming anybody, although I should admit it was probably not entirely convenient for my parents that they came to collect me later in the day from Braemar at such short notice.

Nobody knows how to prevent idiots from doing stupid things in the mountains, nor what to do with idiots who have nearly killed themselves in the mountains with their stupidity. Signs can be placed prominently at the start of access routes, describing good mountain practice in many languages and in no uncertain terms, but they will be ignored by those who know better or believe such principles do not apply to them. I find it difficult to conceal feelings of great disdain towards all those who think they will not be affected by mountains, people whose attitude so disconnects them from reality that they believe they could climb **Ben Nevis** in winter wearing only summer jogging clothes. No doubt, such people will continue to be vilified on social media for their irresponsibility, and some of them might learn to make more sensible choices in the future. But it will make no difference to the ones who did not need to be rescued, who successfully got to the top in baffies or sandals and returned safely without incident.

Having decided to defer to the weather, I awoke the next morning to more promising skies. My yearning for the hills was aroused again and I really needed to get away, so I drove to the end of the road in Glen Lochay and access routes to ***Beinn Heasgarnaich***. I thought I might take a wee walk up the glen to see what opportunities presented themselves. I arrived at about three-thirty. It was a fine afternoon. A man with binoculars told me he had seen pipits, ravens and a buzzard. Two women wanted to know where I was going to camp, what I would be eating, if I slept well alone in the mountains, whether the weather put me off. I told them I was going to put up my tent wherever I found a flat bit of well-drained ground by the burn up the glen, beyond the last buildings. I told them I would be eating rice with vegetables, crackers, nuts and dried fruit, with porridge in the morning, and that I like to sleep out on my own with only the odours of the ground, the sound of the weather and the burn to occupy my attention.

About two hours later I made camp on a moraine by a burn coming down from the south east shoulder of **Creag Mhor**. A little later it started raining. Light pitter patter soothing as I basked warm and dry among the fumes of wet ground. It rained all through the night and into the next morning. Listening to the noises of the mountains, reflecting and carefully thinking things through in an effort to make peace with the usual demons, now mixing with the many insecurities and confused emotions arising from my mother's impending demise, unable to articulate much of it. At about midday I wrapped up against the weather, packed a few supplies in a daysack and went for a walk up the glen. I did not know where I was going, nor what I was going to do. It had stopped raining, but it was still gloomy and dreich, with clouds shrouding the highest mountain tops.

This glen is one of many ripe for repopulation. People lived here for centuries without the benefits of modern technologies and infrastructures. There is no reason why they could not do so again. All estate and Hydro Board tracks could easily be improved and the public road from Glen Lyon extended into Glen Lochay, and then taken all the way through to Crianlarich by the north side of **Ben Challum**. The outlines of shielings can be seen at many places in the upper glens, ruined farmsteads pepper the lower strath; there is plenty stable land where new buildings could be constructed, space for cultivation by the river, good pasture on the lower slopes of the enclosing mountains, and on the upper slopes a recently planted forest of indigenous trees, which could be extended. People could live here easily. All it would take would be the will to make it happen.

While contemplating these things and walking towards the watershed to Strath Fillan, I looked up to the left and saw a stalker's path zigzagging to a bealach between two hills, and above that a ridge to the top of **Meall Glas**, a minor Munro that is more usually climbed with its neighbour **Sgiath Chuil** from Glen Dochart to the south. I had not had this little mountain in my sights; clouds were now lifting, I could see the summit and that I could easily get there.

I crossed peat hags and clambered over a burn past the remnants of shielings to reach the start of the path. Zigzagging up I began to experience the extent of the mountains that contain this glen, dark imposing cliffs patched thick with old snow, high summits reaching into the wet gloom. At the end of the path, the ground became very boggy but there was a clear route up the side of the mountain. It was grassy and steep, sodden from rain and melting snow, and very slippery. On the round shoulder at last it was a gentle stroll to the summit, where there were views between layers of cloud south into Balquhidder and **Ben More**, west to **Ben Challum**, north to *Creag Mhor, Beinn Heasgarnaich* and Glen Lyon, and east to *Sgiath Chuil* and *Meall nan Tarmachan*.

I returned to my tent by a slightly different route, following the shoulder as it became a tighter ridge before descending, soaking up the height. As soon as I was inside my tent, it started raining again. I was still warm and dry, with plenty of food and the noises of the mountains to occupy my mind. In the middle of the night, nature called. When I emerged into the darkness to answer, I saw stars twinkling between thin clouds moving quickly past, illuminated by the moon. In the morning it started to rain again. It rained heavily all the way back to the car, cloud was down to ground level, the colours vibrant and dense in the wet.

Back at the carpark, I read through an information board explaining to visitors how the land is managed, what sorts of animals and birds live here, and why there is a newly planted forest of indigenous trees. The glen is used to graze cattle and sheep. When the new forest is mature it will serve as the upper border of grazing land and provide cover for wildlife. Pleasant illustrations of flora and fauna illuminated the presentation, prominently articulating the usual narrative of custodianship. During the stalking season the herds of red deer who live in the upper corries are hunted and culled, and from the twelfth of August every year the grouse who live among the heather on the moors and lower slopes are slaughtered. The Scottish canned hunting industry is usually overshadowed by the obscenely rich and morally degenerate killing elephants, giraffes and lions in Africa. The Scottish variety is nevertheless well established, and, as information boards like this all over the country proudly attest, it is the mainstay of the highland economy, it provides employment and serves a vital ecological function by culling an animal that otherwise has no natural predators. Or so the story goes.

That things are at the moment as they are makes this cosy picture of Scotland's green and pleasant land more plausible. But that mountain agriculture is dependent on rough grazing and canned hunting, does not mean that there cannot be other ways of doing things. According to the information board, only two permanent shepherds work the farm at the centre of the estate. It is explicitly stated that:

The farming here is really a continuation of the extensive sheep farming that replaced the shielings system in the latter part of the 18th century.

Once again I was shocked by the extent to which Scottish history is so summarily erased, that the most repressive episode of our past is sanitised for tourists and visitors using the little word *replaced,* all sense of development hereafter reduced to a *continuation,* the cultures of the past to a *shielings system* and the complexities of modernisation to *extensive sheep farming.* Imperialist values are never difficult to find in conventional narratives about how the present condition of Scotland came into existence. In this case, they underpin and reinforce the fundamental message of improvement: those who own the land know what they are doing and are working to look after it responsibly into the future by cultivating forest and culling animals.

Demonstrably many more people than two once lived in this glen. Shielings were where the people lived during summer as their livestock grazed the common land in the upper glens. During the winter they returned to the lower straths to live in cottages round farmsteads or townships, or *balies*. At all times the people were under thrall to the landowners and were required to pay tribute and ground rent, and if necessary fight against the landowner's enemies. During the course of many centuries, there was a complex infiltration of the ancient Highland Clan cultures by the Norman feudal system, conflating the roles of chief with landowner, making it possible for the people to be cleared from the land in the name of improvement, to make way for sheep, thereby fuelling the enormous changes of the Industrial Revolution and the continuing project of imperial colonisation overseas. People were too expensive and sheep were more profitable. The labour provided once by people was increasingly available from machines. Despite being partially Anglicised, traditional highland cultures were associated with Catholicism and insurrection and were considered to be a threat to the British crown. The atrocities of Culloden marked the beginning of an explicit effort to destroy Highland culture and to subjugate the population of Scotland under the same self-important and entirely fictitious notion of Britishness that was subjugating native populations the world over. The colonisation of Scotland is probably the first movement of the British Empire.

The *replacement* referred to, of one *system* by another, was not an event, rather a long and traumatic process that exists still, as highland landscapes continue to be depopulated, *replaced* by tourist attractions and temporary throngs of itinerant visitors consuming scenery, seeking some romanticised vision of things past. While land management is focused on the overproduction of a few prey species, the bulk of the actual land is denuded of its natural flora, denatured, and used exclusively by the privileged to indulge their bloodlust, protect their sense of entitlement and preserve an image of dutiful custodianship. The paths taken by walkers and climbers up and down mountains and through glens are marginal and insignificant in relation to the vast tracts of land used exclusively for killing, and through which magnanimously, we are granted access. Almost inevitably we defer to powers that have made it thus.

At least the atrocities at Rossal are now commemorated with a degree of decorum and no longer presented as part of our *heritage*. The stories on information boards such as this reveal a more incipient malaise, a more diffuse denial of the violence wrought upon this land, an example of what during recent decades has come to be known as ethnic cleansing. Deliberate efforts made by political forces to destroy a people or culture are by no means confined to the past, nor executed by powers other than ours in foreign countries. The same principles of political economy were explicitly deployed in my own lifetime by Thatcher during campaigns against Scottish working-class culture and tradition. The continuing existence of this cleansed land is testament to a carefully maintained historical blind spot, that the people who lived here are the ancestors of the working classes deliberately emasculated and dispersed first by

Thatcherism and now by predominant neoliberal ideologies of globalisation and austerity.

In principle there is no reason at all why many more people could not come to live in the glens round here and to build communities together. There is no reason why there should not be libraries, schools, tradespeople, writers and creatives, poets and musicians, pubs, community centres, hospitals, retreat centres, care facilities, and any manner of dwelling spaces for all kinds of family and domestic arrangements. No reason why new roads should not be built and state of the art power, service and communication infrastructures not laid down. No reason why lots of people could not build lives in this glen and many others like it, much better lives than were once endured here, for surely the worst effects of even this foul weather could easily be attenuated by advances in modern technology and engineering.

In practice however, there is very good reason. The land is owned by private capital and expected always to turn a profit. The point of land is for it to be owned and for it to generate income for the owners, not for it to be inhabited, nor afford shelter and provide life. That this is taken for granted is only testament to the extent to which our consciousness has become as denatured as the land itself, infested by neoliberal economics. The usual monetary calculation is deployed; the fewer people required to work, the greater the profit, which will, by some unexplained magical force, trickle down to everybody else. The stupidity of history, of our complicity in its lumbering processes, is to believe that we must carry on as we were because that is just the way things are, which is always an improvement on what has been.

None of us is born with an understanding of the history of where we find ourselves, of how present circumstances came to be as they are; it might be easy to be taken in by the assumptions underlying the selected facts so glibly presented on this board next to the carpark at the end of Glen Lochay, to see the current arrangements as the only way of maintaining custody over the land and of caring for the national ecology. But if we look carefully, we will always see the traces of the past on the ground, the truth of which is very much more complex and violent than presented to visitors. And for as long as we defer like sheep to capital and its bland hagiographies, we will never know what this land could provide. For everybody, not just a privileged few. Nor are we ever likely see a truly natural ecology on these denatured hills.

I drove home in the rain and went back to work the next day, cycling round the city, delivering stuff.

## Gleann Calliche

### 16th to 18th April 2016

At about the same time as my friend and colleague, Iain Kennedy, announced that he had cancer of the oesophagus and would have to undergo an operation to have the tumours removed, not to mention about a foot of alimentary canal, I got the results of the blood test I had a few days after climbing **Ben Vorlich** at the end of March. I was generally healthy, but the PSA had risen from 0.5 to 4.8, indicating that when the medication is taken away, the disease comes back. Quickly. I knew this cancer was aggressive, but I had not expected it to return so vigorously quite so quickly. It came as a bit of a shock. Now though, for the first time in my experience of cancer, I had a buddy who was able to help put matters into perspective.

I told Iain about the rising PSA and its mental effect and he told me a story. When he first talked to the boss about his diagnosis and how it would affect his work, he said that it felt as if he had been hit by a train, but that he quite demonstrably had not been hit by a train. It reminded me of what Paul Kalanithi wrote in *When Breath Becomes Air*. Before he was diagnosed with cancer, he knew that one day he was going to die, but he did not know when; after he was diagnosed with cancer, he knew that one day he was going to die, but he did not know when.

Some cancers have immediate and painful symptoms, others can have none at all until they have spread throughout a body; Iain's tended more towards the former variety, mine more the latter. No matter how severe or debilitating the physical effects of the disease, we both knew that living with cancer is essentially mental. It is hard work not to be overwhelmed by the dark emotions a cancer diagnosis brings with it. Some people speak openly of their experience, many others keep their own counsel. Iain and I both enjoyed sharing our experiences of the disease, being able to talk about it more freely, often with a dark humour that would shock eavesdroppers. Our friendship became part of being alive with the disease, laughing at it, not letting it dominate life.

The rising PSA was like being hit with Iain's train. Again. Every time the PSA rose it hit me. But there was nothing to see. This disease is invisible. It existed only in my head as what the doctors were telling me about it. Apart from the disappearance of the side effects of the medication, nothing had changed. I felt no different. There were no sudden debilitating symptoms interfering with my life. The cancer appeared to be contained within my prostate and had not shown much sign of spreading any further than slowly enlarging lymph nodes in my groin and near my aorta. I was always conscious of being told more than three years previously that I would be dead within three, but of course I did not know when I was going to die.

My mother on the other hand had an inkling.

Since the beginning of her decline, every doctor who was called upon to examine her could do no more than say that she was elderly, that all her complaints and ailments were signs that her body was gradually not working any more. An X-ray showed that her heart had swollen, from which it was concluded that this one organ was now doing all the work of keeping her alive, while the rest were slowly shutting down. One Friday she announced that she wanted to be taken into respite care again. She was given a nicer room with a better view, more secluded. We brought her television and settled her in. Whereupon she told me to get out into the hills. Of course I had a plan ready, an idea of where next to take my troubled soul, to make space and settle my chaotic mind.

At the very end of Glen Lyon, there is a cluster of mountains more conveniently climbed from Achallader on the road to Glen Coe. They can be seen from the viewpoint on the brae down from Rannoch Moor to Loch Tulla where they dominate the southern skyline. From the south and east, they are hidden among several other peaks, but they can be seen well along the road from the end of Glen Lyon to Glen Lochay. Encouraged by my unexpected ascent of **Meall Glas**, I wanted to come at this cluster from the east. The drive up Glen Lyon is always worth it for the journey alone, but it eats away hours. After the end of the road, there is an estate track along the northern shore of Loch Lyon towards places where tents might be pitched. The weather had not improved much since my visit to Glen Lochay and it had become much colder, which meant snow flurries down to low altitudes and more continuous falls on the summits. My reservations about being out in the winter had dissolved, quite confident I would be able to look after myself, on my own, without a companion.

I parked at Pubil then walked round the north shore of Loch Lyon, the water level much lower than the upper limit of the dam, revealing ancient sheep pens, habitation and dykes. The usually bleached stony shoreline had been partially reclaimed by living ground. Where a stream enters the loch from the north, the highest extent of water forms a significant bay; the water level was however so low that it was exposing further remnants of what once were pastures on land that was probably also good for cultivation. The land above the upper water line is used now entirely for *extensive sheep farming*, which has quite demonstrably replaced the *shielings system*; all fences, buildings and access roads are part now of the infrastructure of grazing sheep, as well as connecting with stalkers' paths and grouse butts. Hydro works have partially concealed evidence of this *replacement* with water, with traces now preserved along the sterile margin, revealed only when the water level is low.

I turned right along the bay then followed the river, taking the western fork into a shallow V shaped glen, still along a well-maintained estate track. The only plausible camping space was at the very end of the track on the other side of the burn near the foundations of an old building, on a grassy bank scattered with detritus from a storm gully coming off ***Beinn Mhanach***. I pitched my tent, ate supper and prepared for the night. The noise of snow on a tent is very much gentler than even the lightest rain, only the hardest icy blizzard snow does the pitter patter, mostly it is a kind of soothing swish, a brushing sound as it gathers then slides off under its own weight. Unlike water, which runs straight off, snow can accumulate on a tent, putting pressure on materials, and has to be knocked off from time to time lest it freeze and stiffen.

In the morning it was still cloudy but there were hints of blue behind passing squalls and flurries of fine snow. The flank of the mountain was just outside the tent, beckoning me with almost two thousand feet of continuous upward slog through dead winter grasses into snowfields and swirling clouds. It would be the start of a traverse of the ridge between ***Beinn a' Creachain*** and ***Beinn Achaladair***. The ground was dusted with snow. If there had been no blue to be seen in the sky I would probably have thought twice, but the weather at that moment looked quite promising, I felt up to the task and wanted to get up the mountains.

It was indeed a long hard slog, but on the way, the sky opened out nicely to offer views south and east to snow garnished peaks and shining lochs. White clouds flew past on a stiff north westerly, sometimes carrying squalls of tiny snow. The mountains to the west seemed to hold onto the cloud, and to darken into threatening clumps, while in the east there was open blue behind tall, slowly moving towers of cotton wool. Near the summit I entered a squall of almost invisible frozen needles. The ground was turning from grass to bare rock, encrusted with iced up meltwater and old frozen drifts, now dusted with new flakes. Crampons were not necessary and I carried on. Visibility was not brilliant, but it was good enough to navigate by eye, trusting also the memories of extensive preparatory map reading. I reached the summit of ***Beinn a' Creachain*** before ten thirty. It was still snowing, but there were glimpses through layers of cloud to the far reaches of Rannoch Moor and the peaks of the Black Mount, Etive and Glen Coe. I could also see the route ahead.

I did not hang around at the summit and followed the well-trodden walker's path first north to where it splits, with one branch descending into the northern corrie of the mountain and then to the road at Loch Tulla, and a western branch towards a rounded ridge, with on one side grassy slopes descending to the head of *Gleann Cailliche* where my tent was pitched, and on the other, a series of corries, cliffs and buttresses plastered with thick cornices and cracked drifts. I clambered happily off the summit cone to follow the path west, sometimes crossing substantial snowfields. The views remained tantalisingly partial as squalls continued to pass over just above my head, throwing down more varieties of prickly precipitation. Nevertheless I had a good perspective of the route to the next summit. It was a long walk over easy ground with the lowest point just above eight hundred metres on the last bealach to ***Beinn Achaladair***. I was all the time conscious of not straying too far north into the cornices for I could see how easy it would be under such limited visibility to get confused by white, sometimes only a wall of unstable looking snow against a background of cloud, just waiting for a sudden wind, thunderclap or thaw, or a stupid human being to turn it into an avalanche.

The last climb to the summit of ***Beinn Achaladair*** was less work than I had expected. I reached the top just after twelve, two separate piles of stones, almost as high as each other at either end of a little ridge. I visited both, unable to remember which was the actual summit. The weather was now closing in. There was no view. The snow was becoming wetter, sticking to my rain jacket more tenaciously than bouncing off. I decided I had to descend quickly to the next bealach rather than continue to follow the ridge and then curve back to the next summit, which under more favourable conditions I most certainly would have done.

It was a very steep descent over rocks and scree, leading to a flat corrie scattered with lochans and boulders fallen from the heights above. Lower down, the snowflakes were much wetter and thicker, becoming sleet, lying grey on the ground. As I came over the lip of the corrie, I could clearly see a wide bealach, there was a fence line and a gate at the watershed between the catchments of Orchy in the west and Tay to the east. The ground was boggy and wet, and the snow had turned to rain, although it had also eased to reveal more open skies behind passing clouds. I had the wind at my back on the gentle climb up ***Beinn Mhanach***, reminiscent of my windy walk up ***Glas Tulaichean*** the previous year. I reached the summit at about two. It was wet and windy and there was nothing to see. So I carried on along the ridge looking out for the first way down through the crags and gullies of the north face of the mountain to my tent in *Gleann Cailliche* below.

Then the sun came out, suddenly and briefly, to reveal wonderful glimpses in all directions of rainbows against brown mountainsides and the underside of clouds, although nothing panoramic. After rejecting several snow-filled gullies, I found a more gentle slope into a small boggy hollow where waters gather into the burn that led down to my camp. Whereupon the weather closed in again, something between sleet and rain, wet and cold. The final few hundred metres of descent were hard work over rough unstable ground, with an increasing wind coming down the glen. I was glad of flatter ground at the bottom and looked forward to resting warm in my tent. Then I realised that I would have to turn it round. I had pitched it when the wind was coming up the glen from the east, it was now slicing down from the west carrying with it squalls of lumpy rain, which meant that the front would be open to the weather.

Turning a tent and contents is easier than it may seem. As long as everything is well bagged and zipped up or just bulky, and there are no loose items lying about, it is simply a matter of zipping up the tent, pulling out the pegs, repositioning it and pegging it out again. It is a good idea to remove the heavy stuff, but it can be done full. When it is windy, it becomes a little trickier. Only once did I allow a bit of a tent to fly away during such a procedure, but I got it back after fishing it out of a shallow river. With this new tent, it was quite straightforward, but in these fierce squalls inevitably stuff got wet. I was tired and I stumbled about, did things in the wrong order and wasted energy, but I managed. For the rest of the afternoon I rested, warming up inside my sleeping bag, looking out on the glen intermittently obscured by wet snow and rain. In the evening the wind died down and the sky cleared. I had a peaceful night.

The morning was beautiful. Warm air, blue skies, light clouds hanging high above the summits. There was a definite sense of spring, the almost odour of new growth about to burst through the dormant ground. I dawdled on the way back down the track, taking photos and examining the land. At the car I changed out of my boots and drove a bit up the road towards Glen Lochay to find views of the mountains I had just climbed, thick with snowbanks, glittering in the sunshine. Tempting though it was to take the shortcut over the hill into Glen Lochay, I knew that the road surface on the other side would now be so broken up by cattle and weather it would not be worth the hassle, nor the risk of being unable to proceed with nowhere to turn. So I returned down to Glen Lyon and the long road home.

On the way, I stopped for a bite to eat at an outdoor equipment shop in Perth and phoned mother. She was being well looked after and felt safe. She was calm and lucid, pleased that I had had a good trip into the mountains. I agreed that I would visit at the weekend to tell her all about it, that she should call whenever she wanted. The next day I was back in the city delivering stuff on my bike.

## *Glen Clova*

### 11th May 2016

In her declining months my mother told me that one of the happiest periods of her life had been living with her father on his farm at Kinnaird, next to a gully on the south flank of the Sidlaw Hills looking across the Carse of Gowrie and Tay Estuary to the hills of north Fife. Here she could walk freely in the countryside while coming to terms with how she had left behind her mother and her home in Edinburgh. On the farm she could enjoy the simple things in life, experience the animals and get to know her father after a period of estrangement. I remember my grandfather and his farm well from childhood, collecting eggs from under the chickens, feeding orphaned lambs, being taken to the top of the hill above the farm, and for the first-time experiencing views of distant mountains, learning about the perspective of height. From the moment she noticed it was becoming a passion, my mother encouraged me to get out into the hills. Although she never came with me deep into the mountains, she was a keen walker herself. For all of her active life she started the day with a brisk walk, usually to the high point on the path over the hill to the next village. She and I shared many walks together, along beaches, through woods, to the tops of hills and up glens and back. We continued with this until a walk meant round the corner to see the sunset, or a run in the car to potter somewhere nice, and finally from her chair to another part of the house.

At the end of the week, after I climbed the peaks round *Gleann Calliche*, while she was in respite care, she demanded to be taken to Ninewells Hospital in Dundee. Authorities in Fife wanted to take her to Kirkcaldy, but she was insistent and got her way, as she usually did. I visited on the Saturday at the care home and followed as she was taken by ambulance to the hospital. I waited while she was checked in by a kind nurse, who listened carefully and noted everything she said. One of the questions on the nurse's list was who was the most important person in her life, to which she answered that he was not here. Only I knew she was referring to my father Bryan, who had died more than ten years previously. The nurse looked a little confused and my mother moved her on to the next question.

After she settled in, we sat awhile talking, just being together. She was breathless and tired, sometimes dozing off, but present. She held my hand and talked quietly, once asking as she drifted back from slumber: "Are you there, mother?" All the signs were right in front of me, she knew she was on the way out now, she wanted to be here in Dundee because that is where her father came from, not Kirkcaldy where her husband died. I knew it would be soon, but I did not know when nor what it would mean. It was the last time I saw her alive. When my brother and sister-in-law visited the next day, she was still sharp and lucid. In the wee small hours of Monday morning I received a phone call from the ward telling me I should come to the hospital. Half an hour after sharing a cup of tea and a chat with a night nurse, her heart stopped working. She had made it abundantly clear that under no circumstances was she to be resuscitated. When Shona and I arrived at the hospital, she was lying in a side room, very peaceful. She was certainly not alive, but she seemed not yet to be dead. Her presence persisted. I sat with her.

My maternal grandfather, John Spence, was born in Dundee in 1890, son of William Spence and Jessie Ewing, and grandson of William Robertson Spence, shepherd of Glen Clova. While John Spence was still only eighteen, the younger William died leaving John the family grocery shop. Some years later, this merged with the dairy business belonging to John's mother Jesse's brother, Andrew Ewing. The joint enterprise was called *The Buttercup Dairy Company*. Initially my grandfather looked on his uncle as a mentor, but quickly the two men became solid business partners and then lifelong friends. The company moved its centre of operations to Edinburgh and during the 1920s became the biggest producer, distributor and retailer of fresh dairy products and groceries in the country, with a chain of shops and a very particular recognisable livery, from the highlands of Scotland to the first towns in the north of England. My mother was the third and last living child of John Spence and Mary Woodrow, one of three sisters who grew up in a flat at the Meadows end of Marchmont Crescent in Edinburgh. The family home was a villa on Grange Road.

Mary's first child died during her confinement and had to be cut out of her lest she also might die. To describe this procedure as traumatic would be an understatement. Interested readers are referred for a full description to the opening pages of David Mitchell's novel, *The Thousand Autumns of Jacob de Zoet*. Consequently, she suffered post puerperal fever and then postnatal depression. At about the same time, John's brother Willie Spence and his brother-in-law George Christie were killed in action in the Great War, after which his sister Etta was left alone to care for two young boys. My mother always said that these were the events from which all subsequent family trauma arose.

Her sister Janet, known as Jenny, was born in 1920 and grew into a snobbish, entitled heiress with too many suitors. My mother grumbled sometimes that her sister had never done a day's work in her life. She married one of the sons of a wealthy laundry family, who had spent the war as a lieutenant commander in the Royal Navy defusing mines at sea, and who needed at least a bottle of whisky a day to function. They lived in a house in Ravelston and had no children. My mother's brother William, known as Bill or Boy, was born in 1924 and was immediately smothered by his mother until the two had each other wrapped around each other's fingers. He grew into a dependent mummy's boy, who despite being offered every opportunity to succeed in the family business, failed to shine in any way, and got himself into numerous situations from which had to be bailed out. He was also rather too fond of the drink and died estranged from his family in a squalid flat in Gorgie.

Eleanor, my mother, born in 1931 was rejected by both her mother and sister. She said that she had never known any affection from them and told me often that she believed this was why she herself found all expressions of affection very difficult.

At the age of five, little Eleanor contracted ringworm. This was a condition known more commonly amongst the lower orders, and my grandmother believed it would bring shame to the household were it to be revealed in society, so she consulted the family doctor, who prescribed the standard preparation *Thallium Acetate* as a topical application, with the purpose of epilating and then treating her scalp of the fungal infection. Within several days Eleanor was bald, as expected, but she was also paralysed from the waist down, confined to a wheelchair, utterly dependent on a mother who despised her, a teenage sister who resented her and a brother of eleven whose affections were becoming rather less fraternal that they ought to be. My mother was one of the last to be prescribed this stuff; less than a year later, after a massive review of heavy metal toxicity in a Scandinavian Medical Journal, *Thallium Acetate* was reclassified from medicine to poison, and removed from pharmaceutical production processes.

Very quickly, my grandmother discovered a fashionable clinic with a critical attitude to drugs and all treatments based on unnatural ideas about what is healthy. My mother became a patient of this clinic, which had rooms at the West End of the city. It was owned by the Thomson Family, which some years later established a much more extensive centre for natural health on the outskirts of the city at Liberton in Kingston House. I knew Kingston as a child, where my mother visited every year, as my father joked, to dry out. I was myself a client and feel sure that the decline of my asthma had a lot to do with this. My mother's regular visits continued until it closed during the nineteen eighties, after which she continued to visit its practitioners in other places. She was committed throughout her life to the principles of this *Nature Cure*, and for good reason.

My mother's paralysis took nearly a year to clear, her hair grew back more quickly. The treatment was described as detoxification; not some modern fad advertised by glossy brochures, involving special juices, extracts, infusions or potions. This was a matter of slowly encouraging natural healing processes to do what they do, a broad diet of cleansing foods combined with gradual manipulation of paralysed and atrophied tissue. Not long before he died, the last surviving member of the Kingston practice, Sandy Milne, told my mother that her entire life had been a kind of detoxification, the natural result of her exposure to so much toxic *Thallium Acetate* at such a vulnerable age. The implication of this being that my mother's slow healing had had an effect on my own development. He also told her that at the winding down of the clinic at Kingston, her notes had been among those submitted as of exceptional interest to the Royal College of Physicians of Edinburgh for permanent archive. Despite several requests, I have never been able to confirm if these were ever received in good order. Upon her return from the clinic, no longer wheelchair bound, my grandfather recognised my mother's considerable sensitivity and substantial intellect, aware of the family dysfunctionalities that were affecting her so adversely, and arranged for her henceforth to be cared for by a nanny. Catherine Agnes Grey remained with my mother as the Second World War broke out her school evacuated to Galashiels, then throughout the war and afterwards until she went up to University. My mother told me that her nanny was the nearest to a mother she had known; even from quite a young age I knew this, still unable to grasp what it meant. As I grew older, I came to know much more.

Before I got the call from Dundee crematorium that mother's ashes were ready to be collected, I already had a plan to take her to the top of some mountains. She had left my brother and me a simple note with a few locations she wanted her ashes to be scattered and asked that we take her to some other nice places too before we laid her to rest next to my father in St Andrews. Given the albeit distant family connection, and proximity to Dundee, after picking up the urn, I drove to the end of Glen Clova.

It was a glorious day of emerging spring, blue skies and white fluffy clouds. I parked in the usual place, booted up and strolled towards Glen Doll Lodge with some of mother's ashes in a plastic box. Here I turned left over a bridge into the forest towards the Klibo Path, and after a reflective uneventful wander through the trees, emerged onto the grassy slopes of the mountain. Up ahead at the back of the corrie, there was a cliff encrusted with old snow. The path slanted along the flank of a shoulder separating this corrie from the next, and at the top emerged above a flat boggy bealach with one mountain to the left and the other to the right.

At the top of the path I was already at a height of over two and a half thousand feet, overlooking the eastern edge of the Mounth, the plateau to the east of the road through Glen Shee to Braemar. Looking north, views were opening up over the White Mounth, the mountains I climbed the previous year with Colin and Fergus. From here the going was straightforward, firstly with a slight dip and then a slow rise to the summit of **Driesh**, where I left a handful of mother's ashes on the ground and let some dust blow into the wind. Then I dipped back down to the bealach and followed the path to the summit of **Mayar**, where I did the same. From here I began the return by the circular route towards Corrie Fee. Where the first spring of clear pure water gurgled from the ground, I hollowed out a hole in the peat with my heel and buried some more of mother's remains. The rest I poured into the water bubbling up from inside the mountain, taking her down into the River South Esk, past Kirriemuir and out to sea at Montrose where her essence would merge with atmospheric cycles. In the heights of Glen Clova, a bit of my mother will always remain, surrounded by smiling mountains.

The descent into Corrie Fee was steep and complicated, sometimes traversing precipitous slopes under imposing outcrops and always involving careful placement of feet, a bit like the descent into Glen Doll from Jock's Road, but a lot steeper. At length the path levelled out into a flat grassy corrie with a wide burn meandering over its floor, surrounded on all sides by steep cliffs and crags. Noises echoed in the bowl. It is a place much visited by day trippers and I met a few on the way down. I stopped a bit before the path plunges back into the forest to admire this beautiful place, slightly disappointed that I did not have a tent with me so I might pitch up for the night and soak it up some more. I needed to get out again, to sleep in the heart of the mountains, find somewhere to contain my grief.

When my father died at the end of 2005, I realised quite quickly that I had in fact lost my parents, that my grieving mother was a very different being from one half of a collective identity presented to me from the first moments of life as *parents*. Hereafter she had to learn to be herself again after nearly fifty years of marriage, I had to get to know the widow; the woman who gave birth to me and who was married to my father was now gone. It became obvious after my father's funeral that my mother and I would have to do our grieving apart, in certain respects I was too much like him and it became too easy for her to project on to me all the unspoken resentments she harboured against her recently deceased husband. After I returned to The Netherlands, I kept in touch with my mother on the phone, but I did not visit her in Scotland for three years, by which time she had found herself again and built up a new life.

By most standards my parents had a good marriage, but the final years of my father's life were not easy for my mother. He had been diagnosed with colon cancer in 1999, which was treated by resecting the diseased tissue, and then with a course of chemotherapy. This had given them five good years together, during which they travelled a lot and shared their enjoyment of ballet, opera, classical concerts, exhibitions and so forth. But it all came to an abrupt end when fluid began to build up between my father's pleural membrane and his lungs. After a biopsy confirmed that this was a result of metastatic colon cells that had lodged themselves in there, he was admitted to hospital in Kirkcaldy to have the fluid drained and was once again given a course of chemotherapy. Everything appeared to be going well, but his behaviour was becoming erratic. Whenever I phoned from The Netherlands, my father would be animated and pleased to talk, while my mother was troubled, having become burdened and resentful of the care he was expecting her to provide. The only bright side she could find in her darkest moments was that at least this time she was not cleaning up shit.

He called one day in October 2005 to ask that I come to Scotland, which I did as soon as I could arrange cover and book a flight. He did not look nearly as poorly as I expected, but he was clearly drifting in and out of a kind of delirium, and my mother was reaching her limit. I stayed at home for two weeks, helping her cope and trying to keep my father occupied. One of the last duties he felt necessary to perform was to ensure I knew the emotional conditions my mother had endured as a girl, and later while the two were courting, the circumstances of her departure from her mother. He asked that I drive him to the harbour at St Andrews, where we watched the moon rising through brindle clouds over the East Neuk. The North Sea boiled and roared. Despite the fact that I knew he was probably dying, I did not quite realise that this was the farewell conversation of father to son.

He explained to me that he had made full provision for my mother's further maintenance, that everything was in place for her safety for years to come. He then wanted to know if I knew what had happened before she left home to stay on the farm with her father. I was unsure what he meant until he mentioned the death of my mother's mother, the mother-in-law he never had, the grandmother I never knew, the one whose influence continued to be felt long after her demise. Of course I knew, I reassured him. My mother and I had always enjoyed long conversations during our walks, and she had told me many stories from her past, especially about the emotional games played in her family. It was all of this that persuaded her she should move away to make a new family of which to be proud, rather than repeat damage established in the old.

The first time I heard the story was at Kingston, I told him, the time she suffered a sudden acute swelling of her joints. It was a beautiful day in late August 1982, sitting on a bench under an ancient ivy weaving round an even more ancient yew. I had since heard several versions. Of how my grandmother threatened to kill herself if her daughter ever moved away, of how all mother's friends and relations kept telling her that she had to escape her mother's bullying and emotional control, that she had to make a life of her own and think of a career, of how it was only when the family doctor told her that she really should take a break for the good of her own health, that she decided to travel from Edinburgh to Errol by train to stay for a while with her father on the farm at Kinnaird, and of how by the time she got there, news had already arrived that her mother had sealed every door and window in the kitchen, switched on the gas and waited for nature to take its course.

I was quite frank, emphasising the guilt this surely brought forth in my mother, suggesting that I gestated inside that guilt, that the original sin of my life was much less theological than empirical. I told him too that I had once lost a good friend to suicide in the Netherlands and recognised immediately the very particular grief suicide brings forth. Even though I was not aware of ever knowing anybody who committed suicide, except the grandmother I never knew. I said I had learned a lot from the experience. I wanted my father to know that these feelings were very old, that as an infant I must already have been immersed in the effects of my grandmother's suicide and the emotions my mother experienced in its wake, that these were the emotional foundation of my subsequent journey into consciousness, and furthermore that I did not begin to be aware of this until I was twenty three, after my mother first told me the story.

My father seemed reassured albeit a little disarmed, leaving a slight impression that he had understood not a word of what I had said. He was not a man accustomed to speaking so openly about his emotions and intimate experiences, nor the private events in others' lives. It was also not always obvious whether he was conscious of being in a particular emotional condition at the same time as he quite evidently was, as if he was ashamed of owning up to any kind of emotion at all. But he was also a very good teacher with a reputation for listening and I could not imagine he had missed the point of what I had told him. For I knew that despite his emotional reticence, he was often moved to tears by the beauties and graces of the world, and he was clearly very sensitive. He had reason for resentment too towards my mother's mother, because she never considered him a suitable match for her daughter; even though he had been a grammar school boy, highly civilised, well-educated, intelligent and cultured, he was from the artisan classes and had not been to a school of the same standard as her daughter's (the same system continues to flourish in the Nation's capital contributing to the perpetuation of the same old attitudes) which was for my grandmother enough for him to be struck from the list of potential suitors. It may have been his natural reluctance to talk about how he felt, but I believe too he was simply being kind. I never knew him to harbour grudges, to express any resentment towards his wife's late mother, nor anybody else really.

At the time of our conversation by the sea, he was apparently unaware of what I knew of my mother's past, which seemed to imply he had not asked my mother whether she had talked to me about it, although more probably he was in such a condition of confusion he was unable to remember what my mother had told him. In any event, it was these things he wanted me know. At the end of his life he wanted to make sure that I knew exactly where she came from, and perforce where I came from. After my mother's death, the answer she gave to the question of who was the most important person in her life became so much more poignant. She often said that he had always supported her, allowed her to speak her mind without any expectations of what a woman should do or say. Of all her suitors, he was the only one who did not want her to become a little version of himself, expect her to follow him into a career in the Military, the Civil Service or the Foreign and Commonwealth Office.

They gave up their dream of buying a caravan, borrowing an Aberdeen Angus bull from her father, and using its issue to finance an itinerant life of casual insemination. Instead they chose to work together in professional positions with the rest of the population who, it was said, had never had it so good in the new post-war Welfare State, participating with the rebuilding of a society not long since ravaged by global war, now determined to care for all of its citizens from the cradle to the grave, despite an impeding sense of wider conflict and conflagration hanging over from some bit of the past, threatening to disturb the general order of things into the future. He knew her better than anybody, he looked after her, he made sure she would be looked after when he was gone.

Before I returned to The Netherlands, my father's condition deteriorated. His periods of confusion and distress became more intense, he wandered around the house, fell out of bed, knocked stuff over. My mother and I together were unable to cope, not up to the work his care required. He was taken into hospital and did not return home. Back in The Netherlands, I kept in constant contact with my mother, who was told eventually by a doctor that the final days were upon us, whereupon I booked a flight. When I arrived at the airport, my brother called to say to meet him in the city rather than travel immediately to the hospital in Kirkcaldy. It still had not dawned on me. He sat me down on a bench at Haymarket and said that our father had died a couple of hours earlier, as I was somewhere above the North Sea on my way to see him for the last time.

In the telling of her stories my mother always emphasised that she was unable to express affection because of how her mother treated her, that she was never able to grieve her mother's passing because what she actually felt was relief and rage, and why this engendered both an enduring sense of guilt and an inability to become angry. These were the conditions of my gestation. The emotional substrate of my existence. The reason my father wanted to make sure I knew all about the circumstances under which my parents were married, what it must have been like for the infant who came into this world. The non-genetic inheritance, this residue of the past. Damage.

The peace of Corrie Fee is sometimes disturbed by echoes of even the quietest conversations, which resonate within its bowl. I do not believe I audibly wailed or howled that afternoon, but my grief echoed long and deep as I sat beside the stream in the sunshine, passing the time of day with visitors. My brother and I were now the last generation. We had inherited the family home and its contents, amongst which a substantial archive, and a wee bit of cash. Our parents had done a good job, but the effects of their absence were beginning to overwhelm me.

## *Balquhidder*

### 14th to 16th May 2016

It was a weekend in early summer, or maybe it was still late spring, when the hills were crowded. The weather was stunning. Blue skies, still warm air. Perfect for enjoying the great outdoors and distracting myself from the task of sorting through a houseful of stuff. Despite the hardships she endured and the damage she carried, my mother had enjoyed an incredible life, only one small part of which was bringing me into the world. The spaces that emerge after a person dies are very often unexpected, new perspectives are revealed and experiences reconsidered. My mother had no particular secrets, but every item in the house was soaked up with memories and emotions; from the suitcases in the attic full of letters from suitors to her favourite paring knife in the kitchen drawer. Many things can easily be given away to charity shops, or just thrown out. But it is not easy simply to clear out an entire house, lived in for so many years, then sell it for cash. When there is no future, it is not easy to wipe away the past like this and to start again. I could not contemplate giving up the very thing I had returned from The Netherlands to find. Home. Somewhere safe to die.

Despite the grieving and an impenetrable pile of stuff, not to mention continuing pressure from doctors to think seriously about taking the medication again, I was in a good position. I had as much work as I wanted or could handle, my time was more or less my own, the disease was not yet making its presence felt, and I had resources for a few years yet, enough to be able to die doing what I love. I bought myself some more mountain equipment, mainly clothes, and decided that this is what I would be doing with my spare time and any extra cash, indulging my passion for climbing mountains. I also still had an awesome old Volvo, which was becoming good at taking me all over the country and negotiating the squiggles and humps of the many single-track roads necessary to get to parking places near access to mountains.

From the tops of the Mountains of Glen Lyon, the twin peaks of **Ben More** and ***Stob Binnien*** dominate the skyline to the southwest. Behind these there is a large expanse of gnarly land reaching through the Trossachs to the shores of Loch Lomond, through which no roads pass. At the northern most corner, there is a bundle of five Munros. These are accessible either from Glen Falloch by the road north from Loch Lomond to Crianlaraich or from the end of the road in Balquhidder, at Inverlochlarig.

Inverochlarig lies at the end of such a road, beyond the north shore of Loch Voil, under the south face of ***Stob Binnien***. At the entrance to the estate, there is a substantial carpark with access to mountains and tracks through glens. I parked before lunchtime, walked past the estate buildings onto a track north then struck up the side of the mountain in front of me, pathless over crunchy old grass and intermittent bog, rising along the edge of a gully. It was a slow climb with a heavy pack, becoming hotter in the sun but cooled by a breeze. I stopped often to catch my breath and establish a sensible pace. Intending to camp out high, I was in no hurry. Looking down to Loch Voil, I recalled other visits here; with friends after graduation in a borrowed car, on a picnic one summer long ago with my parents high in the woods on the north shore, watching a family of buzzards wheeling about, screeching at each other.

    I got to the summit of **Beinn Tulaichean** at about four, quite suddenly emerging from a steep section under a crag onto a short rising ridge. People were sunning themselves. I passed the time of day and followed the path north towards a shallow bealach, where there was a clear route all the way to the top of the next mountain. I could see many people either on the summit in the distance or walking along the path. The sky was blue, the wind had dropped, a few fluffy clouds hung in the air high above the horizon. I reached the summit of **Cruach Ardrain** a little less than an hour later, after leaving my pack behind a boulder on the route down to where I was intending to camp. I took many photos of brown mountains, still scattered with snowbanks before returning to my pack to then negotiate a way down to a plausible route up the mountains to the west, and a place along the way near running water for the night.

    This was complicated, lumpy ground. I was following what appeared on the map to be a shoulder of the mountain, emerging from the bealach where I had left my pack. The detail was a complex series of descending gnarls that took in a little hump called *Stob Glas*, from the round top of which I was able follow a dry gully down until there was flat ground near a barely trickling spring that seeped into a deep grassy pool of pure clear water. I pitched my tent facing the direction I intended in the morning to travel, to come off the south east slope of *Stob Glas Beag*, to cross the flat bealach towards a geographical feature intriguingly named on the map, The Convention, and along the underside of the northwest face of **Beinn 'a Chroin** to a shoulder leading to the summit ridge.

    It was a quiet place to camp. I was at an altitude of about seven hundred metres. There was no wind. No sound of running water. The seepage from the nearby spring was noiseless and all water ran from here over soft ground through moss and peat. The rivers in the glens were not significant enough to make any noise that would rise this high. The sky was open. I was alone. After eating and taking photos I drifted in and out of sleep, still waking from time to time to remember again what had happened. I tried to stop myself remembering things to tell my mother about the journey, for she always wanted to know, then I gave up and started to talk to her, quietly to myself.

    In this silence I was confronted with an absolute, one of the elementals talked of by Neill Gunn and Nan Shepherd, a silence so vast and all-encompassing it overwhelms all experience, an essential and benign void that reflects back every minute bubble of awareness, returns every segment of thought and tissue of consciousness into the solitude of a living body. This tent, perched on the edge of a mountain, perfectly pitched, always prepared for the next step of the journey. This body purposefully disciplined to have brought shelter to this place, to be able to survive under the protection of geodesic aluminium and technical fabric, relaxed and at rest. Here was a peace I had never before met. This was an absolute silence that pushed all sense of being anything other than this perceiving body, this perspective, into the realms of fantasy; all pretension to self, ego, identity or any other of the abstract categories with which we learn to clothe ourselves become irrelevant, laughably useless. All these thoughts just a kind of noise. I felt the full contradiction of encountering this void, knowing that by doing so, being conscious of this, there was thus existence and perforce no void. I lay with these thoughts rattling about in the silence of the world, trying to hear anything but the rustle of my breathing or my pulse, with no success, left alone with the random noises of a mind reflecting back on a complicated life, seeking sense, talking sometimes to my recently deceased mother.

In the morning the sun shone bright and early, colouring the flanks of the mountains deep orange. I struck camp and followed my plan, concluding along the way that The Convention most likely referred to a flat piece of ground with slopes around it in the form of a minor amphitheatre. From here I followed a grassy gully to a ridge and then to the summit. I emerged suddenly onto a flat table scattered with protruding rocks, gnarls and lumps, with a clear path west toward what appeared to be another two flat summits. There were people sunning themselves. I asked which summit was the highest. They thought it was the middle one, but said there was some doubt, which is why they had come this far. They looked at my pack and warned me vaguely of scrambly bits ahead.

The first drop to the middle summit was substantial and at one point very steep, involving a backward descent of a rocky chute, looking through legs to find footholds. At the bealach there was a gradual climb to a flat ridge pocked with gnarly crags and concealing little pools of crystal water. This was indeed the summit of **Beinn 'a Chroin**. More people were sunning themselves. Somebody else made a remark about the steepness to the west. I said I would see what I found and do what I had to. I was not worried, but I was beginning to wonder. After all, these people had all come from this direction and had recent experience of the path along which I was about to walk. It was a well-trodden path scooped out of the earth. If so many had come this way before, surely it must be straightforward enough.

The immediate descent from the summit was indeed a bit challenging. At one point, I was not able to see any foothold ahead on the way over a round crag; eventually I persuaded myself to drop one of my poles, which since **Ben Vorlich** I always carried with me, onto the ground below to see what kind of gradient was at the bottom. Correctly judging a gradient from directly above is never easy. The pole landed and did not roll, so I lowered down my pack and let it drop the last metre, then found an easy way over the crag. Again there was a gentler climb to another high point, after which a stroll along a flat ridge followed by a very steep decent to an altitude of about eight hundred metres. From here I followed a gently rising path punctuated by gnarly crags over which a degree of scrambling was sometimes necessary. At the summit of ***An Caisteal*** people were sunning themselves and passing the time of day, mostly discussing which of two gnarly ridges to follow north back into Glan Falloch.

In search again of the peace of the previous night, away from these crowds, I came off the summit west and south, following a shoulder running between two gullies taking water to either side of the watershed below. I was on the way to the last mountain in the cluster, dropping to an altitude of about six hundred metres and climbing again to about eight hundred, where I found a flat piece of ground next to a dribbling water source. Above was a steep grassy slope of terraces. I pitched my tent quickly and climbed the last section unburdened, reaching the summit of ***Beinn Chabhair*** at about half past four. There was nobody here and clouds were beginning to gather. The views were nevertheless unspoiled. South to **Ben Lomond**, west over the peninsulas of Argyll, east back to the bundle I had just climbed, to **Ben More**, ***Stob Binnien*** and Balquhidder, north to pointy peaks I did not yet recognise and just visible on the distant horizon, the great bulk of **Ben Nevis**.

I returned to my tent with the tally now risen to forty-nine, already searching my knowledge of Munros for something special for number fifty. In the morning, the cloud was thick and all sunshine blocked. It was colder. I packed and descended into the glen to the south, then back to the car. The next day I uploaded a clutch of summit selfies to a hill walking Facebook page and watched as the number of likes rose to more than a thousand, which rather took me by surprise. A couple of days later a journalist from the *Dundee Courier* got in touch to ask if he could do a story about me. The next day a sympathetic article appeared in print, which is now archived at the website, describing my efforts as inspirational.

A [Fife] man who continues to defy cancer has called on others to enjoy what Scotland's great outdoors have to offer after bagging five Munros alone over the weekend.

[He] was told back in October 2012 he would probably live no longer than three years after being diagnosed with a malignant and aggressive form of prostate cancer.

Almost four years on, however, the 56-year-old is very much still with us and is focused on climbing as many Munros as he can before his illness makes it impossible.

Having conquered numbers 45 through 49 in the space of just two days in glorious sunshine on Saturday and Sunday, [he] is already planning number 50 with the firm belief that fresh air and the tranquillity that Scotland's countryside can bring is helping him live life to the full.

"I was living and working in the Netherlands when the doctors told me I had cancer and the first prognosis I got said I would only have three years, at which point I decided to do a lot of work on myself," he explained.

"It changed my life and I decided to come back to live in Scotland from Utrecht thinking I was going to die.

"When I got back here the medical approach was slightly different and the doctors thought I could maybe benefit from radiotherapy, which seems to have held it at bay.

"But cancer at this level is an entirely mental thing. I don't have any debilitating symptoms, but it is a purely mental struggle.

"At the moment I'm reasonably fit and healthy, but I know one day the cancer will change that so I'm trying to climb as many Munros as I can.

"My abiding passion is walking in the Scottish mountains, and I've done it for a long, long time.

"I do it to keep myself alive, to keep myself strong, and to keep myself level headed basically.

"There's a discipline needed to do it and if I can encourage others to do the same then great."

[His] other passion is cycling and he can be seen negotiating the streets of Edinburgh by bike as a freelance messenger.

[He returned to messenger work] in 2014 after working for more than a decade in the Netherlands with [...] a collective messenger company he co-founded.

He also has an avid interest in philosophy and has written a collection of aphorisms which summed up his thoughts after being given his bleak prognosis a few years ago.

His exploits in climbing the Munros with cancer ha[ve] inspired hundreds of people via social media in recent days, [which is] something that [he] should be proud of.

"Scotland has absolutely spectacular scenery," he concluded.

"Yes, the weather might not be the best sometimes but when it's good the scenery is always spectacular.

"It's available to everyone and more and more people should take advantage."

[His] efforts have been described as "inspirational" on the Scottish Hill Walking & Wild Camping page on Facebook.

Scores of people have left messages thanking him for his photos and positivity and wishing him luck in bagging as many Munros as he can.

[Craig Smith, *The Dundee Courier*, 18/05/2016]

After such a glowing testimonial, I began to see that being an inspiration would become part of what inspires me and that it brings with it a degree of responsibility.

My mother would have been very proud.

## Creag Meagaidh

28th to 30 May 2016

Once upon a time, on a journey by bike homewards from the far northwest, I had to choose at Spean Bridge whether to take the road through Laggan to upper Speyside and then south along the A9 corridor, or to follow the coast to climb through Glen Coe over Rannoch Moor to Orchy and then to squiggle through the glens of Breadalbane. The Laggan route seemed intuitively to be shorter and more straightforward, although I later discovered that there is hardly any difference between the two. It was already mid-afternoon when I left Spean Bridge. The strong rainy wind at my back blew me all the way up the hill to the dam, which was spewing out a thick parabola of white water into the gorge below, and then it blew me along Loch Laggan until it was time to find somewhere to sleep for the night. During the search, I investigated a track to a deserted farm surrounded by sheep and short cropped grass, rejecting it because it was too exposed and sheepy. This was before the formal declaration that in Scotland we have the *right to roam*. Despite deeds of title conferring the concept of *ownership* to persons or other legal entities on areas of ground, *access* to the land is now free. Under certain conditions and provided we take responsibility not to break the law or wander through people's gardens, we can go where we wish and camp out. In those days, this was still only a tradition, not yet enshrined in law, a principle with which it was possible still to disagree, or which must compete with or defer to more important principles, like the rights of ownership. I had been accustomed from the start of my journeys into the great outdoors to visitations to my camps from those who did indeed disagree and believed I should not be there without permission. Concealment was always an issue in any place near roads or farmland and I did not therefore want to camp here, so visibly next to an albeit unoccupied farm in a field full of sheep. Eventually, I found a sheltered clearing in the woods behind the eastern beach of Loch Laggan where nobody would see me. It was not until I was on my way up *Creag Meagaidh* that I realised that the visitor centre on the National Nature Reserve was once that derelict farm.

What a difference twenty-five years make. Where once the only vegetation was short cropped grass, clumps of heather and tussocks of reed too indigestible even for sheep, there are now regenerating flora, young forests and new pastures, bird hides and nature trails, with ample parking facilities beside fields of cattle, little brown sheep and horses, and well-built access tracks of solid grit. The path towards the mountain follows one of the nature trails through an impressively flourishing infant native forest, steeply at first until it reaches a more mature patch of trees, then more gently as it turns towards the impressive northern buttresses of the mountain. Here I met a woman who recognised me from the internet. She was one of many on the way down the path after a day out, more than a little sunburned and absolutely exhilarated. The path turns southwest and flanks the underside of a long shoulder with ***Carn Liath*** (another one) at one end, and ***Stob Coire Poite Ardair*** at the other, bristling with cliffs, crags and clefts still holding sheets of old snow. On the other side of the glen, the round east shoulder of ***Creag Meagaidh*** gradually steepens into cliffs and enormous buttresses. At the end of the glen there is a deep corrie concealing a dark lochan, the grassy banks of which have seen many camps. This is where the manicured path ends. The northeast face of the mountain is popular terrain for climbers with a series of almost symmetrical buttresses and gullies slanting for over a thousand feet from the summit plateau; the walker's path onto the plateau above rises almost as precipitously over loose scree and rough unstable ground towards a nick in the ridge known as The Window.

Scrambling up slopes of scree and deluged rocks, mud and melted snow towards The Window was more of a struggle than I had expected. All the way, surrounded by massive cliffs and buttresses above a perfect corrie lochan. It is no wonder it is popular; even if I did not have the stomach for it, I could see many ways of climbing up the gullies and buttresses behind the lochan; I could see the potential of deep snow in gullies and iced up rock. Something I was still myself anticipating with a degree of trepidation. I knew that many forthcoming Munros would involve a lot of airy ridges and careful scrambling; my brief loss of balance on ***An Stuc*** and the slight scrambling in Balquhidder were nothing in comparison to what was to come. I recalled an ascent of ***Bidean nam Bian*** via the front of the middle of the three sisters in Glen Coe and back via the Lost Valley, in the worst possible weather with the same people with whom once I took a minibus from Glen Lochay to the Glen Lyon Road to park for a spindrift ascent of ***Beinn Heasgearnaich***. I remembered ridges long ago in Cluanie associated with a sharp dread, but could not recall precisely where. And once on ***Mullach Coire Mhic Fhearchair*** in Fisherfield, when the vertigo became so intense that I had to hug the ground, unable to bring myself to stand proud of the summit.

At the top of the scramble, the path flanked above a deep snowbank filling a cavity, further up the snow had melted away to reveal a sharp cleft of round boulders, which appeared to be sinking very slowly into a giant hopper. The path emerged at last onto the southern extremity of the plateau of the *Monadhliath*. In the distance, far on the horizon, the peaks of Affric, Claunie, Kintail and Knoydart. In the foreground, the first headwaters of the River Roy. To my right was the path up ***Stob Coire Poite Ardair***, to my left the northern corries and cliffs of ***Creag Meagaidh***, dripping with tiny glaciers. I was spoilt for choice. The ground before me was perfect, well drained grassy hummocks, interspersed with low outcrops and large snowbanks. I chose a spot facing where the sun would set, pitched my tent and put my food on a low peep with fuel sufficient to burn out at about the same time that it was ready. Then I bounced up the mountain without a pack, joyous, first over a tumbling boulder field behind the tent, then on an easy path along the northernmost of the round shoulders that come together in the grassy plateau of *Creag Meagaidh*.

What a magnificent mountain this is. My favourite had always been ***Braeriach***, but I was now reconsidering. I reached the summit at about eight, where the views were clear to the south towards **Ben Alder** and west to Glen Coe and Lochaber. The two pointy peaks next to Loch Trieg, the *Easains*, looked particularly intriguing. This is a high mountain, but it is not prominent. From the outside, it is visible only as one of many shoulders reaching down into Lagganside, from which the summit is invisible. From distant summits it appears as a nondescript lump on the horizon at the edge of the vast expanse of the *Monadhliath*. From the top however, the whole of the central highlands is on display. From the distant humps of The Cairngorms and Atholl Hills to the pointy peaks of Lochaber, Knoydart and Cluanie. The sky was clear and the sun warm, despite gathering clouds on the western horizon. I hung out for a while at the summit, pleased with myself, content that this was a good way of celebrating fifty Munros with cancer.

I was back at the tent just after eight-thirty. My supper was cooked and only needed to be warmed through. I was content and peaceful, hoping for a colourful sunset and starry skies. Clouds on the western horizon however subdued the sunset and I slept through the night unaware of the sky. In the morning the air was clear and warm with the sun casting long shadows down the broad glen in front of me. I got myself together quickly. I had arranged to meet friends at the top of ***Creag Meagaidh*** at three o'clock. I wanted first to get to the summits of ***Beinn Teallach*** and ***Beinn a Chaorainn*** and calculated that if I left my camp at eight, I would have enough time.

I followed the underside of the northern flanks of ***Creag Meagaidh***, past melting snowbanks and down to a little glen to the back of ***Beinn Teallach***, which I climbed by following beautiful grassy gullies intermingled with boulders and craggy outcrops at a very pleasing gradient. The views from the summit of this, the smallest Munro, are magnificent. All of the Nevis Ranges, The Grey Corries, some Mamores, Glen Coe, the intriguing *Easains*, **Ben Alder** and the high Laggans.

The drop down to the bealach to ***Beinn a Chaorainn*** is steep but short. The plod up the north west shoulder of ***Beinn a Chaorainn*** is long and steep, but once up on the plateau, the walking is easy again and pleasant with only a slight drop to the bealach between it and ***Creag Meagaidh***. This is a massive plateau surrounded by cliffs and corries with many shoulders and ridges. I was a little late at the summit, but I met my friends. We shared biscuits and tea and watched dark clouds building up over the Grey Corries and Loch Trieg, then decided to get off the hill before the rain came down. We said our farewells on a big snowbank and they returned to the carpark. Just as I got back to the tent, the rain came down, heavy, plopping against the tightness of the fabric. Inside I was warm and dry so set about preparing food and settling down for the night. The rain passed within an hour or so, leaving temperature inversions in the glens below and thick air refracting the light of the lowering sun into myriad shades of orange and violet behind a black serrated horizon.

The next morning I pottered around the intricate snowbanks beneath the northern cliffs of *Creag Meagaidh*, taking photos of meltwater dripping into pools before packing up to climb the short distance to *Stob Poite Coire Ardair*. The round summit was shrouded in thin cloud, which dispersed into wisps as I walked along the ridge towards *Carn Liath*. Somewhere along the way the sky opened up into summer blue with high clouds sailing by. It was a straightforward and most enjoyable wander. The descent into the regenerating forest of Aberarder, behind the visitor centre, much less so.

At first it is a matter of carefully taking the right bearing off the round top towards where the path down is supposed to begin. Having found the path, matters improve slightly until it negotiates an extremely boggy hollow round an outcrop before plunging down again into the regenerating forest, whereupon it is swiftly inundated by new growth and eventually turns into the storm gully of a burn. It emerges at last onto the broad path I took on the way to The Window. At the junction, there is a little cairn indicating the start of the old walkers' path, a hangover from times past, before there was a National Nature Reserve here, before the sheep had been taken away. It appears to be the only plausible route up and down *Carn Liath*, but it is not a path I would choose ever to take again, unless it is improved to the same standard as the others. There is something oddly ironic about so much improvement and woodland regeneration now obliterating an old path up and down this mountain, almost as if it had not been properly thought through.

## *Mullardoch and Strathfarrar*

### 18th to 23rd June 2016

I had always intended to be away on some sort of expedition this midsummer, simply because my next oncology appointment was planned for late June and I needed to prepare for it. As far as I was concerned the fact that the Westminster government had decided to stage a referendum at exactly the same time on whether the United Kingdom should remain a member of the European Union, was irrelevant. I was not going to vote anyway, for I refused to pander to the images of Europe framed by the Faragists, nor participate in this reduction of the complexities of European politics to a binary plebiscite, particularly when those most vociferously in favour of cutting links with the biggest free trade area on the planet were often fuelled by ignorance, xenophobia, delusions of grandeur and past greatness. The campaign appeared to be predominately financed by neoliberal extremists, hyper rationalist incels, disaster capitalists and hedge fund managers. Of course, I was always aware that there were definite issues relating to the centralised powers and bureaucratic complexities of the EU, but having lived on continental Europe for so many years, I was also sure that the principles of the EU remained pacifist and cooperative, pragmatically founded on a shared desire never again to allow rivalries between nation states to erupt into war. Meanwhile, the rhetoric of British Nationalists was very often warlike and triumphalist, relying heavily on a putative collective experience of standing up to the Germans and beating them at their own game. Despite vociferous claims to the contrary from British Nationalists, I refused to accept that this vote was in any way similar to the referendum of 2014 on whether or not Scotland should become an independent country; the relationship between the British government at Westminster and Scotland was very different from the relationship between the allegedly United Kingdom and the European Union.

With this expedition I wanted to move into unknown territory and bag a few of the top fifty summits, those above 1100 metres, or about 3600 feet. For some weeks I had been poring over maps of the vast tracts of land between Inverness and Kyle of Lochalsh through which no roads pass except at the coast. The twelve Munros surrounding Loch Mullardoch caught my attention, and the four along the north edge of Glen Strathfarrar. I noted that vehicle access to the latter is granted along a private estate road from nine to six, except on Wednesdays, when the gate opens at twelve, but only during summer; in autumn there is more limited access and in winter the road remains completely unconnected to the public network. Access is granted at all times of the year to walkers and cyclists. I was intrigued.

Looking at the Mullardoch circuit on the map, I figured that a clockwise circumnavigation would be most sensible, starting with **Toll Creagach** and working west past **Tom a' Choinich** towards **Carn Eighe**, **Mam Sodhail**, **Beinn Fionndlaidh**, **An Socach**, **Sgurr nan Ceathreamhnan** and **Mullach na Dhieragain**, before then crossing over the end of Loch Mullardoch to traverse the four along the northern shore. I calculated that in the worst case, I might be out for four nights, but thought three more likely, although I was in no hurry and, as always, my journey would depend on the weather. I left the city at eight in the morning and after a leisurely journey I was walking away from the dam at Loch Mullardoch at about three in the afternoon. It was a beautiful day.

Initial access was not obvious. The car park at the south end of the dam is surrounded by hydro installations and crags garnished by dense undergrowth. A little way back down the road there is a track from which a rough path emerges into a sporadic forest of native pines and deep undergrowth. The path quickly deteriorates and disappears, but it is easy enough to find a route through the trees to the short grass and random boulders of a gently rising gully, to the final slopes on the way to the bealach east of **Toll Creagach**, after which it is but a stroll to the summit. I was there before six. It was still warm and there was hardly a cloud in the sky. I lingered a while. This is a flat unremarkable summit formed by no less than five round shoulders coming together. I was surrounded by unfamiliar peaks in all directions and content.

I sauntered along the obvious path west. After more than two kilometres walking over a wide expanse of round stones, tussocks and gravelly ground, I reached a narrow bealach at an altitude of about eight hundred and seventy metres, after which there was a slightly steeper climb to the summit of **Tom a' Còinnich**, a rather more pointy, but basically round topped pile of stones formed by three blunt spurs coming together. I reached the summit at quarter to eight. The light was lowering and there was a haze building up on the horizon, but it was still warm. I followed the path down and west along a narrowing arête to *Tom a' Còinnich Beag*, and then south west over *An Leth-Creagh* towards the bealach under *Sròn Garbh*. All the way I could see an exposed path along a crest to the sharpening ridges and pinnacles on the approaches to the prominent summit of **Carn Eighe**.

Before nine, I had pitched my tent at the base of the path up *Sròn Garbh* and was eating supper with views into the depths and heights of the northern corries and ridges of **Carn Eighe**. The sky was clear but there was cloud gathering to the west. At dawn, the sun shone pink under heavy clouds on the northern horizon; when I arose the cloud was down around the tent, blowing past and swirling in updrafts. Quickly I packed up while my gear was all still dry and scampered up the sharp ridge to the summit of *Sròn Garbh*, with the mist cocooning me against its exposure. It was an easier climb than I had anticipated. The ground on the top was the familiar stones and gravel, but soon the little plateau sharpened and the path curved through assorted pinnacles and crags, past *Stob Coire Dhobhnuill* and *Stob a' Coire Dhobhain*. I was in cloud, but there were intriguing glimpses of sunshine and light above. In the vague hope that the sun might burn off the cloud, I waited at the summit of **Carn Eighe**, which I reached at about eleven-thirty, beside two rucksacks, presumably left by two people on the spur to **Beinn Fhionnlaidh**. I really wanted to get a view from the top of this mountain, it was a massive walk to get here, up and over progressively higher summits, tops and ridges. After a while of no sign of the sun coming out at all, I headed off in the same direction over large round rocks and crunching scree. Knowing that I would return this way, I left my pack a little way down from the summit. As I emerged from the cloud at the bealach, the rain came down. I met the owners of the rucksacks as they were coming off the summit of **Beinn Fhionnlaidh**. They had just spent their second night out near the summit of **Mam Sodhail**. Earlier in the morning I had met a couple who had spent their second night out near the summit of **Carn Eighe** and the previous day I had met a group of three men who had been round the whole circuit with only one night out. Evidently, I was going round the wrong way and taking far too long over it.

My plan from here was to return to my pack and traverse round the back of **Carn Eighe** to the bealach between it and **Mam Sodhail**, then to follow the path over the mountain to find a place to camp on the other side of **An Socach** in preparation for the next day's scramble up **Sgurr nan Ceathreamhnan**, the traverse to **Mullach na Dhieragain** and crossing Loch Mullardoch to ascend another **An Socach** before finding somewhere to camp for the final night. But the weather turned nasty and I had to rethink. I missed the bealach between the two peaks and almost gave up completely, but decided simply to climb up and up until I found the summit ridge and then work out where I was. I came out beyond **Mam Sodhail** and backtracked; I found the summit and sheltered for a bite to eat inside a square hole in the massive round cairn. It was now three-thirty and raining quite heavily. I noticed, as I left the summit, a substantial series of deep pools in a cleft only a few metres from the summit that would rather undermine the idea that the highest body of standing water in the country is to be found near the summit of **Ben Alder**. Under other circumstances, I might have stopped to examine this more closely to see if it might be puddles rather than pools, and taken photographs, but the rain was getting unpleasant, lumpy on a sharp wind. My priority was getting off the mountain to flat grass in the glen below.

The 3000-foot drop into *Gleann a' Coillich* was hard, steep and exhausting. There was nevertheless comfortable well drained grass by the riverbank when I got there. I put up the tent in the rain and battened down the hatches. With warm food, goose down and a drying wind between showers, I felt safe, miles from anywhere, mentally preparing to climb the other three Munros surrounding the glen the next day with this as a base camp. I slept well. When I awoke, the day did not look promising. The summit of **An Socach** was only intermittently visible and seemed hardly worthy of inclusion in Munro's tables, just the highest point on a gnarly spur between the giants of **Mam Sodhail** and **Sgurr nan Ceathreamhnan**. The latter was shrouded down all its many ridges, and I could only guess where they came to a point. I do not know what time I left, but it was after I concluded that the weather would neither get better nor worse during the course of the day.

It was a day of ridges, scrambling and lots of air below. There was not much to see at the summit of *An Socach* but gnarls. The climb up ***Sgurr nan Ceathreamhnan*** was sometimes a bit steep and scrambly, but there was nothing to see at the summit. I regret not properly scrutinising the map to learn of the complexity of this mountain because, rather than coming off the same shoulder I had climbed from the east and curving north to the spur to ***Mullach na Dhieragain***, I continued west to meet what I thought was the northern shoulder, teetering first across a precipitous arête with an enormous boulder in the middle. I looked at the map again and realised my mistake, I was on the West Top, the lower of this mountain's two summits. I decided, rather than retrace my steps back over the arête, to continue along the north shoulder to *Stùc Bheag* before descending across the corrie between it and the spur to ***Mullach na Dhieragain***. It reminded me of the mistake on the passage between the final two summits on the **Ben Lawers** squiggle. As I dropped into the corrie, I came out of cloud to find myself wandering over a spooky landscape of rocky detritus, slabs and boggy holes, still plastered in places with dirty old snow. On the ridge at last I looked east to see the vast flanks of ***Carn Eighe*** and ***Mam Sodhail***, under a lightening sky. At the summit of ***Mullach na Dhieragain*** the sun came out.

The descent back to the tent was easy and relaxed. I slept well that night. The next morning, the weather looked more promising. I packed dry and headed off down the glen to the end of Loch Mullardoch. The level of the water was very low and evidently had been for some time. New growth was reclaiming bare peat, scrubbed clean by years in the service of hydroelectricity, now exposed again to air and seeds. It was easy to walk over the head of the loch and to wade the rivers. But the cloud was descending again. My powers were being tested. I regretted not being further than this after three nights out. Maybe if I had thought through my route better and if the weather had not hit me so hard on ***Mam Sodhail***, then at least I would have spent a night out here near the end of the loch, making the assault on the last four on the north side a little easier.

I persevered up the gentle south western slopes of the second ***An Socach***. The cloud parted again for a while and I got my first good view of the summit of ***Sgurr nan Ceathreamhnan***, of how I traversed it and then came off along the wrong shoulder, and of how I crossed the corrie to get back to the spur to ***Mullach na Dhieragain***. An impressive peak indeed. The weather deteriorated significantly at the summit of ***An Socach***, with intermittent horizontal rain. When the route to ***An Riabhachan*** emerged into view from time to time, as clouds sped past, it seemed to involve quite a lot of clambering through pinnacles, following paths that clung to precipitous slopes, and a final push to the summit ridge of ***An Riabhachan*** involving some rather exposed scrambling. The path down from the summit was also challenging and I was beginning to stumble a bit. Again I almost gave up. The rain was wet and the wind strong. Through the cloud below I could see the northern shores of Loch Mullardoch tempting me with gentler camping ground and a bit of a path back out to the dam. But I persevered. Taking each stride at a time. Mindfully placing each footstep, following a well-trodden path through difficult terrain and weather while remaining indifferent to how *difficult* they might be. At the final climb to the summit ridge of **An Riabhachan**, the scramble was indeed steep and exposed, but it was easy enough to find a safe way up. The summit ridge is over two kilometres long and no doubt affords splendid views. But I saw nothing but rain. My priority now was to find somewhere to make camp.

Coming off the ridge to the bealach to **Sgurr na Lapaich** was scrambly and stumbly. The weather did not let up. By the time I found a place to pitch my tent at about eight hundred and fifty metres on a shelf of ground under the lip of the bealach, I was wet, hungry and tired. I was nevertheless able to create a haven of dry warmth under the tumult of weather, but I was uneasy. My reserves were low. I thought again about giving up, then realised that giving up here would mean simply to stay put, to succumb to exposure. Throughout the night it rained. In the morning it rained. I packed wet knowing that all I had to do was climb the 300 metres to the summit of the last of the giants, **Sgurr na Lapaich** and then descend to the gentle ridge leading to **Carn nan Gobhar**, a much lower peak with a very different character. Although it felt as if this would require more effort than I had in me, after all these nights out on the bare mountain, anticipating the exhilaration of gaining the summit drove me forward.

There were nights in the mountains in my youth that were more challenging perhaps, under wind, rain, searing heat, ice storms and blizzards, infestations of midges, flies, clegs, in a similar tent pitched all over this country, from Durness to The Mounth, from The Trossachs to the Outer Isles. But now, because of my condition, the challenges seemed more prescient, brought more sharply into focus. I was faced with a stark choice: succumb or live. In my little tent I can always create the warmth required to keep me alive and I always have enough food and fuel for emergencies, but I was running low. I always know too that from wherever I camp, I can look at a map and see that in an absolute emergency there will be a way down into easier weather and safer ground, but from here it was a long, complicated trek down to the lochside and from there a long trudge back to the car. I keep my wits about me and I know what I can and cannot do. But I am also stubborn. Which infuriates my nearest and dearest, and at the same time makes it possible for me to continue, never to succumb, always to live.

After this fitful night, and even in this weather, I gathered myself together. I knew not to give up, not to succumb. So this is precisely what I did. And as I walked triumphantly past the summit of **Sgùrr na Lapaich** in horizontal rain, then clambered down tumbles of stones, along squiggly paths, over boulder fields, under dark cliffs, and tried to avoid slithering over gravelly mudslides on the way down the other side, the clouds began to burn off and to reveal the summer underneath.

I have found myself often going back to this journey over these giants of the wilderness, and in particular to the bealach between **An Riabhachan** and **Sgùrr na Lapaich**, where I find again my strength, my stubborn refusal to succumb, this elemental motivation to live, to celebrate this chance to be alive and breathing, this precious gift of life. When I feel there is no point, or that I might as well give up, I go back to this bealach, preserving warmth using the last of my resources, rationing myself and always aware that I might still need something in reserve, preparing for the next part on the journey.

When at last I got to the approach to **Carn nan Gobhar**, the sun came out properly. Clouds separated to reveal blue skies and spectacular scenery. This was my reward for the testing of the previous four days. I reached the summit before one and snapped up photos of the surrounding hills as they brushed off the last of the cloud. I began to see what I had just done, surveying the horizon round the might of Loch Mullardoch. On the way down I dawdled a lot and sat beside burns bubbling through rocky gullies under clouds of insects. Back at the car I dried out all my stuff before packing, then headed to the campsite at Cannich where I pitched my tent, showered and went for a feed at Slater's.

I thought that I should probably have a bit of a rest day before deciding what to do next, but when I awoke, to a beautiful woodland dawn with open skies and twittering birds, I decided not to waste the good weather that the day was undoubtedly going to bring. So before nine in the morning I was first in the queue at the gate to Glen Strathfarrar. This place is an absolute gem. I am tempted to keep the details of my traverse of the Strathfarrar Munros to myself, to preserve the mystery of the locked gate. Somewhat reminiscent of the Glen Lyon Horseshoe; six peaks, of which four Munros, but on a much grander scale and further into the wilderness. It is an easy circuit with views of every mountain in the north of Scotland, and layers of ridges south over Mullardoch and Affric to Cluanie, Glen Sheil and Knoydart. It is a bit of a slog to the first summit, but the route thereafter does not drop much more than two hundred metres. From the last summit there is a majestic stalkers' path round an echoing corrie, over a moor scattered with boulders, and then through quiet woodlands to the pristine splendour of Glen Strathfarrar, after which there is rather a long walk back along hard asphalt to the start. I managed to drag myself away from this beautiful place just before the gates were closed for the night.

The following morning I tuned into the radio to discover that my country had voted by a substantial majority to remain within the European Union, while the neighbours to the south had voted marginally to leave, thereby dragging out the entire allegedly United Kingdom. I drove home via a quick trip up and down Glen Affric, listening to the radio for as long as reception held up, beginning to experience the extent of the political upheavals that had taken place while I was chasing down demons in the mountains. Here were the first movements of an almighty train crash of events and forces, which those with a sense of history have been observing in very slow motion ever since, in assorted conditions of disbelief, horror, anguish and despair. Back in the immediate world of my life though, unaffected for the moment by what history was yet to unveil, I had to confront the progression of the disease. The PSA doubling time was shortening and the disease was beginning to make its presence felt.

My oncologist is a very nice man who recognises my will-power and sheer bloody-mindedness as important aspects in the management of my disease. At our appointment when I returned, he showed me a recent abdominal MRI in which was clearly to be seen that my prostate was now mush. The internal structure and architecture of all other organs were on the other hand perfectly visible, but as a result of the radiotherapy over two years previously, my prostate remained inert. Which meant that the exponentially rising PSA value must have been caused by rogue prostate cells finding their way into my lymphatic system. This was evidenced further by a number of slightly enlarged nodes, in particular around my aorta and in my groin. So it was back on the combination of *Bicalutamide* and *Decapeptyl* for me, which would result in chemical castration within a month, no more testosterone would be produced anywhere in my body, thereby holding at bay the rogue replication of prostate cells, whether in my prostate or anywhere else. At the same time, my sleep would be permanently disturbed, every two hours I would be overwhelmed by a flush lasting up to five minutes, I would become depressed and lacking in motivation, my libido would die and my emotional responses would flatten out while from time to time I would experience uncontrollable urges to bawl like a baby. My life was again a choice between progressing metastasis or chemical castration.

The journey of the previous week was often challenging. I scrambled up steep craggy paths, traversed sharp ridges, saw a lot of air beneath my feet, all while carrying a substantial pack. I felt the sheer exposure of the mountains, why nothing much lives here, right up high. I was forced into myself to find my most essential powers and resources, and I learned important practical lessons. Although I was sometimes scared, I was able to recognise the fears I experienced, to separate them out, to distinguish those that had to do with the actual circumstances of the present, with the mountain, the weather and the challenges to my capacities, and those that had to do with other stuff, with the ordinary inventions of an active mind looking back on an unsatisfactory life, and those that had to do with cancer. Back in the real world, the fear, exposure and exertion of being in the mountains seemed nothing in comparison to the prospect of the hellish effects of chemical castration.

## *Schiehallion*

### 13th **August 2016**

I was beginning to feel cancerous. There was a gnawing nondescript ache deep in my chest and a general feeling of sickliness, possibly the result of an enlarged lymph node in the vicinity of my aorta, which had been visible on scans since the diagnosis. After my return from Mullardoch, I resisted the injection until the end of July, by which time the PSA level had risen to a little less than twenty, confirming a doubling time of about six weeks. I was waiting silently for the medicinal effects to kick in, for even although I knew the side effects were going to be nasty, I also knew that the progression of the disease would be suppressed and that this cancerous feeling would go away.

*Schiehallion* is one of the most prominent mountains in Scotland. It is the fifty-ninth highest summit; it is shaped like a shark tooth and there is little of comparable height nearby. It can be seen from most summits in the southern highlands and even from one or two north of the Great Glen, as well as from many locations in the central belt; it is often the topic of hot discussion at summits about whether or not it is visible. Unless there is another mountain in the way, it usually is. I cannot remember when I first climbed this mountain, nor how often, but it was before the construction of the big car park at Braes of Foss and the wide manicured path from here to not far from the summit. In those days, there was a potholed layby and a mucky plod over a field into boggy moorland before an ancient walkers' path found its way through an increasingly rocky landscape. The return trip used to take anything up to seven hours; now it is hardly more than four. The starting point is already above one thousand feet, making this, on paper at least, one of the easiest Munro ascents.

My brother and I have always been close and we had a lot to talk about and organise. I was coming to the opinion that the best thing for me would be to move into the family home. Shona and I had been living in a rented gardenless main door flat in Edinburgh's West End since my return from The Netherlands. This was extremely handy for work and the facilities of the city, but it was too small. Increasingly I wanted to get back to the country, back to where I came from and to make use of the family house, at least until stuff was sorted out. In any case we all still believed I did not have much time left and that I really needed a safe place to live out the remainder of my life. These were difficult conversations, and it took me a while to convince my nearest and dearest that this would be a good idea. From my point of view, it was a no brainer. All I needed was to come to some arrangement with my brother, who jointly owned the property. It made sense to him too, not only would immediate responsibility for looking after the house and the dispersal of family stuff be deferred until some other arrangement became necessary, the value of the property would increase with somebody living in it, making improvements and keeping the place alive. In any case, he had his own house and family to look after. Of course, had the situation been reversed, I would have had no problem with my brother occupying the house. Shona decided that the sitting room would be more homely with a wood-burning stove and invested some of her capital (which my brother and I later repaid from our inheritance) and I made a start on decorating the important rooms. I thought it might be possible to call this place home again, even though I still had no clear sense of the future, just a gradual decline into the ignominy of premature death, in which case familiar surroundings would be exactly what I needed. To hammer home the issue a local tomcat decided that I was now going to be his human being and that this was now where he was going to come back to. Whenever I returned, he was waiting, full of purring friendliness and searching for a warm lap to sit on.

In the vicinity of my birthday I wanted to organise a group ascent of **Schiehallion**, but my brother was the only one able at short notice to come along. Which gave us the opportunity to talk things through. It was a fine day for climbing **Schiehallion**, the mountain of the fairies, with the summit cone shrouded in cloud and the heat of the sun dampened by haze and a slight wind. The glens and forests of Perthshire were utterly resplendent, green and alive, highland cattle munched slowly, surveying the world through ginger fronds, creating picture postcard shots for visitors in an almost perfect elision of domestic bliss and natural harmony. We left the carpark about half past twelve and trundled up the path through ripe bracken, bristling with butterflies and rabbits. It was busy. We stopped once for a bite to eat before entering the cloud, enjoying views and chatting with passers-by.

When the maintained path comes to an end, an old walkers' path scrapes through shattered quartzite and random boulders. This bit of the mountain is as difficult as it always was; those with no knowledge of the old way up complain that the path stops here. It is indeed a sudden change, but this is just how the ground is at the top of this mountain, and until the construction of the path, it was all like this, if not worse. The mountain's prominence moreover exposes it to everything the weather throws at it. Often it creates its own little micro climate under which the summit becomes a howling deluge while all around remains calm. And even before the end of the path, walkers are troubled by false summits for a distance of about a mile along the crest, which in mist become all the more infuriating. We reached the summit in fine wet cloud at about two thirty and had some late lunch in the lee of one of the chaotic slabs that have been piled here by forces unknown. The northern flank is a steep scree of large boulders, the southern a sheer drop of a couple of hundred metres onto another steep slope of scree. Sometimes the mist thinned enough to see down, but mostly we saw only the rocks we sat on.

We returned the way we came. The discomfort in my chest and the horrible nausea were not made better by the achievement. Climbing mountains does not make the disease go away, although having it does not make climbing mountains impossible. My body would feel like this, were it delivering stuff in the city, plodding to the top of a mountain, or sitting peacefully reading a book. I did not like it at all, not only because it was an unpleasant continuous feeling, but also because this is in fact the visceral experience of the disease. This is what cancer actually is. Exactly the same as how it was during the summer of 2012, before I knew it was cancer but was already developing serious suspicions that there was something very wrong going on inside my body. Already it engendered a sense of foreboding, of something so badly damaged that it could never be repaired. Fucked up.

## Stob Binnein

### 30th August 2016

The drugs kicked in. I felt better and I felt worse. I no longer had a nauseous lump at the centre of my being, but I was now insistently reminded of my condition by the side-effects of the medication used to control it, troubled continually by prickly heat and volatile emotions, challenged at every turn to manufacture my own motivation. Always in danger of falling into a pit of despair, conscious that only my mind could now motivate this body, and even then, with the depletion of testosterone, that it was often incapable, impotent. I consider myself fortunate to have learned at my mother's knee that a mind is a vital force of health and well-being. Sometimes though, with this disease and this medication, my mind wandered into some very dark places indeed. There is an excellent Dutch word for this, for which there no equivalent in English, *kankeren*.

On the face of it, being fluent in a language spoken by fewer than twenty million people, the greatest majority of whom are packed onto reclaimed land amid the unstable delta of one of northern Europe's greatest river systems, does not have much value beyond the borders of said delta. Being bilingual does however bring many advantages. Any particular language community will assume that, for all practical purposes, the things indicated by its language are actually there in the world. This usually extends into a more general feeling that the things a language outlines are just the way things are, and that translating into a foreign language is simply a matter of finding the correct foreign words for the things a native language outlines. The first lesson of moving into a new language community is realising that your native language certainly does not set the standard of sense to which all others will defer; the second is that there are many things in the world you did not know about because your language does not have words for them, and conversely that many of the things in your world simply do not exist for others.

There are obvious, immediate and profound psychological consequences of exile which never go away. The gradual processes of becoming bilingual, of learning not only the grammar and spelling rules that formally describe a language, but also the social conventions and cultural practices that give it sense, bring with them many valuable lessons: understanding that no language is able precisely to represent the stuff of the world, nor articulate every possible emotional condition; that independently of those who use them, languages have lives of their own, traditions and characteristics; that what they mean depends on a great deal more than the intentions of their users; that they can both circumscribe and liberate consciousness; that they can both ensnare and enlighten a mind, both confuse matters or clarify thinking. More prosaically, becoming bilingual makes it possible to think differently. Being bilingual has allowed me to experience the stuff of the world around me and to express my emotional condition in ways unknown to my native language. It means having a greater repertoire of meaning to play with, and perforce understanding.

Barring regional vernaculars, Dutch is almost but not quite entirely phonetic, in the sense that what is written down is a representation of what is spoken, there is a more or less one to one correspondence between graphemes and phonemes. Despite also being technically phonetic, English is notorious for the number of words with many different pronunciations, the most obvious English grapheme with multiple phonemes is probably *ough*, which can be *uff*, *off*, *ow*, *owe* and *oo*, not to mention *uch*, *och* and *ooch* in Scots. Dutch does not have anything remotely like this; with one or two minor exceptions each grapheme has a unique sound. Dutch is also very literal and works according to well defined grammatical rules and conventions, unlike English, which can be rather slovenly, is frequently figurative and often open to vigorous misinterpretation. Dutch is nevertheless extremely expressive and can be a wonder to behold in full flow. Subtle differences of meaning are expressed using a particular emphasis, by careful ordering of words or by precise placement of prepositions. Dutch can depict with only a few well-chosen words what would take whole paragraphs in English.

In English, profanity is commonly expressed with old fashioned words for fornication, bodily fluids and sexual organs. Dutch has a less euphemistic attitude to sex and bodies than English and swears most effectively by using words for disease. The most offensive insults involve asserting that others are presenting symptoms of something infectious, or exhorting them to come down with an incurable disease. The most common are *pest, tering* and *kanker*, respectively the plague, tuberculosis and cancer. *Kanker* is also the basis of the verb, *kankeren*, which has two principle meanings in common discourse: to complain or whinge endlessly and demonstrably; and to eat away from the within, to gnaw, suppurate, rumble, fester or putrefy. For whatever reason, Dutch is replete with words for complaining, but this one is the ugliest and most pejorative, signifying something dark and unpleasant just beneath the surface utterly indifferent to the effects it has on the world around. If somebody is sitting in a corner *kankeren* then everybody else in the room knows about it, and the atmosphere is intense and nasty. The double sense of *kankeren* perfectly depicts what cancer actually does. It is there all the time, inside, festering and demanding attention; sometimes it breaks through the surface to take over all discourse, to spoil the atmosphere and drag everybody into its spiral of doom. There is nothing in English that comes even close to the resonances of *kankeren*.

I can say in English that I am having a *cancer day*. But this would be just another euphemism designed specifically to avoid the full effects of the disease, to give it a safe signification that conceals its reality, allowing others to give me space to do what I have to. When I experience such *cancer days*, I become resentful and have to burn off negative energy, to calm my troubled mind, and find some escape from the mundane tribulations of ordinary life, which often seem trivial in comparison to the insistence of the disease, but which are as they are, just plain ordinary. I still had to work to keep myself in food and fuel, living in the country and working in the city was turning out to be less than ideal, and my good intentions to sort through the family stuff were given low priority during redecoration. There was also an awful lot of it, which became overwhelming sometimes and added to the incipient sense of futility and despair that seemed always to be just below the surface, *kankeren*.

I felt myself extremely fortunate though to be living in Scotland, in possession of a sturdy vehicle and extensive knowledge of many beautiful places within easy driving distance of home. On these *cancer days*, I knew of no better antidote than trudging up a mountain, preferably one involving an unremitting slog from base to summit. There are several such slogs within reasonable driving distance of home, most prominently the twin peaks of **Ben More** and ***Stob Binnein***, which dominate the landscape around the Trossachs and Crianlarich. Once I climbed the two together on a fine spring day of blue sky, warming sun and still air; I was planning now to climb them separately on *cancer days* and to make good use of the unremitting slog required for each.

*Inverlochlarig* lies at the end of a squiggly spur west from the A84 trunk road north through the Trossachs. It runs along the banks of Loch Voil under the Braes of Balquhidder, one of the most staggeringly beautiful bits of Scotland. It is a place I know from picnics long ago with family and friends and more recently not long after my mother passed away when I climbed the cluster of five beyond the end of the road.

From the carpark at Inverlochlaraig to *Stob Invercarnaig*, at the end of the south shoulder of ***Stob Binnein***, there is a very steep path, apparently vertical near the top, that rises nearly two thousand feet in less than a mile. It begins straight as a die, through bracken and sheep pasture then continues upwards through heather until it crosses a fence. Hereafter it zigzags and squiggles as it negotiates a series of outcrops and minor cliffs. After this there is a slow steepening trundle through interminable hags and then a little steep section before a rocky ridge to the summit. This is perfect topography for mindfully placing feet one in front of the other without being distracted by views; the purpose being to remain always in the moment, mindfully moving over the ground, not allowing cancer monsters to take over, remembering what a body can do, when it puts a mind to it.

This is exactly what I did. At the summit I was disappointed by a truculent little cloud that appeared to be anchored to its craggy outcrops, and I was disappointed again on the way down to look back and see the little cloud had dispersed into nothing. The thought of returning for a view occurred, but I dismissed it and carried on with the descent, still mindful of every footfall, securing myself to the ground. At the bottom again, I looked back, impressed that I had found a way up such an imposing hillside, reminded again how easy it is to forget what a body can do, no longer troubled by Dutch words for disease.

# Derry Cairngorms

**13th to 16th September 2016**

Some feelings never decline. Certain experiences are so intense they always lurk at the edge of consciousness, to recur whenever the events that brought them forth are recalled. They never lose their edge and remain visceral. Like the moment my brother told me that our father had died, or when my phone rang at three in the morning from a Dundee number and I knew my mother was gone, or numerous moments during my time as a bicycle mechanic and messenger when I injured myself or crashed stupidly. Or when I locked myself out of the car at the Linn of Dee car park, in a light drizzle and swarms of midges, at two in the morning wearing only pyjamas and crocs.

From the moment, I climbed out the rear flap of the Volvo to answer nature's call and heard the mechanism click, I feared the worst, but went about my business in the hope I was wrong. When I tried to open the flap again and it did not budge, I was overwhelmed by panic and my mind ran riot. Every time I remember this, it all comes back. Exactly as it was. Complete panic. I tried again, this time with more force. No movement. Irritatingly it was not properly closed, just not openable. All the other doors were also locked. It was a long walk in Crocs back to Braemar, and then what would I do? My money, ID and phone were all in the car. Could I hitch all the way home to fetch the spare key? Could I knock up some of the others who were probably asleep in vehicles in other bits of the car park? How was I going to explain this? What could they do to help anyway? How could I have been so stupid to have let this happen at all? Why had I not got out to piss using one of the regular doors? For then, opening the door would have tripped the central locking mechanism and unlocked the whole car.

Even as I headed up Glen Lui the next morning, the bewilderment, shame and fear were still rattling around my head. During the rest of the night, the memory of it all disturbed my sleep, awakening me in terrors. So I was glad to be on the move, the car locked, the key safe in my pocket and everything I needed on my back. The weather was warm and close. Thin cloud swirled around the high peaks holding back the sun. I worked up a sweat quickly, augmented by *Decapeptyl* flushes. Every time I stopped to cool down and freshen up by a burn, I was attacked by midges. Adrenaline kept me going. In my head I knew I was not locked out of the car in the middle of the night, but every time I remembered that I had been, my heart pounded. I plodded on, trying to maintain a balance between speed enough to waft off the midges while not overheating, telling myself that I really was no longer locked out of the car at two in the morning wearing only crocs and pyjamas in a fine drizzle and clouds of midges.

I had taken the path out of the car park through the woods to Glen Lui, and at Derry Lodge crossed the river to regenerating forests in *Gleann Laoigh Bheag*. At Luibeg Bridge I followed the glen north along a faint path rising gradually through boggy heather. The cloud was low but not thick, and the air was dense and humid. I was beginning to believe I might not be locked out of the car wearing only night clothes. In an effort to avoid the midges I plodded forward without break, stopping only to refresh my water bottle. It is not a steep climb and even if the path is not well defined, it is clear that many boots have been this way before. I followed the right of the burn along the bottom of the enormous west flank of **Derry Cairngorm**. To my left, the flanks of ***Carn a' Mhaim*** and the arête to the great round shoulder of ***Beinn Macduibh***, ahead the little promontory at the south edge of the high plateau, keeping its tip in the cloud and darkening the implausibly long drop into out of sight corries and lochans beneath. The ground flattened at length into slabs and scattered boulders and then steepened a bit before the broad bealach between **Derry Cairngorm** and ***Beinn Macduibh***. Somewhere on the other side of this was a path from the latter down to Loch Etchachan, my goal for the night.

At the bealach there was thick cloud to ground level. Visibility was not good, so I had to trust that I would find the path on the way down the rocky slope. It began raining slightly. I had crossed the threshold into The Cairngorms' private climate. I was getting tired, having not really stopped to rest or eat since leaving the car and still having to remind myself from time to time that there was no need to stress, that I was not locked out of the car in the middle of the night in swarms of midges and a light drizzle wearing only crocs and pyjamas. The mist on the other side of the col was much thicker and the loch took rather longer to appear than I anticipated, but it was there, just as I remembered it, calm and still. First, I crossed the causeway at the outflow from Loch Etchachan into Little Loch Etchachan in search of flat ground next to the path down to the Shelter Stone that I thought I remembered from another visit to this place, but found nothing well-drained enough. So I returned over the causeway and plumped at last for a grubby bit of ground between some boulders that had evidently been used often before. Despite my initial doubts, it was a good place; sheltered, flat, near water and peaceful. There was however nothing to see outside but mist and soggy ground, so I ate and settled in for the night.

The next morning there was still mist, but it was thinner and the sun shone through sometimes, suggesting I was still within The Cairngorms' micro climate, holding onto the weather as surrounding countryside basked in glorious sunshine. Optimistically, I strolled up the path to the summit of ***Beinn Macduibh***. The path is easy to follow and leads all the way to the top, where the cloud was now predominantly below me, swirling in updrafts from the depths of the *Lairig Ghru*, pouring over the escarpment of ***Braeriach***, revealing only the tips of the high peaks and offering only glimpses of the plateau. I lingered awhile utterly in awe of this place, the second highest point in Scotland; presently the cloud cleared and I saw the enormity of the plateau. Red and grey stones piled above shallow bowls of darker ground where water gathers into green banked channels before plunging off precipices. There is not much to this summit, and were it not for the big cairn and trig point, its precise location would not be obvious. It must be one of the least prominent in the country and is unquestionably one of the bulkiest mountains in Scotland. I returned the way I had come and swung right before the path dipped back down to the loch, so I could continue along the round north shoulder of **Derry Cairngorm**. Again the cloud was thin at the top, but this peak was not high enough to peek out into the sunshine. Disappointed that I had not had a view, I returned to my tent, whereupon the sun came out and the enormous splendour of Loch Etchachan burst forth.

Loch Etchachan nestles at an altitude of about 930 metres in a flat corrie that also forms bealachs between ***Beinn Mheadhoin*** (pronounced Ben Vane), **Derry Cairngorm** and *Carn Etchachan*, the highest point on one of the eastern shoulders of ***Beinn Macduibh***. The outflow is east into Glen Derry and it is fed predominantly by a substantial burn, the source of which is high on the plateau less than a kilometre from the summit of ***Beinn Macduibh***. It is backed at the west by sheer two hundred metre cliffs, while to the north the ground rises slightly and then plunges two hundred metres to the banks of Loch Avon and the tumble of building-sized blocks of stone that over millennia and centuries have fallen off *Carn Etchachan* and the Shelter Stone Crag, and under which there are cavities big enough to shelter tired bodies. It is not a deep loch; for most of the winter, it is frozen solid and in the summer the water is so clear that the bottom appears sharp and clean, the surface invisible. It is surrounded by gravelly stones, tussocky grass and squelchy peat, concealing stunted trees; tiny pines, rowans and birches hugging the ground like heather. I spent the rest of the day hanging out in the sunshine, taking photos and exploring the margins of the loch. Near the end of the day a party of two tents and three people made an encampment not far off, one of whom came over to introduce himself. He was a guide and the others his clients. We had an interesting conversation as light faded.

The next morning, I awoke early to a glorious dawn of pink light painting the cliffs behind the loch. I ate my usual breakfast and bounded the short distance to the top of ***Beinn Mheadhoin***. This is a remote peak and it is concealed by many others, but it is high, only twenty-five feet short of four thousand and the thirteenth in Munro's tables. All along the flat summit there are prominent weather-beaten tors of pink granite, known as the *Barns of Beinn Mheadhoin*. These are similar to the rock formations on the *Bynacks*, some of which are known as the *Barns of Bynack*. Further east on the massive plateau of **Ben Avon**, apart from the summit, there are several high points, all of which are similarly graced with these rather incongruous lumps of rock.

The highest point of ***Beinn Mheadhoin*** is at the top of the most easterly of its barns; the path through the others is reminiscent of the wild west, gravelly ground, round stones, tussocks of tough grass, strange rock formations. It took me a while to figure out which was the best way up the summit barn, and indeed where the highest point was. Many feet had evidently clambered all over it and found ways up to many viewpoints. There was a fierce wind from the south west and the air was warm and thick. But it was cloudless. Ridges faded in layers to the horizon, with the most distant recognisable hills The Lomonds near my home in Fife. I found a way up the barn's highest point and stood bracing into the wind. It was not yet nine in the morning. The exhilaration was intense. I laughed out loud with the sheer joy of being here in the very heart of my favourite mountains, surrounded by old friends. Although **Cairn Toul** and the **Angel's Peak** were hidden behind the great bulk of *Beinn Macduibh*, *Braeriach* was peeking over flat ground of the plateau, a dip where snow lies thick in winter and melts through gravel and mosses to be filtered clean, seeping and bubbling out again into the burns of *Feith Bhuide* and *Garbh Uisge*, before pouring down gullies and slabs to feed the depths of Loch Avon. A couple of patches of eternal snow nestled still under cliffs.

I was standing at an altitude higher than the bulk of the plateau, able to see forms on the ground that I had hitherto only seen represented on maps, or walked over. To the north the green expanse of Abernethy with the North Sea glimmering on the distant horizon. Beneath and to the east, my route for the rest of the day, towards *Beinn a' Chaorainn*, with *Beinn a' Bhuird* and the barns of **Ben Avon** in the far distance. South, the pointy summit of **Derry Cairngorm** and the Caledonian forest of Glen Derry, evidently now expanding and healthier than when I first saw it twenty-five or so years previously. The sun shone strong, beckoning a day of heat. This high desert is a fascinating viewpoint, well worth the effort of getting here. I hung out for a long time, taking photos and being alive. I had almost forgotten that I had locked myself out of the car in the middle of the night wearing only crocs and pyjamas in clouds of midges and a fine drizzle.

Back at the tent, I was reluctant to leave this beautiful place, so I went for another wander round the loch. At about midday I dragged myself away and trundled down the path into *Coire Etchachan* following the outflow of the loch. The first drop is over crags and is a little tricky, but it settles into a steep downward slog on a gravel path to Hutcheson's Hut, where I stopped at about one to shelter from intensifying heat. A thermometer in the shade outside read twenty Celsius. Inside it was warm but not scorching. I sat on the doorstep for a while snacking and preparing for the next stage of my expedition, the search for a nice place to camp on the southern slopes of *Beinn a' Chaorainn*. I had a clear view from here of what this would entail; to follow the path for a while on its way back down into the forest, but to traverse left at about the altitude of the *Lairig an Laoigh*, heading for the path towards Abernethy, then finding a way up one of the gullies coming off the west flank of the mountain.

It was a slog. The ground was rough, then steep and then interminably haggy. It took a while before the burn I was following flattened out onto ground that was not squelchy, tussocky, gravelly or wet. At last I found an almost perfect spot, on soft grass with the burn at my ear, not far below where it bubbled from the ground. I pitched my tent facing northeast and bounced up *Beinn a' Chaorainn*. This is not a small mountain, but it is dwarfed by the high tops to the west, which were beginning to collect cloud again, their summits partially veiled by haze. The barns on **Beinn Mheadhoin** protruded strangely along the horizon. It looked like it was raining above the heart of the mountains, over Loch Etchachan. To the northeast and south the views were clear. I was particularly drawn to the vast expanse of flat bog to the east with the lumps of **Beinn a' Bhuird** and **Ben Avon** behind. I had once thought of combining these two giants with this summit and **Beinn Bhreac**, but looking at the ground now, I saw that it would be no fun at all finding a way across the featureless morass from here. The way south to **Beinn Bhreac** was also characterised by many hags and little pools of glittering water. I felt the exhilaration again at the end of the day, standing in the warm wind on top of another mountain, looking across a cavernous pass to the summit from which I had seen this summit at the start of the day.

I returned to my tent, ate and slept well. In the morning I lingered. The weather was again fine, but the high peaks to the west continued to hold onto their own little climate. The route to **Beinn Bhreac** was indeed a squelchy plod over tundra with no respite. Eventually I found rocks on the northern flanks where I could sit for a snack before the final crunch over piles of round stones to the summit. The high Cairngorms were still rumbling with their own little climate, while I sat in warm sunshine looking down on the forests of Glen Derry and Glen Quoich, beginning to plan a route up **Beinn a' Bhuird** and **Ben Avon** from within the latter.

The descent was straightforward to the first of two clefts that cut through the shoulder between Glen Quioch and Glen Derry, after which I found a path slanting diagonally into the latter. On the way down I met a man with a timid Labrador called Archie who walked into the heather to the end of a long lead as I chatted with his person. He was like that with everybody, the man told me.

Back in the forest, the heat of the day was captured now under the canopy and cooled, the ground less boggy and more deeply carpeted with shrubs, heathers, new growth and mosses. I once camped in a blizzard in a clearing near here by the river. As far as I could see, there were no clearings now, only forest. Birds and insects fluttered about in a vibrant ecosystem protected by ancient pines. The owners of the land here have culled the red deer back to only a few small herds and the effect on the forest is remarkable. In comparison to the barren wastes through which I had been wandering the last few days, this was a verdant paradise, and judging by the number of young trees at and beyond its fringes, it is expanding. I sat once or twice on the way through the forest and again at the bridge near Derry Lodge. In the heat of the sun, the flushes seemed to return. Whereupon I realised that I could not remember being bothered that much by the flushes since making camp at Loch Etchachan. If only it were so in the city.

With another five Munros added to the tally I trundled happily back to the car, at which point I remembered that I was not locked out, that after the initial panic, after all the images of walking through Deeside in pyjamas had overwhelmed me and I had shaken myself into the present, I saw that I had of course left all the windows slightly open, to ensure I would not suffocate as I slept in the back. I looked inside and could see the keys lying in the middle. I could also see walking poles almost within reach. I thrust my arm as far as it would go into the gap between the glass of the window and the door frame, then I did the same with my other arm. Gradually I forced them through the gap. I could feel my strength creaking at the window mechanism and damaging the innards of my forearms. I reached one of the walking poles and pulled it out triumphantly, then wondered what I was now going to do with it. My arms were scraped and bruised and I could not reach the keys using the walking pole as a hook. This act of desperation had resulted only in painful forearms and potential damage to my beloved old Volvo. But then I remembered that on the door handle on the driver's side, next to buttons that operate the windows and rear-view mirrors, was a little button that operated the central locking mechanism. I walked round to the driver's door, on the way finding a stick with the right shape of squiggle at the end, so I could then gently reach down to depress the crucial button. There was a satisfying clunk as the car unlocked. I opened the door and returned to my sleeping bag to begin the process of convincing myself that I was not locked out of the car at the Linn of Dee at two in the morning, in swarms of midges and a light drizzle, wearing only pyjamas and crocs.

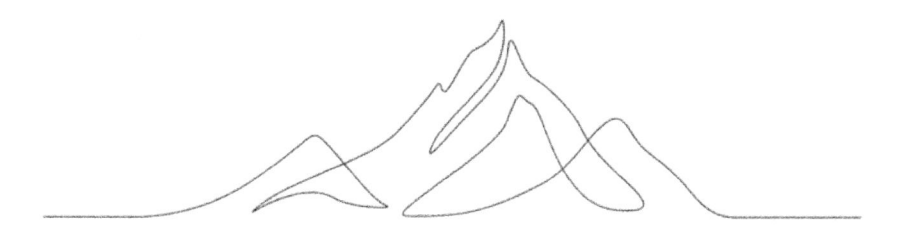

## Buachaille Etive Mor

### 19th September 2016

My friend Janine informed me towards the end of the summer that she would be visiting from The Netherlands for a day to climb a mountain. She had booked a ticket arriving early on the eighteenth of September and departing late on the twentieth, leaving plenty time, she told me, to get to the highlands, find a mountain to climb and then do some sightseeing on the way back to the airport. In purely logistical terms she was absolutely correct. Arranging the weather would on the other hand prove rather more challenging.

I picked her up promptly and drove towards Glen Coe, on the way describing several options, which were boiled down by the time we got there to either a visit to the Lost Valley followed by an attempt on the summit of ***Bidean nan Bian***, or the ridge of ***Buachaille Etive Mor***, which because it is Scotland's most iconic and photographed mountain, she immediately recognised as soon as it came into view. I drove down the glen to show her the Three Sisters and the entrance to the Lost Valley, and then back to The Kingshouse, after which she chose ***Buachaille Etive Mor***. We found a place for the tent on the other side of the old bridge from the hotel; I cooked us a meal under gloomy skies as, much to Janine's excitement, a number of deer wandered past, unbothered by our presence. Part of a small herd that has learned that passing human beings often leave an edible residue.

The weather was not entirely promising, but it was not as bad as it might have been. In the morning, although the tops were shrouded in mist, it was not actually raining. We left the tent and parked in one of the crowded, pot holed spaces on the last bend up from Glen Coe, from which we followed a path to a bridge across the river and access to the mountain. There is a well-worn path that becomes progressively steeper and more slippery as it ascends towards a bealach not far from the highest summit on the ridge, ***Stob Dearg***. Janine was immediately thrown in at the deep end with one or two slightly tricky sections, but judging by the enormous smile on her face and the poise with which she negotiated the terrain, I was assured of her mountain sense. I never had any doubt about this, for she is an experienced world cyclist and former athlete, quite accustomed to the perils of terrain and weather, although never until today in Scotland.

The summit of ***Stob Dearg*** was flatter than I had expected. We arrived at about the same time as several others, two of whom, a couple of older chaps emerging through the mist from the top of Crowberry Ridge. Presently a familiar croak grew louder in the cloud, swooping round our heads. Then a raven landed and walked purposefully to the pinnacle stone on the small cairn, where he stood for some time posing for cameras and preventing anybody else standing at the very top. It was a good ten minutes before he wandered off and we were able to reach the actual summit. I have gendered this bird male because he was very large with pronounced trousers. No doubt, his arrival at the top of this mountain had something to do with him knowing that there are often food fragments to be found here in the wake of human beings, which is no sign of maleness, but his manner on the ground was reminiscent of male raven dominance displays. I like ravens. They are said to be protectors and I am always pleased to see them. It was a real treat to meet this enormous bird just hanging out at the summit. I explained to Janine that she should not expect a welcome from ravens at the summit of every Munro, although it is unusual never to see any. She was happy to be at the top of her first Munro ever.

We returned to the bealach to prepare for the most difficult section of the journey. In the old days, **Stob Dearg**, the highest and most easterly point of the long ridge of **Buachaille Etive Mor** was the only Munro. In recent years, the most westerly and third highest prominence on the ridge, **Stob na Bròige**, has been added to the list. According to purely objective criteria, this does not make a lot of sense. Between the two Munro summits there is another peak, *Stob na Doire*, which is only eleven metres lower than the highest; between this and both of the other two, the ridge has a lowest point at about the same altitude. *Stob na Doire* is without question the most impressive and challenging of the three peaks and it seems likely that the decision to appoint **Stob na Bròige** as Munro had more to do with encouraging baggers to traverse the entire ridge, thereby mitigating erosion, than with any great difference in character between it and **Stob Dearg**.

It is a steep climb up and an even steeper climb down *Stob na Doire*; the summit is pointy and precipitous; it was hard work getting to it and off again, but there is no way round. Again Janine was tested and came through smiling. We ate a late lunch on a flat grassy hump near the last bealach as the sun came out. The walk out and back from here to the summit of **Stob na Bròige** was easy in comparison to what had come before. There were no waiting ravens, only splendid views under dispersing cloud into Glen Etive and towards the fjords and islands of Argyll. We were not challenged by terrain again until descending the bealach into the glen separating the two *Buachaille Etive* ridges. The ground was not only steep and the path often broken and slippery, there were sections of scrambling over wet rocks requiring care and attention, where tired legs could easily stumble and where in winter ice could build up transparently to shroud the rock.

We reached the flat of the glen with tired legs and contented smiles then made our way back to the road, which we had to follow for a mile or so to get back to the car. We returned to the tent, changed and went off to The Kingshouse for a good feed. In the morning the weather was marginally better and we had time to drive down Glen Etive and back before heading to the airport. I had never visited and knew it only from modern mythology as a secluded place popular with so-called *wild campers*. So I was keen to investigate;

it was also a nice way for Janine to witness the complexities of Scottish recreational land use. Near the start of the long descent to sea level from the heights of upper Glen Coe, there was a green Land Rover parked on the verge. A chap in full tweeds was leaning against it as he levelled a high-velocity rifle at a point somewhere up the hillside. A man wearing faux military camo stood in attendance.

I was less enamoured with Glen Etive than its reputation would suggest I be; it is surrounded by impressive cliffs and buttresses and in the upper sections there are several places where I would be happy to find a roost for the night if I were passing through on my bike, but most of the possible camping spaces I saw were overused. In any case, being essentially a cul-de-sac I would never be likely to be *passing through*. Lower down the glen, there are estate buildings, hunting lodges and holiday cottages; the extent of fencing along the roadside would make immediate camping or parking impossible and there are notices indicating that this is in any case not permitted. At the end of the public road there is a gate to a track to an old jetty and a damp patch of grass by the shore, set aside for campers. It is undoubtedly a spectacular location; **Ben Starav** thrusts three and a half thousand feet from sea level as the flanks and slabs round Loch Etive make roads impossible from any direction other than the way we had come. But it is gloomy and dank, and again the only space for tents is overused, with too many grubby firepits and who knows how many deposits of human excrement in surrounding brush and heather.

Janine and I both decided that there is something spooky and unwholesome about this place, that, even though we were glad to have visited, neither of us would seek a roost for the night here if cycling past the road end, that the grassy banks of the river behind the Kingshouse Hotel are much more handy. On the way to the airport the sun came out and we made a deal; next time she felt like climbing Munros, she would stay for longer and I would arrange better weather.

# Ben More Dochart

**11th October 2016**

South of the summit of **Ben More** there is no point higher anywhere on the British Isles. Getting there is an unrelenting slog of over one thousand metres, the longest continuous upward path in the country, more continuously steep even than the path up **Ben Nevis**, which levels out at 600 metres and employs many zigzags. The path up **Ben More** goes straight up from the start without any levelling off at all and only very minor zigzagging nearer the summit ridge.

The last time I climbed this mountain was in the late winter, sometime at the end of the 1980s, with a group of university colleagues. Then, the ground was still frozen and there were considerable snowbanks near the summit necessitating crampons. It was a glorious cloudless day with a warming sun and a promise of spring. Today, clouds were down to about 3000 feet with intermittent spatters of rain, the summits of surrounding hills were only sometimes barely visible. The ground was mushy, thick with grasses grown strong during a long summer. Then, I was on a traverse of both **Ben More** and ***Stob Binnein*** starting at the kink in the A85 at the bridge over *Allt Coire Chaorach*. Today, I took the tiger route up **Ben More** alone, starting from Ben More Farm, straight up and straight back down again.

I was having another *cancer day*. I had to get out of the house and away from the mundane chores of ordinary life because my mind was festering badly, turning over all the stuff that cancer brings. My motivation was low, hot flushes disturbed everything every two hours, my sleep was a mess, the black dog snapped continually at my heels. It was also the four-year anniversary of being told that I would probably live only three. Every day alive in this strange limbo felt like cheating death, that it could come upon me at any moment, that the medication would stop doing its work and allow the cancer to spread unfettered into all the organs of my body. Being confronted so urgently with both my own death and the manner by which it is likely to unfold, and having lived an unsatisfactory life that disappointed all the expectations with which it began, filled me with a kind of regret it is difficult to articulate, a combination of grief and rage that turns into resignation, a deep sense of loss, always in danger of inducing a particularly nauseating form of self-pity.

So in the middle of all this, what better way to clear my head than bag another of the high peaks. And in the process, show myself that life is still worth living, that it is still possible to get this body to do stuff in spite of its medically induced lethargy, to get it to the top of a mountain where the air is clear, the ground challenging, and where the views of the world put things into perspective. On the way up I almost gave up when the rain came down fierce and prickly, but I stopped to take stock and adjust my clothing in a hollow under an overhanging rock used by sheep, and then continued, concentrating not on the summit and the reasons I was climbing the mountain, but on every individual step.

The present can be overwhelmingly filled with mental anguish and disturbance or with the forms and textures of rock, mud and grass, with the best places for feet, with the bodily adjustments every step requires to move on successfully to the next. And so, slightly over two hours after I left the car, I reached the short summit ridge. I was filled with joy, grateful that I am alive at all, privileged to be able to experience this place, in awe that there is such a life as this among the enormity of creation.

On the way down I stopped once or twice to snack and gaze out over the world, now familiar mountains coloured shades of pink and purple by layers of cloud pierced by the light of the lowering autumn sun, laughing with pleasure at the beauty all around, no longer troubled by thoughts of cancer and death.

## Ben Avon

### 24th and 25th October 2016

I wonder sometimes how my life would have turned out if I had camped under an old red pine deep inside Glen Quoich on the way back from the heights of **Ben Avon**, rather than yomped back to the car at the Linn of Dee, to arrive well after it was too dark to see where I was going. I figured I had to get back, unpack and give myself a day to recuperate before going back to work. I look upon it still as being the more responsible choice, deciding not to pitch my tent under that tree in the perfect spot in the forest above the confluence of two mighty branches of the river Quoich, each quite evidently capable of hurling substantial rocks about and rising to levels very much higher than the moment. I sat here for a very long time, almost deciding to pitch my tent, drawn somehow to the future that awaited me by walking back to the car, and yet held back by the sheer majesty of the place. And so it was that hours later I walked back in total darkness along the narrow road from Linn of Quoich and overshot the entrance to the carpark at Linn of Dee, which although irritating was nowhere near as stressful as locking myself out of the car in the middle of the night. Responsibly, I made it home in plenty time to get a good night's sleep, recuperate and sort out my stuff for work the following day.

The weather in Scotland's mountains during November and early December is quite often utterly atrocious, so I was pleased to find a window of opportunity before the deluge to complete the easternmost Cairngorms, which I was thinking would likely be my last outing of the year, although I was not ruling anything out. It would depend. I was also on the point officially of moving into the house in Fife, where I would have enough to keep me busy when the weather got bad and I could not get to any summits.

I parked in the early afternoon and took the familiar path out of the carpark at the Linn of Dee through the woods to Glen Lui. Less than a kilometre along the track from the bridge over the river, at a ruined township, I followed a faint path right beside a burn leading up to a sharp cleft in the hill and through to Glen Quoich. *Chlais Fhearnaich*, as it is called on the map is an odd feature, similar to one to the north I passed by on my way off **Beinn Bhreac**. Two steep slopes of scree, scattered with stunted trees, converge to create a straight valley, cutting fifty metres or more into the height of the ground above. Apart from a very handy path, it contains a slender lochan of peaty water that drains into Glen Quoich. I am sure it was formed by the same natural forces that have created every feature of these mountains, but it seems almost deliberately to have been constructed as a passage between the two glens, as if a mighty axe had cleaved the ground.

At the exit to the cleft I saw the wonderful vastness of Glen Quioch. Ancient pines spreading over grassy pastures and heather clad moorland, garnished by alders, birches and rowans, clean white boulders lining the riverside sometimes spreading out beyond the banks where there have been floods and cascades. Autumn colours bursting through under a blue sky, still warm in the sunshine. I walked down to the track and turned up the glen towards a meadow nestled between two branches of the River Quoich, then forded the river and followed the track to the start of a path into the trees towards the gully of *Allt na Beinne*. Here was the start of a long walk up onto the high plateau of **Beinn a' Bhuird**, a mountain I had visited once before during one of my journeys towards Speyside; from Glen Clova over the White Mouth through Royal Deeside to the Slugain Gap, over the summit and down its northern shoulder on my way to follow the River Avon upstream into the heart of the high Cairngorms. The views from the top are incredible in all directions and I was looking forward to seeing them again.

There was once a plan to exploit this mountainside as a ski centre, during the consideration of which an ugly zigzag track was scraped into the edge of the southwest shoulder. This has now been expertly relandscaped, covered over with peat turf and heather plants, leaving only the old walkers' path, which rises slowly above the burn, flanking this southwestern shoulder of the mountain all the way to the summit. At the point where the gully turns from a steep-sided gash between two shoulders of the mountain into a flatter corrie, I left the path in search of a level patch of ground. Where the burn meanders among lumps of grassy peat and is joined by bubbling feeder burns, I found a flat space to pitch my tent, just over three thousand feet, facing south to the hills of Atholl, with the twin peaks of *Beinn a' Ghlo* prominent under a darkening sky.

The long night began at about six-thirty. I was warm inside and kept myself occupied until I found sleep. During the night nature called once or twice and I emerged into the cold to answer, but there were no stars, just the gurgling of the burn. There was hardly any wind. Light returned at about seven-thirty to encourage me into a new day. It was cold, the edge of the burn was iced up, hoar frost garnished the grass. The sky above me was now open, but to the south a front was gathering and heading in my direction. It took a while to get myself fed and moving, during which time I watched the start of a thin front of cloud wafting over the mountain tops leaving remnants hanging in its wake. The air became dense with suspended water; not yet drizzle, it condensed as it came into contact with anything solid and immediately formed glistening trees of frost. As I packed up the last of my stuff and plodded up the burn, parallel to the path, I saw another walker heading up the hill, lightly packed and fleet of foot.

To the summit from where I was camped was about two miles rising a bit less than a thousand feet, a most agreeable gradient along the course of the burn, past its source, seeping from beneath boulder fields and onwards to a plateau of red gravel pocked with round stones and tussocks. In better weather

I would have made a detour to the south top of the mountain and then followed the edge of the eastern precipitous cliffs to gaze down into the eastern corries, which contain a number of secluded lochans, but cloud gradually engulfed the plateau so I went straight to the north top and highest point. On the way the cloud to the west parted sometimes to reveal the familiar horizon of **Derry Cairngorm**, *Beinn Macduibh* and the barns of *Beinn Mheadhoin*, with layers of cloud dangling among them. The cloud was definitely thinning and the sun behind strong, suggesting it would only be a matter of time before it burned off. But I saw nothing from the top, only thick hoar frost and a dusting of snow. The other walker caught up with me not far from the summit and we walked together thereafter through the gloom. This is not a prominent summit, only the highest point on a flat expanse of scree, gravel and grassy peat where water gathers before plunging over cliffs. Lest we stray too far north towards one of these, we took a careful bearing off the summit, about fifteen degrees north of east towards the subsidiary top *Cnap a Chlèirich*, before then dropping due east through screes scarred by mountain bike tracks to a bealach known as The Sneck, at which point the sun came out and all cloud evaporated.

I dumped my pack behind a boulder and yomped up the side of **Ben Avon** with my companion. Much like *Beinn Mheadhoin*, the summit of **Ben Avon** (pronounced *Ben A'an*) is a long plateau marked by granite tors; more expansive and at the very edge of the high country, rather than bang in the middle. Much like on my visit to *Beinn Mheadhoin*, the wind on top was fierce, though the air was much less thick and it was colder. There was a dusting of hoar frost at the edges of rocks and paths, which was rapidly melting away in the bright sunlight. Only at the highest point round the summit tor was the frost thick, so thick and frozen almost to deny a safe passage over the rock to the highest point, a flat slab facing slightly southwest with perfect views over the enormity of *Beinn a' Bhuird*, which, like *Beinn Macduibh*, is only the highest point of a flat plateau. All along its eastern extremity, a series of vertical cliffs into dark corries, punctuated only by The Sneck, the bealach to **Ben Avon**, and obscuring views of the rest of the high Cairngorms still holding onto their own weather. To the north and east the long brown expanse of the plateau, blending imperceptibly into the low hills of whisky country and the green farmland of coastal plains.

After pottering around for long enough at the summit, I headed back to The Sneck with my companion who then trotted on ahead with his light daypack as I dawdled with my overnight rucksack. We were both heading back to the Linn of Dee carpark, but I was not sure if I was going to stay out another night and he was a lot younger and fitter than me. The Sneck is a remarkable place, similar in many ways to the bealach between *Beinn Bhrotain* and *Monadh Mor*, a gentle rise on the south side from the sprawling Caledonian forests of Quoich, with sheer cliffs on the north into a dark northeast facing corrie draining into the River Avon, higher than many Munros, with views upwards to surrounding peaks. The difference that this is more expansive, even more vast and backed by forest, making the bealach at *Monadh Mor* feel cosy and intimate by comparison. It is the low point of a deep horseshoe of sheer cliffs, in places more than two hundred meters high, stretching for about three miles from near the summit of **Ben Avon** to *Stob an t-Sluichd*, the end point of a spur from the north shoulder of *Beinn a' Bhuird*. There is no way down from here to the north, which is why I had to travel via the summit of *Beinn a' Bhuird* and then follow the northern shoulder that I walked past all those years ago.

The ground along the top of The Sneck is flat, pleasantly scattered with rocks and outcrops ranging in size from an armchair to a small building. There is a real feeling of being a long way from anywhere. It would take me maybe four hours to get back to the car from here if I put my mind to it, but realistically, without pushing it, five. There is another way out into Royal Deeside, the way I came before, via the Slugain gap, which would take about the same time. To the north, the only route is first to climb back over the summit of *Beinn a' Bhuird* for about four miles to get to Glen Avon, after which it is not far to the road end at Tomintoul. To the east, the summits of Ben Avon peter out along several shoulders and into the wild empty moorland of the Lecht and the gentle glens of West Aberdeenshire. I wanted to stay here forever, or at least pitch my tent and stay out one more night.

After picking a way from The Sneck through the boulder strewn slabs and grasses of the upper corrie of *Glas Allt Mòr*, I stopped for a breather and to adjust my clothing on a bench of a boulder in preparation for the rest of the descent. There was a better path now all the way down from here. The sun would be below the horizon in about three hours, it would be getting dark in four and there would be no more light at all in five. I had a long walk ahead of me and I did not want to rush. This is a most beautiful part of the country, majestic and almost Canadian in scale, heading into one of the last vestiges of ancient Caledonian forest on the east of the mountains. A big enough space perhaps for reflecting on a difficult year. The weather was mild, the colours gentle, the mountains smiled, maybe I would find somewhere to pitch my tent for one last night out. Maybe not.

My Munro bagging adventures in the eastern Cairngorms were now almost complete, which contributed perhaps to my reluctance to hurry on home. I had only two Munros on this side of the *Lairig Ghru* left to climb now; **Carn a' Mhaim**, which I could combine from the Linn of Dee with **Bod an Daemhain** at the southeast edge of the western plateau, after which **Cairngorm** itself, which I could pick off easily enough from the Ski Centre. No need to go to the lengths I once took to get to the top of a mountain; my notion of an expedition had changed a great deal since my youth.

Once, my motivation was both refreshingly childlike and realistically adventurous; the journey I have already described here, starting from Glen Clova and passing by every Munro on the White Mounth before coming down into Deeside, then plodding over the Slugain Gap and up to the Sneck, over *Beinn a' Bhuird*, and finally north to a bridge over the River A'an, to turn back upstream to find Fiandouran Bothy, all of this was *in preparation for* climbing **Cairngorm** from the bealach above the start of Strath Nethy, known as The Saddle, during a predicted period of particularly fine weather. Having completed my goal, and passed the time of day with a small congregation of dotterel on the plateau, I walked out via **Beinn Macduibh**, down the path to Loch Etchachan, past Hutcheson's hut to Glen Derry, then right at Luibeg towards the southern expanses of the *Lairig Ghru* to the White Bridge, to follow the Geldie Burn to the bridge over the River Eidart and finally down Glen Feshie. After which I came through the forest to Drumguish found the road to Kingussie and stopped for lunch and a pint (or two) at the Star Hotel before taking a train home. It took me about a week.

I wanted now to hold onto all of this, contain every one of these expeditions through these mountains in the vast bowl of rivers coming together into forest before me, to keep it all alive forever and never know anything else.

A lot had changed in a year since I camped high on **Meall nan Tarmachan** contemplating temperature inversions and the enormous complexity of things. I had a lot to deal with now; a lot had changed too in the six months since mother had died. I was now the last generation, one of those without living parents.

Somewhere along the line, I was making a deal with Karma, that in exchange for being alive, my life would be just as ordinary and extraordinary as anybody's, that I would suffer the same joys and disappointments, the same misfortunes and luck, the same tragedies, comedies, accidents and hilarities, that my life would proceed through the same stages and periods of growth, development, decline, decay, degeneration, epiphany, and celebration as all others.

I was coming to understand very deeply how privileged I was. Not only in a material sense, which had taken me somewhat by surprise, for I had no idea until this moment in my life what it meant to own property, nor to have more than a couple of thousand in the bank.

I was perceiving things differently. These mountains, the view of their vastness from the top of Ben Avon, all these plateaux of bog and gravel, studded with tors, these remote corries and precipitous cliffs, all now different. Closer to home. Inside. Incorporated into this mountain being I carried within. It was not really surprising that I wanted to stay here rather than return to the city to deliver stuff.

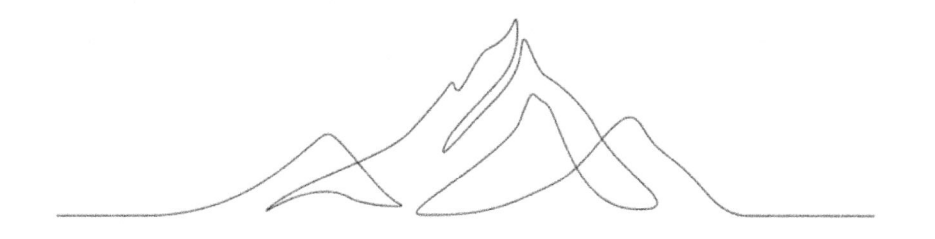

# 2017 ignorance

## Meall Ghaordie

### 22nd January 2017

It was cold and still. Layers of cloud hanging in the glens, clinging to the summits. The ground was stiff and frozen, lightly dusted with snow. Slumbering winter grasses, dead bracken, leafless trees heavy with frost.

I left the car by the roadside in Glen Lochay just before eleven and followed the path all the way up the mountain, where I sat cross legged, eating lunch of carrot and broccoli, dipped in humous, protected from the cold by windstopper, down and fleece, and from a slight wind by a ringed cairn encasing the summit trig point.

If the ground had not been so frozen, large sections of the path would have been a great big squelchy mess and the ascent would have taken longer. It is not difficult to see why some Munro guides are rather less than enthusiastic about this mountain, for the path follows an easy gradient with very few obstacles, and it took me to the summit in only two hours.

I imagine that the views of afar from atop this mountain are quite spectacular, but I did not see any. What I experienced instead was the ground beneath my feet, the stillness of the mountain and the life that clings to it, even up so high, even in the depths of winter. Despite the season, there was hardly any snow, much less than would be expected, but where remnants lay, under crags or in little gullies, it was as hard as rock.

I sat at the summit for half an hour with only the sound of rustling clothing and the occasional contented croak from a ptarmigan. There is no better way of bringing a troubled mind to rest than the experience of real silence. For when confronted by an absolute lack of noise, in a well-protected body, it is impossible to conclude anything other than that all the noise in a head is only in the head. That there is nothing out there, signifying who or what is inside, no evidence anywhere of internal existence, let alone internal turmoil, just the beat of a heart and the rhythm of breathing.

And so I encountered an enormous sense of peace and well-being. As I returned back along the path the ptarmigan fluttered along behind me, cackling and croaking with some song of celebration, or trying to tell me something. He stood for a moment on a rock at the edge of the still monochrome landscape, illuminated only by mist diffused sunlight, continuing his crackly song. I turned to look at him.

When he finished his singing, he stood looking around, puffing up his feathers, being alive in his home. I do not know how long we stood there together, sharing this mountain top. I kept expecting him to fly off, that my slight movements would startle him, but he was not bothered by my presence, not showing any sign that I existed in his world at all. Presently, he turned to look at me and cocked his head slightly, at which point I smiled and turned down the path.

As I emerged from under the mist, the colours of the glens, this morning diluted by the frost, were vibrant in comparison to the black and white landscape of the cloud shrouded summit. The beauty of the planet never ceases to delight and does not depend on open skies of blue.

I remembered an old Zen epithet about what you find at the top of the mountain being only what you bring with you, and was given cause again to reflect upon the sense of peace I had found there, and shared with a resident ptarmigan.

I was coming to understand how special it is to be alive at all, what a privilege it is to be human, and how we waste this life if we do not experience the beauty of every moment, no matter how grey the skies or insistent the noise from within.

Maybe my mind was less troubled than I thought.

## Sgiath Chuil

### 27th January 2017

During the second half of 2015 when I was enduring *Decapeptyl* injections, my PSA never rose above one, even at the end of the six-month cycle. During the equivalent period in 2016, my PSA never dropped below three and it was back up at four before the end of the three-month cycle. From this I concluded that the disease was becoming active again, that it was beginning to adapt to the medication's suppression of testosterone. Under these circumstances I was beginning to make a significant decision that would set the course of my life for the next two years and beyond.

The road along Glen Dochart from Killin to Crianlaraich is one of the fastest in the country. Traveling from my home in Fife towards any mountain in the northwest, this road is unavoidable. Until very recently there have been no permanent speed cameras and never have I seen anybody pulled over. With one or two critical exceptions, where geography requires the road to take sharp corners, it is straight and broad with excellent sightlines. It is reasonably paved and even has a bit of a shoulder to make room for cyclists. There are several places over a stretch of about eight miles where cars can be parked for access to mountains or picnic sites on either side, amongst which the path to ***Sgiath Chuil***.

I wanted to maintain complete ignorance of what medical science knew of my disease, to give no priority to external or objective knowledge over the experience of my body, my original private mindfulness. At the same time I was happy to continue to have my blood monitored and to be scanned, and if there were ever any sign of extreme metastasis or other indication of rapid decline, I was prepared to be informed of this so I could reconsider my decision. It was my intention to offer whatever was happening in my body as data or evidence; here was an opportunity to observe the progression (or otherwise) of the disease in its natural state, so to speak. My motivation was quite simple; I was getting fed up with drugs and their collateral damage; treatments that worked for a while and then stopped, of being always in a limbo of expectation where whatever I was likely to be given would one day stop working, leaving me to my own devices, either to succumb gracefully or to come up with something else. I wanted no longer to be dependent on medical opinion, no longer to have my health contained by the deterministic logic of disease progression, nor to have my life defined by a career as cancer patient. I wanted simply to live a healthy life of mountain climbing and delivering stuff in the city, while acknowledging the existence of the disease but without having *cancer* hanging round my neck like the proverbial albatross.

**Sgiath Chuil** lies on the south side of Glen Dochart and is usually climbed in combination with **Meall Glas**, the little mountain I climbed by accident from Glen Lochay to the north at the start of 2016. The approach to the two begins at the other side of the River Dochart from the road at a farm called *Auchessan*. I looked at the map and thought I remembered it, then hit the road. A bit less than two hours later, I parked near a bridge to a farm under some trees in a layby raised slightly above the level of the road. I booted up and wandered down the track. Almost immediately I failed to reconcile what I was seeing on the ground with what I could remember from the map. Very soon I saw I was parked in the wrong place, in a layby on the other side of the river from the farm at *Inishewan*. So I returned to the car and drove to the right layby.

There was an important precedent. From the first diagnosis in the autumn of 2012 until the end of spring 2013, I maintained an obsessively strict diet, which I believed would sustain my body's natural resources and give the cancer nothing to feed upon. I cut out all foods that leave what is called an *acidic residue*; all processed food, caffeine, alcohol, sugar, all meat and dairy. I ate only fresh fruit and vegetables, nuts, seeds and wholemeal bread, almost entirely organic, inadvertently vegan. I continued two or three days every week to deliver stuff on my bike and to look after my little workshop. I also began to prepare for dying, firstly by shutting myself away from all others except clients and colleagues, then by writing my little book of unclassifiable aphorisms, and finally by gathering my stuff and preparing to return to Scotland. This was not an easy time, but I had good friends on my side who accepted my stubborn idiosyncrasies. At the start of this period my PSA had jumped to 139 from 96 in only a few weeks, in the aftermath of a prostate biopsy, from which a Gleason Score of nine was recorded, indicating malignant, aggressive and incurable disease. At the end of the period the PSA had risen only insignificantly to 142. Which meant that for five months, throughout a Dutch winter, still working as a bicycle messenger, mechanic and wheel builder in the fine city of Utrecht, with a healthy diet, lots of exercise, good friends and a positive attitude, I was able to hold at bay an aggressive and malignant cancer. I decided therefore it was time to apply similar principles at home in Scotland. Clean out my diet, clear out the nonsense in my head and keep my body moving.

My walk up **Meall Ghaordie** the previous week had given me a taste of winter; I was now on a mission to bag straightforward nearby peaks and pile up the tally; **Sgiath Chuil** was an obvious candidate. I was also remembering my father who would have turned 86 on this day. The last new snow had fallen before the turn of the year, after which there had been a sustained thaw with little rain, leaving only scattered patches in the usual crevices. It was eleven-thirty before I was on my way from the correct carpark in the direction of the correct farm on the north side of the River Dochart.

I was not only fed up with the bleak trajectory onto which I had been placed by medical expectation, I was also resentful that establishment medicine was interested only in dishing out drugs to suppress the symptoms of disease, without the least interest in causes, nor finding an actual cure. The treatments I was offered had always been essentially palliative, suppressing and postponing an inevitable decline. The only hope, as each new treatment would work for a while and then stop, was the future development of new drugs. Even although hormone-based cancers are incurable, they can be managed successfully using a variety of treatments, which offer a good quality of life. Prostate cancer is well known as one most men die *with* rather than *of.* I knew all this. It was rapidly sounding like an ideological trope and not in the least bit reassuring. It was this from which I wanted to be free. To find something more honest, grounded in the experience of being human in a complex world, less mechanical and happy clappy.

It was a beautiful morning of open blue skies and wispy clouds. There had been a severe frost, although where the sun shone on the ground this had already melted into dew. I passed by the farm heading east into open pasture following a track. At a gate and a bridge over the burn coming off the mountain, there was a field of lazy highland cattle steaming gently and munching on silage. From here I followed a rough path, up the left side of the burn into a wooded gorge towards the brown hillside. The ground was hard and quite steep, but not as boggy as it would surely become at the end of a day in this sunshine.

To complicate matters, my mother had brought me up with the principles of Nature Cure, according to which good health is achieved by eating properly, by deep breathing and good exercise, not by taking drugs when something did not feel right. I was inoculated against the usual diseases just like the rest of the population; during my childhood doctors were sometimes summoned, but more often, when I became ill, I was simply put to bed and expected to get better. My mother always explained that this was nature's way, that I should learn to trust my body's healing intelligence. She also explained that it followed from the principles of this *Nature Cure* that conventional medicine had got a great deal wrong about the classification, causes and treatment of disease. These notions became my normality, *reinforced* by my experience of being ill and getting better again without the need for doctors and medicines. I developed thus a *practical,* rather than *abstract*, knowledge of my own body and its capabilities from a very early age, and I learned indeed to trust its natural intelligence. Given her own experience as a child, it is not surprising she brought me up this way, and I am very grateful that she did, but it has not always made my life easy; I have often found myself in conflict with established opinions about health and disease because I do not share established norms, values and assumptions. To complicate matters further, despite his intelligence and critical faculties, my father was happy, like most of the rest of the population, to accept without question that medical science gets things right, that taking pills to relieve symptoms is not in the least problematic. Apart from having been brought up by a mother who held doctors in high esteem, *socially*, my father felt that my mother's ideas were too inclined to make a person feel guilty for not adopting healthy habits. My mother on the other hand understood the principles of Nature Cure as a way of taking responsibility for her own health, that we are all endowed with natural healing powers that will care for us if we feed them properly. This fundamental principle, perhaps it is an *elemental*, has been with me for as long as I have been conscious; my health is my own responsibility and I should trust my body to teach me how to look after myself.

It is a very gradual climb up this little mountain from the end of the gorge, but the path is not good. The bogginess was however frozen into a reasonably solid walking surface. Mountains all around were deep brown and pale ochre; out of the slight wind the sun was warming. During the course of my ascent, cloud gathered from the south in layers, filtering the sun's rays into spectacular shafts through gathering haze. These were fine conditions for contemplation, as changeable as the turns taken by a mind wandering through difficult ideas and their origins in early learning.

*Illness* I learned was a misnomer. According to conventional medicine, that which is called illness or disease is based on classifying clusters of symptoms. Nature Cure taught me that these were exactly that, symptoms of some underlying issue in a body, a *dis ease* within a person; not a thing that had invaded a body to disturb its normal functioning but rather the expression of this particular body's reactions to its current conditions; its inherent ability to maintain healthy functioning. The crucial implication of this was that every illness was unique to each individual, each was living in a unique environment, each had a unique biography and each would thus respond uniquely. Of course, because I lived in a world where something else was taken for granted, I asked my mother about the clustering of symptoms and in particular about the effects of *bacteria* and *viruses* on bodies, about how the ideas of cause and effect engendered by these ideas of disease, bacteria and viruses, all seemed to go together. These were after all the predominant ideas of the time, its common sense, and I could not but pick them up. She explained that, according to the principles of Nature Cure, bacteria and viruses do indeed exist, but are just everyday constituents of the environments through which we all move, that they are often already in our systems doing good work or being flushed out by our bodies' natural healing processes. When we become ill it is simply a sign our healing powers are not up to the task of flushing out all toxins, under which circumstances a body becomes more susceptible to the products of viral or bacterial reproduction and is sometimes overwhelmed, the observable symptoms of which are considered to be the *illness* and then treated with medicine. Medicines therefore actually suppress natural healing processes, not even touching underlying *dis ease*, the reasons why a person has become unwell. Debilitating symptoms are a sign that it would be better simply to take to bed where the natural healing intelligence can do its thing. When a body feels unwell, this is because it needs to rest, to find shelter and keep warm in order to preserve resources and concentrate on healing.

At the summit there was still a thick hoar frost clinging to grass and dusting rocks. The snow concealed still in northeast facing crevices was rock hard. Wisps of condensing vapour wafted over the flat gnarly landscape behind the summit. It was two in the afternoon. The sun was already lowering behind thickening layers of cloud over **Ben More** and *Stob Binnein*. I walked north along the flat plateau to another top. The air was still and the severity of the cold held at bay. I was hoping for snow now with this gathering cloud, but it did not yet look heavy enough.

My mother was describing, using a vocabulary left over from an earlier time, before the emergence of what has become the medical establishment, what is now called *the immune system*. The history of medicine tells of a schism that took place at some point during the nineteenth century after which modern scientific medicine became possible, and which persists today as a tension between the motivations of physiologists and clinicians, between learning about the natural history of disease and controlling it by whatever means necessary, eradicating it or managing it. *Nature Cure* originated before this schism, when clinical judgements were always based on a natural scientific understanding of how particular individuals become unwell and were affected by sickness; treatments were focused on stimulating a particular body's inherent resources. Modern mechanistic, reductionist medicine is a consequence of prioritising control, of getting bodies up and about as quickly as possible, at the expense of natural observation and allowing time to heal.

I pottered around the summit for a while taking photos of the changing day. The bright sunshine of the morning was gone, leaving gloomy light behind grey clouds made pink as the sun descended. I walked slowly down the mountain, aiming for an alternative to the route I had taken in the morning, which I figured would now be a slithery mess, and steep to boot. As I dropped altitude, the layering cloud drifted north, presenting again clear blue skies mixing with the mists of the evening.

I was trying to decouple myself from establishment knowledge of my disease in order to experience its movements from the inside; learning to live with it, to know what it wants and how to keep it in its place, even to fall in love with it. I was going to eat well, exercise properly and come to terms with why my body had reacted this way, what made possible this *dis ease* in me. There was something I did not like about the attitude of these modern doctors, something artificial, almost as if their first priority was not to their patients but to something abstract. Once upon a time a doctor would tell terminally ill people to set their affairs in order. What I got was a piece of emotional blackmail. And for all the great care and compassion of the oncology team in Scotland, the preparedness to accept my own vitality as an important element of the way the disease is managed, the medical trajectory remained trapped by the same dichotomy; take the drugs later and die now, or take them now and die later. I was open to anything, desperate even, to escape this mechanical view of my life and to subvert the determinism it engendered. I wanted also to expand my knowledge beyond the sterile dichotomy into which I had been born, between the principles of my mother's Nature Cure and my father's pragmatic acceptance of establishment medicine, to deconstruct it, tease out the emotional residue from the damage, expose and articulate the ideas and relations holding it together. I was prepared now to delve as deeply as necessary.

I dallied and took many photos of **Ben More** and *Stob Binnein*, gloriously dominating the landscape, with their triangular summits casting fascinating shadows in the gloaming, enjoying the peace of the place and preparing again for ordinary life below. Approaching the edge of the woods at the end of the gully, I swung right to follow a fence surrounding a plantation down until it met a track coming up from the farm. It was a boggy mess all the way and I slithered all over the place, stabilised by walking poles and content with my achievement, for the moment distracted from the dichotomies in my head by concentrating on not falling on my arse. I reached the car before sundown and drove home. On the radio I heard snow forecast for the weekend.

Throughout my thinking about these things, I always felt the proximity of my father, not as some ghostly external presence, nor even memory, but as an *integral part of who I am*, listening carefully and taking note, writing things down in preparation for conveying the essence of matters to his pupils, but never intervening, just as he never intervened when my mother took me along to Kingston (a centre that followed the Nature Cure method) to treat attacks of asthma. My mother told me that the two had often had vigorous disagreements about things medical, which is hardly surprising, and that in his final months when she had been caring for him, he had been quite nasty, scathing and cutting, but during my upbringing he seemed always to me to be respectful of my mother's ideas. He could see for himself that her visits to Kingston were good for her; he said simply that the Kingston method was not for everybody, by which he meant himself and most of the rest of the population. Presumably also he was able to discern that I had taken on board many of Nature Cure's principles, while coming to my own conclusions on life's many mysteries, and of which a great many had been formed under his own influence. He was aware that I was not simply swallowing an ideology, but using *general principles* taken from many places to work things out for myself. Always he left me to find my own way; I think he remained slightly in awe of what became of the little being he had made with his beautiful young wife all those years ago. Whatever else, he is always here as I write.

## Glen Shee

### 29th January 2017

As predicted, there was an enormous dump of snow on a front blowing over from the northeast. It began falling towards the end of the day after my visit to ***Sgiath Chuil*** and continued into the next morning. These would be perfect conditions for bagging the cluster of three to the west of the ski centre in Glen Shee, two of which are only whiskers above three thousand feet and bristling with ski infrastructure, qualifying them as among both the ugliest and most boring of Munros. The starting point at the ski centre lies at over two thousand feet, making this moreover one of the easiest triples in the country; with this weather they would become a lot prettier and more interesting. On the way to the ski centre it became clear that I was not going to be disappointed. Above fifteen hundred feet there was thick new snow. Even in Fife there was a covering, which became thicker as I drove north out of Dundee, always melted off the asphalt with salted grit, thicker again coming out of Blairgowrie and then packed hard on the relentless climb past what was once called the Devil's Elbow. I was surprised to see hardly any skiers about; the chairlifts and ski tows were idle. Perhaps this sudden dump had taken everybody by surprise. There was even room to park directly outside the ski centre café.

It took me about half an hour from here in a straight line upwards through deep firm snow to the summit of **The Cairnwell**. It is not pretty here, even when every bit of concrete and rusting steel is as garnished with windblown ice sculptures as surrounding rocks and crags. I did not hang around and followed the northern shoulder off the mountain in search of a good line towards the summit of ***Carn a' Gheoidh***, the nearest high point on the plateau of glistening snow to the southwest. No paths were obvious and all fine detail of the surface of the ground, minor gullies, crevices, crags and outcrops had been filled in or smoothed over, with nothing protruding through the surface.

In the distance a lochan, now frozen over, sparkled under intense light. On days such this protective eyewear is vital, for the rays of the sun are low and intensified by reflecting snow crystals and come at you from below as much as from above. On the northern horizon the familiar profile of the Cairngorm plateaux, dense white with the exception of the glistening rocky protuberance of ***Bod an Daemhain*** at the entrance to the *Lairig Ghru*. Near the top of ***Carn a' Gheoidh*** I almost put on my crampons, but found a way through soft snow and hard rocks to the top. For a while I shared the summit with a number of others quietly gazing at views of snow smothered mountains in all directions. Even in the glens of Perthshire to the south there was a covering, blackened by roads, habitations and the shadows of woodlands. The air was crisp and cold, the sun shone bright.

I saw my final goal for the day, ***Carn Aosda***, standing out from the white, just like its neighbour **The Cairnwell**, ski infrastructure bristling up its flanks to the summit. I retracted my steps to the shoulder between the two mountains where at length I turned along a bare path sheltered behind a fence, put there to ensure snow drifts deep against it, giving skiers more to play with. At the start of a track to the third summit, I decided I should have a breather. Reaching into my pockets, I could not find my phone. I danced about for maybe five minutes beside a rock near the fence rummaging through my pockets, looking for my phone, until I had to conclude that it must have fallen out somewhere as I stumbled into a snow filled hole on the way back from ***Carn a' Gheoidh***. My coat pocket must have been unzipped. What a stupid thing to have done. It was however gone. Never to be found. I plodded on, resigning myself to the loss, annoyed that losing a phone nowadays takes away so much more, stuff upon which I had become, like everybody else, dependent. Most immediately, I could not phone my old friend who lives now in the next glen to arrange delivery of a copy of my little book. No contact with Shona until I got home. All my photos. Gone. Happily I download regularly onto a hard drive so it was only photos from today that were lost, and all my important data was backed up in secure digital clouds. So the loss was actually only mildly inconvenient. And the cost of a new phone.

The path up ***Carn Aosda*** was ugly and often stony, not made prettier by my mood. The summit is not a place to which I am desperate to return. On the way back down I found myself encumbered by more fences being used to hold back snow, but then I discovered a way down via a gully and, as I descended, began gradually to notice the liberation of being without connection to the digital aether. Optimistically, I asked at the café if a phone had been handed in, then drove home via a visit to my old friend, who was very easy to find by old fashioned methods, following road signs and asking people.

Despite a certain relief that I was no longer connected to the digital aether, free of the need to respond to notifications, responsible only to myself, I had to get a new way of communicating with the world. Apart from any of the rest, I needed a phone for work, so I visited my mobile service provider, where I had a chat with a young man who had a good offer on a new phone, attached to a new two-year contract, with a great deal more data than I was getting, for only slightly more than I was already paying. And so forth. So I agreed, signed the papers and answered his questions, one of which was if I knew of any reason why I would not, within the next two years, be able to pay the agreed amount every month. It gave me pause. For I did know of a very good reason why I might not be able to continue paying every month. I was already well over a year beyond the time I was given to live. I asked the salesman rather whimsically about death. To which he replied straightforwardly without my needing to go into any detail, that under such circumstances special rules apply. Thoroughly professional.

So I had a new phone, but I still had a cancer that was likely becoming resistant to the medication. I had latched onto the fact that there were *significant differences between two measures of PSA taken at exactly the same moment at the end of two otherwise identical six-month cycles, an obvious difference of degree and also a difference in kind*, from less than one on a steady baseline to nearly four on an exponentially rising curve. As usual, I was convinced of my own reasoning. It was perhaps true that I would not know for certain if the cancer had become resistant unless I took the medication again, but given that it seemed no longer to be keeping the level of PSA down, it followed that the cancer or some of it was now at least indifferent to the medication and therefore that there was no longer any point in taking it.

Always there was a lingering sense that now I must be entering the final phase of the expected trajectory. Despite being told by oncologists in Scotland that newer treatments would become available, my mind was stuck still inside the logic of the first prognosis. Despite much knowledge and experience contradicting the message, most palpably being still alive, the brutality of the dichotomy of the choice with which I was first presented was scarred deep in my mind, debilitating, except as a challenge to find another way. Any fool with access to the internet knows that alternative cures for many diseases are available at the end of a few clicks and a credit card payment. Most prominent of the more credible and respectable of these are preparations derived from certain varieties of the hemp plant. Many people of good conscience had been suggesting I investigate these ever since I first made public my diagnosis, and I always knew they were there as a possibility, so I began now seriously to investigate.

To cut short a complex story of snake-oil, overpriced too-good-to-be-true miracle cures, and technical discussions about the many varieties available, what they do and how they work, I was put in contact with a pharmacist in a foreign country who offered different courses of treatment for different conditions. He could send me what I would need at my own risk for a not unreasonable price. He warned me, however, that what he does is technically illegal in his country; I already knew that if I were to take possession of his product I would be breaking the law.

Reflecting upon this, my most salient response was rage; that any plant-based preparation could become a banned substance seemed odd enough, but to ban one with healing properties seemed at best bizarre, and at worst plain nasty. Sufficient anecdotal evidence of its therapeutic effects must surely now have suffused into the body politic, bent attitudes a bit and at the very least stimulated further research. But no, the law continued to declare that possession of a particular plant and all preparations derived from it is illegal, because they all will have allegedly dangerous, hallucinogenic and narcotic effects. All are lumped into the category *drugs* by the herd mentality and take on all the opprobrium this entails, bringing along associations of inveterate recidivism, moral depravity, addiction, petty crime and the breakdown of the social order. The idea that such a *drug* might have any therapeutic power at all was utterly anathema, threatening; only medicines approved by government health services, medical authorities and insurance companies may legitimately be used to treat disease. The efficacy of these medicines is guaranteed by having been developed according to the strict procedures and criteria of science, which is, as we all know, the best way of understanding what is going on and organising society in general, not anecdotes from the internet.

During my conversation with the pharmacist, he told me that his stuff is quite straightforward to make domestically but there are no guarantees of its efficacy; that I would also have to work on my diet, to practice relaxation, meditation and breathing techniques, and to rid my life of stress. All good advice, much of which I already followed; though living with cancer is stressful enough, now it was exacerbated by an arbitrary border between legitimate and banned substances, and by an actual border that an actual preparation would have to cross if it were perhaps to help against the progression of my disease and maybe even cure it. It was very difficult not to rage against the banal stupidity of this particular cog in the big machine, not to believe that anybody standing in the way of my getting hold of this possible treatment for a disease that will otherwise kill me was just being a dick, mindless, indifferent, ignorant, robotically following rules because they are rules.

If I had not been a cynical curmudgeon with no illusions about the power of the pharmaceutical industry, the dominance of dependency culture within medical institutions, and the moronic reductionism of the disease model of medicine, I would have been at a loss to understand why nobody, at least not in the respectable scientific literature, has actually inaugurated a more rigorous research programme, to compare and contrast different blends taken from different strains of hemp plants, to observe how different bodies respond in the treatment of all sorts of conditions, and to record their effects. From the point of view of science, there is absolutely nothing standing in the way of such a programme of research. Absolutely nothing. So there must be reasons why it does not take place.

Any such research would be conducted by pharmaceutical companies with a view to producing medicines, because that is what the law says must happen and what society expects. That medicines cure disease is a fundamental truth of our society, doubting this puts the doubter in direct conflict with almost everything. The products of pharmaceutical processes are the end result of very costly research and development that keeps a great many people in employment. In order for these costs to be recovered, therapeutic substances and their constituent elements must be patented and licensed, *owned*, mass produced and sold in carefully controlled and regulated markets. Which means that the precise chemical compositions of the active ingredients of any naturally occurring substance that appears to offer therapeutic benefits must be isolated, correctly described and if possible synthesised. Research is always focused on finding *the one* active ingredient, the *singular chemical* with the therapeutic effect from which products may be manufactured, the magic bullet, philosopher's stone. If however it were to be conducted according to the narrow view of legitimate science favoured in our societies, here is where any research into preparations of hemp would falter. For the active ingredients cannot be isolated in this way; they are too numerous and too intricately combined to be separated. There would be no point in placing a patent on any one molecule because no one molecule does the work, there is simply no single active ingredient. Rather the stuff is a blend of over one hundred active chemicals, which unleashes a so-called *cascade effect*, whereby the different molecules work in untold combinations over the period during which a body soaks them up into every corner of its many cells and systems, unleashing the dormant power of endocannabinoid processes. Patenting every one of these and their many combinations would not be realistic; knowing how it all hangs together is quite simply ruled out, marginalised and made invisible by the dominant reductionist methodology of pharmaceutical research.

There appeared to me to be an unholy alliance between the unquestioned power of the pharmaceutical industry, unquestioned to the point of invisibility, and a kind of reductive morality, which is often associated with *science* as such, but is more strictly analysed as a pervasive *scientism*, the notion that *the only correct understanding of anything is scientific*. This appeared to me as some sort of *assemblage*; a complex knot of barely acknowledged moral assumptions, ideological tropes, conceptual distinctions, power relations and bad habits. But it was not reducible to any one of these.

Most prominently, the reductionist ideology of atomism, according to which things are made up of smaller things, so that it becomes impossible to understand and, perforce, to replicate a substance without knowing the precise composition of its constituent building blocks, right down to the molecular level. Next, the medical model of *disease as a thing that invades a body to incapacitate it*, that *can only be* expelled by judicious use of the correct substance or surgical procedure. Then, mechanistic theories of biological function that rule out any agency in a body, reduce the complexities of nature to regular processes and universal structures that can be modelled by algorithms, and that relegate consciousness and mental life to irrelevance. Finally, and more generally, predominant ideas of *the economy*, according to which wealth is created for the whole of society when the most rapacious, venal and self-serving of its members are given free rein to exploit the labour of others, and as a consequence of which individual motivation must always be dedicated to earning money, so that all human activity becomes subsumed under an abstract value that has nothing to do with that activity.

It took me the entire two years of my new mobile contract to even begin to unpack any of this. Eventually, I would also need the space created by hospitalisation and recuperation to articulate what it all meant to me, to relate it back to the conflict between my mother's ideas about nutrition and disease and my father's pragmatism, and to find my way through the complex of old emotions and resentments it embodied. It remained nevertheless festering within, *kankeren*.

In the meantime, I was on the point of asking the foreign pharmacist to send me his stuff, to risk being arrested. In my more belligerent moments I wanted actively to take it to court, to publicise the absurdity for all to see. What did I have to lose? But I did not want to get caught and would never be so courageous as some when taking their case to the press; the most prominent in recent years being the mother of a child with severe epilepsy, who demanded that a substance demonstrably able to reduce the intensity and frequency of epileptic seizures, and thus improve the immediate health and well-being of her child, be removed from the illegal substances list.

And yet, if I got away with it and anybody asked, I could just say that I was using many kinds of supplements and natural preparations in my diet, like ground turmeric, ginger, spirulina powder, bee pollen and hemp oil. None of these could be considered as anything but food.

I believed I was out of options. If I did not find some way of keeping the disease at bay, it would rapidly spread through my body. And I would die, which I did not want.

Not yet.

I was far too young.

There were far too many mountains still to climb.

## Ben Dorian

### 12th February 2017

Although I was intermittently enraged by the reductionism of medical science and its exclusions, and became exercised sufficiently often to hold forth about why I was doing what I was doing, I had about a month until my next visit to the hospital when I would have to confront any of it. In general I was concentrating simply on being alive, enjoying my time with Shona, taking trips in the campervan, finding space for a home in the house I was brought up in, and travelling in my old Volvo back and forth to the city and to the start of paths up mountains. During this time, as well as recording ascents, I used my blog more and more to document the experience of refusing to fit into the box created for me by establishment medicine. Sometimes also I wrote earnestly believing I would be contributing to some burning political debate, but in retrospect I was mostly just getting stuff off my chest. In any event, the blog became a partial phenomenology of being deliberately oblivious to what the disease was doing to me as much as a record of bagged Munros, a kind of *diary of ignorance*.

Meanwhile, I was becoming increasingly influenced by the Kagyu tradition of Buddhism, which came out of Tibet from 1959 with the first wave of exiles. In particular I was studying the life and work of the Second Akong Rinpoche and attending teachings at Samye Ling Monastery and its satellites, where I met a number of excellent teachers and wise Lamas. This was the beginning of my final departure from the Western tradition of knowledge into which I had been educated and upon which most of normal discourse, conventional wisdom and common consciousness is inevitably based. I was becoming aware of the power of Buddhist teaching to undermine all that is taken for granted by the Western mind, while at the same time offering practices that make a real difference. Hitherto I had been a student of what are sometimes called immanent critiques of reason, places where the Western tradition of thinking undermines itself, or where one of its fundamentals can be used to destabilise another, or where it looks beyond itself for something that it is not and that is yet required for it to function. Now I was encountering very different ways of thinking, based not on the many reductions, dualisms, separations and disconnections of Western contemplation and experimentation, *nor on any critique of these*, but on compassion in all conduct towards all sentient beings, a rigorous mind training and candid analysis of what a mind actually is, how it fits in with, or not, the causal forces of the world, or *karma*.

I tried to get away to tick off another mountain as often as I could, but the weather did not always oblige. Inevitably I had to work on days with glorious weather, which I knew would offer glorious days in the mountains. Apart from switching between cycle and van delivery, both of which are much more pleasant when the weather is fine, I was proofreading a couple of PhD theses, written by non-native English speakers, which though rewarding was taking up a lot of time. Sometimes I delivered as far as Stirling, bringing me so close to mountains I could smell them; from most of the hills and ridges round the city, snow-capped peaks were visible on the distant horizon. At home in Fife, the southern Grampians are always present behind the Sidlaw Hills and the other ridges beyond the Tay estuary; from my study window I could see the Lomond Hills prominently topped with snow.

The mountainous regions of Scotland were parsed in my planning into short days out. At most, it was a two- or three-hour drive to everything south of Bridge of Orchy, Aviemore and Braemar. So although I was ripping through them, I still had a lot of choice when windows of opportunity arose. Sometimes I drove away from home knowing that conditions were not ideal, but always hoping that it would not be as bad as forecast. On the day I headed towards **Ben Dorian** and *Beinn an Dothaid* (pronounced Ben an Doe), the cloud was forecast to be broken, but the wind severe, with gusts of over 40 mph, which would make walking on any summit much more challenging. And yet I was not put off, still hoping for the best.

Access to **Ben Dorian** and *Beinn an Dothaid* is via the railway station at Bridge of Orchy. From the extent of parking, it was obvious I was not the only hopeful. Under a tunnel and through a gate at the end of the southbound platform into a sheepy field, which immediately becomes the mountainside, the path forges upwards above the bank of a substantial burn in a gully, towards a corrie backed by cliffs and packed with snow. Cloud was swirling round the summits; the snowline was about fifteen hundred feet, a sharp line on the ground, like a tidemark, separating brown wet land from white frozen land. When I got to it, there was a short margin of squishy wet slush and slithery snow, after which it became deep, firm and crunchy. As I climbed, my feet began more and more to slip on ice beneath the snow or to fail to crunch securely through the upper layer. It was time for crampons.

Behind a house-sized boulder affording generous shelter, I came upon a man crouching in the lee, squeezing a small mongrel into a smart new coat. The dog scampered over to say hello and then proceeded to roll about and slither in the snow, apparently trying to rub off his new coat. The man began putting on crampons. We struck up a conversation as I did the same. Up ahead, in the back wall of the corrie, thick with snow and its prominent features obscured by gloom and flurries of spindrift, a group of about a dozen was receiving instruction in using crampons, digging snow holes and roping themselves together. There was a stretcher lying amongst their kit suggesting they were recruits to a mountain rescue team, I vaguely remembered a van with MR livery parked with the other vehicles in the car park below. My new companion and I struck on up through the snow, glad of spikes on our feet and this fellowship, not yet feeling the need to rope ourselves together, though he told me that if it became necessary he did have a rope with him. We walked together for the rest of the day, while the dog continued trying to rub off his coat by slithering in the snow.

The climb to the bealach between the two peaks was made easier by firm snow, but once we got onto the exposure of the ridge, the going became very hard work indeed. Wind saps energy like nothing else. Standing still becomes a kind of mindful leaning; great effort is always required to compensate for buffeting blasts of unpredictably fast-moving lumps of air. As far as we could, we kept to the leeward side of the ridge. We were both glad of spikes on our boots; I held my ice axe at the ready in case I were knocked over and had to dig in. It was not actually snowing much, but there was considerable spindrift whirling about violently. Strangely, when we reached the first high point, *Carn Sasunnaich*, the air fell still. We speculated about why this top should be called The Englishman's Cairn and my companion, being English by birth, ventured cynically that it would be because this is where the weak decide they have made it to the summit and then return without checking. I took a photo of him standing at the summit of this Englishman's Cairn, gritting his teeth into a smile, before we carried on into the teeth of the gale, which suddenly seemed even more intense. There had been a flatter section further down where the wind had ripped through so fiercely that we both privately thought this ascent might not be such a good idea after all, but carried on relying on the implicit support of the other, a collective momentum. Now on the short summit ridge it was worse. But we did not give up. We were far too near the actual top and the ground was level enough. We fought through the wind until we found the air at the true summit to be again strangely still. Although this was not called the Scotsman's Cairn, he took my photo standing against layers of grey light and dazzling wet slabs on distant hillsides. We decided to return through the conflagration to *Carn Sasunnaich* where we found shelter in the lee of a crag and were able to sit in peace for a bite to eat.

Conversation was easy. I liked his cavalier attitude to weather and willingness to persevere, and I was impressed by his extensive knowledge of the mountains. He had already completed a round of Munros and was now concentrating on the minor lists, endeavouring to tick off as many unclimbed summits in a year as his age at last birthday, with the occasional return trip to a favourite Munro. He was retired from a successful career, with a solid background in science, well-informed and thoughtful, with an interest in mindfulness, now doing what he loved best. A man after my heart. We had both planned to climb the neighbouring peak, **Beinn an Dothaidh**, but on the way back down the ridge to the bealach it was clear that our bodies had been sapped of all the energy they had at their disposal for the day, and we returned along the path to Bridge of Orchy as the sun fell behind banks of cloud hanging in layers between the hills. At the same boulder, we stopped to remove our crampons. The dog kept on his coat until the bottom of the hill. The snowline had risen to about two thousand feet while the margin of mush and muddy slush was broader and more slippery. Looking back up the path, we saw busy clouds right down into the bowl of the corrie and a lot of snow flying about. Coming off the mountain, not continuing on to **_Beinn an Dothaidh_** had been a wise decision.

This was an epic day out that I was glad to have shared. It took me out of myself, forced me to think about how to talk about the nonsense in my head and how to respond to poignant questions, or to remain silent, holding it all in suspension, thinking it through for coherence and sense before blurting out some brain fart. Again I was put in contact with the elements. *The company of this gentle, intelligent man* pulled me away from the pits of despair and dissipated the furies of resentment, brought peace to my mind, even under the onslaught of a hellish sidewind. Before we left the carpark, we exchanged numbers and agreed to keep in touch.

## The first Geal Charn

1st **March 2017**

I always began to get a bit twitchy if, for whatever reason, I had not been out for more than a couple of weeks. My obsession was teaching me quickly that *weather* is always the limiting factor for *anybody* doing *anything* outside in Scotland. It is of course the same everywhere, The Netherlands had its own extremes, a particular favourite of mine was *ijzel*, a thin layer of frozen invisible water covering every surface, everywhere. Outside movement of any kind without pavement spikes becomes impossible. Not everybody realises though that weather conditions can be so extreme in Scotland, that people will die very quickly if badly protected; perhaps rather less quickly if equipped with the most scientifically advanced, insulated clothing. There are times when it is simply suicide to venture into mountain areas. Which makes the work of Scottish Mountain Rescue teams all the more heroic and praiseworthy. The people who volunteer to help those in distress for whatever reason under these conditions represent the very best of what this country makes of people, for most will say that, despite knowing they are saving lives, it simply has to be done; you can't leave people to die in the mountains knowing you could've done something about it. We'll all work together, help in some way with phone calls or cups of tea or battling through blizzards, searching for souls in distress.

The biggest challenge to an ordinary Munro bagger like me is finding weather windows. Careful observation is necessary. It was becoming my experience that highland weather is divided into distinct areas, which often sustain different miniclimates and weather types. One or two regions, notably Skye and the Cairngorms, maintain distinct climate *systems*. The line of the Great Glen from Inverness to Lochaber defines a distinct western region where fronts from the northwest back up a bit and can often be piled with cloud for months on end. The northern bits of the country, in Sutherland and Assynt, are sometimes on the other hand bathed in sunshine for the same time. Southern mountainous Scotland has a small western bit round the Trossachs and Arrochar, and reaching into Lochaber, where it rains all the time, and a rather larger bit to the east, which is split along the A9 corridor; if it is horrible to the west of this, it is not always nasty to the east. Likewise there is a division on the western edge along the Laggan corridor to Lochaber; if it is nasty to the north of this, it is sometimes clear to the south, and *vice versa*. On every free day I had, I sought out places with the best weather, but often there was nowhere within easy reach where it was anything but appalling.

I was getting a little anxious about a forthcoming meeting with my oncologist, during which I was going to tell him about my decision to remain free of medication, while allowing myself still to be tested and scanned though not to know any results. I also wanted to emphasise that even if I did not want to know anything, Shona did and I had no problem with this, so she should be granted access to all test results and information pertaining to my case. This did not seem to either of us to be complicated, nor unreasonable.

The next Munro on my list was a bit further away than I anticipated and was one of the borders of my imagined weather map. Access is from the end of the public road at Garva Bridge next to the young river Spey as it comes out of the Corrieyairack Pass. On the map it does not seem far from the village of Laggan, but the drive feels interminable and seems to traverse several distinct topographies, passing through a diversity of forest, farmland and heath. At the end there is a wide parking space, and a bridge over the Spey, on the other side of which the public road stops, but an unmaintained road continues towards the pass, one of General Wade's, built during the eighteenth century to expedite movement of government troops in their systematic destruction of Highland cultures. There is a lot of infrastructural work going on in this glen still; a little north of the old road there is parallel access between windfarms up the glen and on surrounding moors a new substation further down. When I arrived at the carpark just before twelve, there were already several vehicles parked.

My oncologist is a nice man, more sympathetic and sensitive than others I have met, more able to see me as a human being describing what is going on in this living body, less inclined to see me only as a disease. He works nevertheless in a system of health care, so he can only do what its protocols permit. And underlying everything he says, there is never anything other than absolute certainty that the disease will progress, that the function of medical science is to manage the disease until such time as it is no longer manageable, after which palliation will be the only option. This cancer of mine has always been regarded as malignant and aggressive, not something that will ever be cured. All ideas I have ever harboured about making the disease go away have been regarded with everything from polite scepticism to disdainful ridicule. It had been suppressed and burned out, but it came back each time, so it would be easy to conclude that its progression is indeed inevitable. But I never gave up hope and I tried not to be intimidated by the reductive determinism of medical science. My oncologist made this a little easier. I was not however sure that he would understand my latest desire to remain ignorant of test results, to be both medication and medical knowledge free.

There are four Munros called **Geal Charn**, all of which are located within a fifteen-mile radius. There are also countless other Corbetts, Donalds, Grahams and unclassified peaks with the same name, which means *White Hill*. This is the most northerly of the four **Geal Charn**, situated at the southern edge of the *Monadhliath*, just at one of my imagined borders between regions of weather. The path up is a straightforward plod all the way to the top. I crossed the Spey, turned right and followed the track on the other side, then crossed over a feeder burn with the access road and immediately followed a path along the east bank of the burn beside a plantation. The path meanders through pasture for a while and then crosses another burn, after which it is an ordinary trundle up a blunt shoulder to the summit. The going was not always easy, with mixed patches of deep heather and mud. As I rose the ground became less squelchy and more garnished with snowbanks, which at about two and a half thousand feet became general snow cover. It was a beautiful day indeed, despite the gathering clouds; when the sun came out and the wind dropped it was warm like spring, but when cloud blew over it was bitter cold.

The snow became progressively thicker and more resistant to the weight of my boots; the top layer blowing off, carving fascinating whorls and drifting round protruding rocks. My feet made a satisfying squeak as they sunk into the snow. My mood improved. As always, being up here on the brink of climbing another mountain, where the view from the other side begins to present itself, all woes and worries, all the nonsense in my head, evaporate. The cloud is high above the summits, there are passing squalls and the sun is warm. I reached the summit at about two-thirty and lingered awhile, turning round the horizon. The Cairngorms were mainly smothered in clag; grey squalls billowed up in thermals above a vast expanse of white, gullied dark by glens, over the *Monadhliath*. Only **Creag Meaghaidh** to the south and the Laggan Hills on the way to Lochaber was consistently graced by sunshine, sparkling joyously with iced-up snow, plastered smooth into every crevice. Maybe there was something in my division of Scottish weather.

On the way down I thought to take a different route, first to the bealach towards *Beinn Sgiath*, whereupon I discovered that the flat shoulder on the way down from here was a great big boggy mess, sometimes still garnished by squelchy snow banks. I slithered all over the place and tired myself out, cursing my decision not simply to return along the same route, where the nice snow lasted longer and the ground was nowhere near as boggy as this. It was however what it was and I persevered, flanking back to the burn again before the ground became too steep at the end of the spur. I was back at the car at about five and made myself a cup of tea before hitting the road home. It was light later now, spring reaching higher up the mountains, leaving winter only in the very tops. I was ready for the conversation with my oncologist.

We talked through the current state of the disease and the medical options. It was a long and difficult conversation that revealed not much we did not already know. The PSA value was rising again despite the influence of the medication, a slight rise, but the first indication that the cancer has reached the next stage, that it was becoming resistant to the medication, changing from *locally advanced metastatic prostate cancer* to *hormone resistant metastatic prostate cancer*. There were new drugs available that I should take. Firstly, I should continue with the medication to which the cancer appeared now to be becoming resistant, in combination with another which I had taken before, and to which the cancer became resistant over two years previously, and with a new one, which will work in a different way from the other two to block testosterone production. Secondly, there are assorted chemotherapies and radiotherapies further down the line.

I listened carefully and asked questions, from which I was able to understand why he believes what he believes, why the medical options are such as they are. Other issues were discussed, amongst which was how to attenuate the side effects of the medication. In this context, he mentioned a particular drug which sometimes works, sometimes not, but nobody knows why or how. He said that it was a matter of trying stuff out to see if it works and to use what seems to help best. Assorted herbal remedies and tinctures that may or may not help were mentioned. Sage, black kohosh, dandelion root. For some men they work, for others not. From here, it was a short step to discussing whether or not any similarly herbal or plant-based remedy might help in maintaining the health of a body or maybe even keeping the cancer at bay, some substance not produced by a multinational pharmaceutical conglomerate, but rather a domestic preparation of the essential oils of a plant, comprising many different elements and compounds. This part of the conversation was more difficult. Actually it produced more heat than light, which was never the intention of either Shona or I, and he had to think of his next patient, so he brought it to a close. What I was being offered was a combination of highly synthesised chemicals. He had nothing else to offer.

His position was straightforward. No research is being conducted, nor is it ever likely to be conducted into whether or not naturally occurring, multi-molecular substances, working in combination with each other, might be efficacious in the treatment of any disease, let alone cancer. All anecdotes about certain oils and tinctures are just that. Anecdotes. They do not meet the scrupulous criteria required by the health service, and nobody within the system was going to fund any more systematic research with a view to producing more convincing evidence. The onus was on those who believe that something else might work to undertake or to fund others to undertake research.

Meanwhile the profile of my disease was well documented. This much I knew and no more. The level of PSA was doubling about every six weeks. It was measured again at the hospital. Eight weeks previously it was 3.9, so I would expect it to be about 9 now. And six weeks after that about 18. If I were to start taking any kind of *alternative* substance, and if there were to be any deviation from this six-week doubling time, I wondered if there would then be reason to believe that the substance in question might be having any kind of effect on the progression of the disease. Offering myself up as an experimental subject in a study being undertaken by nobody, the outcome of which only I would only ever see, the consequences of which only I would ever comprehend. Trying to justify my stubborn refusal to engage with conventional medicine, to fly the flag for mother's wisdom, holding onto a rather perverse and borderline narcissistic piece of logic, that if I could only prove medical science to be wrong, then it would focus its resources in other directions and bring forth a real cure for my disease.

There was clearly a whole series of flaws in my reasoning, but the clinical question remained open, *entirely an empirical matter*, it remained to be seen whether anything else, some stuff not on the pharmaceutical menu, would have any effect on the disease. Even if medical science was not prepared to address the question, I was. It was my life. I was perfectly capable of trying stuff out to see what works, but I needed a natural baseline, to have flushed out the drugs, to be eating well and keeping busy.

I wanted to free my mind of the inevitability engendered by the concept of *disease trajectory*, to have no medical knowledge of this whatsoever, hereby removing from my life any reason to react to it, nor become pulled into this particular spiral of negativity.

What did I have to lose? It was exactly what medical science does after all. Try stuff out to see what works.

The only difference being the source and essential structure of the stuff being tried out, and upon whose authority.

## *Stùc a' Chroin*

### 11th March 2017

Twice I had failed by other routes to reach the summit of this mountain. The first time upon seeing the exposure on the path from the summit of **Ben Vorlich** with very tired legs at the start of 2016, and again at the end of the year, when I was on my own for Christmas as Shona was in Canada. I really wanted to get up a Munro, but the weather was consistently awful for the duration of her absence. Nevertheless I made an effort, clambering up from the path out of Callander in dreich cold and glum daylight, watching a family of red kites parsing the moors, to cloud level at about two thousand feet before deciding to call it a day. I was getting a bit fed up of not yet having been able to get myself to the top of this mountain, so I adopted a different strategy. To come at it from behind, via the ridge from *Beinn Each* and to take a completist with me, who would know the way.

Since returning to the family home, I was in touch again with one or two friends from my school days, one of whom, upon returning from many years in the Merchant Navy, had settled down and done a round of Munros at weekends. He was now looking for companionship for the odd return trip to a summit. Let's call him Neil.

Although the weather did not look brilliant, the forecast was for clearing skies in the afternoon. We arrived at the carpark by Loch Luibnaig at about eleven and sought the path through the trees at the side of a gully that drains into the loch near Ardcullarie Farm. The path is steep and made more challenging by many exposed roots adjacent to a drop into a ravine. The path levels off a bit before leaving the forest, then strikes off right at a prominent cairned junction upwards to the summit of *Beinn Each*. It is steep and slithery, but it is a good way of gaining height quickly.

We entered clag at about two and a half thousand feet, following the path as it wound its way round the mountain. By the time we reached the summit of *Beinn Each* we had become somewhat disoriented; what seemed to be the intuitively sensible path that we should be following from here was on the wrong bearing completely. Evidently there was some magnetic anomaly in nearby rocks or something, for all our devices pointed in what felt like the completely wrong direction. But unbeknownst to us the path we had taken up the mountain wound us right round the back of the summit to join then with the path coming *back* from ***Stùc a' Chroin***. In our misty minds we had arrived from the south and would have to continue straight on to find our way north, whereas what we had done was walk round the summit, until approaching it (almost) from the north. So we walked on forward in what we thought was the right direction for a few meters, then stopped. The ground was not right and there was hardly anything of a path. We checked our compasses again and saw what we had done, then returned to the summit to look for a path different from the one we had used to get here. It was not easy to find. Visibility was not good, but it was there, meandering over a fascinating landscape of knobbles and cliffs, finding a way through melting snow, boulders and gloopy peat.

In the thick still mist, navigation was a challenge. Neil took bearings at regular intervals to make sure we were not going in the wrong direction. We could also follow the remains of an ancient wrought iron fence, perched along the crest of the ridge between the summits of **Stùc a' Chroin** and *Beinn Each*. There is also a reasonable path alongside this old fence. From time to time I consulted the excellent OS app on my iPhone, which despite the clag and gloom was able at every moment to pinpoint our exact location.

Despite the thickness of the mist, the challenges of navigation were overcome and we enjoyed a very pleasant afternoon together, easily reaching the summit of **Stùc a' Chroin** in less than four hours, where we saw the yellow disc of the sun through thinning cloud above our heads and the ground beneath our feet.

Thin though it was, the cloud did not seem to be going anywhere, nor breaking up. It was cold and damp at this altitude so we did not hang around. On the way back, we missed out a return to the summit of *Beinn Each* and dropped instead diagonally into Glen Ample for a gentle walk out over the pass back to Loch Luibnaig, making a round trip about seven hours.

# Glen Lyon

### 9th April 2017

The first weekend of April, Shona and I were at the end of the north fork in Glen Lyon in the campervan. It was mainly dreich, but we witnessed black grouse gathering in a lek and a hen harrier sweeping tight and low over hummocks in search of a morsel. We had a good walk along the north side of *Loch an Daimh* to a sheepy pinewood by some old buildings. On the way back I made a detour onto the southwest shoulder of ***Meall Buidhe*** in a vague effort to reach the summit, but it was too foggy above two thousand feet and I had not properly prepared. So I came down again for another night, cosy in the campervan.

A week later after a couple of nights at a resort in Aberfeldy at a stag do, I had nothing better to do on the way home than return to the north fork of Glen Lyon. The weather had improved. But not much. It would be a pity though to have come this far and not to visit a couple of unclimbed Munros. Although none of the others at the do were at all up for mountain climbing, I knew that I would be climbing a mountain with the forthcoming groom, for he was Shona's future son-in-law.

A major attraction of climbing mountains round Glen Lyon is Glen Lyon itself. Getting to the end takes a long time; every hump, hill and bend on the road is there to be savoured. Looking from Aberfeldy, the mountains are simply impenetrable towering lumps; even from Fortingall driving along the River Lyon past fields of sheep and horses, there is no indication of what is to come. Then quite suddenly the road has been hacked out of the side of a sheer cliff, very narrow and hugging the curve of the river with only a low, square-stoned dyke as parapet above a narrow linn and an inclining cliff face for a roof. Despite the rocky steepness, the ground is lush and verdant. The road then climbs high through gnarly woodland, dense with mossy undergrowth, oaks, birches and a few red pines. As the river prepares to come plunging down through the gorge, the road emerges into the first pastures of Glen Lyon, nestling between the flanks of **Ben Lawers** and ***Carn Gorm***. It is now flat and much less squiggly until Bridge of Balgie, where the road splits, with one branch heading south to Loch Tay and access to the **Ben Lawers** clusters, the other onwards up the glen.

The most sensible way of proceeding from here would be to follow the road on the floor of the glen, but this is private, blocked by a gate house. The public road rises steeply along the flank of the hill into woodlands where it becomes a complicated switchback through lumpy ground and mixed woodlands with spectacular views of surrounding mountains and the opulent splendour of the land beside the private road below. Happily there are one or two well-chosen places to park and to admire the views, for it is certainly not possible on this road to drive and watch scenery at the same time. As the road settles down again, just before the private road merges with the public road up the rest of the glen, there is a junction right. From here it is a steep climb almost immediately past a farm and round a lochan, up again into high mountain country, passing through a gate on a steep rise with impressive views back into Glen Lyon. After flanking a ravine of pines and winding through lumps and moraines, the road ends at a dammed loch, on either side of which there is a small Munro. The altitude is already four hundred meters. On a good day, it takes at least an hour to drive here from Aberfeldy.

I parked by the dam at *Loch an Daimh* (pronounced Loch an Deff) with hope in my heart that the cloud would burn off and I would get views. I was also nursing a slight hangover; despite my dietary discipline, I had imbibed a few shandies to celebrate the coming union and stayed up rather late playing poker. The only way of climbing these mountains is from the lowest point on the quickest route between them. The only choice is which to do first. I went for the southerly of the two, **Stuc an Lochan**, the summit of which lies at the end of an impressive horseshoe of a corrie with sheer cliffs facing north and a lochan at the bottom. The cloud blew past at about three thousand feet, with little gaps when there were glimpses of a horizon. The best views were down into the lochan in the horseshoe corrie and on the return along the path down the length of Glen Lyon, dappled in sunlight.

It was not much more than three hours before I was walking past the car again on the way to the path up **Meall Buidhe** for the second peak of the day. I was by now feeling positive about the decisions I had made to remain medication free, but I was still troubled by demons. Being reliant only on my own powers, working to make sense of how my body is on the inside *on the basis only of how it felt*, without any kind of external or objective sources of information, would be a continuing challenge. I would need to gather my wits about me, think very carefully about my experience and remove myself from the disagreements between my parents. I would need to become much more mindful of my own reactions, and to bring the theory and practice of my Buddhist leanings into much closer harmony.

The path up the second mountain of the day is easy to find and straightforward. Unfortunately by the time I was above about two and a half thousand feet mist was swirling about and obscuring views of any feature beyond a few hundred metres away. It was an uneventful and uncomplicated ascent with one or two boggy sections, but with a reasonable walkers' path all the way to the summit. Again, I was back at the car in less than three hours. After which, I had plenty of time to enjoy the return journey down Glen Lyon and be home in daylight. It was beginning to feel as if winter was finally over.

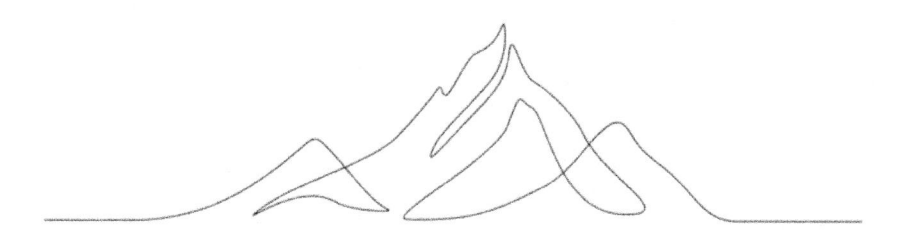

## *The Great Moss*

### 22nd to 24th April 2017

From the moment I arrived back to live in Scotland with Shona, I was thrust into the heart of a bit of the Scottish Tibetan Buddhist community that was suffering an enormous loss. I did not realise at the time that the loss was felt all over the world. While he was visiting Tibet in the autumn of 2013, the cofounder of Samye Ling Monastery, spiritual leader and friend to many, Akong Rinpoche, along with his retinue, were attacked by a disgruntled and deranged former monk who believed Rinpoche owed him money for painting work undertaken at Samye Ling many years previously. Rinpoche and two others were stabbed to death.

At the time of his murder, Shona and I were planning my final trip back to Scotland. She was going to fly to Amsterdam where we would stay for a couple of nights in a cheap hotel, with something classical at *Het Concertgebouw*; then we would have a few more nights in Utrecht to pack my remaining stuff into the old Dutch Volvo and to say my farewells. Because Shona had never visited there, and because everybody must at some point in their lives experience the intensity of this most amazing city, we drove to Paris, for a long weekend in a wee hotel in the heart of *Montparnasse*. After this, we took a ferry across the Channel to visit an old friend from school who lives in Kent, and then a few more nights wiggling north back to Scotland, stopping where we fancied, which turned out to be nights in Lincoln and a village hotel in North Yorkshire. After this, Shona expected we would be able to visit Samye Ling on the way through to Edinburgh, where she could introduce me to Akong Rinpoche. All of which happened according to plan, except there was no Akong Rinpoche.

The last time she had seen him, she told him about a new special person in her life. He tied a blessing cord into the shape of a little figure, tied this round another blessing cord, blessed it and gave it her to give to me. This is all I have of him; when I arrived in Scotland, I met only a great sense of grief, a gap in the lives of everybody who knew him. Only gradually was I able to learn about his life from others, listening to memories and stories of his extraordinary legacy, why he had meant so much to so many, amongst whom Shona.

Despite never having met him, from the first moment I arrived in Scotland, he became a vital presence in my life. I read all his books, the first of which, *Restoring the Balance*, was inspired by a wish to offer simple ways of healing from what he had learned from many years observation as a porter at a London hospital, to be the major sicknesses of Western ways of thinking and being in the world. Although the book is naively written, it is one of the most profound denunciations of Western morality I have ever read. When read in the spirit with which it was written, it offers the kindest, most practical advice about how to restore a natural balance in a life disrupted by bad habits.

There are three components to this restoration of balance. First, to review life with a view to simplifying it; second, to begin an activity that will bring peace and relaxation to the mind; and third, to develop a realistic world view on the basis that nothing lasts. At first sight these might seem straightforward enough; thinking them through more thoroughly presents some rather radical proposals, while challenging quite a lot of what is taken for granted by the Western mind. Rinpoche states that "in society every human is brainwashed in society's ways, with many conditions and little freedoms". This is neither an excuse nor exhortation to smash society, which is neither desirable nor possible; rather it is reason to learn how properly to use the precious fact of being human, despite the restrictions of society. To be mindful. Looking mindfully within is not however just being aware of the mistakes or negative side of our lives. Mindfulness involves seeing the whole picture with a mind that is well-nourished, discovers the vital healing force within, by which the restoration of balance is possible, and *then* finds the right balance for itself, for *that particular mind*. What works for one mind will not work for all.

There was something very familiar about this. Reminiscent of Nature Cure's polemical attitude to the customs and fads of medicine and society, and its insistence on examining each *dis ease* in a person as unique to that person. Rinpoche explicitly challenges us to be mindful of society's delusions.

> Until the mind is aware that appearances may be deceptive, that social customs are quite superficial and need not be taken as solid and consistent, it will hold on to prejudiced beliefs about others.

Rinpoche says that of the *mind poisons* known to his tradition, he has observed that there are three with particular toxicity in the west: *ignorance*, not knowing what we need; *desire*, using more than we need; and *hatred*, destroying what we do not want. The most difficult task is overcoming selfish, egotistic conduct and ways of thinking, even coming to realise the extent of ego's dominance is an achievement. Egocentricity stands in the way of both coordination and cooperation, while projecting itself onto others. This sustains a fundamental ignorance, that there is a solid separable self-entity and that this alone is who we are. As long as we believe that who *I am* is who *we are*, we create *others*. What is required is *selflessness* (and thus also *otherlessness*) leaving only universal love and compassion.

At the turn of 2014 into 2015, the second New Year since returning to Scotland, I was at Samye Ling with Shona on a meditation retreat led by an old student, friend and colleague of Akong Rinpoche, Ken Holmes. Here we met a couple who were camping in a damp, sunless and lumpy field at the back of the temple, let's call them Chantal and Chris. We struck up a friendship quite quickly because they were obviously outdoor people and Chantal was Dutch. I knew immediately from the way she spoke English where she came from and addressed her fluently in her own language, which was always a good way of breaking the ice. I was also the only one who had correctly pronounced her surname in many years. Chantal, it turned out, had already completed two rounds of Munros, one entirely in winter; Chris was a former outdoor leader with a military background. So we agreed that we must one day climb mountains together, but since at that particular moment they both lived south of the border, it would have to wait until next they were in Scotland. It was Chantal and Chris who I met at the summit of **Creag Meagaidh** in May 2016. Chris was still stuck somewhere in the Black Country, always on the lookout for employment north of the border. But Chantal had moved to live in Aviemore, so it was much easier for us to arrange a mountain.

It was many years since I had been up onto the Great Moss, or *Mhòine Mhòr*, a vast expanse of mossy grassland, peat hag and ancient rutting grounds at an altitude of three thousand feet or so, on the southwest corner of the west Cairngorm plateau, surrounded by several of the highest mountains in the country. Over the years, I have come here from all directions; along the ridge of *Sgòr an Dubh Mòr* and **Sgòr Gaoith**, down from the high plateau of *Carn Einich*, clambering up a cleft in the wall of cliffs round *Loch Einich*, up the estate track from Glen Feshie, and along the length of the River Eidart from its confluence with the River Feshie, one of the least visited glens of the Cairngorms. The *Mhòine Mhòr* is a place dear to my heart and I fancied camping up there for a night or two, to try out my new rucksack, climb two of the high Cairngorms from the back, as well as the two most westerly on the plateau. I suggested to Chantal that on her day off we climb **Sgor Gaioth** together from Achlean, the only route I had never taken, before I then camped out.

During previous months, I sought counsel from two Lamas about how to deal with my condition. The daily effort of a cancer diagnosis is entirely mental; though I was now also beginning to feel the effects of the medication not working any more, of the disease itself sloshing around my lymph system. Or so I imagined, and because I was refusing to know test results, my imagination was challenged to focus only on what it perceived within my body, and my mind often took this into anxiety and panic. Once there is metastatic cancer in a body, it is difficult to imagine twinges, pains and symptoms as anything but an expression of this. I was also afraid of dying, of the pain and anguish this would bring, and of the transition to whatever lies beyond this incomprehensibly beautiful, irrevocably fucked up world. Although I did not put it quite like this to any Lama.

In the rough and tumble of so many outings with my tent, I had now almost worn out the seventy-five litre rucksack I bought to replace the sixty-five litre version I bought after coming back from The Netherlands, the one that turned out to be too small for my purposes, both good value for money and manufactured by *Vango*. I still have the smaller of the two, but I sold the larger one for a good price to a mother in need of equipping her daughter for a first Duke of Edinburgh Award outing into the unknown, and a bit unwilling to fork out a great deal more for something she might only use once. I needed something more robust anyway, with even more carrying capacity. So I invested in a *Lowe Alpine Expedition*, which expands to ninety litres and, though pricey, is extremely well designed and manufactured with some very useful features. It had been in my sights ever since I replaced my old daysack with one of its smaller cousins just after my trip up **Ben Dorian**. I expected never again to need another new rucksack. This was its first trip out. It was so big that I did not need to pack it properly, and just threw in all my stuff, separated into coloured stuff-sacks. Everything fitted in loosely and the rucksack remained comfortable on my back. So I was quickly satisfied with it as a product, though so badly packed, it looked very lumpy. I looked forward to using it for longer expeditions and learning how best to take advantage of its superior capacity.

I told the first Lama I met, Tulku Ogyen Nyima, that I had come to see him because I had been impressed and inspired by an element of a teaching I saw him giving at Samye Ling, in Tibetan and translated simultaneously, that the *either/or* mentality is the greatest obstacle to clarity of thought he had encountered in the west. Not only did I agree with this *without reserve*, but from a completely different starting point, I remember enjoying the flow of his thinking, unencumbered by any dialectic, dualism or dichotomy. He told me that he had forgotten now what he had then said, but that he would help me as he could. When I told him I was scared of the development of the disease and the dying it would bring, he told me simply, there is nothing to be scared of, that the moment of death is no different from any other, that we must prepare ourselves for the dissolution of our bodies but not dwell there. He offered breathing exercises and told me about books that might help bring my mind to rest. He then wanted to know about what kind of philosopher I was. Somebody had told him that I was a philosopher. I explained that in so far as I am a philosopher in any formal sense, rather than just a human being with an active mind who likes to think stuff through, I might claim to belong to a distinctively Scottish tradition of contemplation, which for centuries has based itself on rigorous analysis of experience, maintained a sceptical attitude towards established knowledge, and gone off periodically to continental Europe to educate itself further while escaping the stifling sectarianism and class divisions that inhabit these islands. I emphasised however that because I had been educated in the Western tradition, it was difficult for me to shake off the idea that there is an external world to which I am related as subject, or the inclination to believe that things being as they are is more important than what they are turning into. Or something like that. He was genuinely interested and asked one or two searching questions, which left me thinking. Our conversation would have been more expansive I am sure had I been able to understand him expressing ideas in his native Tibetan. I took his advice and obtained the books, which were very helpful. When I can, I also practice the breathing exercises he suggested with my meditation practice. I left him a copy of my own little book.

We left Achlean at about lunchtime, a short drive for Chantal who was now successfully at home in Aviemore and beginning to experience the joy of living with the Cairngorms in her back garden, while enjoying her new job at an adventure holiday company. After many years working in a call-centre somewhere in the English Midlands, this was paradise. The forests of Speyside are by any standard staggeringly beautiful; the new owners of Glen Feshie estate are for example proactively rewilding, in the first instance by encouraging the return of native Caledonian forest through the complete eradication of all red deer from the estate. Beneath ancient gnarly old pines and collapsed weatherworn tree skeletons there is fluffy young growth thrusting through heather and juniper. I am happy that in my life I have seen this process underway; that trees are returning is one of the few things that gives me hope for this country, not only because I like trees and know that their regeneration always brings forth changed ecosystems and climates, but because I see here a new kind of ecologically aware landowner, untainted by the perfidious habits of Britishness, prepared to fly in the face of land management fashion and to oversee the reestablishment of a more fitting ecology.

The second visit was together with Shona to His Holiness Lama Yeshe Rinpoche, Abbot of Samye Ling and brother of Akong Rinpoche. We had been told that his attitude to cancer had been able in the past to help many others. He invited us into his audience chamber saying he always forgets what he says, so we must never hold him to anything. There was a glint in his eye, a big smile breaking out, but he said seriously that he would help as he could. Immediately he turned to Shona and told her rather sternly that she had to stop asking me how I am, to stop in this way giving the disease any ... he could not remember the right word in English and knocked on the wooden arm of his chair with a knuckle to indicate what he meant. Solidity, I ventured. Yes that was it, not give the disease solidity. He repeated the word *solidity* several times, with joyful emphasis on the second syllable and the last two elided into one. Then he turned to me and said that in a universe where everything changes, even cancer can change. I blurted out that I did not want to die, whereupon he laughed in my face.

The spell was broken; the fear of death and dying evaporated. Everybody dies; it is absurd, not to mention a bit stupid to want not to die. I responded rather defensively that I knew that one day I would die of course, but that now was just too soon. He told me that I was not dead yet, that now I am very much alive. Which, in fact, really was all I needed to know. I do not remember exactly what more was said, but I do know that his words were seeds sewn deliberately to have an effect specifically on those to whom they were addressed, not to be written down and preserved. Shona and I both took away from the meeting a great deal. More importantly we left with a great sense of joy, for he has the most beautiful happy smile, a very infectious laugh and the most joyful attitude to life of anybody I have ever met. I could imagine too from his countenance a bit of the charisma of his late brother.

The path towards the Great Moss and **Sgòr Gaoith** squiggles through tall heather and regenerating pines for a few hundred metres before entering mature forest, after which it flanks the side of one of the western shoulders of the plateau. It rises out of the trees hanging high above a sharp valley cut deep by millennia of meltwater. The weight of my pack was well distributed and did not hinder the effort of walking. Sheets of snow shimmered in the sky above Glen Feshie further back, we set a good pace, catching up and blethering in Dutch. It was good for us both to speak Dutch; after many years exile in England, Chantal spoke of The Netherlands sometimes in the way I spoke once of Scotland. She was happy now to call Scotland home in a way I once called The Netherlands home. There was also now something else, I also found myself empathising directly with Chantal's sense of exile, missing the ordinary stuff in The Netherlands that is different from the ordinary stuff here in Scotland. Sharing the experience of being Dutch in exile. It is said that any return from exile is either glorious or ignominious; mine was marginally more the former than the latter, but I had not been expecting to feel exiled from the country where once I was in exile.

Before we reached the plateau, the snow passed. There was a bright blue sky with white clouds hanging high above the summits and occasional grey squalls scraping over tops, dusting the ground as they passed. There was not much new lying snow, only old banks in the usual crevices and sagging cornices teetering against cliffs. The view from **Sgor Gaoith** is one of my favourites; the outline of *Loch Einich* below is exactly the same as its shape on the map, on the other side, the enormous flanks of **Braeriach** and *Carn Einich*, blending into boulder fields at the edge of the Great Moss and the route towards **Cain Toul** and **The Angel's Peak**, and beyond to the nondescript humps of **Monadh Mor** and **Beinn Bhrotain**. To the south a clear path was visible towards **Mullach Clach 'a Bhlair**, though the peak itself was not obvious. The southern horizon beyond was crystal clear. To the west and north, layers of cloud and squall over Speyside and the brown round hills of *Monadhliath*.

The effects of both Lamas' words worked their way through my consciousness as I carried on avoiding the deterministic narrative of medical science, able still to climb mountains and experience the great outdoors, learning to liberate myself from conceptual contradictions and mental acrobatics by not giving the disease any solidity, by celebrating the fact of being alive now, of this experience of vitality and health, without allowing any idea of disease, or any ancient metaphysical dogma about deterministic forces to overwhelm my life. Contrary to popular opinion, Karma does not mean that everything is laid out in advance, rather that we are all now, always have been and will continue always to be, active participants in the causes of things, which means that sometimes our conduct is affected by forces, and has effects, of which we are as yet unconscious or of which we quite often never become aware. Which does not mean we are powerless; on the contrary, for as long as we are *mindfully* alive we are free. We just need to train ourselves to understand what this means, to learn where a mind can create a prison for itself, or become infected with poisons, overwrite the ordinary experience of being alive with abstract conceptual gobbledygook; perforce to concentrate not on any abstract notion of mind, but on the actual unique mind that has been bestowed upon each and every one of us by each and every precious human birth.

We came off the summit of **Sgor Gaoith** in bright sunshine chatting happily. At the crossing of paths, we said farewell and Chantal returned to her car. I continued south, looking for a place for my tent and to complete the eight kilometre walk to **Mullach Clach 'a Bhlair** before the sun went down. To say this mountain is not prominent would be an understatement. After following an old estate track scraped out of the ground, final access to the insignificant summit cairn is over thick green moss and stones. Looking back it is easy to see that this is indeed the highest point of this corner of the Great Moss, but it is not obvious why it should qualify as a Munro. According to the map there is a drop of less than a hundred metres between here and ***Sgor Gaoith***. Which means that this mountain must teeter on the edge of qualifying criteria, but here it is, on Munro's list. After leaving my pack and yomping there and back, I found a nice place to camp by a gurgling burn at about three thousand feet and settled in for the night.

In the morning I walked due east towards the twin peaks of **The Angel's Peak** and ***Cairn Toul***, a gentle stroll of about seven kilometres over easy ground on a very agreeable gradient. Unfortunately the view from the top of both peaks was of cloud and horizontal snow. Just as I was coming off the second summit, the clouds lifted to reveal the sheer scale of these incredible mountains. There is little more humbling in Scotland, more able to set one small life into perspective, than standing at a height of eleven hundred metres and looking *upwards* to peaks all around. If I had not been to these summits several times before and seen the vast chasm of the *Lairig Ghru* beyond, I would perhaps have returned just for the view. I was content though to admire the brief view I did get; at the rocky bealach between the two summits and through the bealach between them and the high plateau of *Carn Einich* as I was coming off the south shoulder on the way back to my tent.

The most obvious victim of Lama Yeshe's specific advice would be the career as inspirational cancer patient I had built up since deciding to come out about my condition four and a half years earlier. At the very least it would have to be tweaked, and if necessary ditched. It would be too easy to become dependent on some sort of anti-cancer-identity, and perforce on the disease itself, thereby giving it a rather unhealthy kind of solidity. More difficult perhaps, and yet also more in keeping with Lama Yeshe's advice, to acknowledge the disease quietly but to concentrate on the ordinary business of being alive, not to give it any more solidity than an idea or a memory.

The two Lamas each in his way also demonstrated something more important, with such a cavalier attitude towards what they say, challenging my ideas about the importance of solidifying ideas into cleverly constructed combinations of words, forcing me to focus on the moment not as something to be preserved or archived, to be described and written down, but as *being alive*. There is no need really to make anything solid at all, every word uttered, every gesture and expression, has its meaning only at the moment of its existence. And sometimes there are just moments, with no meanings, just existence. *Meaninglessness*. A fine idea to take to a tent for a night under a blizzard.

It was already cold and I knew the weather forecast predicted a further drop in temperature. After dark, the wind got up and it started to rain. Sometime later, the noise on the tent changed and I knew snow had arrived. For the first time ever I did not go out into the night to answer nature's call, but instead used one of my cooking pots, which I tipped out steaming into the blizzard. In the morning I punched off a layer of ice from the tent, cooked my porridge (in a different pot) and got myself together slowly under blue skies filling up with squalls. I put on all of my clothes because it seemed like the best way of staying alive, and packed up the rest of my stuff, the only trace was a dark tent-shaped patch surrounded by snow.

Not that I did not want to inspire people, to encourage others to get out there and experience the mountains, to develop the bodily habits, mental skills and common sense principles necessary to be alive in these places, perhaps to encounter *elementals*. This was the whole point of my blog, *It's shite being Scottish*, to underscore the ironies of this snippet of a rant spoken by a character in the film version of *Trainspotting* by Irvine Welsh, to make use of the enormous space freely available at the end of the road, or behind a railway station in the middle of nowhere, despite the petty resentments of ordinary life and the political realities of being Scottish.

But I would be changing my attitude. No longer would I climb mountains *with cancer*, neither in spite nor because of the disease, neither in order to struggle against it, nor to prove to myself that I am winning. I would climb mountains because they are there, using the summits only as a way of getting out of the house and taking myself on new journeys into wild places. Weather permitting, the 282 Munro summits are simply places to visit with a view, high points from which new perspectives can be created, expansions of knowledge of this most beautiful country. Or so I tried to convince myself.

Great curtains of snow danced with the wind over the landscape, awaiting mountains high enough upon which to fall. Back down again in the forests of Glen Feshie, the snow became more general, beginning to settle as if it were still winter. The blizzard continued as I drove south through Drumochter, on the other side of which, into the gentle slopes of Glen Garry, with new growth pushing green through ochres and browns, a bright blue sky, high white clouds and all snow vanished, there was no doubt that on the contrary spring had arrived.

## Glen Shiel

8th May 2017

Having promised Janine better weather for her next trip, she promised to come for longer so we could take advantage of it. As the date of her arrival approached, the forecast was indeed excellent, so I decided to travel a little further afield, to revisit a popular ridge, a section of which I once traversed by accident.

Before I left to live in The Netherlands, by way of farewell, I took a series of long walks through the mountains, one of which began at Glen Finnan and came through Knoydart to *Loch Cuaich*, at which point I ran out of food and decided that instead of trying to hitch home along the interminable road from Kinloch Hourne, I would climb over the ridge to the north, on the other side of which was a much busier road where I would have a much better chance of getting a lift. Inadvertently I climbed some of the Munros on the south Glen Shiel ridge, though I was not sure how many. I was right about the road, for almost immediately I got a lift all the way to Stirling, where I slept under bushes in the middle of a roundabout until first light, when I was moved along by Forth Valley's finest in the direction of the railway station. I spent the rest of the day resupplying my rucksack, I had a hot bath and got a good night's sleep then hitched back to where I had left off my journey north through the mountains. Again, one single lift. Now from an archaeologist on his way to a dig on Lewis, who decided to travel via Skye rather than Ullapool so he could drop me off. At this point in my life I was still an aspiring academic with a particular interest in Michel Foucault's use of the word *archaeology* to describe his historical method, and we enjoyed some fascinating conversations, none of which I can now remember. After he dropped me off, I climbed to the summit of ***A' Chralaig*** and pitched my tent facing the sunset. In the morning I awoke to a sea of cloud beneath, which burned off as I traversed the ridge to ***Mullach Fraoch-choire***. From here I dropped down into the glen behind the Affric Youth Hostel for the night and the next day took the path past the Falls of Glomach to then wended my way round the back of West Monar and over Glen Carron to Torridon, by which time the weather had turned nasty again and there was snow dusted on the heights of the mountains.

Although the snows I had experienced on the Great Moss had become general north of Drumochter and for a few days dumped a load on the highest bits of land, the transition towards summer was underway. Only the usual banks of old snow remained on the mountains, and although there were still frosts early in the morning, spring was well established. It was a much happier welcome for Janine, driving north and then west along the Laggan corridor and north again until Loch Oich, west over the pass into Glen Loyne, where Loch Loyne now submerges the old road, and then down to the confluence with Glen Morriston under the massive wall of Cluanie Dam. This road offers the most spectacular views of any in Scotland and remains the nexus of one of Scotland's most scurrilous political crimes, for it is along the side of this road that Glasgow lawyer and political activist, Willie MaCrae's car was found with his murdered body inside it. There are many worse places to die than under this horizon with the pointy peaks of Knoydart and Kintail behind boundless forests and lochs, scattered with ancient habitations, impenetrable except on foot or by boat from the sea on other side.

We parked at the end of the spur to the old road back to Invergarry, drowned now on the other side of the ridge. We camped just before the bridge over the upstream end of Loch Cluanie. Another tent was pitched a little further off; I felt we had the better spot. We ate my usual gourmet mountain fare and caught up with the gossip from back home, reinforcing my sense of exile from The Netherlands. I lived there for more than half of my adult life, it would seem a bit odd if I did not now remember with affection living there. I missed the pragmatism, the eternal cycling and the grown-up thinking in public discourse. I missed the dry humour, the linguistic tomfoolery and the advanced sense of satire. I missed my friends, being part of something and building bicycle wheels. It was good to remember my old life with a special friend visiting from what had happened after I left it behind.

It was beginning to look as if the most common demographic category of my summit companions was Dutch women. If we completed four, maybe five of the South Glen Shiel Ridge and the next day a couple on the north side of the glen, then it certainly would be. We were blessed with wonderful weather for both days. This rather made up for Janine's experience on *Buachaille Etive Mor*, which she looked upon as a test, or rite of passage. We were up early and underway before nine, at the same time as a number of others, some of whom apparently chose to follow the old road to its highest point and to begin the ridge from the bealach at the very start of the ridge. This seemed to us the more gradual and longer option, and we could understand purists wanting to do this. It took us a bit more than two hours to get to the first summit by a more direct route, through the corrie to the bealach between the two easternmost summits of the ridge.

We reached *Creag a' Mhaim* just after eleven, where we were met by a small passing cloud, which scattered a consignment of drizzle to cool us off. After this minor and somewhat incongruent precipitation, the sky opened up completely and all cloud dispersed. The sun was warm and there was little wind. Looking west, I began to recall my journey in the other direction all those years ago, though I was pretty sure I had not visited this summit, and had descended to the road from the next on the ridge.

This was one of those days in the hills that will always remain burnished in memory. For the next five hours we wandered west along the South Glen Shiel Ridge, stopping at Munros and viewpoints to gaze in wonderment at mountains and shimmering horizons in every direction. This is rightly considered to be one of the most spectacular traverses in Scotland. When we got to the second Munro, **Druim Shionnach**, I remembered the way I had descended into Glen Shiel, off the northwest flank and then along the northeast shoulder back to the bridge. From this summit I would be retracing my steps from all those years ago, still not sure of how I had climbed up from the depths south of the ridge.

With one of two minor exceptions, the going was easy. To the south, steep grassy slopes into Easter Glen Quoich with the chaotic complexity of buttresses and crags on the north side of **Spidean Mialach** and **Gloeuraich**, and Ben Nevis on the hazy horizon directly behind. To the north of the ridge there are numerous precipitous cliffs and buttresses hanging above dark corries and tiny lochans, with the main road to Skye and the Outer Hebrides below and the high peaks of Cluanie, Affric and Mullardoch behind. To the west, our view as we walked, was more sublime than I can put into words. The sea shimmered, appearing to hover above the pointy peaks of Knoydart and Kintail, the horizon indistinctly blending with the haze into the serrations of the Cuilins and the Small Isles.

There is a well-trodden path to follow and the ground presents no serious obstacles. By the time we got to the third Munro, **Aonach air Chrith**, it was hot. I remembered sitting here once before in similar weather contemplating my future life in The Netherlands, looking down on the road wondering whether to go down as quickly as possible or first to wander east along the ridge a bit further. In those days I had absolutely no interest in ticking boxes; I did not know how many of these tops were above three thousand feet, nor how many of these were Munros. I was simply there on the way through to somewhere else. It is only now in the writing that I am able to reconstruct the journey I took. Somewhere along the way to the next summits was the point I reached on my way up from Glen Cuaich, but I still did not recognise it.

The next Munro, **Maol chinn-dearg**, and fourth of the day was my hundredth since I had returned from The Netherlands. Janine was a worthy companion for this achievement. From here we could decide whether to descend into Glen Shiel and back to the tent or to continue to the next summit on the ridge where we could also descend into the glen, or again continue further. It was not quite three in the afternoon. We sat for a while in the sun with great big silly smiles on our faces, then decided to carry on to the next summit. On the way I recognised the route I had taken before, up the edge of a grassy gully, marked on the map with a tiny zigzag path into *Coire na Fienne*. This meant that I had been to three of the Munros on the ridge before. At our fifth summit, **Sgurr an Doire Leathain**, Janine was happy to call it a day and to sit in the sun for a while with a great big silly smile on her face before descending into the glen.

A young man with a beard, a full pack and a spring in his step passed by on a mission to get to **The Saddle** before sundown; he had started in Fort William at first light, over fourteen hours earlier. In the time Janine and I were sitting in the sun at this summit, he had reached the next. I do not believe I was ever as fit as this. I had almost persuaded Janine to continue, for it was not that far, but she was right, it would take us much longer to get there than this young man and we still had the descent to think about; five Munros in a day was not a bad tally and the sun was still warm.

The descent was straightforward but it required care, it had been a long day and we were planning another the next. We dropped northeast into the glen and found a way across the burn while it was still possible. On the other side we were onto the watershed and no longer needed to cross any river on the way to the road, where we stuck up a thumb and got a lift back to the end of the spur to the tent. We had no doubt that the weather was going to be good the next day too and so decided to eat at the tent rather than sample the fare at the Cluanie Inn. My gourmet mountain risotto is after all filling and nutritious. In the morning there was an open sky and a thick frost, but also an emerging glow of sunshine on east facing mountainsides. We had discussed the options for the day and decided that the best would be **Ciste Dubh** with perhaps **Aonach Meadhoin** on the way back; rather than **A' Chralaig** and out and back to **Mullach Fraoch-coire**, both of which I had climbed before, or either the Sisters' or Brothers' Ridges in Kintail, which seemed a bit ambitious. We set off in good time after a hearty breakfast.

It was a straightforward plod up the glen to a flat bealach of hags and dark lochans separating the three peaks of **Ciste Dubh**, *Sgùrr an Fhuarail* and *Am Bàthan*. On the other side of this was a clear path up the first, initially quite steep and then rather sharp and a bit daunting. I did not share my apprehension with Janine, but soldiered on, knowing it was all in my mind. There was no wind, an open sky of blue, a warm sun and a well-trodden path. Up ahead though the view was of a very sharp ridge, with on one side a grassy slope and on the other steep cliffs. This is a very common profile in the highlands of Scotland, but this one seemed particularly sharp; not much further on, the crest along which the path was traced, changed from a pleasant rising incline to a steep exposed clamber. I walked on ahead, from time to time looking back to see Janine conscientiously placing every footfall, methodically making her way. At the steep bit, I concentrated only on the ground beneath my feet and did not give the fear any practice. The fear was nevertheless there, inexplicably infecting my mind with potential disasters, pumping adrenaline into my blood. At the summit we discovered a small flat plateau with an obvious cairn. It was absolutely glorious weather. We rested content surrounded by sublime horizons and sun-drenched mountains.

This was the first time I had seen the Mullardoch peaks clearly since I had climbed them instead of voting in the EU referendum. I was particularly keen to gaze at the profile of **Sgùrr nan Ceathramhnan**, which was just on the other side of the deep glen to the north. Beyond this, the long summit of **An Riabhachan**, another summit I remember only from the middle of a storm. Immediately to the east, on the other side of a vast chasm, was the long precipitous ridge connecting **A' Chralaig** with **Mullach Fraoch-coire**. Behind that and south, the bulk of the Grampians shimmering into the hazy horizon, with the big mountains of Lochaber most prominent. Behind the Glen Shiel Ridge south and to the west, the chaos of pointy peaks in Morvern, Sunart,

Morar, Knoynart, Cuiach, and assorted islands. To the west there were perfect views of the Kintail Sisters with the great lump of **Beinn Fhada** in front. It was difficult to take it all in, so benign, the views so staggering, the beauty was almost terrifying, too much to bear. We sat awhile eating lunch with great big silly smiles on our faces, contemplating the return route. Already the idea of finding a way back along that ridge gave me the squiggles.

From the summit we could see easily the route towards **Aonach Meadhoin**. It was back the way we came, at the end of the same ridge, which viewed from here did not even begin until we dropped down an almost sheer face of scrambly gravel pierced by rocky outcrops. As long as I looked north along a dipping shoulder of the mountain and ignored the apparently sheer drops on all other sides, I was fine. I figured that the flatness of the top contributed to the apparent steepness on all sides. Taking the path again did not make me feel good, but I worked my way through it, concentrating on each and every step. Once we were beyond the worst, we looked at each other and confirmed what we already knew but had yet formally to agree, that we were definitely going up **Aonach Meadhoin**.

To get there we first had to get to the top of *Sgùrr an Fhuarail* and then descend to a bealach before the ascent to **Aonach Meadhoin**. We had it in our legs and made good time, again overwhelmed by views all around, the still benevolence of the land. Light clouds fluttered by on thermals and dispersed into nothing. The summits of both of these peaks are also flat, but also more expansive, as if twin pointed cones had somehow been sliced off, and they only differ a few meters in height, the farther is tallest. Though exposed, the clambering on the way produced no fear, only great big silly smiles. We sat at the summit of **Aonach Meadhoin** awhile contemplating the only possible route back to the tent, via *Sgùrr an Fhuarail*, save continuing west along the Kintail ridges where there is only one safe descent between here and the west end. Maybe next time.

From the summit of *Sgùrr an Fhuarail* we turned south along a broadening shoulder, looking down on the glen we had walked in the morning, on the other side of which the third peak of this triple, uninteresting to us because it was not a Munro, but certainly a mountain with a fine profile. We had met one or two on the way who were including it quite deliberately. There are times when the goal of ticking boxes creates exclusions, reduces perspectives and introduces arbitrary hierarchies. It was too late in the day in any case and what we were doing continued to be pretty much as good as it gets. The sun was warm, there was a very slight breeze, the season was too young for midges. The ground beneath our feet became steep and more grassy as we descended, slowly and surely, gradually levelling off on the approach to The Cluanie Inn, where before returning to the tent, we had a slap up meal of traditional Scottish fare. Janine very much enjoyed her broth, vegetarian haggis and cranachan.

We slept well. In the morning the weather was again fine. Perfect for the journey south. As we struck camp I discovered that the battery of my old Volvo was dead. The first sign that there was some bit of this old car's electrics that was damaged somehow and leeching power without any of the sensors noticing.

I had jump-leads and Janine found a generous couple who drove their van within reach of the car. We thanked them, wished them success on their traverse of the ridge and drove off recharging the battery into the morning, glowing and empowered by our experience of the previous two days.

There are only two ways south from here; to Spean Bridge, Laggan and the A9 corridor, or through Fort William and Glen Coe towards Stirling and the Trossachs, both of which I was experiencing quite regularly these days and Janine had seen before. So I took a slight detour, first to the south end of Loch Ness, then up the road on its eastern side into Stratherric and the northwest flank of the *Monadhliath*, through low lumpy hills, strangely shaped lochs, scattered with copses of stunted bushes and little plantations.

About ten miles south of Inverness, at a hamlet called Woodside, there is a tiny road east over a moor onto a high pass and down into Strathdearn. I have used this when travelling by bike to avoid the conflagration that has become of Inverness, a lovely city, but vehicular chaos. On the descent there is a very steep section into pasture and woodland that could be Alpine, there are one or two gates and several cattle grids. After the high road joins the road along the River Findhorn, the route connects to the old A9 at Tomatin and with the new fast road just before *Slochd*. In addition to this little diversion along a seldom visited route, I was able in this weather to transport Janine down through Strathspey with the mighty Cairngorm plateau still snow-capped behind, then up to Drumochter and down again through Glen Garry, Tummel and Tay to Perth, and onward to the airport in time for her flight home. All of which thoroughly made up for any disappointment she experienced on her trip to **Buachaille Etive Mor**.

## The Mounth

### 17th to 19th June 2017

At the end of the day I climbed The **Cairnwell** cluster at Glen Shee and lost my phone in some hole in the snow, I visited an old school friend who lives now in the next glen, let's call him Cliff. He suggested that if I were ever going to climb the six Munros to the east of Glen Shee, I could park my car in his garden. So I took him up on the offer.

I had not long returned from a weekend of teachings given in London by His Holiness the Seventeenth Karmapa, his first ever visit to these islands. I travelled to London by train and met another old friend, let's call him Henry, who very generously lent me the key to his flat on the ground floor of a faux Art Deco block not far from the King's Road, very handy for the event, which was taking place in Battersea Park on the other side of the river. It was good to see him again after so many years, so much water and so many bridges. He also lent me a lanyard with readable card, access to what he called *Boris Bikes*, enabling me to cycle throughout the hugeness of this city free of charge on bikes available more or less all the time at numerous parking points, the only good thing Johnson ever did as Mayor, or so I was told.

Although the forecast was for clear skies, the weather did not look promising. The midges were voracious as I unloaded my stuff from the back of my car in Cliff's garden. Without further ado I loaded it back into his and he drove me to the lodge at end of the estate track, beyond the end of the public road. I said I might be two nights out but no more, said farewell and traipsed on over the moor through deepening heather and increasing rain. I was heading in the direction of a way up onto the plateau of the Mounth, marked on the map as a faint squiggly path. It was a steep wet plod that became increasingly engulfed in cloud. The forecast was better than this so I was a bit glum as I found a damp though comfortable patch of flat ground for my tent, made some food and settled in for the night.

The opulence of Knightsbridge and Chelsea grated slightly in comparison to the simplicity of his Holiness' teaching, and the balmy warmth of London seemed now continental in comparison to this sodden hillside. These transitions and differences are nevertheless testament both to the elemental diversity of things and their interconnectedness, which was the most basic theme of His Holiness' message.

The Karmapa is by any standards a significant presence in the world, second only to the Dalai Lama and his likely successor as spiritual leader of the Kagu tradition of Tibetan Buddhism. He was educated according to the Tibetan way from an early age because he had been recognised as the seventeenth incarnation of the Karmapa lineage. (Those uncomfortable with the idea of reincarnation or the arcane processes by which the reincarnations of specific Lamas take place, must nevertheless accept that in Tibetan culture and society reincarnation is absolutely crucial, that it is simply taken for granted; sceptics may if they wish make sense of what happened as a simple recognition that the infant Karmapa was seen as a particularly gifted child and was therefore given the best his culture had to offer, in much the same way that gifted children are quickly recognised and looked after by their parents here in the west.) After leaving behind a simple nomadic life with his family on the Tibetan plateau, he was taken to the ancient monastery of the Karmapas, where he learned mediation techniques, became familiar with ritual practices, learned about discussion and the power of ideas, while studying the ancient texts. A more rigorous philosophical training would be hard to find. When his position within the borders of China became untenable he took his seat to Nepal, though he has never himself been able to stay there. After many years exiled in India it became possible for him to travel further afield and to bring his teaching to a wider audience. His interpretations of the Buddhist message within the complexities of these interesting times are of great interest to very many.

My experience of teachings hitherto had been more intimate, often involving meditation practice and ritual; here it was more like a convention. A cynic might also have observed that His Holiness was promoting his new book, *Interconnected*, copies of which were available for sale amongst the usual merchandise of little Buddhas, ritual items, prayer flags, meditation cushions and texts. I bought two copies of the book, one for myself, the other I left in the Chelsea flat for Henry and his wife. It is a fascinating book, making use of the Buddhist notion of *Interconnectedness* to dissect the major issues of our times. Like Akong Rinpoche's work, it is both very kind and a profound denunciation of Western ways, offering straightforward practical solutions to many social and political issues. It is a significant and sophisticated contribution to general understanding, well-researched and written very carefully in collaboration with a team of advisors. It therefore becomes itself an example of *interconnectedness*.

It was a long night with mist obscuring all views of anything. I was pretty sure where I was; although I have often gotten it wrong when pitching up in thick cloud, I had a fair idea that when the cloud rose I would be looking out on **Tom Buidhe** and **Tolmount** from a position not far from a tiny long lochan. It got light early but the cloud did not begin to disperse until eight. I was bang on though. Looking out towards **Tom Buidhe** and **Tolmount** from the middle of a plateau of peat hag, now drying out nicely for the summer, resplendent with cotton grass and little brown birds. Ptarmigan gurgled nearby. I had already eaten so left my tent and bounced over shallow hags to **Tom Buidhe**, which I reached before half past nine, an unremarkable mossy hump scattered with round stones. Cloud was persistently hanging just above my head, giving the plateau a roofed character, penetrated by shafts of intense sunlight. Half an hour later I was standing atop **Tolmount**, a more interesting grassy hump pocked with sharp protruding rocks. I sat a while as the cloud lifted and dispersed on the wind, then I turned southwest and curved round the steep slopes on the north edge of the plateau over grasslands scattered with hags and piles of round stones towards **Cairn of Claise**, which I reached at eleven. This is the highest point on the crest of an ancient boundary marked by a drystane dyke, in remarkable condition for three and a half thousand feet and built atop piles of wobbly stones. I noted my brief visit to this place for the record, with cloud again now almost low enough to touch, then followed the dyke north before turning to the spur of *Carn an Tuirc*. Another pile of stones, larger, pinker and more angular than the grey round screes of the others. I was at the very edge of the Mounth now, looking down into the slopes of Upper Glen Clunie towards white squalls washing past the Cairngorms. From here I returned to my tent over happy grasslands and hags, passing beneath piles of stones on the summit of **Cairn of Claise**. I had lunch, rested a while and packed up for the final two peaks of the day.

Throughout the event, His Holiness sat cross-legged on a throne in the centre of a stage. Along the sides of the hall, CCTV images were available for those with a restricted view as he spoke through a mic, sometimes in English but mostly in Tibetan, each chunk translated by an assistant. The first thing he said was how disappointed he was not to have been welcomed to these islands by Akong Rinpoche, who had been his friend and teacher during very difficult times for everybody in Tibet. From the audience reaction to this, it was clear that there were many in the hall who had known Akong Rinpoche well and missed him terribly. There were also assorted high Lamas and elderly sages, amongst whom His Holiness Lama Yeshe Rinpoche, Tulku Ogyen Nyima and Ringu Tulku, as well as many regular exiled Tibetans in traditional dress, Buddhist nuns and monks in robes, one or two of whom I counted now as friends. Chris was also there, come down for the weekend from the Black Country with the news that he had found work in Scotland and would be moving to the Forth Valley as soon as he found somewhere to live.

His Holiness took as his source *Eight Verses for Training the Mind*, which were spoken by Geshé Langri Thangpa in the eleventh century of the common age, and written down by others to be preserved for posterity. Here were to be found the most important lessons for our time. More concise, he said, than the better known *Thirty-seven verses on becoming a Boddhisattva*. This is not the place to go into the fine details of Buddhist theology, but His Holiness' most important message was understanding the precious gift that is human existence and to use this with compassion for the benefit of all sentient beings. He was particularly keen to emphasise finding compassion for those, by whose actions others are made to suffer or take offense. To consider their condition as another variety of suffering. In this way we learn not only that nobody has a monopoly over suffering but also about what makes us react. He was most emphatic, even the cruellest behaviour should be regarded as an opportunity for training the mind. It is a bit flippant perhaps, but not entirely inaccurate to say that whereas Christianity asks us to consider the plight of the unfortunate and downtrodden, Buddhism challenges us to have compassion for despots and sadists. However, whereas the former promises salvation, the latter offers only opportunities to learn. Buddhism does not promise any kind of salvation to the faithful, no blissful or eternal afterlife, only an eternal recurrence of the same, in the knowledge that there are always ways of bringing a mind to rest in the midst of it all, understanding the causes of human suffering and understanding that this is improved by living a life of compassion.

I struck camp at about three as clouds rose and dispersed on the wind. At last the full glory of a summer afternoon high on a mountain plateau. Hares flopped about, ptarmigan croaked, ravens played their games in the air. I climbed past the eastern flanks of **Cairn of Claise**, down again to a bealach where the path up from Glen Shee joins the plateau. From the last track towards **Glas Maol** I could see the ski centre below and the top of a winch; I had forgotten that one of the major reasons for climbing these mountains from Cliff's back garden was to avoid ski infrastructure. The summit of **Glas Maol** is the highest point on the Mounth, a flat grassy hump with views from the Lomonds to **Lochnagar**, from Montrose to the *Monadhliath*. It was already after half past four and I had not yet decided where I was going to spend the night. But it did not seem to matter.

Just off the top of **Glas Maol** the landscape changes quite abruptly from predominately round flat and grassy to exclusively rocky sharp and steep. The dyke continued along an increasingly gnarly ridge of broken stones of many sizes, beside which there was an increasingly challenging walkers' path clearly visible to the top of **Creag Leacach**. On the way I met a couple who had given up before the summit because after five Munros already and such a long way back to their car these sharp rocks were just too much at the end of a hard day. The woman was limping quite heavily. I wished them a safe return and found my way gingerly to the summit, where I was regaled by views into agricultural Angus and Perthshire, with Fife as clear as a bell behind. This must be the mountain I can see from the top of the hill above my house. Immediately beneath the summit, nestling in a hollow in the scree was a little pool of crystal-clear water surrounded by flat mossy ground facing east to the sea. This was obviously where I would be spending the night. I had told Cliff to expect me after at least one night out; if I was not back after two nights, then there was probably something amiss. With this perfect camping spot at the summit of my sixth Munro of the day, I was going nowhere, knowing I would be safe and nobody would be worrying.

One of many methods of learning meditation involves concentrating on only one element of the environment, one speck of experience; or to focus only on the ambient breathing of the body, a heartbeat or the fleeting ideas of a mind. The last of these I found difficult, having learned throughout my life to do the complete opposite, to gather together and pursue thoughts and ideas and to arrange them according to the values of rational legitimacy and truth that are favoured in the west, on the assumption that something can then be done with the result. Such fully formed opinions are the currency of both philosophy and political discourse, of personal identity and group allegiance. They become the flags that people carry, their uniforms and badges, coextensive with their sense of who they are. But they are made of fleeting insubstantial nothings.

Concentrating on the actual stream of consciousness in a mind, whether as a way of learning meditation or just being mindful or interested, teaches that every thought is transitory and insubstantial, even the ones that seem to be really, really important.

Differences of opinion are partly a consequence of the brute fact of us all being different, occupying a unique trajectory of experience through life. They have been encouraged in our culture, at least up to a point, as the motor of discourse and the engine of social change. For as long as people identify with opinions, differences will become personal, which is always going to be political. Arguments about whose version of reality gets to wield power are real and often involve actual warfare, state oppression, media manipulation and defending the moral superiority of some present state of affairs, no matter how wicked and beastly. At the level of interpersonal relations the situation becomes very much more complex, easily mixed up with unresolved passions, half understood science and hearsay; positions become easily polarised and emotions frayed.

In some way, this is all commonplace, easy to accept, the normal everyday reality of being human, what is known to Buddhism as *Samsara*, the eternal cauldron of confusion to which consciousness is subject. Because this is a kind of normality, it becomes quite straightforward to point out the delusions and mistakes of others, especially when these are objectively or obviously so delusional or mistaken that they cannot be called anything else. It is more compassionate however to endeavour to understand why others believe and act as they do, even if this goes against what has become normal or morally acceptable. All of which would suggest that it is never a good idea to identify with an opinion or to take the opinions of others personally, nor to hold it against somebody for having unconventional opinions. In the grubby business of everyday life this is however easier said than done, becoming mixed up with unconscious reactions over which we have no control. I am nevertheless sure of two things; that ideas do not care who identifies with them and that holding ideas makes no difference. Ideas exist irrespective of whether anybody believes them. Conduct is what is important in human relations, whether motivated by notions of the mind, blind obedience, habit or visceral urges. Conduct. How we behave towards each other.

I like Cliff. He is well-read and self-contained, and lives at the end of a glen in a house he built with his bare hands. But I do not like the work he does, as a ghillie for the estate, which sometimes causes friction between us, or marks out areas of conversation we would best avoid. I should be more precise: I do not like it that this is work that is offered round these parts, that this kind of work exists at all. Which has nothing to do with Cliff, only with those forces offering the work, a long history of short-sighted, rapacious land management and ethnic cleansing. If Cliff did not do the work, then somebody else would. Once, because I asked, he described in great detail what he does to a recently despatched stag while the animal is still warm, and I listened with great interest and slight revulsion, impressed with the care he takes preparing a carcass, his pride in getting the job done properly. I understood that things being as they are, this work must be done by people who know how. And yet I continue to believe that things *could be otherwise* and that Cliff's extensive skills would still be productively employed if the land were put to other use. I am also very fond of Henry. We had some fun times together many years ago, but our paths diverged, we live now in completely different worlds and our opinions are often diametrically opposed, although by no means always. Again, these are territories into which we know better than to allow our conversation to wander. But when he explains to me exactly what he does and the assorted projects in which he is or has been involved, I can find nothing but careful thought, integrity and enthusiasm, a real sense of understanding the future.

It was a quiet night contemplating why some differences make the ordinary differences between us more pressing, more inclined to engender old passions and external, political conflicts, while other *differences between us* remain *utterly benign*. Here is the front door to the *wilderness of mirrors*, for each of us sees on every other what we would prefer ourselves not to be. This was one of the reasons I always I tried to hold back from talking about other people at all; I wanted always to avoid individualism, not to become embroiled in stupid arguments about who should take responsibility for the words. Instead I sought clarity of mind without erecting the individual as the centre of consciousness and the building block of society. I wanted to find sense to my thinking while understanding that being able to describe this at all is a delicate task, made possible only because I am a political animal and knowing that contemplating the vicissitudes of language can ensnare a mind and obscure the truth as often as illuminate.

I lay with the tent front open to the night drifting into sleep under fascinating light and billions of stars. Towards dawn it clouded over, which was disappointing, but no big deal in the grand scheme of things. I packed and made my way off the summit cone of **Creag Leacach**, south to a little rocky stub and then skirted in front of a subsidiary peak. I was still not far below three thousand feet, with quite a long walk ahead of me. I turned onto the eastern ridge, following a fence until I reached a low bealach, from which I descended into a broad strath with a lazy meandering burn on its floor. Presently I picked up a track towards the estate lodge. It was hot and clammy and the track dusty.

At last, sitting comfortably in his kitchen with a nice cup of tea, Cliff said he had briefly wondered if he might not have seen me the evening before. His wife looked at him with a quizzical expression, did he *really* think I would only spend the one night out up there? A wise woman.

## *Bidean nam Bian*

30th June 2017

For some months, I had been communicating with the man I met going up **Ben Dorian** at the start of the year, on the matter of when we would meet up again to climb mountains. Let's call him Martyn and his dog Coll. It took us a while, but at last we found a mutual window of opportunity and decided to visit Glen Coe. We agreed to meet at the confluence of our routes, from which we would proceed in one vehicle.

Once upon a time I climbed *Bidean nam Bian* with the same bunch of academics I have mentioned before, or at least as part of a group led by a particular professor of psychology and one of his postdocs. I took part in four of these outings, based from an outpost of Edinburgh University department of physical education at Firbush on the southern bank of Loch Tay. Only our trip over **Ben More** and *Stob Binien* was during fine weather. *Beinn Hesgearnaich* was in assorted densities of mist, snow and spindrift all the way. There were blizzards on a trip over *Beinn Glas* and **Ben Lawyers**. The assault on *Bidean nam Bean* remains however the most radical thing I have ever done in the mountains.

There were six in the group I think, maybe eight. Our leader assured us as we walked up the burn towards the Lost Valley in fairly typical Glen Coe weather, sheets of torrential rain, that if we struck up right towards the towering buttress of the middle of the Three Sisters, we would find a way through its terraces to the ridge of *Geàrr Aonach*, where there was a path onwards up the mountain and then a circular route back down into the Lost Valley. At the time I took all this on trust. The slabs on the opposite side of the gully were pouring in one vast waterfall, whipping up in the wind, turning to spray and adding to the general deluge. As we climbed through the terraces along a path that was surprisingly well defined, the weather deteriorated from rain to sleet to prickly ice. It is all a bit of a blur now, but I remember on the way round standing on two distinct summits, between which it was very hard work, and for most of the way wearing crampons. I also remember a friend of the good professor, an academic philosopher, from time to time asking in a most splendid Edinburgh accent, whether what we were about to do was entirely wise, most memorably at the point where the path plunged through cloud down a sheer wall of frozen snow into the Lost Valley. This was just before his bunnet blew off towards Glen Etive in a sudden gust, never to be seen again. Apart from following the bunnet, the only way back down was via the wall of frozen snow.

Martyn and I would be following a route more or less the reverse of the above, with the important difference that we would *not* be coming off the front of *Gèarr Aonach*, but following a climbers' path out of the corrie under *Stob Coire nan Lochan*, and we would first be visiting **Stob Coire Sgreamhach**, the highest prominence on the southeast corner of the massif, and its only other Munro. From my previous experience here I was sure that I had climbed two Munros, but I now understood that *Stob Coire nan Lochan*, the first peak on the route I had taken before is not classified as a separate Munro, which rather surprised me.

Glen Coe is a place people stop to gawp at the mountains or take short walks in the vicinity of car parks. The weather was fine as we left the car, but it was already getting on for lunchtime so it was busy. The path had been improved greatly since my last visit, taking us steeply, but securely towards the Lost Valley, even as it found a way through the forest of birches and house-sized boulders in the gorge. The Lost Valley is always worth a visit. Meadows and scattered stones in a long flat valley surrounded by precipitous slabs and unstable scree slopes, often drenched for days on end by sheets of torrential rain. The arrangement of stones on the valley floor is in continuous flux as the mountains are worn away by weather. It is said that the MacDonalds of Glen Coe secreted away their cattle in this place, although I find it difficult to imagine how they persuaded the unfortunate beasts across the ravine of the River Coe below and up through the boulder filled gorge.

Apart from having a height of more than three thousand feet, Munro's criteria of inclusion within his tables were entirely qualitative; each peak must have its *own distinct character* with a *sufficient degree of separateness from its neighbours*. His legacy is therefore notoriously difficult to manage and results in endless discussions and periodic reclassifications. Which is testament only to the difficulties of putting into practice qualitative criteria and how this mixes immediately with the vicissitudes of human relations. Barring earthquakes and avalanches, measurement and mapping technologies are sufficiently advanced for there to be no significant disagreements about which points on the surface of the land protrude above three thousand feet, the only matter of discussion is how to separate these into *significantly* protruding peaks. It has to be said however that the official heights of Munros maintained by the SMC differs slightly from the continuously updated lists of summits maintained by the Relative Hills of Britain, and there are one or two differences with the heights recorded on OS maps. Without getting bogged down in details, these differences are not great and do not much affect the overall rankings; this does indicate however that even in matters that on the face of it should be quite amenable to objective evaluation, there is ambiguity.

All the minor lists employ entirely objective criteria of inclusion, the most extensive of which, the *Marilyns*, a name about which authentic Munroists sometimes get a bit miffed and haughty, demands no height criterion, only a vertical drop of at least 150 metres on all sides, or what is called 150 metres *prominence*, bringing in a large number of islands and low hills in un-thought-of places, and interestingly excluding a significant number of Munros. There are well over one and a half thousand of these in the British Isles. Lists of mountains and hills below three thousand feet, the Corbetts, Donalds and Grahams, also all employ objective criteria of both height and prominence. Only Munro's tables are decided upon by committee. Not that there is anything wrong with this, the thorny problem of implementing Munro's criteria of inclusion cannot in practice be addressed otherwise. It does however lead to anomalies and oddities.

The path out of the Lost Valley rises gradually along the northern enclosing shoulder from a large rock protruding into the flow of the burn, which I remember being encrusted with ice and the path round it impassable without again putting on crampons. Of course today the weather was utterly benign and the large protruding rock presented no problems. We tootled along getting to know each other, gradually leaving behind the crowds who were here only for the Lost Valley. Coll the dog ran about fully engrossed in his universe of scent, stopping only to stuff his nose into deep grass in search of rodents, one or two of whom he managed to catch, much to Martyn's dismay. No terrain presented him with any difficulty as he scampered about, getting rather too close to the edge of precipices for my comfort, although Martyn was not bothered, so I assumed Coll knew what he was doing as well as Martyn did. The path wends towards *Bealach Dearg*, where it becomes very steep and deteriorates into slippery gravel. This is what lay under the vertical wall of frozen snow I descended all those years before. We arrived at the bealach and turned left towards **Stob Coire Sgreamhach**, whereupon the clag came down. We stopped for a snack behind some rocks. It was not cold. But it was dreich.

I had already encountered anomalies. **Buachaille Etive Mòr** is one long squiggly ridge with three major protruding points at heights of 1022m, 1011m and 956m, with drops to 875m and 860m respectively between. The two Munros at either end have a prominence of 147m and 94m, while the non-Munro between has a prominence of 136m and is undoubtedly the most challenging of the three. **Mam Sodhail** and **Carn Eighe** are about the same height, are separated by a drop of barely 140m and lie at a distance of less than 1km from each other. A fit person in good weather can walk between them in less than 15 minutes. And yet they are separate Munros. A similar remark could be made about the twin peaks of **Cairn Toul** and **The Angel's Peak**, with prominences of respectively 151m and 116m. **Mullach Clach a' Bhlair** on the Great Moss is barely 100m above the lowest point towards it and **Sgor Gaoith** and is about as prominent (in the non-technical sense) as the middle of a field. No doubt each of these pairs is made up of mountains that have their own character, each being the highest point of a separate series of ridges and corries, or on a completely different kind of landscape. Which being the case it would make sense if the two summits of **Sgurr nan Ceathreahmnan** were classified as separate Munros.

We got to the summit of **Stob Coire Sgreamhach** at about three. There was nothing to see but clag so we toddled off to **Bidean nam Bian**, which we reached in less than an hour without any difficulties. But it was now raining quite persistently. There was nothing to see at this summit either so we took a bearing and clambered off the edge of the mountain towards *Stob nan Coire Lochan*. Here the fun began. Here was the hard work I remembered from last time. There is a path of sorts but the ground is steep, rocky and exposed, and the traverse is as challenging as *Stob nan Doire* on **Buachaille Etive Mòr**. We came out of the clag at the bealach and climbed into it again on the way to the summit, which we reached at about five after more rocky, though less steep, clambering. There was still nothing to see, so we descended steeply again towards *Geàrr Aonach*, whereupon the cloud cleared and suddenly we could see we were still high up the mountain, surrounded by precipitous slopes, cliffs and very gnarly ground, with a long way back to the car.

If it is true that the aforementioned pairs of mountains can only be separated by their character, then so too must it be true of **Bidean nam Bian** and *Stob nan Coire Lochan*. The latter is only the third highest point of the great massif behind Glen Coe's three sisters, so perhaps it is rightly not a Munro. And yet the very much lower and equally integral to the massif, **Stob Coire Sgreamhach** *is* classified as a separate summit. If anything, the walk along the ridge from **Sgreamhach** to **Bidean** is a lot less challenging than the traverse from **Bidean** to *Stob Coire Lochan*. By as many criteria that I can think of, there is a *sufficient degree of separateness* between **Bidean nam Bian** and *Stob nan Coire Lochan* for the latter to have a recognised character that can be classified as a Munro. It is a fine mountain with a prominence of well over a hundred meters, replete with corries, buttresses and pinnacles all of its own, and it is separated from its nearest neighbour by a steep edged arete, which is much more challenging than the gentle stroll required along the round ridge between the two existing Munros.

Emerging from the cloud we were better able to see the route ahead and the great amount of air beneath our feet, buttresses and terraces, great slabs and chutes and chaotic detritus on shallower slopes. I could see the path towards the route I had taken before; we flanked left towards a flatter area sheltering lochans and places where climbers gather. Martyn assured me that along the side of a waterfall emptying the lochans was a path down into the glen next to the Lost Valley. Of course he was right. Initially the path squiggled through some complex terrain and then settled in to flanking the glen all the way down, high above the burn. On the way, Martyn pointed out coloured figures on rocks on the other side of the glen, climbing between the terraces on *Guala Làidir*. I would never have noticed them; it was only when they were pointed out that I could see what they were doing. Martyn had been watching them for a while and knew exactly what they were doing. He asked if I had done much climbing and I told him honestly that I had no experience at all of anything involving ropes and very little of narrow ridges. So, he observed, I had never been along the *Aonach Eagach*, the ridge we could see on the other side of Glen Coe, the famous one. One day, he suggested, he would guide me along it. I looked at the thing and already felt my legs wobbling. Think about it, he said, when the weather is still and clear, when there are views and the going is easy. I agreed, but said that for the moment I was on a mission to zip through the peaks to the south of the Laggan corridor.

We did not reach the car until nearly eight, which at midsummer is still full daylight. What a fantastic day out this was. Although the weather could have been a lot better, I had made a friend with whom I could enjoy climbing mountains in the future. We agreed to keep in touch. I had a feeling that before very long I would be clambering along the *Aonach Eagach*.

## Loch Treig

4th and 5th July 2017

At the north of Loch Treig, at the end of a spur from the main road from Laggan to Spean Bridge, there is a hamlet called Fersit. This is a place worth visiting for its own sake; overnight parking is discouraged, but there is space for walkers' vehicles and it is recognised that a circuit of the Munros enclosing the loch, or just the loch, is less rushed with a night camped at its south end.

The usually reliable Mountain Weather Information Service (MWIS) offered an eighty percent chance of cloud free Munros in this area, with the proviso that a bank of cloud would be encroaching from the coast and obscuring summits in the Nevis Ranges and possibly further, but exactly where it would border the more open skies to the east, was difficult to predict.

I drove away from home under a blue sky with white fluffy clouds flitting past high on a summer breeze. From the final stretch along the Laggan corridor there was a good view of the encroaching cloud, gathering over The Grey Corries and hanging onto the very tips of the pointy *Easains*. Undeterred, I proceeded with my plan and took the potholed squiggly road to Fersit. I arrived at about midday and booted up. There were many midges, but the breeze was enough to keep them off. Lush summer foliage of bracken, birch and grass painted the mountains green all the way to the summits. Loch Treig glistened in the high sun.

Despite being high and appearing pointy, the route up the *Easains* has only one or two steep sections. At the end of a gravel track through birchwood from the carpark, ATVs have found a way up through muddy pastures scattered with cotton grass. On the ridge ahead there is a pillar, something to do with hydro works, which makes a good point for which to aim. It was steep, sometimes I found myself walking along ATV tracks, but I was mostly following my best judgement. From the pillar it was more level, but still boggy. The views ahead and all around were spectacular, more impressive to the east where there was much less cloud. The summits of the *Easains* were still capped with cloud. I plodded on, happy with my new rucksack's ability to carry all I needed without me much noticing the weight. There is another steep bit a little further on, zigzagging through crags onto *Meall Cian Dearg*, after which it is a gentle stroll all the way to the summit of **Stob a' Choire Mheadhoin.** I walked into clag at about three and a half thousand feet and into a rather surprising conflagration of weather. So much for eighty percent.

There was no respite until I emerged again on the way off the southern shoulder of **Stob a' Choire Easain**, not even on the bealach between the two summits, from which I was able only fleetingly to glimpse the splendours of cliff and buttress hanging over glens below. I was at the first summit at about quarter to four and the second about half past. It was thick and cold, tiny needles of rain felt too hard for water. It was a disappointment, but a reminder never to expect anything from the weather and always to prepare for the worst. These two were immediately added to the *return list*. I kept moving until I was on my way down on the other side, stopping only to take grumpy wet selfies and screenshots of locations. As soon as I was out of the cloud the sun warmed again, but the ground was steep, grassy and wet.

There was time enough still in the day to find a way off the ridge and to choose a nice place for the night at the south end of the loch. It was however a long slog. I should have followed the crest of the ridge further, all the way down perhaps, but I missed a kink eastwards and took a straight route beside a quartzite seam that soon petered out, slithering through long wet grass and tiring myself out. Here I felt for the first-time dampness seeping into my boots; layers of leather and Goretex creased too often in the same way and beginning to yield. Three years seemed not very old for boots, but on second thoughts, with a hundred and thirteen Munros behind them, they were not doing too badly, and I would probably not have to replace them until the weather deteriorated into winter, which was not going to be happening any time soon. As I looked back, I saw the last wisps of cloud drifting off the summits. Typical.

At the bottom there was a path along the bank of a very pleasant little river downstream towards Loch Treig. I was further away from the loch than I thought and was getting weary, in need of finding a roost for the night, but it was warm and dry. At length, the path veered off from the river over a pasture dotted with gnarly old trees and then delved into a dry gorge, very narrow in places and with smooth walls of twenty feet at least. The river now skirts the pasture above the entrance to the dry gorge and plunges fifty feet or so down a substantial waterfall into a narrow cleft before emptying into Loch Treig. Once upon a time a lot more water certainly flowed past here.

From the dry gorge the path emerged into bracken strewn pastures, past sheep fanks and dipping cages towards the old farmstead of *Creaguianeach*, apparently in use, but by whom and for what purpose was not obvious. I crossed a bridge over another river at the bottom of a little gorge feeding into Loch Treig, to the right the start of a path towards Glen Nevis and Fort William. I plodded on for another mile or so until I crossed the next burn coming off the hill into the loch; nearby I found a perfect spot for my tent. Flat short cropped grass on thick earth, well-drained, and high on the bank, looking north over Loch Treig towards **Beinn Teallach**. A way further off, nearer the loch, was a minor encampment of two small tents with washing line and dinghy, somebody staying here for the duration maybe. There are worse places to spend a summer; in an emergency the jetty at Fersit is a short boat trip away. Down by the very edge of the burn, in a gravelly hollow by the feeder burn, there was another encampment of two rather oddly pitched tents. But none of the occupants of either made themselves known to me, or even visible, and I spent a peaceful night alone under the stars.

In the morning I was up and away in good time; it had been cold at dawn and I was raring to go. The sky was open with only light clouds high above the summits. I followed the track over another river draining into the loch, and turned south uphill in the direction of Corrour Station, for a while parallel to the railway line until it bridges a burn coming out of the glen between ***Beinn na Lapp*** and ***Chno Dearg***, where there is the start of a track directly towards Loch Ossian. Immediately I struck off from the track for a long gentle plod up the western shoulder of ***Beinn na Lapp***.

It was a beautiful morning of light breezes, warm sunshine and white fluffy clouds hanging high above the land. The ground was very easy, stunted heather and low flat rocks scattered with gravel on a gentle gradient. Views gradually opened up all around. Ahead I could see a figure moving slowly towards the summit. It appeared to be a woman on her own, but I was not sure. I caught up quite quickly. It was indeed a woman, rather elderly, extremely focused and deliberate, but very slow. She said she had come from the station at Corrour; she was polite but was in no mood for conversation. I wished her well and continued. On the final section, near the summit of this little Munro there is a substantial pool of clear water in a cleft between blunt rocks angling out of the ground amidst peaty grasses. A fine place to rest or pitch a tent I thought. But I had other plans.

At the summit I paused to admire the views of familiar horizons and mountains to the east and south, and the chaos of pointy peaks and ridges west towards Etive and Mamore, the Glen Coe and Nevis Ranges, with the *Easians* now entirely free of cloud. I was particularly drawn to the profile of ***Ben Alder*** and the two peaks I climbed on the way there from Rannoch back in 2014, with behind this on the distant horizon, as clear as a bell, the sharp point of ***Schiehallion***, the nondescript lump of the Glen Lyon Horseshoe and then the familiar profile of the **Ben Lawers** squiggle. West of this, over the vast expanse of Rannoch Moor to the big mountains at the end of Glen Lyon and the beginnings of Orchy. All of these now old friends, each holding onto an important part of my life, waystations on my healing journey, stepping stones to the present. I waited at the summit until the elderly woman arrived, thinking she might be more forthcoming. Somehow I felt drawn to her, sensitive to whatever was troubling her. I felt sure that her demeanour was more than simply determination. She nodded good day to me and a number of others who were sunning themselves at the summit, then repaired to a place of solitude at the edge of the steep northern slope of the hill. I have always wondered about her story.

This mountain is most often climbed from Corrour Station, or the Youth Hostel at Loch Ossian, and there is a circular walk down a minor ridge to the east end of the loch where a route begins to ***Sgor Gaibhre*** and ***Carn Dearg***, the two I climbed on my way to **Ben Alder** in 2014 from Old Corrour Lodge. I was going in a different direction though, and had quite a long day ahead of me. I followed the main ridge northeast looking for an easy slope to the north down towards a sensible place from which to climb ***Chno Dearg*** and thence ***Stob Coire Sgriodain***. I could find no such route so plumped for a slanting descent between two deluge gullies. It was hard work, this very steep downward gradient with full pack, and I was glad at last to find a spot to sit in the sun for lunch. I was making good time.

It was a peaceful place, looking down the glen to the hump of **Beinn a' Chlachair** and the pimple of **Creag Pitridh**, two mountains that I was planning to get up in the very near future with their neighbour, another of the **Geal Charns**. I sat quietly, reflecting on the journey, on how I had come to this place and of the places I am planning still to visit, the expectations I had of the future. I had then a moment of revelation difficult to describe, but which infused me with a vitality I could not contain. I came upon myself. I was able evidently to think about the future. Also to make decisions that will bring about favourable events, rather than to sit around waiting for the inevitable to work out its course. It felt as if this was the first time I had been aware of doing anything like this since the diagnosis when the future was taken away from me. This was the moment I realised that the first victim of cancer is in fact *the future*. I felt a definite shift. I was making sensible decisions that connected with many other matters of importance in my life. I felt truly blessed to be alive at all, not because I believed that the grace of God is shining down upon me, although it may well be, but because at this moment, in this place I see just how extraordinary any of it is, that the precarious existence humanity thinks it has secured for itself on the surface of this planet is a most unlikely, marginal happenstance within an infinite creation, beyond every power of comprehension. The mountains before me smile in the summer sun. Tall grasses swoosh in the wind and water gurgles over rocks.

I come upon myself thinking this and become aware of the fact of thinking it. I am therefore pulled into a reflexive spiral, from which I am able to escape only by proposing either that all these thoughts (including this one) have been put in mind by forces beyond understanding, or that I have just made it all up inside the echo-chamber of wandering consciousness. At which point I grasp that either alternative is as miraculous and bewildering as the other, and I am left again to focus on the present, on smiling mountains, strangely inoffensive midges, the enormous variety of grasses and tiny delicate flowers decorating every nook and cranny in the rocks. A cascade of joy, grief and rage all at once, overwhelming and expanding my consciousness in every direction. I look to see the waters of the burn move on again and I am overcome by an emotion I do not understand.

It was a hard slog up from here, though I felt replete, utterly infused by my experience by the burn. I did not understand it, did not know how to describe it, and as it faded into memory I could not even be sure that it had happened at all. I went back through trains of thought, hoping to hold onto a timeline, but

I had a notion that what I had just experienced lay *perpendicular* to what I had learned to call *time*, that all those trajectories of thought cascading over each other and the overwhelm of emotion, had taken place in an instant between moments, in *the void*. I tried to reconstruct what was going through my mind just before I realised again that I had a future, that *by reflecting back from a point of presence to a past present in which it was declared that there is no future, I was exposing a contradiction*. The very fact of this *now* being after a *then*, which was itself once a *now*, means that this *now* would *then* have been in the *future*. From which it follows that from now there is also a *future*, which will become a *past*. *I am a living point on this logical progression*. Perhaps this was my own way of making sense of Lama Yeshe's wisdom, his bald assertion that I am alive *now* and that this is really all I need to know. It was in any case a reminder of my temporal mortality, an element of which had been taken away from me, and which upon its return changed things. In another sense, I was no longer living in the past where there was no future, but in a present in which the future is whatever I make of it. All of which was quite straightforward in comparison to what came next. Apparently, as I sat eating lunch between two mountains at the meeting of waters in the summer sun, thinking stuff through in great cascades, I encountered *timelessness* as an actually existing presence viscerally impacting on my life. Touching the void as *elemental presence*. My Western trained mind grappled with the contradictions as I plodded up the hill. Near the top I disturbed a herd of hinds who turned to watch, but who were otherwise unmoved, as gradually the gradient eased and I emerged onto a broad plateau of drying hags and grasses.

I left my pack behind a big stone and walked to the summit of **Chno Dearg** over grassy ground scattered with rocks. I was exhausted by the climb, even though the last few hundred meters were weight free. What a wonderful mountain this is, even more impressive than the last, with views emerging north to **Creag Meagaidh** and east into the remote Laggan Munros beside **Ben Alder**. I returned to my pack then found the way to the next summit, **Stob Coire Sgriodain**. The ground was more complex than appeared from the map, with sections of rocky outcrops, peat hags and a gnarly ridge. I was getting tired now. It was still hot and I had a long way to go. I rested again at the lowest point between the two mountains next to some pools of still water on the very edge of drinkable. After recuperating awhile I found a way through a section of gnarls to the summit, at which point I forced myself to sit down and stop properly for a while. The weight of the experience at lunch was much heavier than I realised at the time and I needed just to sit with it.

This is also a marvellous summit, with clear views over Loch Treig to the *Easains* and Nevis Ranges. The summit is long and rocky but there was a grassy place to sit looking southwest over the loch beside a chaotic pile of broken slabs under the summit, which from this viewpoint was also a chaotic pile of broken slabs. Far below was the line of the railway and the shimmering loch, on the other side the proud *Easains* in front of the Nevis Ranges, resplendent in the summer sun. I hung about for a long time and took many photos of horizons.

The way down is long and in places arduous, over rocky terraces at first towards a grassy gully under some impressive crags to the beginnings of a burn, which eventually enters the forest in a little gully not far away from where a wobbly gate takes the path. Suddenly in the forest the path takes on a completely different character, a long avenue of mature pines with a dense canopy protecting the soft ground beneath from wind and water, where a massive diversity of grasses, mosses, shrubs and small trees flourishes. Shafts of sun illuminated mossy stumps and undergrowth, tiny lochans were sometimes visible through the trunks. The path emerges among cottages at Fersit and follows the road back over a bridge to the car park. It was half past six, a bit less than two hours after leaving the summit of **Stob Coire Sgriodain**.

On the radio as I am driving home, I hear a piece of music called LAD, composed by Julia Wolff, in a transcription for electric guitar by Sean Shibe recorded in Anstruther during the East Neuk Festival. As soon as I get home I seek out a recording of the original, scored for nine pipers. Its layering of sounds, note-bending and joyous dissonances, moving to *piobaireachd* and then to jig mirroring the cascades of my mind at lunch between the mountains, mimicking the resolution of emotional turmoil. Except that the pipers stretch out to ten minutes or so the expression of an experience that took place between moments, in the absolute infinity of emptiness from which consciousness emerges to make stuff solid in what we think of as time.

# Bare Mountains

### 18th July 2017

A few days after I wrote up my ideas about anomalies in Munro's classification in a blogpost about climbing **Bidean nan Bian**, I linked the post during an online discussion about anomalies in Munro's classification at a mountain climbing group on the Facebook. In reaction to this, somebody told me to keep politics out of things and demanded that group admin remove the "offensive" post. I was rather taken aback, for I was not aware that these opinions would be so controversial. Then I was reminded that for those unencumbered by any sense of irony or unfamiliar with *Trainspotting*, the blog's title, *it's shite being Scottish*, was maybe a bit pungent.

I felt compelled to write an extended rebuttal, by way of analysis of the snippet in question and its relation to mountains. I called the post *It's (not) shite being Scottish*. The parenthetical (not) was intended to demonstrate the irony of the tirade from which the phrase is plucked. In the process, I articulated the essence of the message I wanted to convey to the world at my blog. Which is not I suppose terribly surprising. I had not just chosen the title randomly; I have long understood the full significance of these words.

At the time of writing the post in question, the design of the blog displayed prominently the entire tirade uttered by Renton immediately after his exclamation that it's shite being Scottish. It was perhaps this that had caught the attention of the one so offended. It does after all contain two "fuckings" and a few minor expletives, and makes reference to an imperial relationship between England and Scotland. I had simply forgotten that not everybody knew that the title of the blog is a quotation from *Trainspotting*, nor that not everybody would get the irony of using this phrase as the name of a blog about climbing mountains.

It was hot. I had a day off and a burning desire to tick off more mountains from the list. I was still thinking through my experience of two weeks earlier, letting it resonate, for the first time in nearly four years *making plans for the future*, realising what this means, having somewhat unconsciously held in suspension a notion most people take for granted. From my resting point between **Beinn na Lapp** and **Chno Dearg** two weeks earlier I could see down the glen to the round whaleback hump of a mountain, with to the left of it a wee pointy one, respectively **Beinn a' Chlachair** and **Creag Pitridh**. Behind these was another of the **Geal Charns**. All three are accessible via the bridge over the channel between the two bits of Loch Laggan, at the entrance to Strath Ossian and Corrour estates.

Irvine Welsh's *Trainspotting* follows the adventures of a group of friends from Edinburgh as they negotiate the squalor and depravity of heroin addiction and urban deterioration. It is a ground-breaking book at many levels: it confronts directly issues faced by working class youth abandoned by authority and the state; it is predominately written in phonetic transcription rather than correct English, faithfully representing the actual language people use, with extensive use of words that only a few decades earlier were considered so shocking they broke the law; the grammar and punctuation are idiosyncratic; there is no strict narrative but rather a series of tableaux or fragments which combine together to tell the stories of the characters; and, perhaps most importantly, despite the subject matter often being quite harrowing, the book is absolutely hilarious.

It was published in 1993; arguably it inaugurated a shift in Scottish Culture away from a kind of elitism, within which being properly Scottish involved some kind of heroic connection with the landscape (materially, linguistically or symbolically) and towards something more historically relevant, material and demythologised. Certainly it stands as a testament to the troubled times these islands suffered during the transition from the 1980s into the 1990s. It is a book about progression, renewal and hope in the context of a world careering towards the millennium without any clear sense of purpose.

I arrived late with indigestion and a grumpy head at the parking place beside the entrance to the estates. The track towards the mountains crosses the wide river coming out of Strath Ossian and keeps to the east, gradually rising past a plantation and into open moor. There were only three colours visible; green grass and trees, blue water and sky, and scorched white rock. The track was stony and dry. My indigestion settled down as I settled in to achieving my goal for the day, still grumpy. It was getting hotter by the minute and even this gently rising walk-in was already bringing me out in sweats. After I passed the end of a lochan, the ground flattened out in front of the flank of **Beinn a' Chlachair**. Absolutely nothing was happening. A slight wind, but no cloud. Only my walking kept the midges at bay. While passing a flat round bog of cotton grass, I struck south off the track following the line of a burn. About a kilometre further, this petered out into a flat hag, pocked with tussocks and bogwood. At the edge, another burn flowed off in another direction, more substantial, emerging from a gully rising straight up the side of the west shoulder, which I followed all the way up. It was a long sweaty slog. When the ground levelled out at last, I turned left along a round ridge scattered with white rocks, becoming more dense as I approached the summit. Suddenly it was windy; I began to enjoy the cooling off.

*Trainspotting* was made into a film directed by Danny Boyle starring Ewan McGregor as Renton, which manages more than adequately to convey the spirit and humour of Welsh's writing without becoming trite or sensationalist. The phrase *it's shite being Scottish* appears only in the film, at the start of what became, or at least so I thought, a well-known tirade, which is a sanitised version of a much darker passage in the book. It is filmed at a familiar spot for mountain people, just to the northwest of Corrour Station on the path to *Leum Uillem*, a hill that fails only by a few feet to make it into Munro's tables, and is a favourite of Corbett baggers.

At this point in the story, Tommy is not yet using heroin and is keen to get his friends clean; the character will later die horribly from toxoplasmosis because addiction has compromised his immune system, while the actor will become typecast in a hospital drama set in Seattle. He has persuaded three of them, Spud, Renton and Sick Boy, to take a train out of the city to go for a wander in the great outdoors. When he turns from marching purposefully towards the hill to see his companions unenthusiastically nursing hangovers on a flat wooden bridge and taking a hair of the dog, Tommy remonstrates with them for their lethargy, to which Spud responds shivering, "Tommy ... this is not natural man!" Tommy then sweeps his arms around, exclaiming: "it's the great outdoors, it's fresh air!" After some banter from Sick-Boy about Tommy's precarious relationship, he asks almost rhetorically the most crucial and perhaps the most difficult question asked of any Scot: "does it not make you proud to be Scottish?" At which point Renton holds forth.

> *It's shite being Scottish! We're the lowest of the low. The scum of the fucking Earth! The most wretched, miserable, servile, pathetic trash that was ever shat into civilisation. Some hate the English. I don't. They're just wankers. We, on the other hand, are colonised by wankers. Can't even find a decent culture to be colonised by. We're ruled by effete arseholes. It's a shite state of affairs to be in, Tommy, and all the fresh air in the world won't make any fucking difference!*

Tommy then shrugs and walks away from the mountain to join the others as they trudge home.

It is a short, slightly absurd scene that perfectly illustrates Welsh's dark sense of humour and dense irony. The viewer is suddenly transported to the middle of nowhere, without any context or preamble and in complete contrast to everything else that is going on in the narrative. The *great outdoors* is presented as something alien and irrelevant to the lives of characters who are suddenly thrown into it inadequately prepared. Commonplace notions about the benefits to health of being outside, of the challenges of both extreme sport and traditional outdoor recreation are rejected summarily. Representations of Scotland based on this empty land and its beauty are suddenly held in suspension. Any ideas we might hold about national identity that are based on this landscape, or on our ability to eke out an existence from its soil, or to climb to the summits of its spectacular peaks are dashed against the reality of Scottish consciousness.

We are riven by sectarian conflict not of our making, which we allow to continue because it has become normal. We find ourselves at the rough end of an imperialist relation, encouraging us to be servile and pathetic. But it does not matter because we can still get hammered and we will still be mates. This scene is not written in order to advocate this opinion or celebrate anything about this attitude. It is a work of fiction; there is no reason to believe that either Boyle or Welsh believe the words that Renton speaks. They work together in order to display, to document and to reveal. So we are left wondering as viewers why we see only this very short glimpse of the mountains, why Boyle took Welsh's characters to this place to give Renton this epic rant, only to have them all walk away, why they put in this scene at all, if not to expose more of the hypocrisies that intersect Scottish consciousness.

Finding or making a path through boulder fields is never easy. Every step has to be carefully placed as every rock can wobble unpredictably, risking stumbling and injury. Experience teaches well, but everybody can fall over. In this heat the challenges were intensified. I could see somebody near the summit, coloured clothing contrasting starkly with the bleached rocks and wobbling on the haze. The ridges of the high Laggans and **Ben Alder** behind shimmered. The sun shone hard bouncing off slabs and water. By the time I got to the summit the other was long gone. There was nothing much here but piles of hot white stones. Spectacular though the views were, colours were all washed out by the intense light. I clambered on round the summit cone east in search of easier ground, which came eventually at the start of the broad eastern shoulder of the mountain, though the ground remained sporadically stony. At a shallow bealach before the end of the shoulder I could see northeast to the path I wanted to reach and the start of the route up *Geal Charn*. Instead of seeking out the climbers' path down to the south and round the end of the shoulder, I traversed some rather rough ground under outcrops on the northern side of the mountain, which was in shadow now and relatively cool. At the first water, I drank copiously and filled my bottle then trundled off to find a place to rest and look out over the bare landscape. The wind was now quite strong, whipping through the bealach from the south, both cooling and dehydrating.

I did not believe that linking my blog would disturb cyber ethics or offend anybody. The reaction of this one person though illustrated perfectly why sometimes it really is shite being Scottish. It was as I and others at the site had suspected; the reaction was to the header, not to the content of the post about anomalies, describing it as "nationalistic tripe" and demanding that admin remove the link, since this was a site about mountain climbing not politics, emphasising that if I wanted to talk politics I should go to a political site. It was politely pointed out by others that this person had missed the irony, that *"it's shite being Scottish"* is a quotation from *Trainspotting* and that, if anything, the sentiment expressed in the tirade is profoundly *anti-nationalistic*. Anybody familiar with the passage in the book upon which it is based will have little doubt about this:

> [...] *It's nae good blamin it oan the English fir colonising us. Ah don't hate the English. They're just wankers. We are colonised by wankers. We can't even pick a decent, vibrant, healthy culture to be colonised by. No. We're ruled by effete arseholes. What does that make us? The lowest of the fuckin low, tha's what, the scum of the earth. The most wretched, servile, miserable, pathetic trash that was ever shat intae creation. Ah don't hate the English. They just git oan wi the shite thuv goat. Ah hate the Scots.*

I pointed out that the imputation of this sense of *political* as opposed to *apolitical* was itself a political move, which was summarily rejected as sophistry. Somebody so privileged as to be able to fence off politics from ordinary life, to think of politics as only a competition between political parties for power, so sure that this position is good, true, natural and right that any attempt to relativise or challenge it is simply unthinkable. As far as this person was concerned I was introducing politics into matters that are properly not political, thereby sowing division, which is more or less what appeared from where I was sitting what the other had already done by demanding that my post be removed, without ever having read it.

Here then was a perfect example of *the shiteness of being Scottish*; exactly the point of Renton's tirade. It is possible for a person to pick up a mere snippet of any text or film, to denude it of its context, rip out its nuance and irony and take it to mean whatever purpose it can fulfil in some battle against an imaginary evil enemy. We have come to accept this as normal, which means it becomes necessary from time to time to engage with accusations based on absolute fantasy, dreamed up in the warped imagination of British nationalism or some other delusional ideology, and to become sucked into pointless arguments with those who either do not listen, have lost their grip on reality, have forgotten about reason, or have already firmly made up their minds. Events are so often presented and described deliberately to separate and divide that those standing on either side are blissfully unaware of their complicity. Reason and logic are irrelevant to discussion. Discourse takes place for other reasons.

In the wind, clouds began to billow up from nowhere and fizzle out again. From my resting place I crossed the path and struck up the broad shoulder of my second ***Geal Charn***. Nearer the top there were interesting outcrops, but the ground was predominantly grassy intermingled with screes and boulder fields. I was at the summit before three, where I sat for a while admiring the views over Loch Ericht to familiar horizons, looking if I could see any of the other ***Geal Charns***. The big one between here and **Ben Alder** was clearly visible, as was the one behind Loch Ericht, but the last on the edge of the *Monadhliath* was not easy to pick out. I was getting weary now of all this sun and the wind was becoming hard work. I found a route off the summit on the leeward side in the direction of ***Creag Pitridh***. Near the bottom, I found a very good line and just avoided descending too far into the wrong glen by skirting along the top of a steep drop of crags.

At the bealach between ***Creag Pitridh*** and ***Geal Charn*** I briefly contemplated not bothering to go to the summit because I was now becoming very tired and I was still a long way from the car. No amount of nourishing, energy-rich dried fruit spurred me along. Water slaked my thirst but my mouth remained parched. It took me all of ten minutes to reach the summit though, where I took a few photos and chose a route down towards the nearest burn and the path back to the start. It was a long haul through thick grass over rougher ground than appeared to reach a stalker's path which led to the estate tracks again past the end of *Lochan na Earba*. Looking back at the mountains, they appeared now exactly as they had at the start of the day, smooth and featureless, the same green blue and scorched hues, except the shadows were falling more on eastern slopes and I recognised where I had been. I did not get back to the car until nearly seven o'clock. It had been a strange day; despite being stunning, the weather was extremely challenging and the landscape empty, leeched of all colour, almost lifeless, austere and harsh.

Welsh has said that he writes in order to find out about his characters, to see what makes them tick and to understand why they act as they do. I cannot think of a more honest, civilised and humane approach to writing fiction, nor a more compassionate attitude to the multiplicity of consciousness to which human *Being* can become subject. It does not matter if Boyle or Welsh first came up with the exclamation *it's shite being Scottish*, maybe it was Ewan McGregor, it encapsulates Scottishness completely and it has served me well. But it is ironic! I regret the necessity of the parenthetical (not) in the title, just because somebody missed the point. It's shite being Scottish? Spoken by an angry junkie going through cold turkey, dragged unwillingly and inadequately prepared to the margins of an imaginary wilderness, and who has not the faintest idea where he is? Aye. Right enough.

Not everybody realises that some of us understand the irony of our condition, that when we climb mountains we already know that we are only able to do so because they are denatured; denuded of their natural covering of forest to make way for sporting estates, to which we are granted only restricted access. It is Spud who speaks the truth here from the bottom of his bottle, for this landscape really is not natural. Not everybody sees this condition as the direct consequence of political decisions made by those in the past who called themselves master, and those in the present who have taken on the responsibility of government and authority. And because some realise this and others do not, our culture remains riven.

I make no secret of my support for Scottish autonomy nor for radical land reform. I am also a civilised human being and I believe that it is not only possible but also absolutely necessary to discuss anything with anybody without personal allegiances or the defence of identities getting in the way, which is as far as I am concerned the very essence of reason. I refuse to engage in sectarian argument and when confronted by accusations from people who should know better, I try to explain errors and demonstrate using example and argument. Which is precisely why it is shite being Scottish, for people do not on the whole respond to reason, but are trapped inside disputes and conflicts not of their own making, without realising this to be the case. Renton's tirade expresses this condition perfectly, while its setting in the so called "great outdoors" points to the inescapable fact that there are vast tracts of empty land out there, bare mountains available to all, waiting for anybody with a mind to do so, to discover that on the contrary, it is not at all shite being Scottish, that actually it's fucking awesome!

## Exposure

### 25th July 2017

People used to tell me they would be frightened, alone in the mountains, particularly when camping out. My usual response was that there is nothing to fear except axe wielding maniacs. Sometimes I also had to ask when the last time was they had heard of an axe wielding maniac running amok in the Scottish Highlands.

There are nevertheless often very good reasons for fear in the mountains. Circumstances can arise when a body is pumped up suddenly with the rush of adrenaline, when its heart beats faster, its breathing becomes more insistent, and its muscles tense up, poised for immediate action. When a foothold becomes suddenly less stable than first seemed, when clouds billow up from nowhere to obscure all sight and confuse navigation, when a route turns out to be much more complicated and scrambly than anticipated, rocks and grass can be slippery, many minor events can result in the natural reflex called fear. And all of these are overcome in subsequent moments, as circumstances change and the body in question moves on. Fear is at this level a natural and useful bodily response.

It is not however the same as the many fears that fester in an imagination and that have nothing to do with immediate circumstances or with any actual danger. These are the most complex and difficult emotions to understand and overcome. For they are built up over many years, from the first moments of experience, using resources available in the body politic; ideas, stories, rituals, habits of conduct, morals, images, linguistic forms and so forth, grounded on long forgotten infant experiences, the expectations of others and significant events. Of course the physiologic responses and bodily changes are much the same, but these are triggered not by immediate conditions, but by an idea or a memory or some other notion of the mind.

As we came down from ***Bidean nam Bian*** the previous month, my new mountain buddy Martyn suggested that one day he guide me along the *Aonach Eagach* on the other side of the glen, which he had traversed several times before and wanted to revisit. This ridge has a reputation that precedes it. It is regarded by some as the trickiest exposed ridge scramble on the Scottish mainland, although it is said by others to be quite straightforward in comparison to one or two Welsh and English ridges. When viewed from below, from within the cavernous basin of Glen Coe, traversing the *Aonach Eagach* would appear to involve negotiating a mess of crags and narrow ridges, with sheer descents into dark clefts between protruding pinnacles and columns, with no obvious route down from the top, if ever it became necessary to find one. One of the major reasons for fatal accidents here is people trying to find a way off. Although both Munros along its length are accessible easily from behind, the best way of experiencing them is to traverse the ridge between. Guidebooks warn of exposed scrambling and technically difficult sections that need to be taken seriously. Mention is made of ropes.

Anybody engaged in the obsessive project of bagging Munros is always several steps ahead in the planning, and I had been aware of this ridge for some time, knowing that I could always bag the two Munros it connects together independently from different starting points. More recently, I had been steeling myself, beginning to think that maybe I should give it a go. So when I got a message from Martyn suggesting a trip to the *Aonach Eagach* the following week, I did not immediately reject the idea, and knew, in fact, from the moment that I thought about doing it, seriously, without giving any influence to fears that might arise on the basis of its reputation, without being scared off by my imagination, that I would be there. Having clambered together up the Lost Valley to *Bealach Dearg* and then along the high ridges of **Bidean** before descending into the corrie in front of *Stob Coire nan Lochan*, I felt confident that he could be trusted when he told me that I would be fine. He also said he would bring a rope.

After an evening reading walk reports and watching YouTube videos of *Aonach Eagach* traverses, I decided I should stop because it was terrifying me. For the days before the trip, I was niggled by a fear of terrible accidents, but confident that there would be nothing to worry about. After all, in spite of a few fatalities, many thousands of others have made the traverse without incident or mishap.

It was a glorious day to be in the mountains. Which meant that it was busy. As we walked up the path from the car park towards *Am Bodach*, many others could be seen up ahead. At the summit and starting point, dubbed by the mighty Muriel Gray, Brown Pants Hill, I could see what I was about to experience and knew immediately what Muriel meant. From this distance the ridges to the two Munro summits appear as sharp edged and smooth with very visible paths perched along the crests and precipitous drops on either side. The first difficulty is a steep diagonal descent of about thirty metres over stable rock with lots of foot and hand holds, but with a great deal of air beneath, onto a narrow path on a sharp grassy ridge. Martyn said that this is considered to be the most technically difficult section. He went on before me to make sure my feet were well placed. At the first proper ascent, up an enclosed gully, he suggested I go on ahead. At the top he gave me some advice: *always try to remain upright; climb first with your head, then your legs and then your arms; always know where a hand or foot is going to land before you move it; never have more than one hand or foot on the move at any one time.*

After that it was just practice. The route is very easy to follow, over shiny rocks, scarred with crampons and where there is earth, along deep rutted paths. On the way there is only one place to stop for a breather, the summit of the first Munro, **Meall Dearg**. From here there are excellent views of the Mamores and Nevis ranges on one side and the enormous bulk of ***Bidean nam Bian*** on the other, and along the rest of the ridge over Ballachulish to Sunart, Knoydart and Mull. There were moments along the next section where I was briefly consumed by the screaming habdabs, particularly atop a section known as The Crazy Pinnacles, but I discovered quickly that as long as I kept moving and remained mindful at every moment of where my limbs were clinging to the rocks, there was no fear at all. After a while it was just like any other day out in the hills in good company. We chatted about stuff, admired the views, which are absolutely spectacular in all directions, and passed the time of day with the many others we met. Although it seemed that most were travelling east to west as were we, a few others came from the west, sometimes creating blockages where courteous relations became strained. Though on the whole there was a spirit of camaraderie among those we encountered.

Just as I thought it was all over, I experienced a brief wobble during a descent into a dark narrow cleft where there was a queue of folks clinging to a ledge, waiting to stand on a narrow column projecting out of the void between two massive pinnacles, from which the route continued again, up a steep gully out onto the ridge. There was a party using the gully to practice roping together. We waited patiently above a long drop onto a nasty looking scree slope merging into cliffs and terraces hanging above the busy road through the glen. The queue lengthened behind us. By now I was quite accustomed to standing on my very own column of basalt, about the diameter of an oil drum but well over fifty feet tall. It was unnerving but there was nothing to fear. The air was not sucking me down. With the previous two hour's experience behind me, the ascent of the gully presented no problems, and all fear dispersed as I scrambled up and out into safety and the approaches to the second Munro, ***Sgorr nam Fiannaidh***.

Looking back along the ridge, now having traversed its pinnacles I could see its serrations more clearly, that it is not smooth at all, and I understood why it is considered to be such a tough challenge. It is a sustained and intense scramble that requires commitment, attention and care at every step, it involves sometimes walking along a crest of rocks less than a metre wide with a sheer drop on either side and sometimes climbing up and down rock faces with much air beneath. But the rock is stable, the route is obvious and it is nowhere near as scary being up there negotiating the pinnacles as it is sitting at home dreaming up disasters, anticipating accidents and imagining the worst.

Quite near the start of the route, before the summit of ***Meall Dearg***, there is a projecting spur known as The Chancellor, to which there is a path down from the main ridge. Just looking at that path as I passed it by was enough to make me silently weep in terror. Martyn had shown me a photo of his daughter standing there happily waving back at her dad. He suggested as we passed by the access path that I too pop off for a portrait. I declined politely, but now rather regretted it. Looking back along the ridge at the end of the route, I became aware that actually walking upright along the top of the crazy pinnacles with thousands of feet of nothing on either side and climbing up and down steep rock faces did not at the time fill me with terror at all, just momentary flashes of fear that dispersed as if on the wind. Only now, reflecting back and remembering, could I discern any residue of the fear I once experienced in anticipation of the journey.

Martyn assured me we would not be descending the extremely hazardous Clachaig Chute, nor continuing to the Pap, but instead taking a more sensible and direct route, sliding through scree to the floor of the glen and then walking back to the car. Despite recognising that this would be a great deal quicker than anything else, I was a tad alarmed as the mass of stones moved around me and its surface fluctuated between solid and something else. Once was I caught up by a large stone that I had already dislodged or had been dislodged by another I had dislodged, to be clattered painfully on the shin. I almost cursed Martyn for this rather reckless method of descent, but I got into the flow, developed a technique for avoiding being clattered on the shin by previously dislodged bits of scree, and began to see him as seriously hardcore.

I always knew that fear is largely imaginary, but I was not always very good at not giving in to it, at preventing fear from motivating my conduct, colouring my judgement and obscuring the reality of what lay before me. My experience on **Seanna Bhraigh** had perhaps been exorcised by walking the *Aonach Eagach*, left me with a sense of achievement, a great feeling of satisfaction that enabled me more easily to contemplate Torridon or even The Skye Munros.

And with this, an unfamiliar sense of disappointment, that if this is the toughest Munro scramble on the mainland, then I have nothing to achieve here now. Which of course would be to take far too narrow a view of achievement. For every journey into the mountains offers lessons. Walking the *Aonach Eagach* did indeed relieve me of a burden, showed me how easy it is to be terrified by absolutely nothing.

I was in touch now with a kind of clarity, more able to disconnect fear from all thoughts or emotions about what lies ahead, be it in the next moment or the unknown void faced by us all, more willing to trust that whatever lies along the path, no matter how dangerous it appears from a distance, no matter how exposed, it is well trodden and there is no need to be afraid.

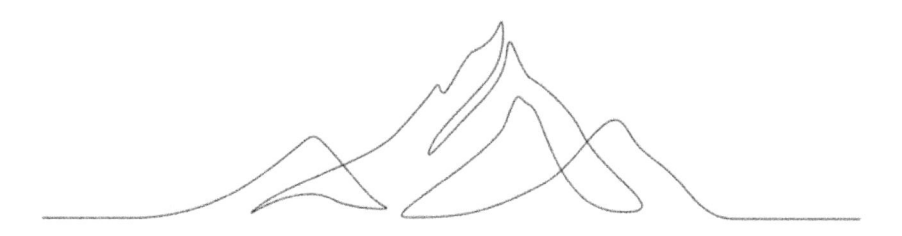

## *A tale of midges and tourists*

13th August 2017

I should have known from recent visits to Glen Coe that twelve-thirty in the afternoon of the busiest Sunday in August would not be the best time to find somewhere to park before climbing **Buachaille Etive Beag**. Apart from numerous already parked mountain people's vehicles, there were as many hordes of gormless tourists consuming the scenery and striking poses with selfie sticks as midges trying to suck their blood; vehicles of all shapes and sizes came and went with no regard for anything but finding an immediate place to pull in; parking was random and chaotic, traffic was dangerous, lives were put at risk, humanity's more antisocial, narcissistic and venal traits were displayed for all to see. Or at least, so it appeared.

I had been planning a walk up **Buachaille Etive Beag** in Glen Coe with Shona on the way home from our holiday on Barra and the Uists in her campervan. There is a nice gentle walk into a relatively easy ascent, after which she could either attempt the climb or more probably walk on up the glen a bit and meet me again on the way back down. I thought it would be a nice way of finishing off our holiday. But it was not to be.

The previous morning we awoke at Skeabost Bridge on Skye after arriving on the last ferry from Lochmaddy and parking up in the pitch dark, surprised to have found a deserted section of no longer in use public road, the sort of place that is usually snapped up by travellers. On the Outer Isles, midges are a minor irritation that is attenuated by sea air and wind. Not on Skye. After a quick recce of the environs, which included an ancient ruined chapel on an island on the river, we decided to get moving as quickly as possible. We had not reckoned on the true extent of the massive influx of visitors the island endures at this time of year. Never have I seen so much vehicular stupidity within such a short period, an extreme contrast to the courtesy and care on display on the Outer Isles. The strain placed on the island's infrastructures was also palpable. We stopped for breakfast in Broadford and heard horror stories of people sleeping in bus shelters, blocked public toilets, piles of litter and human excrement, and of shops and garages running out of supplies. Back on the mainland, the chaos seemed only to intensify. We had great difficulty finding somewhere for the night among the huge flocks of other travellers searching for a roost in Lochaber, but eventually took advantage of the last available pitch at a very nice, albeit pricey, campsite in Glen Coe village.

I might have hoped that this experience would have prepared me for the traffic in Glen Coe. As I drove into the mess of vehicles in search of somewhere to park, I could feel my hackles rising. Then somebody nipped in before me to a space for which I was obviously aiming and I simply could not deal with the behaviour of the other drivers any more, nor could Shona trust that her van would remain safe in our absence, so we decided on the spur of the moment that I climb the Munros behind the Glen Coe Ski Centre and she take a stroll along the West Highland Way and back. As I attempted to re-join the road, a car parked directly in front of me and its occupants got out to take photos and offer their blood to the midges, without the least regard for my indicated intentions. I experienced a brief moment of real rage, winding down the window and telling them in no uncertain terms to move their vehicle now, or else. Happily, the car park at the Ski Centre is huge and is used on the whole by mountain people parking their vehicles sensibly, rather than for tourists to stop briefly to gawp at themselves with the big shepherd in the background.

It is a short sharp slog underneath ski lifts up to the big corrie basin where the skiing happens and another up the crag behind it. I reached the summit of **Meall a Bhùiridh** in less than an hour and a half, in spite of being caught in a very nasty squall on the way up; though I found shelter awhile behind one of the ski buildings, it was cold lumpy rain carried by a fierce wind that suggested a return to the van for a nice cup of tea. I persevered after the deluge had passed, following the same line taken by the ski-tow. At the summit, the clouds had passed and the views were spectacular.

I met some people who had experienced the squall at the top of **Creise**. They were not happy. I looked over at the high exposed ridge of the mountain and felt their not happiness. I imagined why being caught up there in a squall at any time of year would be challenging. It is long and flat with absolutely nothing protruding. At least at the top of pointy craggy mountains, there are slabs and rocky outcrops that afford a degree of shelter, whatever the wind direction.

The traverse to **Creise** appears large and imposing, with a bit of a scramble at the end, and for a moment I thought about saving it for another day. Only for a moment though. As I approached the summit I met a large party of no longer quite in the first flush of youth Bearsden and Milngavie Ramblers who had just gathered themselves together to enjoy lunch. I suggested that this was a notch above rambling, not that I have anything against rambling of course, in response to which I was regaled with tales of a previous outing to *Stob a'Choin* at Balquhidder, in comparison to which this was a doddle.

There is a steep though easy scramble to the summit ridge of **Creise** after which it is featureless, exposed and only forty meters ascent to the summit, about half a mile to the north. I got to the summit and understood why there is only one way down from here, exactly the same as the way up, for not only is it razor sharp, the flanks steepen into invisible depths on all sides except back along the ridge. There is a much-admired traverse from here to **Stob Ghabhar** in the Black Mount along a couple of lesser summits, which looks like the sort of thing I would want to do were I not fanatically bagging Munros, but apart from that, the only way off is back along the arete to **Meall a Bhùiridh**.

I decided to take lunch out of earshot of the weegie banter of the Bearsden and Milngavie ramblers. Later, on the arête I overtook them, and then some caught up with me again at the summit. They had been here during the squall and were happy to linger on the way back while I took a leisurely route to the van, firstly along the northwest shoulder of the mountain where I encountered a notice for skiers; attached to a pole was a little symbolic skier in a red circle with a slanting red diagonal on top. No skiing. On the other side of the sign was another of those slopes that steepens into precipitous invisibility, opposite the similarly precipitous flanks of **Creise**. In the bowl of the corrie I met a group of Bearsden and Milngavie Ramblers who had become quite exercised by several of their number having been seen taking the chairlift from here down the final section to the car park. They would be making sure that Club records would not register those who had taken the chairlift as having *climbed* these two Munros. Hardcore, I thought, in full agreement.

The path down from here is steep and hard after such a long afternoon of exposure. I could not remember it at all from the way up. Evidently I was in a hurry to get away from the chaos of tourism and find space to articulate a reaction. Just as the van came into clear view, the midges kicked in again, after which I yomped down much faster than was good for me and arrived sweating for a very nice cup of tea that was waiting for me. I had though brought far too many midges in with me so we had to leave quickly and create moving air around us that would keep them off. We witnessed the usual hilarious displays from many others similarly inconvenienced by the incessant presence of these miniscule monsters. One car reversed in great circles with both doors wide open, skidded smartly to a stop and drove off as the doors slammed shut before any midge could re-enter. Quite an impressive tactic. Pod dwellers and campers alike went about their chores and ablutions as best they could. Many midge nets were in use. We drove off to find somewhere to eat, which eventually we found at Victoria Bridge where again the midge level was so intense we stayed only long enough to eat before moving on. We had stuff to do the next day and really had to get home, even though we were still on holiday in our heads.

The peace, tranquillity and sheer unadulterated beauty of the Outer Isles are special. They operate at a different pace from the rest of the country. Their weather is more extreme and intense, the people more resilient, mindful and gentle. The colours of the planet are staggeringly beautiful here. And there are fewer midges. Perhaps the price of passage on *Calmac's* splendid services, even with generous state subsidy, is too much for travellers already forking out a small fortune. Perhaps the facilities are too basic, the centres of population too sparse, the roads too narrow. Whatever it is that prevents the chaos of mainland tourism from infecting the Outer Isles, long may it continue.

The frustrations of returning from this holiday paradise to the realities of the mainland disappeared on the top of the mountain, as I realised that everything had turned out for the best. In spite of coming off the last ferry at Uig in the gloaming, we found a nice secluded spot to park up. In spite of much toing and froing in Lochaber, we found a well-appointed campsite. In spite of chaos in Glen Coe that made it impossible to park where we planned, we were able quickly to make a new plan to park at the ski centre. Shona enjoyed a lovely walk along a bit of the West Highland Way and had a chance to reflect on her own journey. I got to climb another two more of the top fifty, to escape the tourists, to meet with some lovely mountain people and to learn a little more about my reactions: everything turned out for the best after all, there was no need for any of that irritation, rage or annoyance.

Except that this is not only a personal matter. Of course, it is my responsibility to conduct myself with good sense and decorum and to be aware of how my emotional reactions might be inappropriate, unnecessary or insensitive. But these feelings have causes. They arise in specific real-life situations, they are visceral, not inventions of my mind.

Great efforts are being made to encourage people to visit this country. *Visit Scotland* is an umbrella organisation that promotes Scottish tourism. It has a website where the usual gaudy display of shortbread tin Scottishness is wrapped up in anodyne stories about Scottish history, ecology, society and culture, devoid of any political context, all of which omit any mention of the violence, struggle and hardship experienced to this day by many hundreds of thousands of Scots. There is not a lot about midges either. It is little more than an advertising billboard for Scotland PLC and its many subsidiaries, employing the scenery of the land to purvey everything a wealthy visitor might require. A cursory examination is enough to conclude that tourists are expected to consume good food, stay in exclusive accommodation, to enjoy the sunshine on unspoiled beaches, to gaze in wonder at the marvels of nature, to be actively engaged in some outdoor activity that requires (the hiring of) special equipment, and to visit castles, beauty spots and museums. Scotland is here commodity.

The relative value of Sterling against the Euro at the time made it cheaper for Continentals to come here and for Brits to stay at home. The BBC had been allegedly promoting the country, or at least, displaying it favourably, with documentaries and travelogues. The popularity of a certain phantasy historical drama series no doubt also contributed to the increasing numbers of visitors. Under which circumstances, the suspicion must arise that only the purveyors of tourist services are profiting from this overcrowding of public space; no conspicuous effort was being made either specifically to improve the toilet facilities on Skye or the car parking spaces in Glen Coe, or more generally to ensure that infrastructures are fit for purpose, able to cope with the large numbers of people who come here to spend their money.

Predominant ideologies of neoliberalism have us believe that business is good for everybody, that if wealthy people are allowed to become more wealthy, then their wealth will trickle down to the rest of us, that there is no need for complex social planning, or long-term, joined-up thinking, and that the operations of the market, the pursuit of personal profit, will ensure a stable and happy society. This makes about as much sense as giving a dog three sausages to share with his two dog friends, or expecting the motivations of the most venal, rapacious and self-serving individuals in society to ensure the welfare of everybody in society, or believing that midges will stop sucking blood.

## High Laggans

1st – 3rd September 2017

I have been advised not to stuff too much philosophy into these pages. I am also mindful of the advice of my father's old friend in Manhattan, that nobody is interested in abstract concepts hanging on a line, no matter how immaculately arranged or carefully described. Nevertheless, it is necessary at this point to present a potted history of Western ideas that is pertinent to my own story, in particular to my encounter with Buddhism.

For some time I had been preparing for a return to the Holy Isle, where I had signed up for a week's meditation retreat led by His Holiness Lama Yeshe Rinpoche. Although I did not know quite what to expect, I had a very strong feeling that I must attend. Intellectually, I felt as prepared for the challenges of immersing myself more deeply into Buddhist practice as I would ever be and emotionally, I was confident that I would be able to handle every difficult idea that came across my path. I had attended many teachings and learned a great deal, some of which was familiar from my reading of Western philosophy, though expressed in an unfamiliar idiom. Like many others I had notebooks full of scribbled words, evidence of making sense of what I was being taught with my Western educated mind, writing to which I could refer back as a reminder. I was also sure from my experiences in the mountains, that I was developing *practical understanding* of many Buddhist ideas, like *void*, *impermanence*, *attachment*, *karma* and so forth, perhaps these are like Nan Shepherd's *elementals*. I do not know, but I aspired to a different way of thinking, unencumbered by any desire for there to be an *external world* in relation to which I am a separate, independently existing thing in command of a will to act upon and change it.

In the meantime, Chris had moved to civilisation, or at least Falkirk, and he was settling in nicely, raring to get out for a weekend in the hills. Chris is ex-military, a former outward bounds instructor, self-contained, self-disciplined and hardcore, which makes him an excellent companion for any expedition. The next cluster on my expedition list was what I call the *High Laggans*, four of the most isolated Munros within easy driving distance of the central belt and the most southerly of the ridges sandwiched between **Ben Alder** and the Laggan corridor. This would be our first expedition together after at least two years trying to arrange something, so we were looking forward to it. The weather forecast was good; the start of the softening shades and lowering sun of autumn, first frosts and colder winds.

There is always vigorous discussion about which Munros are the most remote. There are many fine candidates, a few of which I had visited, always like this as the high point of an expedition with tent. Although access to these four is within easy driving distance of major centres of population, it would be a very long day bagging them all at once. Even cycling, either from the Falls of Pattack or the railway station at Dalwhinnie, as far as Culra Bothy before the eight- or nine-hour round trip along the ridge and back over the bealach between the High Laggans and **Ben Alder**, would cut maybe three hours from the total, but it would still make for a very long day, rushed, and to my mind, disrespectful of the wonderful remoteness of the place. The bothy is now closed, but there is some very handy grassland in the flat bowl round Loch Pattack.

Chris and I both know that being Buddhist is not like signing a pledge or going to a place of worship with faithful believers at the same time every week. It is not a religion and neither really is it a way of life, nor even a philosophy, although this comes quite close; perhaps it is no more or less than a commitment to be mindful and compassionate in all conduct towards all sentient beings. The *teachings* of Tibetan Buddhism are more concrete; these are contemplations, commentaries and interpretations of the basic ethical commitment; translations into specific contexts, during particular periods of history, by successive generations of Lamas, Tulkus, Karmapas and Rinpoches and recorded for posterity. Such continuous reiteration of the basic ideas for every coming age could indeed be a variety of philosophy, but these *teachings* are not the essence of Buddhism, which remains always practically focused on compassionate conduct towards all beings.

In a certain respect, these Buddhist teachings came into existence according to a process similar to what happened during a similar timescale in the west. Important men thought about stuff, meditated, discussed it and recorded this in texts, which the next generation of important men scrutinised and thought about and wrote some more, continuously overwriting, interpreting and translating to become what we call *history*. It might be possible to make an analogous distinction between the *essence of philosophy*, the practice of thinking things through or reflecting upon existence, and the *teachings of philosophy*, the corpus of literature that has survived the vicissitudes of history to be classified in libraries as Philosophy. Although this might have a superficial appeal and certainly clarifies two meanings of the word *philosophy*, the history of Western philosophy is a great deal more complicated.

Western philosophy likes to believe that it is speaking with a neutral or general voice, that it can express truths independent of who is doing the expressing. From its very inception however, the history of Western philosophy is a story of male voices, the loudest and most powerful of the voices of men clamouring for attention, trying to convince each other that their opinions are most important, according to whatever abstract criteria of importance are fashionable at the time. Philosophy is the most essential form taken by the fittest, most persuasive of the stories men tell each other as they occupy positions of authority within society, which has always been dependent on the labour of others, in particular that of women and slaves, the perspectives and opinions of whom are excluded from the stories men tell. From her readings of the early Greek philosophers, Luce Irigaray has demonstrated persuasively that the first wisdom that these first male philosophers discover, the first power or mystery about which they felt the need to speculate and over which their discourses will henceforth roam, is always cast in the feminine, some kind of Goddess or female power of Nature. However, as Irigaray demonstrates with great precision, in the course of its use, the Goddess is always neutralised, neutered, generalised by the masculine voice, leaving a lacuna or lack at the very centre of humanity's first speculations about itself, where it lives, what it does, why it is here at all and how the stuff of the world hangs together. An absence that points to a fundamental error at the heart of what has come to be understood as *Western thinking in general*, and also now to a vibrant presence which will animate new ways of making sense, properly, with due respect for the reality of the *Goddess*, of the precious gift of life she brings.

When first I read the teachings of philosophy, I did not know about the systematic suppression of women's voices throughout history and the exclusion of slave experience. Despite being brought up by enlightened parents who did their very best to ensure that I learned never to regard men and women as anything but equals, I became a teenager during the 1970s in Scotland and unavoidably soaked up something of the misogyny, violence and prejudice of the times, learning to react from a position of aspiring male entitlement. It was not until the turn into the 1980s that I became aware of any formal feminist analysis or critique.

When I encountered academic feminism for the first time in an undergraduate Sociology course, I quickly accepted the general premise *without reserve*, on the fairly obvious grounds that it was surely correct that any putatively general understanding based only on a particular viewpoint cannot claim any universality, and any that specifically *excludes* other perspectives is certainly not neutral. This was what had happened to female voices and experience under the hegemony of male power. Hereafter, my mental life was never innocent or naïve; I was aware that existence is always *sexuate*, as much later I encountered Irigaray calling it, or *gendered* in more regular parlance, that my voice emerges from a (reluctantly socialised) male body, which I would have to learn to regulate, to bring under the control of an enlightened mind. This was not always obvious to others and no doubt I often failed. Often, too, I encountered conflict and misunderstanding when discussing matters of gender and sexuality, but I remained true to my parents' sense of what is right and wrong, taking my father's polite gentlemanliness as an example of good conduct and my mother's fierce intelligence as an example of intellectual rigour; apart from structural and functional differences between male and female human bodies, differences between what we call *men* and *women* are artificial, dependent on prevailing historical circumstances, just like everything else, which have always put women in subordinate positions and marginalised their experience. My parents were both historians, both the first in their families to go to university, absolutely committed to principles of intellectual integrity and rigour.

I became aware too that writing itself was always the preserve of men. For centuries only nuns in convents or women in positions of great power were able to write about ideas, even after the invention of the printing press and the decline in monastic hand copying, which had hitherto been the only way to preserve writing. From about the eighteenth century and the European Enlightenment, the expansion of society and the beginnings of science, women begin to appear in writing as writers, sometimes disguised as men in order to avoid the usual exclusions and prejudice. Only from the end of World War Two, has feminism been gaining acceptance as a valid intellectual pursuit, though even then in some places only reluctantly and in some places still, not at all. It is only in the last decades, with an expansion of the universities that women have been accorded an intellectual status more on par with men, women's voices and experiences heard more generally while women occupy an increasing number of senior academic positions.

This is not of course the end of the story, for the world of the mind is still intricately entwined with the same systems of male power that have been dominant for two and a half millennia, reproducing the same fallacies and delusions that arise in any exercise of exclusion or vilification. Meanwhile women, whether they call themselves philosophers or not, continue to experience the sharp end of toxic masculinity, which has become adept at finding ways of disguising itself, sometimes even within feminism itself.

The four mountains between **Ben Alder** and *Beinn a' Chlachair* had been on my radar for a very long time. Three of them are above eleven hundred meters, members of the top fifty and always in my sights. On my first expedition after returning from The Netherlands, I surveyed these four from the grassy plateau of **Ben Alder** as I marvelled at what I could achieve despite the disease. During previous months I had been climbing the peaks to the west and north and I had seen them now from many directions. I knew too from journeys through here in my youth about the extensive campgrounds at Pattack.

We walked away from Dalwhinnie at seven-thirty on Friday evening in a cloud of midges along the well-maintained estate track, passing first through an impressively improved gatehouse. It is a pleasant undulating walk through mature plantation skirting above the enormity of Loch Ericht. After about six miles, just before the entrance to the lodge, the track veers right and up to flat grassland where water coming off the mountains gathers into the shallows of Loch Pattack before flowing north and feeding into the east end of Loch Laggan. By now, twilight was in full swing and rapidly turning into night. As we left the track to follow the footpath over flat grassland towards Culra, the last light had gone from the horizon. Three hours after we left Dalwhinnie, we thought it best to stop because we could see nothing beyond torch beams. A sudden breeze blew away the midges as we pitched our tents on top of luscious grass and moss. We chewed the fat awhile, made a plan for the next day then settled in for the night.

The history of Western ideas tells that the earliest Greek thinkers, most famously Heraclitus, emphasised that *change was the essence of things*. Parmenides responded that the truth must surely be unchanging, which meant that only appearance could be impermanent and that there must be a realm of permanent reality beyond. This *metaphysical dualism* , the difference between the *real* and the *apparent*, was formalised by Plato and further developed by Aristotle into the origins of Western philosophy, science and consciousness. In the process of which prioritising solidity, permanence and repetition, separating nature from reason and producing an *external world* full of objects and beings acting upon each other according to recognisable principles. All philosophy hereafter is arguments about how best to reveal the reality behind the appearance of things and becomes, as Whitehead famously remarked, footnotes to Plato. Less well-known, though nonetheless germane is Nietzsche's observation that this *apparent* world is the only one, that the real world has been *lyingly added*.

From the end of the classical period until the beginning of the modern, all philosophy, scholarship and learning was tied to the dogma of Christianity, which was regulated by the Church under the authority of the Pope in Rome. The origins of modernism, which extend into the depths of antiquity with the metaphysical dualism of Parmenides, are made explicit with Descartes, who was able to found a philosophy that would not threaten the power of the Church and could come to conclusions without interfering with God. Descartes achieved this by adding another dualism to the Parmenidean pile: between the material level of matter which moves about according to mathematical principles; and the mental level of mind, all morality, consciousness and relations with God. Despite being almost immediately subject to the most rigorous of philosophical rebuttals by Spinoza, the Cartesian philosophy became probably the most important element of the modern period. And it settled in nicely beside Locke's notion of *improvement*, according to which supplying labour to the material stuff of the world adds value to it. This provided both motivation and intellectual justification for the agricultural and industrial revolutions and contributed to establishing the ideas of future political economy.

There follows what is usually called the Enlightenment, during which modern ideas of individual freedom, reason and ethical conduct are developed to their conclusions. This leads into an unprecedented period of political upheaval, imperial plunder, capital expansion and industrialisation. Darwin, Marx, Nietzsche and Freud introduce respectively *evolution, history, power* and *the unconscious* into the conceptual mix, making it possible to overturn or question much ancient dogma and established thinking. At about the same time, science begins to separate from philosophy, believing it can survive on its own, without any philosophical baggage, working for a living in universities and throughout increasingly tightly administered societies. Moving into the twentieth century, humanity encounters one of its most violent periods: industrialised warfare becomes a thing, atomic weapons are used in anger and concentration camps happen. Science becomes almost entirely instrumental, mixed up in the business of running society, producing stuff for the market, persuading consumers that the stuff being produced is exactly what they want, and so forth.

With the possible exception of Phenomenology, which makes stalwart efforts with its method of *phenomenological reduction*, to keep alive the dream of discovering places of pure knowledge, unadulterated by history or psychology, philosophy does not quite know what to say until the 1960s when it overflows into real life with the explosion of ideas that became known somewhat erroneously and often pejoratively as *Postmodernism*. Throughout the previous two and half millennia, there were a few iconoclasts, notably Hume and Spinoza, who offered treatises that did not fit well with the Platonic tradition, but these were usually regarded as heretical. The philosophy of the 1960s began to change this; to unpick these alleged heresies, to expose and make explicit deeply ingrained relationships between power, reason, truth and the written word that had become so habitual to the modern mind that they were now invisible.

We were awake at six and discovered where we had camped. It was cold and clear, blue sky with pastel tinges at the edges and wispy mist wafting in the morning air. I was facing Loch Pattack and the low hills to Speyside. We left at eight, fully breakfasted and packed for the day ahead. We walked past Culra bothy and up a steep slope beside a small dormant wind turbine. For a while another walked with us. Views opened out to **Ben Alder**, to the great lump of ***Geal-Chàrn*** to the west and into the reaches of Speyside to the east. We reached the summit of ***Carn Dearg*** in less than two hours, puffed out and exhilarated.

The mountains had not yet decided what to do with the air swirling among them but we were hopeful. Mists formed in the glens, cloud blew past, partially obscuring the plateau of ***Geal-Chàrn***, skimming the top of Lancet Edge, a much-admired ridge climb from glen to plateau that we might have taken had we not decided first to climb ***Carn Dearg***. The sun continued to shine strong through gaps in the cloud. The wind was cold and penetrating. It was a fine gradual walk off the summit over easy ground and then a straightforward scramble from the bealach, which although exposed in places presented no problems. As we emerged onto the massive plateau of ***Geal-Chàrn***, the mists dispersed at last and the cloud base rose, revealing the enormity of this place, which is almost as expansive as **Ben Alder**'s, similarly grassy and scattered with piles of stones. We reached the summit about eleven thirty.

The philosophy of the 1960s was in many ways a warning. Having documented the history of their intimate relations, it foretold a future where *power* is disconnected from *reason* and writing becomes less the glue that holds these together and more another creative tool in the expression and expansion of ideas. It pointed out to those who were paying attention that within itself reason is always riven, and that it is legitimate only insofar as we agree that it be so, that its power is not some God-given or natural right, but an expression of what we agree to call reasonable. A reminder that all hallowed values and deeply held metaphysical assumptions are woven into languages and culture, failing always to find a place beyond history, at a distance from the grubby vicissitudes of ordinary life, never quite able to inhabit any plane of universality where the same rules apply in all contexts. Although the contrary was screeched above the discursive babble, *none of this made philosophy impossible*; in fact it made philosophy much more expansive and interesting, offering thought a degree of latitude that had hitherto been ruled out by ancient Greek logic and incoherent abstractions about truth, held together for two and a half thousand years by the politics of writing, by who owns the power to wield a pen and who controls the printing press.

The philosophy of the 1960s had no more or less effect on the circumstances of the 1960s than any other philosophy on the circumstances in which it finds itself, and very quickly became incorporated into a facile pedagogic distinction between *Anglo-Saxon* and *Continental* traditions and perspectives, by which old ideas about truth could be taught to a new generation of enthusiastic young minds at the same time as being able to continue asserting their superiority. The warning was in any event certainly not heard beyond the cloisters of a handful of academic institutions, departments and staff, until it was far too late; even if it had been, it could never have been converted into any force sufficient to obviate or prevent what we are witnessing sixty years later, to wit, the complete and utter breakdown of all standards of rational integrity and reasonable conduct in public life, the emergence of post-truth politics, alternative facts and epistemological narcissism, the society of spectacles, tawdry infotainment and unsustainable overconsumption.

Perhaps though, it was less warning than self-fulfilling prophecy. Here was a reminder that, as Spinoza had already pointed out in the seventeenth century, philosophy is *always* political, and Hume in the eighteenth, *always* historical. There spawned now a great diversity of critical movements and ways of expressing new ideas, most of which took form beyond the limits of what was once thought of as philosophy, in the arts, literature, film, television, drama, cabaret, performance and high culture, and which circumvented and/or challenged the standards of truth and legitimacy that perpetuated or were parasitic upon dualistic ideas, recognising these to be almost always a product or effect of the same forces about which it had become necessary to issue warnings. Philosophy, in the old-fashioned sense, was desperate to start again with a blank slate, but was now painfully aware that after two and a half thousand years of writing scratched on its surface, rubbed off and scratched again, the only available slate was far from blank and had become quite damaged. It was no longer, nor could it ever again claim to be, naïve. In the 1960s, Buddhism was already part of these nascent rumblings, as the first waves of exiles from Tibet began arriving in the west, influencing a new generation of thinkers and academics who were looking for alternatives to the discourses of the Cold War and the hegemony of two and a half millennia of wrong-headed metaphysics.

There have always been reactive forces labouring to identify and demonise radical sentiments or any movement perceived to pose a threat to the established order, always keen to incorporate and neutralise iconoclasm and critique. In recent years these have procured and deployed mass communication media to hammer home the same basic message: that power is benevolent when exercised in the name of democracy, but evil and malevolent when seized by insurrectionists and terrorists. Who are of course, from their own perspectives, fighters for freedom. This crude dichotomy dominates newsfeeds, slicing every echo-chamber into good and bad, us and them, making it impossible to see the nuance of what is actually going on, tying down all discourse into sterile and increasingly polarised feuds between sects. Unreason and demagoguery have taken hold of power; the words of oligarchs, internet influencers and media tycoons are given as much if not greater credence than the considered opinions of experts and scholars. What were once arcane arguments, based on careful readings of certain significant philosophical texts, which presented a progressive or radical message about certain old-fashioned ideas about truth, about how asymmetries and contradictions at the origins of reason have been perpetuated throughout history by the politics of writing and the power of discourse to reproduce dichotomy into new contexts, have been requisitioned now by populists undermining genuine efforts to engage in reasonable discourse about matters that affect everybody. Beneath it all, from identity politics to the narcissism of demagogues, lies *individualism*. The delusional notion, most simply stated by Akong Rinpoche, that who *I am* is who *we are*. Having noted that every being experiences stuff uniquely, it does not follow that the world is composed of a plethora of uniquely experiencing beings, that there is nothing *between us*, no love, no passion, no ecstasy.

The traverse to the next two peaks is easy, dropping gently only two hundred metres or so between each. But the wind was burning cold. After stopping only to mark the event at the summit of **Aonach Beag**, we sat awhile out of the wind at the summit of **Beinn Eibhinn**, eating lunch and chatting with others enjoying the remoteness of this place. Presently, a man returned from the other end of the mountain's long narrow peak, demonstrably clutching a device for measuring the altitude of the ground. We wondered about how it is possible to measure the highest point so precisely when it is actually obscured underneath a pile of stones. He showed us how in this case he made his estimate, following the lie of the land round the cairn to a reasonable height then holding the device at the edge. An estimate. He said he was just confirming that this was indeed the higher of the two high points on the ridge. By all of thirty centimetres. Adding more data to the heap in this shifting world. When we asked him about error margins he changed the subject, insisting before he left on burying a discarded avocado stone *lest it encourage ravens*. I was planning to add it to the base of the cairn, but whatever. We waited until he was out of earshot before bursting into laughter, and then carried on with lunch. Encourage ravens? What on earth could a human being do at the top of a mountain to encourage ravens? And what would be the point of trying to discourage them? It is where they live, truly *in* the mountains, not temporarily *on* them like us human visitors, but in air that swirls among them. We could not in any case see ravens. Perhaps they had seen the measuring man coming and decided to stay away; all we saw were lochs and rivers, patches of forest on empty moors, only the vastness of the land in every direction, visible here from its very heart.

During my more formal philosophical investigations I have been able to express concisely what I believe to be the important principles of things. This was the point of my little book of aphorisms. I also like to pluck snippets from others' works, which express some general truth. One of these has been with me since 1989 when I came upon it in a translation of a book about Nietzsche written in French in 1962 by Gilles Deleuze. It is a terse, challenging expression of the reality that lies behind the appearance of philosophy:

> ... ressentiment (it's your fault) and bad conscience (it's my fault) and
> their common fruit (responsibility) [are not] simple psychological events

> but rather ... the fundamental categories of Semitic and Christian thought, of our way of thinking and interpreting existence in general.

A lot of my subsequent philosophical investigations became teasing out the consequences of this, watching how it works in the ordinary conversations and relations of the world, seeing how we confuse our limited viewpoints for truth, obscuring the actual causes of things in interplays of egos, eliding vocabularies of responsibility and causality and perpetuating numerous dichotomies and exclusions. How often do we hear commentators and respectable scientists alike, talking of a particular factor being *to blame* for a particular phenomenon? Is looking for somebody else to *blame* not just the same as looking for *the cause* of events, finding somebody *at fault*? Both strategies for externalising responsibility or avoiding involvement in the messy business of being alive? Even sophisticated minds slither between discovering the causes of things and seeking out who is to blame or who should take the credit, and in so doing miss the point of Karma.

Remoteness in its common sense is relative, meaning a great distance from anywhere. But there is a more absolute sense of remoteness palpable here at the very centre of the central highlands, an elemental sense of being a long way from everywhere. The Cairngorms are a distant blip on the horizon. **Creag Meagaidh** is an insignificant blip on the northern horizon. The crags, screes and pinnacles of the *Aonach Eagach*, the Mamores, Nevis Ranges, Etive, Orchy, Breadalbane, Glen Shiel, Affric, Knoydart, all minor serrations. No sign of any sea. Only springs gushing clear pure water into rivers, gathering in glistening lochs among forests and moors.

My investigations into Buddhist philosophy had brought me to another terse conclusion. Notwithstanding what Deleuze wrote about Nietzsche or anything that Nietzsche himself wrote about philosophy, it came to me that *resentment*, in the fullest sense encapsulated in the quotation and developed by Deleuze's by now thoroughly influential reading of Nietzsche, *is the very erasure of compassion.*

Quite simple. *Resentment is the very erasure of compassion.* The cornerstone of Buddhist practice is excluded by resentful desire to identify individual causes, culprits and scapegoats. Conversely, any surging resentment, any urge to distribute credit and blame becomes an opportunity to train a mind in the practice of compassion.

Despite feeling that there were moments in the history of Western ideas that were perfectly consistent with Buddhist teaching, I was coming to understand that on the contrary, the very foundations of the former made the latter impossible. I wanted my studies of the history of Western ideas still to have been relevant, and so held on to the slightly less iconoclastic idea that any thoroughgoing critique of Western philosophy would clear the mind, make space for thinking more in keeping with Buddhist traditions of contemplation. The only problem with this is that there exist many critiques of Western reason, few of which result in spaces of quiet contemplation, more usually they lead to some sort of political imperative, that the world being as ghastly as it is, something must be done to make it different.

We retraced our steps and then descended the east ridge of *Beinn Eibhinn* into the glen that runs from Loch Ossian towards **Ben Alder**. We ploughtered about for a bit in peat hags and squiggly burns before climbing through heather to the old path round the mountain and over the pass back to Culra. A marvellous walk under a blue sky dappled with high clouds, surrounded by majestic crags and buttresses, affording splendid views back over Loch Ossian to the ridges of Glen Coe, tiny on the horizon. At the highest point on the path there is an aircraft wreck, driveshaft rising perpendicular from rusting engine carcass among a deteriorating pile of recognisably helicopter-shaped detritus. We stopped on the way down the other side for rest and reflection at a burn by the path, where a gentle wind kept off the midges.

If the weather permits, this is an important moment on any expedition. On the return, sitting by water, meditating upon the day and whatever challenges it has presented, while gazing at landscapes, experiencing directly the silent benevolence of the land, sharing this now with Chris who, apart from being handy in the mountains, is an accomplished artist, and took out his sketchbook. I had certainly come a long way since my first meditation retreat at the turn of the year into 2015, where I had met Chris for the first time, and I have no doubt looking back that I believed I was doing very well, quite pleased with myself. But I was trepidatious about my trip to the Holy Isle.

Returning to our tents, we saw the grass a little further up river was flatter, so we moved, cooked supper, nattered awhile and prepared for the night. We awoke again at six and departed, leaving no trace, just as a gang of inquisitive geldings came over to say hello and to look for sandwiches. Despite rummaging through our stuff with their big round noses, they found nothing and wandered off. We were back at the car by eleven, taking the total walking time to about sixteen hours, spread over two nights camped out at the very centre of this enormous little country. Excellent preparation, I thought, for my visit to the Holy Isle. When I got home, I began carefully packing all I believed I would need into my big rucksack and an old daypack, which I was going to carry back-to-front on my chest. A few days later, I sent my brother all my access codes and passwords and took a train to the ferry terminal at Ardrossan.

## Killing Fields

### 27th September 2017

I could have said that during the middle of September 2017, I spent a week on retreat on the Holy Isle, learning meditation and taking my Buddhist investigations to the next level. But it was rather more complicated than this. I have thought long and hard about how much detail of this to recount and have decided to keep most of it to myself, for I was confronted by my fiercest demons and forced to deal with them. In the spirit of His Holiness Lama Yeshe's advice, I have no desire to give these any solidity with words; how I felt, what I thought and how I reacted as I learned about what really twangs my wire and how to begin to move on, these were all temporary states, I will not allow them to define or identify me. Apart from this, I enjoyed a week in a little bit of paradise and learned a great deal to improve my practice. His Holiness is a master of meditation and teaches well.

A few days after my return, my eye was drawn to an article about a pair of mountains just south of Glen Shiel, the ones I saw with Janine in May from the south ridge, dominating the view towards **Ben Nevis**. I did some more research. They were a long way off, but a straightforward climb from the road beside Loch Cuaich, made easier for being serviced by well-constructed stalkers' paths. If I prepared and got up nice and early I could get there and back in a day.

Eventually, it becomes far too easy to point to the delusions and mistakes of others, especially if these are objectively or obviously so delusional or mistaken that they cannot be called anything else, but it remains more compassionate to make efforts to understand why others believe and act as they do rather than to call them out. At the same time, given we all labour under delusions of one sort or another and frequently make mistakes, it is always a good idea to examine *why* pointing out any particular delusion or mistake is so important. It is a commonplace of most therapies and certainly of psychoanalysis that everything said of another is a reflection of the one speaking rather than the one spoken of. The Buddhist version of this principle, emphasised by the Karmapa in London and expressed in many texts and teachings, is to be mindful always of reactions to every other, to elevate anyone who offends or hurts or who so twangs the wires, to the same status as the wisest teacher, for in this way we see exactly how our own reactions come to dominate who we become, so we can then perhaps begin to make it otherwise, to conduct ourselves proactively, mindfully and with compassion.

It took me three and half hours to drive the 150 miles from Fife to the tiny road past Loch Cuaich to Kinlochhourn, where I found a rutted parking spot, amidst gorse, rhododendrons and highland cattle, wide-horned and characteristically indifferent. The meanings of ***Spidean Mialach*** and ***Gleouraich*** refer respectively to wild animals (not only deer) and the sounds they make. Even without any Gaelic, the word *Gleouraich* looks as if it signifies noise. As I gained the easterly of the two huge corries that lie between them, all I heard was the unmistakable grunt and bellow of stags, echoing and dispersing in the gloom. The cloud was down to just above the summits, but moving past very quickly and not completely obscuring the sun. I had already decided on an anti-clockwise traverse so I could use the more prominently enthused over of the stalkers' paths on the way down, in order to save my knees. Going this way the path is described as faint and indistinct in walk reports, and evidently peters out in the middle of a peat hag. Much better to have this on the way up with an eye on the summit as goal, with a well-engineered path on the way down.

The ground was dry and the colours of the land dulled, so it was difficult to locate the sources of roaring. I disturbed groups of hinds sheltering in peaty hollows, but they just looked at me demurely. Later as I scrambled up a shallow gully through deep heather and crumbly stones, in an effort to keep out of the wind as I neared the summit ridge, I was surveyed by a large heavy-antlered stag and his harem. When the ascent flattened into grasses and shattered rock, I passed over their tracks. His musk hung heavy over the ground, pungent and prominent. The summit was not far off; the cloud was quite thick at the top so I stopped only briefly to mark the event then found the path back along the ridge.

As I came off the Holy Isle, I felt the safety of the community departing; I was left now to deal with my turbulent emotional condition all by myself, unprotected by the tolerance of the Sanga. A wind was getting up and piling water up the Clyde Sea, forcing CalMac to cancel ferries. I waited at Brodick for several hours, churning things over, keeping my distance from everybody. At last on the ferry, I could stand on deck with the elements in my face watching the islands recede and the mainland approach. Coming in to Ardrossan, I witnessed a most masterful display of seamanship. Up ahead there was what looked like a rather too narrow gap in a sea wall, barely protruding above the tide lapping over it and behind which calmer waters of docks and terminal awaited. The ferry was rolling and yawing at great speed towards a point to the right of the gap, with her bow rather alarmingly off the direction of travel and into the substantial sidewind. At just the right moment the captain cut the engines and steered the vessel in a perfect curve through the gap towards the roro ramp, and at just the right moment gunned them into reverse to ensure she came to rest without the slightest bump. Meanwhile, crew frantically threw lines back and forth between ship and quay, pulling out and securing giant hawsers. Without the distraction, I was back inside my head, on the way to a crisis.

The path along the ridge from ***Spidean Mialach*** is very good and it affords views of everywhere, today diminished by haze and cloud, and augmented by bellowing and roaring from stags in the corries beneath. There was a good view from the lowest point on the path of the chaos of broken rock, crags, sheer cliffs, steep corries and unstable peat on the northern slopes of the ridge; the cloud was well above my head, still hazy, the faint outline of the South Glen Shiel Ridge looming on the other side of the chasm of Easter Glen Cuaich. After climbing to the subsidiary peak of *Creag Coire na Fiar Bhealaich*, the ridge undulates gently to its highest point, where I enjoyed lunch in the lee of **Gleouraich**'s handsome cairn. I descended again with the walkers' path onto the south shoulder of the mountain and discovered the end of the stalkers' path, its destination from below, its purpose.

Unbeknownst to me, Shona arranged another audience with Lama Yeshe and so we went again to Samye Ling. He was very stern with me about my reactions, forcing me to think carefully about my future. He repeated something he had said once before; *Europe culture very gone wrong way*. He knew exactly what this would mean to me. The order of the words was crucial: *gone very wrong way* would be a really bad turn on a journey; *very gone wrong way* is a condition of extreme dysfunctionality. If I am to pursue a Buddhist path, I must peel away the pretensions of European enlightenment, find a place where practice is everything, unencumbered by too much thinking, untainted by judgement and fury.

My oldest friends would probably say they have been trying for years to tell me exactly this; that I think too much. But there are others who might say I am able to feel the world in the way that I am thinking about it, which will be subject to continuous change just like the world, that I recognise always, as Yeats so eloquently noted: "We taste and feel and see the truth. We do not reason ourselves into it".

Of course I knew that I often overthought things, reacting angrily from some moral high ground, choosing some scapegoat (real, imagined or abstract) and ranting until I was ranted out. I do not doubt or deny this in the slightest. I also felt though that if it is to be thoroughly appraised, this overthinking, it has enabled me also, eventually, to grow into a more compassionate and humane person. This was now exposed as another blip on the continuous dialectic of hubris and self-effacement, the same resentful ego looking for credit and recognition, evidence of its very own special existence.

On the way home from Samye Ling, somewhere about the sources of the Tweed, a process began that I can only describe as the dissolution of my sense of self, or maybe just the final visceral realisation that there exists no such thing, that there is no *identity*, never will be and never has been. The search to discover or express the authenticity of such a thing and to seek from others validation of this is therefore a futile waste of mental resources that creates unnecessary, artificial divisions between groups of flag wavers each claiming special treatment and validity. Anything with which I choose to identify is external, brought inside by a desire to solidify my being. It is not who I am. A beating heart, a confused mind and indescribable pain, with the trauma of dissolution repeating every now and again until I get used to it, or, at least, until I learn how not to be overwhelmed by it. Real life continues as it must. I went back to delivering stuff, sometimes in the van and sometimes on my bike, still proofreading and climbing mountains, while training my mind more conscientiously to recognise opportunities for compassion in every surge of resentment.

Behind a low wall at the end of the stalkers' path dug into the mountainside, partially paved and with ample room for supplies, sits an emplacement for those whose pleasure it is to cull animals, looking down on a corrie of peat hags and rutting grounds, echoing with grunts and roars. Stalkers are after all those who know where the deer are to be found, so they build paths to enable them more easily to carry out their duties for the owners of the land, their guests and clients. The paths they use are often ancient; the lines they take are not necessarily the ones a walker would choose, often employing substantial zigzagging, which makes it easier for both the horses who carry supplies up and carcasses down, as well as those who do the actual killing to get to places where they can get in their best shots.

I paused a moment to reflect upon this realisation, that my access to these mountains is granted by complicity with this elision of custodianship and canned hunting, that the noises made by the animals here are not what they were when these mountains were named. There are fewer now, much less diversity, no forest cover, only sterile loch margins, denatured ground and retarded attitudes to land management. Not that I am unaware of these things, but this simple shelter scooped out of the ground brought back the reality. I thought for a moment of taking a photo, but decided not to make any use of this facility, not to acknowledge it, to walk on, to give it no solidity.

Here was my challenge. To find compassion for those whose livelihoods depend on a system of land management I despise and that stands in the way of Scottish autonomy; were it not for the continuing existence of this peculiarly medieval attitude to the land, Scotland would already be an independent country, where every citizen would have an option on an acre or two within Nationally administered wilderness and forest areas. More prosaically, my challenge is how to deal with the reactive passions I encounter towards actual material forces of exploitation, oppression, destruction, inertial stupidity, ideological obfuscation and habitual indifference, which either produce suffering, stand in the way of its amelioration or deliberately exclude or undermine efforts to improve conditions for the general benefit of all.

The Buddhist answer remains the same; understand these forces as karma, reactions as an opportunity to learn. If there is something to be done then do it, but know the limits both of what can be done and what you can yourself do, and otherwise, move on. There was, however, something unsatisfactory about this, for it seemed to rule out legitimate discussion, the necessity of activism, collective organisation and autonomous revolt; it seemed to reduce the focus of politics to an individual in a particular relation of turmoil with a specific political situation, a configuration of forces or karmic knot; politics seemed to have become just another individual problem or choice, something for atomised individuals to decide upon without consultation with others in similar circumstances; whatever the *it* happened to be, it was simply a choice between doing something about the *it* or dealing with the *it*, which seemed to me not particularly Buddhist. Where was the power of us, the "ecstasy between us" as Irigaray calls it? Here perhaps was where, according to Lama Yeshe's perspective, I began to overthink things, to solidify and move beyond the purely empirical *it is what it is*; looking for principles or other notions of the mind by which to make sense, judging, unable to accept that this is just how things are and that there is no need for any conceptual apparatus above and beyond to hold it all together, that all beings can only move as they do, doing what they can in the flow of events, making it up as they go along, whether by making what they believe to be rational choices in their worlds or acting by dint of habit.

If there had been no path and I were looking only at the contours on the map to find a way off this hill, I might have dropped into the corrie and skirted the eastern flank of *Druim Seileach*, or more probably followed its crest to the end so I could look back to the ridge of the mountain, and then find a way back to the road in a more south easterly direction. The stalker's path does more or less this with one crucial difference; it is very carefully constructed not along the crest, but on the leeward side of the ridge that encloses the corrie, so that any deer going about their business will be sheltered from all sight, sound and smell of any human beings on the way to shoot them from above. The path is excellent, a remarkable feat of engineering, paved and drained all the way, from clinging high on the edge of the precipitous west shoulder to zigzagging through crags and bogs, always looking down on the sterile white margins of Loch Cuaich. The hazy peaks of Knoydart, Arkaig and Kintail serrating the horizon in pastel shades. The first section of the path is particularly impressive and worthy of a visit for its own sake, slicing along the side of an extremely steep grassy slope into the northern ear on Loch Cuaich, now hardly more than a riverbed again, with another precipitous grassy slope on the other side and empty colourless ridges receding into haze. I find it quite difficult to describe the feeling of so precisely contouring a slope with a gradient just that little bit too steep for comfort, which becomes even steeper below, and yet feeling perfectly secure and in no danger of sliding off.

Not that I was ungrateful for the path; if I had wanted, I could easily still have followed the crest, and it was a relief to be out of the wind following a route I knew would take me safely to the car without having to navigate, nor ploughter over complicated ground. I did after all need to be sharp enough to drive home for three and a half hours. The experience of animals lingered, the musk and bellowing of stags filled the autumn air with the ghosts of those made silent by the destruction of this land at the pleasure of the powerful. The emplacement at the end of the path only hammered home how it is possible for me to be here at all. It does not matter that I detest this slaughter and that I believe quite passionately that the archaic systems of land management that continue to dominate these empty mountains could be replaced with something more sustainable, that deer populations could be controlled in other ways and that people could easily live again in the glens, trees replanted and infrastructures established, while ecosystems develop. The only thing standing in the way of this, apart from the massed powers of the British establishment, is bad faith, a version of an old delusion, that the current state of things is the best they can be, the only natural condition possible. That there is no need to change anything. And yet things are continuously changing, people continue to try to change them in the direction of their ideals and desires or simply *to be the change* they want to see in the world.

A devout Christian once told me that learning Buddhism made her a better Christian. Buddhism has perhaps sharpened my philosophical mind, made it better aware of the confusions to which it can become subject, more viscerally conscious of the resentments that have driven it for so long. Perhaps I also now have a better grasp on the history of ideas, the Western version of *karma*, the causes of things conscious, how we think about who and where we are.

Not long after I returned from The Netherlands I sat talking to a good friend and colleague of Akong Rinpoche about his life and work. An Irishman, recently retired from a successful career as a psychiatrist in Dublin, one of those who had been around during the early years and who was instrumental in getting Rinpoche's methods of restoring the balance recognised as a *bona fide* therapeutic technique by relevant authorities. He told me a story and said it was the best ever explanation of karma he had heard. Imagine a Dublin accent.

An elderly Lama and a young novice were walking through the market. The monk kept pointing out things he thought worthy of comment, coaxing the old man to utter some nugget of wisdom, prompting him to offer some valuable teaching. But each time the Lama just smiled and walked on. After a while, they passed by a beggar thrusting out a cup, pleading for alms, whereupon the young monk exclaimed enthusiastically that it surely must be part of this man's karma that he is a beggar. The Lama turned immediately to remonstrate with the youth, pointing him to the other side of the street, to a bank, where he could go and take out all of his money and give every last penny to the beggar. And that, he said, would also be part of his karma.

There are three lessons I have taken from Buddhism: learning meditation, from which arises not only a degree of mental restfulness, but also a deeper perception of the girth of the present; being nice to people, even really bad, very stupid, delusional, unthinking people who do a great deal of damage or who are deliberately cruel; and *training the mind we actually have to take control of its motivations*, to think proactively rather than to become great repositories of reactions, entirely dependent on the abstractions foisted upon it by the history of Western consciousness.

How to deal with the politics of things continued to trouble me. I had gotten no further than this: if you can do something do it, otherwise move on. I liked the idea of *being the change you want to see, of being the difference you want to make, of making the world again in the image of something better,* mindfully employing the integrity of reason and compassion, but this seemed inadequate against the sheer power, the momentum and inertia manifest in the evils of the world, the absolute power by which they are maintained and the indifference by which they are regarded, if at all, by most human beings. The absolute necessity of collective organisation was nowhere to be found.

I continued to harbour a kind of political imperative; it must always be necessary to do something about the sorry state of humanity, and to hold opinions that will contribute to the improvement of the human condition and the amelioration of the lives of the downtrodden, oppressed and exploited, that the world is something about which something *must be done*. Perpetuating old illusions about the ability of reason to interrupt the flow of Karma.

## The Buddha of Braeriach

#### 8th October 2017

It is deeply ingrained in the Western mind that it is able to control events and to maintain the stability of society. History undertakes this by sustaining those economic forms most appropriate (or *fit*) to the circumstances, laying down moral, social, epistemological and physical architectures that confine and define the responses of individual *human bodies*. In our times, power's dominance over human bodies reaches a pinnacle with scientific medicine, which drills down to molecular, biochemical levels to control the very substance of life.

Sometimes the *mind* that is supposed to be able to control events is instantiated by the gargantuan legacy of scientific endeavour. Sometimes it is the conduct of particular great men, acting with decisiveness and vision; a view, which looked at from another place, may appear as some variety of conspiracy theory, or again only some hagiographical narrative designed to maintain the idea of what a *good thing* the present is, because it was made by all these great men. Sometimes it is the operation of political procedures and collective processes. Sometimes, however, it may appear to be the outcome of blind, obedient, unreflective habit, of minds repeating themselves over and over again because that is what they do.

Since the European Enlightenment, individuals have become intimately involved in these developments; each unique body having been given a unique mind, furnished with the same principles of abstract reason, which it uses to act upon the world. At the beginning of the twenty first century, everybody was involved somewhere, somehow, in using their mind to engage with the politics of something, even if they did not realise this. Scientific methods or some simulation of these are used almost universally to justify and support what they do. Using minds to participate in processes of personal development or social change, or to resist these, has become universal. There is now a politics of everything and anything. At least in public discourse.

Although I might have expected myself to have celebrated this seeming diversity, to be broadly in favour of as many as possible participating in decisions made about social life, from where I was sitting, established assumptions about how the world works, about how minds relate to it and each other and what it all means, were so fundamentally flawed that the whole of society and politics resembled a train crash in slow motion. While all participants seemed to be labouring under some delusion or another, most crucially, that this is not a train crash but the outcome of reason, of individuals exercising their reason and engaging their minds, bending the world to their will.

I was myself as guilty as any, for there were many large bits of the world I wanted to change. I was in full command of reason, my native wit was in good order and my common sense polished up nicely, and I had come to know one bit of the world very well, the bit of it that was telling me that my body was a biomechanical process being slowly shut down by the progression of a disease over which I had absolutely no control. Frantically I wanted still to believe that if I could just establish the falsity of the former and regain control over the latter, then the disease would go away.

Again it was a man I met on a mountain who took me away from the nonsense in my head, brought me down to earth and reminded me of what my mind was actually for. For the weeks after leaving the Holy Isle I had let my mind run itself into the ground chasing down answers for badly posed questions, allowed it to fester in pits of self-indulgent despair and cynical nihilism, given it no reason to think of itself as anything but a frightful appendage, a falsely solidified nothing, without value and of no consequence. It does not seem right to concentrate on such moments of complete collapse and despair, without recalling the epiphanies and sustained mental effort necessary to come through all these crises and to emerge again on the other side with renewed hope and deeper understanding of my own condition and circumstances. It always becomes easier to deal with private demons in the company of others in similar circumstances, even if the demons are never actually talked about.

We recognised each other quite quickly from a mountain climbing Facebook page. I recalled too from an online conversation that he and I had something else in common. We are among the ten to twelve percent of the male bodied population who will experience cancer of the prostate, which is about the same as the percentage of the female bodied population, give or take, who will experience breast cancer. So we had much to talk about, experiences to share. Of course, like everybody else, he took for granted the medical model of disease, trusted the knowledge upon which the medics were basing their clinical judgements, diagnoses and treatment. All of which enabled me to hold in suspension my unconventional ideas about health; I was nevertheless both *medication free* and *ignorant of the results of medical tests*, so I was able to speak from this position without difficulty, adding another perspective to the pile, *being* and *speaking* as one who had chosen, for the moment at least, to follow a non-medical path.

Shona and I were at the farmhouse in Rothiemurchus again, with her daughter and new husband, William. At their wedding in May, I approached all three of Shona's children in turn, explaining that since Shona's father had passed away not long after my own, when I was still living in The Netherlands, I sought *their* blessing to marry their mother; I am a bit old-fashioned in this respect. They were all glad to give their blessing. We did not arrange anything immediately though. Then we had a visit from a man offering to prepare our wills, who explained that these things are very much more straightforward when couples are actually married. So we got ourselves into gear, giving ourselves less than two months to organise everything. This meant that soon I would have a *step-son-in-law*; what better excuse to get to know him better than by taking him up my favourite mountain. He has done a couple of tours in faraway places for Her Majesty and knows a thing or two about multiple martial arts, so I had no doubt that he would be physically able to get to the top of a mountain, and more importantly to see when it might be necessary to turn around.

We left the womenfolk to go for a walk round *Loch an Eilean* and drove to the Sugar Bowl carpark, which nestles in an elbow of the road to the ski centre just at the limit of the thickest forest. On my previous trips out I had not encountered much water nor wet ground, but when I had, it was obvious that my boots were now at the end of their mountain life. Apart from being scuffed and worn down, the soles were now far too pliable, all original rigidity used up, and they were definitely no longer waterproof. I had my eye on a new pair, but I had yet to convince myself that I could justify the price. This is a ritual I often go through with myself when I need new stuff; usually I have a notion of what next I will need and have already sought out and sourced possibilities, often I have decided upon a purchase and reserved a budget, but I wait as the same internal dialogue plays out; is it really what I want or need, can I afford it, can I afford not to have it, is this the right choice, is this a good buy, will it be worth the money? All very commonplace. Instead of this being a pair of new boots' first trip up a mountain, it became my old boots' last, a fitting swansong on my favourite mountain. One hundred and thirty Munros for one pair of boots.

Starting at a signpost on the other side of the road from the car park, dropping steeply down into a gully and up again through a margin of Caledonian forest creeping up the gully to the edge of a flatter moor, there is a good dry path all the way to the top of **Braeriach**  Here is a pasture where reindeer live. I was hoping we could get to see them close by for they are comely beasts, gentle, with friendly eyes and soft mouths, but they were being attended by a human being far away at the other side of their enclosure. A collie shuffled statically in permanent anticipation at a gate by a small shed, awaiting instructions. We walked on up the well-appointed and firm broad path towards the mountain, making short work of the flat ground in front of ski slopes and gradually rising towards the Chalamian Gap. To my great delight I could see young Scots pines growing vigorously amongst the heather, the most profound and immediate consequence of culling almost the entire population of red deer from the high Cairngorms.

What a difference from when I first came this way, in the other direction, on the way back from a yomp up **Beinn Macduibh** when I was just short of nineteen. I had a summer job at a caravan park south of Aviemore. On a day off I hitched to Coylumbridge then walked to the summit of the *Lairig Ghru*, where I struck up the side of the March Burn, allegedly one of the sources of the River Dee, although since all its water disappears under piles of rocks at the summit of the pass, it is not obvious how it would be possible to know over which side of the watershed it falls. I was wearing the traditional garb of a novice, jeans and Doc Martens, carrying sandwiches in a gasmask case. Despite slithering on grass a bit near a snow bridge where the burn cascades over the edge, I made it onto the rocky plateau without incident and easily found the summit of **Beinn Macduibh**. I then strolled over the plateau to Cairn Lochan and walked west along the plateau's northwest lip, enjoying the experience of looking down from such a great height into deep dark lochans surrounded my enormous rocks. I remember it being quite a complicated descent from here over large boulders, which in the corrie formed the banks of the lochan; I had never seen anything like this seen before, water edged by boulders the size of small vehicles and no earth. I sat on top of one of the boulders as water lapped on all sides, in awe of this place, gazing at slabs dipping into the lochan at the back of the corrie. At length I descended further into less rocky ground and followed a rough peaty path coming out of the corrie towards another coming out of the Chalamain Gap and heading towards the road, where I hitched back to the pub near the caravan site where I would find my workmates. These old paths were rather ugly; just the many lines taken by many boots on their way to or from the plateau. They have been replaced now with carefully engineered paths, much wider and with solid foundations, drainage culverts and intermittent paving. The engineered path to the Chalamain Gap stops however rather abruptly, albeit unsurprisingly, at the entrance.

The Chalamain Gap is a rocky fissure about fifty feet deep and a quarter of a mile long, cutting through the shoulder north from the Lurcher's Crag. Along the floor, lie heaps of unstable stones of many shapes and sizes, fallen from the sides, cracked and crumbled by eternal cycles of freeze, thaw, wind and rain. Inside the chasm there is an eerie silence broken only as footfalls echo above hollows in the rockpiles; unlike the path over the summit of the *Lairig Ghru*, which is also a series of piles of stones fallen from on high, there is no noise beneath of gurgling water. It is at points quite a complicated traverse, and probably the most technically difficult section of this route up **Braeriach**. William came through without any difficulty.

At the exit to the gap, the flanks of **Braeriach** and the opening of the *Lairig Ghru* come prominently into view. The engineered path returns and slants down into a deep chasm to cross *Allt Druidh*, where water emerges eventually from beneath piles of boulders at the start of the *Lairig Ghru*. The path rises steeply again on the other side and crosses a flat exposed moraine where once stood a rough bothy of breeze blocks and brick, erected to commemorate William Angus Sinclair, a Scottish philosopher who died near here in a blizzard in 1954. The only thing going for the shelter was the spectacular view north from the door to Rothiemurchus and Speyside. It was however a badly placed refuge, too far from good water and exposed to every wind hammering through the pass. I stayed here once or twice; even at midsummer it was damp and gloomy. It is gone now, demolished because it posed a risk to health, allegedly, or was subject to perpetual unsightly graffiti, leaving now only the memorial plaque to Sinclair cemented into nearby ground.

Hereafter the path winds steeply through a boulder field garnished with deep heather and mud, then climbs zigzagging to the shoulder of *Sron na Lairig*. Here we met our prostate cancer warrior, let's call him Dave. After initial recognition, introductions and chat, he encouraged us to carry on to the summit, for we were clearly maintaining a faster pace than he could manage. William's strength and enthusiasm had pulled me forward more insistently than was perhaps sensible, and I had once or twice suggested he hold back a little to conserve his (and my) energy for the rest of the day, especially during our steep ascent of *Sron na Lairig*. But he was strong and the path was no longer steep, so I felt I could handle the pace, just as long as I had a good break at the summit and dawdled on the way down.

Mist was now gathering. The air still and not cold, no sign that conditions would deteriorate as they had the last time I was here with my Dutch friends in July 2014. There is a cosiness to such conditions that induces quietude. In the gloom I was able to seek out remnants of a crashed aircraft I knew lay on the way to the summit. We both took souvenir blobs of molten aluminium; I found a piece resembling a Buddha sitting cross legged and discovered a spur of metal among the gravel, some lining from a window or control panel, to give to my brother for his collection of random bits of metal and found objects.

At the summit we rested. It was not cold. We sat cocooned by cloud, beside big red stones, grey outcrops and gravely ground. Presently Dave emerged smiling through the mist. A couple arrived from the other direction and another came up from *Gleann Einich*, then went off around the plateau towards **Cairn Toul** and the **Angel's Peak**. It was good craic. At length we departed the way we had come with Dave, chatting all the time, sometimes about our experiences of the disease, about getting into the mountains to get away from it all and how we felt about how all this affected the important others in our lives, and of course, the sorry state of human affairs and the nugatory efforts made by politicians and authorities to do anything about any of it. What my folks used to call setting the world to rights. It was good to let William see that bagging Munros has as much to do with enjoying the company of those you happen to meet along the way as it does reaching the actual top. After all, the spectacular views I had promised him south from the summit of this wonderful mountain towards Deeside and Atholl, of pointy peaks and vast plateaux ringed by enormous cliffs and corries, were nowhere to be seen. Just the ground beneath our feet and the company of strangers, who *could always* become friends.

We came through the Chalamain Gap again, larking about a bit, trying to find stones that had been smoothed down by boots or scarred by crampons and that did *not* also clunk, wobble or move about. It was just a game, but it was good for balance training and strengthening calf muscles. Ahead, we saw a couple approaching the lower entrance to the gully, still on the broad path and packed up for nights out. By the time we were nearing the end of the gap, it became clear that for the moment at least the couple was going no further. They were sitting by a burn emerging from the side of the shoulder nearby, evidently agitated, embarrassed to be seen thus as we walked by, nonchalantly passing the time of day as if the sun had just come out, which had indeed just happened. They were pointing at an OS map and comparing what was there with the ground ahead of them, gesturing with great concern towards the passage through. We did not feel it was our place to do more than smile politely. It seemed private, and none of us had enough German in any case properly to understand what was going on. It did, however, seem that a degree of disappointment was being experienced, since the dotted line on the map signifying *path* was not consistently constructed to the same specification, and at this point, the going through the gap, became sporadic, unreconstructed and unmanageable with such heavy packs. Of course I had successfully traversed much more challenging terrain than this with a big heavy pack. However I remembered paths I had walked long ago in the Bavarian Alps, well-constructed to altitudes much higher than anything in Scotland. I also recalled that on the maps I used, different grades of path were depicted with different grades of dotted line, so I could imagine a kind of disappointment based on the experience of paths in Germany encountering the many varieties of routes on the ground in this country signified by little dotted lines on maps as *path*. We had fun speculating further, striding manfully towards the carpark and looking back from time to time to see the couple still sitting at the entrance to the Chalamain Gap.

We were tired from the day out, looking forward to a good feed and to lounge about in front of a fire at the cottage. The reindeer were still on the far side of their enclosure, but the collie had gone and there was no sign of any human. We said farewell to Dave after exchanging details and drove down the hill past Loch Morlich to Coylumbridge to our temporary home in Rothiemurchus. William was beaming from ear to ear, bursting with stories to tell his new wife, and my mind was much less troubled by self-imposed medical demons, grounded again in conversation and common experience. Not to mention the actual ground beneath our feet at nearly 1300 meters above sea level.

## Ben Cruachan

### 29th October 2017

It was now five years since I had been told that if I did not take the medication, I would be dead in a year, and that even if I did, I would likely die within three. About a month after this, as was my right within the health insurance package I was able to afford, I received a second opinion about the diagnosis at another hospital, which unsurprisingly differed very little from the first, although it did seem to this urologist that three years was a rather pessimistic prognosis, and that five years were more likely.

It is not easy to describe the feeling of bursting through the prognostications of medical science. This was my third. The first when I was still alive a year after refusing to take the advice; the second two years after that, having received a more careful assessment in Edinburgh and a more tailor-made treatment; and now this third, *having lived for nearly a year free of all pharmaceuticals*, looking after my health by eating a nutritious diet supported by natural supplements and preparations, enjoying stimulating interactions with interesting people, climbing mountains and blogging my adventures.

During previous weeks Shona and I had been organising our wedding, which was scheduled to take place on the fourth of November, almost five years to the day since the second opinion gave me only five more years to live. I could think of no better way of smashing through this particular prognostication; for it was the most *wonderful* day of my life. When the registrar asked if I took this woman to be my wife, joyously I exclaimed yes as our guests cheered and threw hats in the air.

The Sunday prior to the wedding, there was a weather window coinciding with nothing in particular to do. It was the first day of the return to GMT; clocks had gone back an hour, daylight would be disappearing suddenly at the end of the afternoon so it would be an early start. I got in touch with Chris and Martyn to invite them on a trip into Argyll, to the heart of Campbell country to climb the big mountain there. Some men have stag dos in foreign countries involving alcohol and outrageous behaviour, some do the same at home. I have never been much of a drinker and now took no alcohol at all, so climbing **Ben Cruachan** with my buddies and whoever else we might meet along the way, seemed like the perfect preparation for the future with Shona, whose family name is Campbell. It was a bit short notice for Martyn who had already made other plans and so it was just Chris and me. And my lovely new *Garmont* X-Lite boots.

We arranged to meet at a car park *en route*, sometime between seven and seven-fifteen. We arrived at exactly the same moment and left again promptly. Military discipline meets messenger precision. At the parking area on the road near the Cruachan Visitor Centre, we squeezed into the last plausible space. Just after nine, we began a steep arduous climb through muddy woods, then over more open squelchy ground fringed with decaying bracken and young trees towards a paved access road and a grassy path along the underside of Cruachan dam. There is a very deep overflow channel at the upper edge, which can only be passed by climbing up metal steps and then walking along the brutal concrete surface of the dam itself. After this, the route round the loch is level for a mile or so, following a track to the beginning of the ascent. The great bowl of the corrie, bright and benevolent, hanging with wispy cloud, opened up before us. It was already a great day out.

We stopped for elevenses by some rocks on the path to the bealach between the main peak and the subsidiary *Meall Cuanail*, along which in both directions parties of happy mountain people wended their way. It was a straightforward climb from the bealach along the most benevolent of the mountain's ridges to the summit. We arrived at about twelve-fifteen to veritable crowds of people sunning themselves with Sunday lunch in the still autumn air. A pair of ravens wheeled and cawed at each other, playing in eddies and updrafts, plummeting past the edges of crags and cliffs, needing no encouragement from any visiting human to demonstrate how awesome it is being a raven.

The views from the summit of this magnificent mountain are incredible. It is the highest of anything around and the most westerly peak above 1100 meters in the southern highlands. It sits on a ridge of several pointy peaks, behind which I could see unfamiliar views of familiar horizons. Since my first sojourn into the hills in July 2014, I had been looking at peaks I could now see *in* the north and east, only *from* the north and east. I had concentrated this summer on bagging everything in Laggan and round Loch Treig and I had nearly completed the major peaks round Glen Coe, which meant that I had now climbed not quite every Munro I could see in the east. I had only ever seen the Etive Munros on the western horizon; from **Cruachan**, Etive was behind me now renewing the view of the east, while the horizon before me was filled with a glistening mosaic of low hills, lochs, coastlines and islands, bathed in sunlight filtered by thin cloud. Utterly sublime. From this angle, the length of Loch Awe is crimped to a short squiggle. Mull and the might of **Ben More** are far away on the horizon, Morvern and the Ardgour peninsula shimmer into Lochaber. The Nevis ranges, Mamores and *Bidean nam Bian* meld into a great jagged lump in the north to the left of **Ben Starav**; likewise Breadalbane, the Trossachs and the Loch Lomomd hills to the southeast behind the end of the **Cruachan** ridge, with **Ben Lui** and *Beinn Buidhe* prominent in the foreground.

After lunch, we took the path off the summit along the ridge towards *Stob Daimh* and soon discovered what an absolute delight and privilege it was to be here on this mountain on such a beautiful day as this. The ridge is nowhere near as scrambly as the *Aonach Eagach*, but there is section of traverse over slabs that requires some care, it is as precipitous on both sides and I would not care to seek a route down from here in an emergency. It is not as randomly stony as the route between *Conival* and **Ben More Assynt**, but there is very little earth and it is a much longer walk. Along the way there are subsidiary tops, from the crests of which the drama of the ridge is made as palpable as the *Aonach Eagach*, the last of these, *Drochaid Ghlas*, affords superb views both back to **Ben Cruachan** and forward to *Stob Daimh*, slightly lower and yet a separate Munro.

On the way down from here, just as the path begins to level off, the ground changes abruptly from predominantly rocky to predominately earthy. It is a clear difference on the ground that justifies Munro's insistence that only mountains with a separate character be classified as separate summits, even if they are lower than the minor tops of immediate neighbours, which is the case here. The path to *Stob Daimh* is straightforward with a wee steep bit just at the end. We reached the summit at about three, my fiftieth summit of the year; the one hundred and thirty first since returning from The Netherlands. We soon realised we would have to make good time on the descent if we were to get back to the car before dark. On the way we experienced the most sublime views of low sunlight lowering through layers of thin cloud, illuminating a patchwork of forest, loch and mountain.

It was easy to find a way down along a selection of paths merging at the edge of a deep slanting ravine and to follow the boggy slopes above the loch. Though it was a long walk after a long day, there was brief respite from mud on the road from the dam before the return to the path through the forest. It was not completely dark when we reached the car at about five-thirty, but almost.

The final week of wedding preparations presented a number of challenges, but everything happened more or less as planned. We had a beautiful day, and our guests enjoyed themselves. A sudden squall of hail appeared at the venue just before the ceremony began, creating rainbows. Later a raven flew over, cawing and croaking happily, which is not a common sight in this bit of Fife.

I was never fond of using vocabularies of struggle or battle in relation to the disease, or at least, if there were battles to be fought, these were rather with the consequences of the diagnosis and my own responses and reactions, not with any disease. I was increasingly and absolutely doubting the prognostications of medical science, gradually understanding the wisdom of the Lama who suggested I give these and the disease absolutely no solidity whatever.

Getting married was the greatest affirmation of this. For despite a pain in my lower back that I later realised was a sign of things to come, I felt better now in myself than I had five years earlier when I was first diagnosed and had no intention whatever of leaving this life for the foreseeable future. I was enjoying it far too much for that.

I had many more mountains to climb, new horizons to experience and a new life ahead with my beautiful wife.

## Ben Challum

### 19th November 2017

In the course of only a few days after meeting Dave the prostate cancer warrior on ***Braeriach***, I received messages from two others seeking advice about the disease. The first from an acquaintance in Utrecht who was being treated at the same hospital where I was first diagnosed, if not by the same team; the second from an old school chum living now on the other side of the big water. Having been brought down to earth on the mountain, I now had reason to translate my wilful ignorance and non-medical experience into languages anybody could understand. It seemed counterintuitive to use this experience of refusal as the basis of offering advice to others who were facing medical choices, but I recognised also that on the way to where I was now, I had become knowledgeable about prostate cancer and its treatment.

The first snows had now arrived and temperatures had dropped. It was time to continue my campaign to bag nearby single Munros while their boggy approaches froze. My sights were set on ***Ben Challum***, a prominent mountain with a serious reputation for squelch, lying to the east of the main road north from Crianlarich, not far from Tyndrum. From this side it appears to have a single round top; from the east, where it is not unreasonably included in the most westerly of the clusters surrounding Glens Lyon and Lochay, the higher summit to the north is much more imposing. Back in the spring of 2016, taking time out from looking after mother during her final months, I camped out for a couple of nights very close to the back of ***Ben Challum***, contemplating bad weather and clearances while accidentally climbing ***Meall Glas***, from where it is a severe, craggy ridge at the western end of the range south of Glen Lochay.

Prostate cancer is the most common to affect male bodies. It has a similar pathology to breast cancer, which is the most common to affect female bodies. Both are hormonal and incurable; the professor of urological oncology told me once that a Nobel Prize awaits the research team that develops a cure for hormone-based cancers. In the meantime, the current state of medical knowledge allows prostate cancer to be managed successfully for many years, and, if it is caught early enough, all tumorous tissue can be surgically resected, or burned out by focused radiotherapy. This is the nub of the prostate cancer problem. *If it is caught early enough.* For by the time that prostate cancer has made its presence felt, it is very often a very long way away from *early enough*.

Paths up Ben Challum from the west begin at Kirkton Farm, parking for which is available on a wide layby that is easy to miss. This is another fast road, similar to the fast road east from Crianlariach, where it is also easy to drive past laybys. Having successfully parked, crossed the River Fillan, negotiated the farm and followed a path to a bridge over the railway line, the hillside opened up at the western edge of a plantation, still frosty and firm.

Despite the existence of many support and campaigning organisations and charities, such as Prostate Cancer UK, Prostate Scotland, Maggie's Centres, Macmillan, it remains much easier for women to discover and discuss the first symptoms of breast cancer than for men to find out about what may or may not be developing in a gland they probably do not realise they have. Without wishing to be vulgar, the explanation seems straightforward enough; breasts are more prominent than prostates and are more frequently examined. Anomalous tissue growth in breasts is consequently more quickly identified than in prostates.

It was bitterly cold, but I worked up a sweat quickly and stripped down to only two and a half layers for the ascent. I was in no hurry and maintained a nice pace over increasingly pleasant frozen ground that ensured the balance of sweating and cooling off was maintained. I was aware however that as soon as I stopped or slowed down to admire a view, the cold engulfed me quickly. It was a fine still day of layered cloud with an increasing wind as I rose; at about Munro height a deep layer of snow was in full development. Fine drifts and interesting ice formations wrapped around protruding rocks; steep slopes to the north and east were thickening; gullies filled deep with soft playful snow.

Undoubtedly, there is more to differences between prostate cancer and breast cancer recognition than with only the physical location of the prostate, its obscure function and its insignificant size (about the size of a walnut). It is not so easy for men to talk about how it feels down below or at the back, and men, at least men of my generation, are not actually very good at knowing *anything* about what is going on inside their own bodies. It often takes the emergence of a cancer or serious illness for a man to begin his own journey into bodily consciousness, towards the medical mindfulness that makes of a cancer patient a *cancer warrior*.

As I rose, the ground became firmer and more deeply covered with lovely new snow. I was in my element again. Fully equipped against this severe cold, pushing through knee deep drifts and enjoying the support depth gives to ploughtering legs. Far too early in the year yet for any snow to have solidified into the icy banks that make crampons necessary, but I had a set with me, just in case. There were only piles of fresh new snow, more deeply spread over northeast facing slopes. I reached the first summit from where I saw that the ground between here and the actual summit about half a mile further north was packed full of fresh snow. It was not obvious under these circumstances what the natural topography of the ground looked like. There was a substantial dip and then another ridge that leads to the summit, but more than that I could not say.

Not everybody realises these things about prostate cancer, perhaps because in general, it develops slowly in men over the age of about sixty, who have by this age other, more pressing, medical issues. My diagnosis was unusually early in my life, while most men who die of old age have some sort of prostate cancer.

In most cases, its growth can be thwarted with hormone suppressing medication, surgery and/or radiotherapy. But the aggressive, malignant varieties, at least according to the statistics, are more swiftly fatal. Statistics are notoriously difficult to use as any kind of estimation of what is really going on in the world, but the best estimates are that between ten and twelve percent of men will have prostate cancer at some point in their lives, whether they have been diagnosed or not. One more interesting statistic about prostate cancer is that over half of men who die and receive a *post mortem* have a cancer in their prostates, even if this had nothing to do with why they died.

After much wading and jolly floundering through deep snow, under the same momentum that had pulled me up the mountain, I was at the summit of **Ben Challum** in little more than two hours; as soon as I stopped, the cold caught up with me. I pulled warm clothes out of my pack and put everything on as quickly as possible, but my right thumb burned in pain with the searing cold, even under thermal gloves. Only when I was able after an ecstasy of fumbling to pull on thick mittens, having zipped up all down and windstopper, did the pain begin to subside and warmth return. This is a bald open summit with no sheltering crags, where windchill is unavoidable and extreme, so I returned to the south top for lunch.

Every man who is diagnosed with this disease is confronted suddenly with his own mortality. A confrontation with a disease that can be managed but as yet has no cure, this is a deep awareness of how precious and precarious a life is. Each of us then travels a different path, depending on the stage at which the disease is diagnosed, but we have this in common. Dave who I met on the mountain has taken a different journey from me, but we both continue to suffer side effects of medical intervention; my old friend from school is also moving into a different future from me, but most likely his disease will have been removed and any residue will be manageable for a long time to come. It was important for me and for each of them to be able to share knowledge and experience of the disease, of the decision-making processes involved and of how it felt suddenly to be confronted with the big questions. These conversations are important not only for the exchange of intimate experience, sharing tales of bodily dysfunction, but because these exchanges have a quality that places them outside conventional male discourse.

The tragedy of maleness is that if such exchanges were brought into everyday discussion, there would be greater chance that prostate cancer might be more frequently nipped in the bud, identified at an early stage, before it gets a chance to spread beyond the gland itself, whereafter its management tends more towards palliation than suppression.

The views from the top of **Ben Challlum** were spectacular, with the snow line at almost exactly at Munro level, making it easy to identify the peaks all around, and far into the distance. To the south, the Crianlarich Hills and **Ben Lui** are dominant; to the west **Ben Cruachan**; in the northwest, **Ben Dorian** in front of the Mamores and Glen Coe melding into a complex layering of white ridges with Ben Nevis massively resplendent to their right. In the east, the Lawers group and the Glenlyon Hills with *Scheihallion* behind; far away, slightly south of east, the Lomond Hills near my home in Fife; and on the northern horizon, just behind *Beinn Heasgarnaich*, the mighty **Ben Alder**. The views on the return are dominated by the pointy giants of **Ben More**, *Stob Binien* and **Ben Lui**, with the ridges of the Trossachs silhouetted between them in the low winter sun.

Imagining what inclusion of more intimate discussion of bodily function among men might look like is not easy. Blokes out on the piss and taking a leak together, one noticing that the other is a bit dribbly and having problems squirting out the last drops, then asking if this has been a recurrent issue and if so suggesting his mate get his PSA checked. Or on a building site, one bloke seems to spend too long in the toilet, to emerge looking pained, and who reveals when asked by a mate that it feels as if he has something permanently stuck up there, some sort of blockage that has nothing to do with his digestion. Perhaps exchanges like this might happen, but I do not think they are very common. The only other, and in fact the most prominent initial symptom of prostate cancer is diffuse intense lower back pain, which can be the result of so many more bodily disfunctions, that prostate cancer does not even make it on to the list. These are the only signs that there might be something developing. After this, the lower back pain becomes more piercing, then the generalised sickliness of metastasis, of some inexplicable ache deep inside, by which time the options for management, at least according to current medical understanding, will have been already limited.

Apart from measuring PSA in the blood, the only way of examining the health of a prostate is with the gloved middle digit of an experienced physician. Just as any good physician can palpate livers, spleens and other internal organs through the relaxed wall of the stomach, the condition of the prostate is easily palpable through the wall of the rectum. The opposite is of course also true; the owner of said prostate becomes aware of the movements of the digit of the physician as it examines, and thus it comes to feel itself, its own shape. Healthy prostates are smooth and slightly squashy, about the size of a walnut; unhealthy prostates are hard and ridged, much bigger than healthy prostates. All of my own prostate experiences are of a hard ridged lump; during my first rectal examination the physician's digit also touched the sensitivity of the gland, which spread a sudden unfamiliar sickliness throughout my body, leaving me discomfited for some time afterwards and unwilling immediately to sit down.

Returning back from the summit of the mountain by the way I came, I was warm and secure. Inevitably the ground was squelchier on the way back down after a day of sunlight. I was back at the car in good time to get home in time for supper, feeling good about myself, thinking about men and their cultures, what they can and do tell each other about the intimate moments of their lives, their problems, pains and private sufferings. Having been both a fully sexed, albeit reluctantly socialised, man during the bulk of my life, having now become periodically desexed over the previous few years and having also experienced the effects of a female hormone analogue pushing my body in the direction of femininity, I had a peculiar view of maleness, and I was happily confident that I had no more illusions about what it is like to be a man, no reason to identify with any kind of maleness, nor defend any male conduct, to stand up for the flag. All I had were the memories of the past when I behaved badly because I was a man, expected women to be a certain kind of being because I was a man, or demanded of them my attention and emotional support simply because they were women and I was a man. As far as I was aware I had sinned no more than was permitted by the culture I inhabited, but of course I live now with the reality of who I was before, the being society made of me, the stumbling and fumbling of growing up in a world where violence against women was commonplace and male entitlement taken for granted.

My imagined conversations between men about how to identify the first signs of prostate cancer were based on my own projections of how men *are* or *could be*; my own experience was nevertheless rather unusual, not perhaps the best basis for such speculation. Not every man enjoys the pleasures of chemical castration, no longer pulled by genital urges, the need to compete, nor any sense that achievement builds up entitlement even further. Apart from gay friends I did not know very many men like me; I certainly could not think of any existing male culture that accommodates intimate prostate examination, nor imaginary exchanges between blokes out on the piss or at building sites. They are nevertheless what must be necessary if the first symptoms of prostate cancer are ever to become as noticeable as the first signs of breast cancer. As far as I am aware, nobody is teaching men about prostate self-examination in a similar way to how women are encouraged to examine their breasts. I would like to think though that one day it might be possible for men naturally to talk to each other about what is going inside their bodies, so that if a man begins to notice something untoward going on, he will be in immediate contact with a culture that can advise, with access to technical discourses that recognise both the emotional and physical elements of the disease.

If the imperative to *be the change you want to see in the world* has any meaning at all, exchanges such as the ones I had recently with my friends and with Dave the prostate cancer warrior are already a contribution to making this so. Nevertheless, they remain private, outside public discourse. We all have to get on with our lives as best we can under the circumstances of our diagnoses. These are too often viewed entirely through materialistic reductionist lenses; the processes of the disease are seen as physical and mechanical, while the emotional and spiritual elements are pushed to the periphery, excluded from its pathology. Consciousness of the disease is reduced to knowledge of the facts as presented by the medical establishment; dealing with the psychological effects of either disease, its treatment or the collateral damage of medication is only to be found by first gaining insight into the actual truth of the condition. Under these circumstances, there is simply no space allotted for any notion that the emotional conditions of male socialisation, whether during infancy, early life, adolescence or adulthood, might actually *contribute to the development of the disease*.

*Prostate cancer warriors* know different; the experience of the disease is very different from understanding how it *works. There was a moment in each of our lives when it began, before which it did not exist and after which it did.* To say, for example, that this moment was the expression of some combination of genes is just a cop out; surely with honest reflection and retrospection, each of us may come to know when circumstances emerged that enabled the first unregulated division of cells that led to their prostate becoming a hard ridged lump rather than a soft squishy gland. Or maybe not. Who could honestly remember how it all started, when precisely his life became so stressful that cancer could more easily take hold of a minor insignificant gland?

Whatever else, each of us knows about the emotional effects of medical intervention, that these will always be more than the resection, suppression or burning out of the disease. There are reasons each of us got it; some of these may still be with us and if they are removed perhaps we can alleviate its worst effects or learn how to deal with our emotions differently.

Among the raft of side effects and consequences of the disease, each of which brings along new series of challenges and consequences, not only for ourselves, but for our nearest and dearest, was now the beginning of breaking down male culture, or at least a little bit of some of it, just at the edges.

## *Mount Keen*

### 2nd December 2017

I was coming to believe I did not have cancer, not because I was not in some sense ill, but because the existence of a thing called *cancer* that was going to kill me was becoming increasingly unsustainable.

I was also being informed that the style of my blog might be putting people off reading further, that my politics were not always to everybody's taste and that if I toned down my rhetoric a bit I might get a wider readership. Despite feeling that Frank Zappa had got it about right with the advice to creative types just to do what you do without compromise and those who appreciate your work will get it, for as soon as you compromise for an imagined audience, you no longer do what you do, I did make changes. After all, I was hardly in the same league as Zappa. So I changed the layout and tone of the blog, moving away from solidifying language and underplaying the egoistic bits; ascents were no longer described as *with cancer* but instead as *since diagnosis*; I also removed from view the complete quotation from *Trainspotting*, with all the difficult ideas and sweary words, from which the title was unashamedly plundered and which some readers apparently found a bit nippy. It turned out that it did not matter much either way; the new layout was more pleasing to the eye in any case and indeed much less *in your face*; there was no empirical increase or decrease in traffic and it appeared that it was still just my writing, my tales of derring-do and descriptions of mountain landscapes that attracted a readership.

Throughout my career as a cancer patient, the struggles had always been with the processes of diagnosis and prognosis, and with the demons of the mind that are exposed in the wake of these. There were of course times that I have no doubt I was very ill, but these seemed now to have receded into distant memory. At the beginning of this year I felt very much worse than I did now, when I learned that the medication was not working any more, when my PSA began to double more quickly than before, and when I had a nasty feeling in my chest in the region of an identifiably enlarged lymph node. Given that I was now free of all medication and that none of these symptoms had become worse, I was becoming genuinely sceptical (as opposed to being simply in denial) that I still had cancer, coming to see cancer less as a physical condition and more as *a state of mind*.

For more than a year, I had been looking after myself using sensible nutrition, good exercise, meditation and assorted dietary supplements. According to the deterministic logic of stage progression, since I stopped taking the medication, the cancer should have spread like wildfire. But I felt nothing of this in my body, and felt better in myself than I had at the start of the year, despite intermittent back pain, which was the real sign that something was not right. Whatever else, these feelings of improved wellbeing were a very good way of learning not to give cancer any solidity.

There were of course many voices asking: *What do the tests tell you? Have you had any results?* Not only actual people asking me about the status of the disease, about test results and about how the treatment was working, but also many methodological voices in my own head hearkening back to undergraduate studies of psychology. Oddly these had been brought now into even sharper focus as I endeavoured to follow His Holiness Lama Yeshe's advice, not to give the disease any solidity; when studying psychology often I could not understand how the thing that the psychologists were measuring was related to the actual life or being of the person or persons of whom it was being measured. Such doubts already made it quite easy not to give the disease any solidity; for in the absence of any measurements and in the presence of wellbeing, it was already not very solid at all.

The clamour for objective truth had become for me part of the problem. I was trying now not to listen to this noise. It was part of that same methodological knot, which had evidently continued to exist underneath other sciences of life. I still found it difficult to articulate, but to put the matter at its most general: I doubted *the power of single quantitative measurements of elements of complex systems to reveal the general condition of those systems.*

There had been a blood test sometime in the summer, and there were some scans too. The deal I made with the oncologists that I be tested only for the data, that I not know the results, seemed to be working well, at least from my point of view. I was quite happy knowing that my physicians had a duty to tell me if they discovered anything immediately life threatening, and since I had heard nothing ... *no news is good news* ...

The value and meaning of the results of tests was in my mind clear. They give only a snapshot of a particular moment in very complex living processes. Without any context, without any idea of how things are changing, they are more or less useless, unless incorporated into a larger context or theory of how things like this change, of what the rest of the world already looks like; such as, for example, mechanistic theories of organ function or deterministic logics of stage progression, both of which my experience was now rejecting.

According to statistical norms, my case seemed now marginal. Big science is not good at dealing with marginal cases. Though clinical science should, I felt, be fascinated by marginal cases. If a person does better than expected according to statistical norms, then there is surely something about that person or some aspect of their life that has made a difference. Which is surely of interest to those charged with improving the condition of all of those under statistical scrutiny. And if they could "bottle" what such a person has, they could surely use it as medicine. Metaphorically of course. Or so I might have expected the logic to proceed.

Even if there had been anybody remotely interested in investigating my case to see if it might help others, they would have discovered quickly that it would in any case be impossible to isolate any one factor, any single item of diet, environment or attitude that had made the crucial difference. Unlike the illusory mechanics of Cartesian metaphysics, I did not believe the world to be the sum of component parts operating according to mathematical principles; it is a complex and continuously changing interconnected whole with which we are intricately entwined, actively involved. Whether it is at this level *rule-governed* or *habit-forming* or old school *mechanistic* remains a matter of speculation, or even perhaps empirical investigation.

Just as there are many ways of understanding the general way that things hang together in the world, there are many ways of doing science, and the meaning of the word *science* has changed considerably throughout its history. It seemed to me at the time that medical science had become one of the most successful ways of controlling populations since Catholicism (this was one of the more provocative aphorisms in my little book) and that it had done so by employing a strict Cartesian division between the mechanics of the body and the mysteries of the mind, that the two were essentially separate and that no effort by the latter to influence the former would affect the mechanical processes of a body in any way.

I was still angry that this was so, for it seemed that this being the case had contributed not only to my condition but to the exclusion of certain ways of looking at it and perforce means of treating it. The methodological criteria employed by the medical establishment of the present takes for granted an outdated and sterile notion of objectivity, founded on the dualistic metaphysics of seventeenth century French philosopher Rene Descartes who found freedom to write in the city of Amsterdam, and it is no longer fit for purpose. Or at least, if its purpose is to manage the progression of disease using statistical analyses of snapshot measurements of assorted aspects of human bodies, on the assumption that these are biochemical machines separated from intrinsic consciousness, then it has a certain social, political and economic function, *and power*, a kind of leverage over human conduct, consciousness and experience.

But if it genuinely believes it is bringing individuals into a condition of health, then it fails. Miserably. Or so I believed at the time. I might even have opined in more radical moments that the only way for bodies to maintain any condition of health and wellbeing is for them to live *outside* and beyond the knowledge imposed upon them by medical science, where diet and emotional wellbeing are far from side lined, but *are regarded as absolutely* crucial to developing lives, and any *dis ease* that a person may encounter should be examined entirely within the specific conditions of that person's life. The challenge was to make a switch from being dependent on some authority in order to avoid being unwell, to becoming actively well, finding the intrinsic powers a body always already has hidden away, to *include* the power of a mind in the efforts of a body ravaged by some disease. A *dis ease* is always of a whole person, comprising this body and this mind together over the years of their particular history.

There are many perfectly coherent *sciences of life*, in a broader sense, than demanded by contemporary norms, that accommodate the place of human beings within the complex interconnectedness of things, without insisting that it is only possible to know anything at all by standing at a distance from life and assuming it is a big machine, no matter how complex. Specifically, ideas about health and wellbeing that are based on nutrition, exercise and mental discipline and that do not rely on drugs produced by big pharma. At a purely intellectual level, I had always been scathing of mechanistic theories of anything except machines and the operation of machinery; my continuing life was now living testament to this attitude.

For I did not need any more objective evidence than this of my own condition. Which on this day took me to the top of **Mount Keen**, the most easterly Munro in the tables, taking my tally for the year to 52, an average of one per week. It did not seem to me that somebody who was extremely ill would be able to get to the summits of one hundred and thirty-four Munros since he was diagnosed with a terminal disease. With so much experience in these legs, my mountain craft and skills were at their peak; no task seemed beyond their reach. I was also very pleased with my new boots.

I arrived to climb **Mount Keen** from the south at the hamlet of Mark where snow was piled by the verges. It was a long flat pleasant walk in, along a good estate track, followed by a few hours ploughtering through snow, with views west to **Lochnagar** and Glen Shee, all shrouded in snow cloud, and of clear skies over the North Sea from Fraserburgh to St. Abb's Head. The sun shone low through thinning cloud above Glen Clova, garnishing the slopes of ***Dreish*** and ***Mayar*** with orange glow, sparkling their crust of snow, as if my mother's gentle smile was still hanging over the hills where I had left some of her remains.

Despite everything I thought, believed, said or wrote, I still found it difficult sometimes not to slot into the logic of medical determinism. At a daily practical level, always living in fear that the ordinary twinges of being alive, that the occasional pains of a body, are signs of the spreading of the disease; that at any moment, one of my vital organs might begin to fail or my body become wracked with excruciating pain. I believed though that with every summit I reached, I actively negated the alleged inexorability of cancer, and undermined the power of medical technocracy to determine my fate, chipping away at the fears it engenders to reveal the ordinariness of life, where there is stuff to fear, to be sure, but it is always real and never insurmountable.

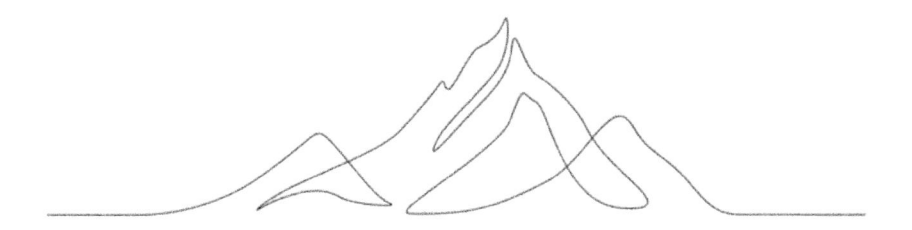

## *An Socach*

### 10th December 2017

It was minus nine when I started the car and scraped off a thick layer of frost from the windscreen. As I parked in a layby in Glen Clunie on the road to Braemar, it was minus six. It did not look as if the sun ever warms this side of the pass into Deeside at this time of year. Dry compacted snow squeaked under my new boots along the track to Glen Baddoch. A dipper flitted over the rocks in the burn, an artery of brown under the white, steaming slightly. At the ford through *Allt Coire Fhearnseagh* I filled my bottle, knowing this would be the last liquid water I would encounter until I crossed over on the way back. It felt warm flowing over my hand. I was on my way to my third, the most accessible, **An Socach**.

My mind was still rummaging around the practicalities of prostate cancer diagnoses in the light of contact from the two men from different bits of my past, both diagnosed recently with prostate cancer; an old friend from school and an acquaintance from Utrecht being treated by the same team who first diagnosed me in 2012. This had brought up a whole lot of stuff, not only residual resentment towards the urologist who had behaved like an asshole, but also my uncommon attitude towards medical science and the effects this has on the decisions I make during life. How could I give advice in good faith about matters medical when I have such a deeply sceptical attitude towards medicine? I would certainly not advise anybody to do what I had done, least of all without knowing all the *facts*, nor thinking very carefully about what it all means. But anything else would seem dishonest.

I began the ascent through deep snow and high heather over increasingly frozen ground, following imprints left by others. At a cairn at about seven hundred metres, having slithered too much to get there, I put on crampons. The sun appeared for the first time over the ridge to the south. From here the snow was deep where it lay, the ground rocky and icy. This mountain is an almost level, two kilometre long, banana shaped ridge with rather steep sides. There is a slight prominence at either end and a little dip in the middle. The farther summit is higher by six metres. The ground is stony and exposed, with very few outcrops or crags so the snow was not lying deep, continuously blowing past and sculpted like desert sand. At the first summit I removed my crampons and began the walk to the far end of the ridge and the highest point, which was difficult to pick out in the low sun in front of the amalgamated bulk of **Ben Iutharn**, **Carn an Righ** and the three Munros of *Beinn a' Ghlo*.

The sun shone low in the southern sky, the air was still, ptarmigan croaked contentedly. Hares flopped about sunning themselves, washing their faces. It was easy going along the top, surrounded by views of white mountains and distant peaks. The air was still and the sun warm. Were it not for the snow on the ground, it could have been summer. It is not the cold that takes heat away from a body, it is the wet, a lack of sunlight and fast-moving air. Sitting at the summit with my flask of soup, the warmth of my body easily held at bay the cold outside, behind down, windstopper and layering. I found myself thinking through my story in Dutch, about my condition and what advice I would offer to one diagnosed with prostate cancer by the same hospital I first attended.

The conditions were extremely peaceful and benign, the benevolent wisdom of the land overwhelming. I allowed my mind to drift as I surveyed the southern horizon and the first words came to me. A farewell letter to my past, offering answers to my own questions and those of many others.

*Zo. Daar zit je dan te zonnen in de sneeuw, lekker warm in je dons, fleece en windstopper, boven op de 135ste berg die je beklommen hebt, vijf jaar nadat je te horen kreeg dat je nog maar drie jaar te leven zou hebben, mits je de medicatie nam, en slechts één zonder. Wat een wonder is dit!*

*Tegenwoordig word ik af en toe om advies gevraagd over kanker in het algemeen, en prostaatkanker in het bijzonder, door bekenden, oude vrienden en mensen die van mijn verhaal gehoord hebben. Recentelijk nog door een kennis uit mijn tijd in Nederland, die onder behandeling komt bij hetzelfde ziekenhuis waar ik behandeld werd toentertijd, meer dan vijf jaar geleden.*

*Dit contact heeft van alles en nog wat weer naar boven gebracht. Ik kan natuurlijk altijd advies geven. Ik ben inmiddels al lang ziek, ik heb meerdere medische behandelingen ondergaan, ik heb verstand van mijn eigen lijf, ik kan goed voor mezelf zorgen met behulp van een dieet, meditatie en het beklimmen van bergen, en ik ben niet bang om over moeilijke dingen te praten. Eerst moet ik echter alle uitslagen van alle onderzoeken hebben.*

*Zo was het, toen voor het eerst prostaatkanker bij mij geconstateerd werd. Voordat ik klakkeloos overnam wat de artsen me adviseerden, wilde ik eerst alle uitslagen hebben, en wilde ik alles te weten komen over prostaatkanker, zowel volgens de medische wetenschap, als diverse alternatieve stromingen. Het was mijn leven. Mijn beslissing. Gelukkig heb ik ook een belangrijk document gevonden, gedownload en uitgeprint: het* European Prostate Cancer Protocol *(het EPCP).*

*Het proces van diagnose is, in eerste instantie, een proces. Niet alles kan tegelijk gebeuren. Het begint met een bezoek aan de huisarts. Dan volgt een reeks afspraken en bezoeken aan ziekenhuizen voor diverse onderzoeken, scans en biopsieën. Om een lang verhaal kort te maken, in een periode van anderhalve maand, heb ik maar liefst vijf urologen gesproken van twee verschillende ziekenhuizen, die allemaal tot dezelfde conclusie kwamen, namelijk dat ik meteen met de zogenaamde hormoontherapie moest beginnen. Meteen. Ze hadden allemaal het* European Prostate Cancer Protocol *goed gelezen. Toen ik het ook las, had ik tot dezelfde conclusie kunnen komen. Het is een protocol. Het maakt niet uit wie het leest.*

*Het is natuurlijk niet normaal dat een gewone burger niet meteen het advies van een expert opvolgt. Er zijn dingen die gewone mensen niet kunnen weten. Daarom hebben we experts die protocollen opstellen. Vooral artsen, die het meeste weten over ziektes en hoe ze behandeld moeten worden. Toch? Maar dat is niet voor iedereen vanzelfsprekend.*

*In Nederland wordt je in het algemeen geleerd om verantwoordelijkheid te nemen voor jezelf, om goede keuzes te maken op basis van betrouwbare informatie. Dit was min of meer mijn standpunt toen de eerste uroloog me vertelde dat mijn PSA-waarde 96 was, en botweg zei: "Ik denk dat het kanker is; we moeten een behandeling opstarten. U kunt gelijk een injectie krijgen bij de oncologieverpleegkundige."*

*Waarschijnlijk was mijn reactie verkeerd. Ik had moeten zeggen: "dank u wel, dokter" en ik had meteen naar de oncologieverpleegkundige moeten gaan voor een hormooninjectie. Dit zou de productie van testosteron in mijn lichaam onderdrukken, en zodoende de werking van mijn prostaat tot stilstand brengen en de kanker op nonactief stellen.*

*Door het lezen van het EPCP, wist ik echter al van de vreselijke bijwerkingen van deze injectie. Verder wist ik dat het geen oplossing was, maar meer een palliatief dan een curatief middel. Op dat moment was er nog geen uitslag van de biopsie en daarom wilde ik wachten. Maar het woord kanker bleef door mijn hoofd spoken. Daarmee was alles veranderd.*

*Een week later nam een nieuwe uroloog vijf monsters van prostaatweefsel af voor onderzoek. De week erna vertelde een derde arts mij dat mijn Gleason-score negen was, oftewel agressief en kwaadaardig, en hij benadrukte hoe belangrijk het was om meteen met de hormoontherapie te starten. Ik herinner me dit gesprek als de dag van gisteren.*

*Ik vroeg of het mogelijk was dat er tijdens het uitvoeren van de biopsie kankercellen vanuit mijn prostaat ontsnapt konden zijn, en of dit een verhoogde PSA-waarde kon veroorzaken. Hij antwoordde dat dat mogelijk was. Om dit te checken, mocht ik mijn bloed opnieuw laten onderzoeken. Ik zei nogmaals dat ik wilde wachten met het nemen van een beslissing over de hormooninjecties. Er was nog altijd, wat mij betreft, onduidelijkheid over een iets te grote zwelling in mijn lymfeklier, wat de artsen zagen als bevestiging dat de kanker al uitgezaaid was. Op scans waren echter nergens uitzaaiingen te zien, en deze zwelling hoefde toch niet per se op kanker te duiden, het kon ook een onschuldige infectie zijn. De sfeer was een beetje moeilijk. Er werd hem gevraagd over wat voor tijdsbestek we het eigenlijk hadden. Zijn antwoord staat nu al vijf jaar in mijn geheugen gegrift: "Drie jaar met medicatie, misschien één zonder."*

*Het is goed mogelijk dat hij dat echt geloofde, dat op basis van zijn ervaring met de desbetreffende wetenschap en het behandelen van patiënten, iemand zoals ik, met deze uitslagen, echt binnen enkele jaren dood zou gaan. Maar om het me dan op deze manier te vertellen? En zo precies? Alsof dit mij ervan zou overtuigen om meteen met de hormoontherapie te beginnen? Alsof hij mij emotioneel probeerde te manipuleren? Ik heb misschien kanker, maar ik ben niet dom. Er is eigenlijk geen keuze hier. Alles is voorbestemd. Het is slechts een kwestie van tijd. Ik besloot erover na te denken, en ik overwoog op een bewustere, gezondere manier te gaan leven. Wat had ik immers te verliezen?*

*Geen andere specialist heeft ooit zo'n specifieke prognose gegeven. Een paar hebben "off the record" gezegd dat het niet zo netjes was van deze arts, maar zijn prognose was de eerste die ik kreeg. Ik heb deze man daarna nog maar één keer gezien. Het was een naar gesprek. Net als de rest van zijn collega's in de Nederlandse zorgindustrie, was hij van mening dat het niet uitmaakt wat je eet, hoe gezond je leeft, en welke supplementen je gebruikt, de kanker overwint alles en zal je uiteindelijk doden. Dit vertelde hij mij op een kleinerende manier. Erg sarcastisch. Eigenlijk was het echt een lul van een vent.*

De volgende PSA-waarde was met 139 flink omhooggegaan vanaf 96; dit kan mogelijk met de biopsie te maken hebben, maar dat is niet zeker. Vijf maanden later, na radicale veranderingen in dieet en levensstijl en zo, is de PSA maar naar 142 gestegen. Direct bewijs, wat mij betreft, sinds het begin van mijn traject, dat niet alles zo voorbestemd is als de wetenschap verwacht, dat je wel iets tegen zogenaamde stage progression *kan doen, simpelweg met wilskracht, met je manier van zijn en doen. En nu vijf jaar later, zit ik boven op een berg. Tja.*

Ondanks mijn twijfels over de wetenschap, ondanks het feit dat ik nog leef en de eerste prognose onjuist bleek te zijn, kan ik het soms niet loslaten en word ik echt kwaad. Ik heb op basis van de prognose beslissingen genomen. Sommige hiervan hebben geleid tot rust en geluk, maar andere tot spijt, verlies en woede. En de prognose bleek onwaar te zijn. Moet ik die spijt en woede voor lief nemen, en dankbaar zijn voor de rust en het geluk? Moet ik vergeten dat ik mijn zakelijke belangen met verlies verkocht heb, dat ik mijn pensioenrechten overgedragen heb, dat ik veel dingen weggegeven heb, veel vrienden achtergelaten heb, en een heel leven opgegeven heb, omdat ik liever terug wilde naar mijn eigen land om daar te sterven, maar waar ik nu nog steeds niet gestorven ben, en zonder alles wat ik ooit in Nederland had, probeer weer een nieuw leven op te bouwen?

Maar goed. Hier zit ik dan, boven op een berg te zonnen, midden in de winter in mijn eigen land, met het gevoel dat ik helemaal geen kanker meer heb, en ik voel geen behoefte om me bezig te houden met uitslagen van onderzoeken en scans, of om meer verhalen te horen van de medische wetenschap.

Het is hierdoor niet eenvoudig om me uit te spreken over het advies dat aan een ander gegeven wordt door dezelfde afdeling, zo niet door dezelfde specialisten, die er bij mij zo naast zaten. Nu ik met de wereldberoemde NHS te maken heb, heb ik een veel betere ervaring met artsen en specialisten, die protocollen niet als bijbel maar als richtlijn gebruiken, en een patiënt behandelen als een mens en niet als een nummer.

Volgens mij is het in Nederland misgegaan door de hervorming van het zorgstelsel in de jaren negentig, toen het ziekenfonds aan de zorgverzekeraars werd verkocht. Als alles op de meest efficiënte manier dient te gebeuren om maar winst te kunnen maken, zijn mensen niet meer dan een nummer, en hebben artsen geen tijd om individuele gevallen te onderzoeken. Ze hebben geen belang bij alternatieve behandelingen, en geen ruimte om na te denken over hun eigen positie in een machtsrelatie.

Mijn raad over dit alles is heel duidelijk. Zorg goed voor jezelf met een dieet, beweging, meditatie en ga bergen beklimmen, of als er geen bergen aanwezig zijn, fietsen, zwemmen, hardlopen, kanoën, wat dan ook. Ga naar buiten, geniet van de aarde, adem het leven diep in, blaas de giffen uit. Zelfs midden in de winter kun je boven op een berg zitten zonnen, en je erover verwonderen dat er überhaupt leven is en dat je het kunt ervaren.

It came out more or less like that. Non-Dutch speakers can be assured that it contains not much that has not already been mentioned, that reading on from here without further ado will not detract in any way from the story. To anybody who insists that readers who understand Dutch are getting something extra, a literal translation is provided shortly. It was in any case most cathartic to have articulated these things in this way, a great help with the demons I met on the Holy Isle.

After lunch I wandered back along the ridge, taking photos of low hanging light over dazzling snowscapes, glittery ground and wind sculpted ice, washed with every hue from deep orange to subtle purple. Tarrying to gaze at familiar outlines on horizons all around, smothered thick in white, I was reminded of how little daylight there is at this time of year. At two thirty I was back at the first summit and put on my crampons again for the descent. The sun had already begun to slide behind the bumps of *Beinn a' Ghlo*, giving the snowy mountains an amber glow. Coming off the ridge, I gazed back at the Cairngorms for the last time, dominating the northern horizon, smiling under their winter blanket, **Bod an Daemhain** dark and prominent at the entrance to the Lairig Ghru.

Stomping back along the path, squeaking again over dry impacted snow, it was obvious that the sun had not been seen here today. Yet it did not feel cold, and my feet were hot from their day's work, happy in their new boots. Back at the car, the temperature read minus eleven. I was very relieved that the engine started. I drove home carefully, my old Volvo doing best exactly what it was designed to do. This was a day that will stay with me for a very, very long time.

And here then a translation of the Dutch above.

So. There you are sunbathing in the snow, nice and warm under down, fleece and windstopper, on top of the 135th mountain you've climbed, five years after you were told you would only have three years to live, even if you took the medication, and only one without. What a wonder this is!

These days, I am occasionally asked for advice about cancer in general and prostate cancer in particular, by acquaintances, old friends and people who have heard my story. Recently from an acquaintance from my time in the Netherlands, who is being treated at the same hospital where I received treatment then, more than five years ago. This communication has brought up all sorts of stuff.

Of course I can always give advice. I have long experience of the disease, I have undergone several medical treatments, I understand my own body, can take good care of myself with diet, meditation and mountain climbing, and am not afraid to talk about difficult stuff. However, first I need to know all information from all tests, which is how it was when I was first diagnosed with prostate cancer.

Before I immediately started doing what the doctors advised, I first wanted to know about all the results, and I wanted to know everything about prostate cancer, both according to medical science and according to a variety of alternative perspectives. It was my life. My decision.

Fortunately, I also found, downloaded and printed an important document: the *European Prostate Cancer Protocol* (the *EPCP*).

The process of diagnosis is, in the first instance, a process. Not everything can be done immediately. It starts with a visit to the doctor. Then there is a series of appointments and visits to hospitals for various tests, scans and biopsies. To cut a long story short, over a period of one and a half months, I spoke with no fewer than five different urologists from two different hospitals, all of whom came to the same conclusion, that I should immediately start the so-called hormone treatment. Right away. They had all also carefully read the European Prostate Cancer Protocol. When I read it too, I could have come to the same conclusion. It is a protocol. It does not matter who reads it.

Of course, it is not normal for an ordinary citizen not immediately to accept the advice of an expert. There are things that ordinary people cannot know, which is why we have experts who set up protocols. Especially doctors, who know best about diseases and how to treat them. Right? Not necessarily self-evident for everyone.

In the Netherlands, people are generally taught to take responsibility for themselves, to make good choices based on reliable information. This was more or less my position when the first of the urologists told me that my PSA value was ninety-six, saying bluntly, "I think there is cancer in there; so we have to do something about it. You can get an injection right away from the oncology nurses."

I believe mine was the wrong reaction. I should have said, "thank you, doctor" and then I should have gone straight away the to the oncology nurses to get the hormone injection, which would suppress the production of testosterone in my body and thus switch off the function of my prostate and shut down the cancer.

From reading the EPCP, I knew about the terrible side effects of this injection. I also knew that it was not a solution, more palliative than curative. At that moment there was no biopsy result so I wanted to wait. But the word cancer kept ringing in my head. Everything then changed. A week later a new urologist took five samples of prostate tissue for analysis, a week after a third told me my Gleason score was nine, meaning aggressive and malignant, and stressed the importance of taking the hormone treatment right away. I remember this conversation as if it were yesterday.

I asked if it was possible that during the process of taking a biopsy, cancer cells could have escaped from my prostate, and if this would be reflected in an elevated PSA level. He replied that it was possible; to check this, I was allowed to have my blood tested again. I said again that I wanted to wait before I decided to take the hormone injection. There was still always, as far as I was concerned, some doubt about a bit too large swelling of lymph, which was instant proof to the doctors that the cancer had already spread. However, there was no further evidence of metastasis on any scan, and this swelling could have come from not only cancer, but also from common or garden infections. There was a rather difficult atmosphere. He was asked how long we are talking about here actually. His answer has stuck in my consciousness for five years now: "three years with medication, maybe one without."

It is possible that he really believed this, that according to his experience of the relevant sciences and of treating patients, with these test results, a person like me really would likely die in a very few years. But to tell me in this way? And so exactly? As if this would convince me immediately to take the hormone treatment? As if he was trying emotionally to manipulate me?

Maybe I have cancer, but I am not stupid. There is really no choice here. Everything is predestined. It's just a matter of time. So I walked away to think about it, and possibly move into a more conscious, healthy life. What did I have to lose?

No other specialist has ever offered such a specific forecast. A few have told me, off the record, that it was not very clever of this doctor, but his prognosis was the first I heard. I only saw this man one more time. It was an unpleasant conversation. Like the rest of his colleagues in the Dutch healthcare industry, he believed that no matter what you eat, how healthily you live, and what supplements you use, cancer rolls over everything and will eventually kill you. He told me this in a disparaging way. Very sarcastic. Actually, this bloke was just a dick.

The next PSA value rose sharply to 139; of course, all we know is that it may be related to the biopsy, we are not sure. Five months later after radical changes in diet, lifestyle and all, the PSA had risen to just 142. Direct proof, as far as I was concerned, *from the start of my trajectory*, that not everything is as predestined as science expects, that you can do something about so-called stage progression, with your willpower, your way of being and doing. And now five years later, on top of a mountain. Well!

Even though I had doubts about the science, even though I am still alive, despite the failure of the initial prognosis, sometimes I cannot let go of it and I get really angry. I made decisions based on the prognosis. Some of these have led to peace and happiness, but others to regret, loss and anger. And the prognosis turned out to be false. Do I now have to accept regret and anger while being grateful for peace and happiness? Should I forget that I sold my business at a loss, that I transferred my pension rights, that I gave away many things, left many friends, and gave up a whole life because I thought I would rather go back to my own country to die, where I still have not died, without everything I had in the Netherlands, trying again to rebuild a new life?

Nevertheless. Here I am, sunbathing on top of a mountain, in the middle of winter in my own country with the feeling that I no longer have cancer at all, with no need to know about results of tests and scans, or to hear more stories from medical science.

Not so obvious then, what I should say to the advice offered to another by the same department, if not the same specialists who handled my case so badly. Now living with the world-famous NHS, I have a much better experience with doctors and specialists who can use protocols, not as a bible but as a guide, and who treat patients as people not numbers.

In my opinion, things went wrong in the Netherlands as a direct result of the changes in the health care system that started with the sale of the state health fund to insurers during the 1990s. When everything has to be done in the most efficient way to make a profit, people can only become numbers, doctors have no time to examine individual cases, they have no interest in alternative treatments, and no room to think about their own position in any power relationship.

My advice on everything now is now very clear. Take care of yourself with diet, exercise, meditation and mountain climbing, or if there are no available mountains, cycling, swimming, running, canoeing, whatever. Go out, enjoy the earth, breathe life deeply in, exhale out the toxins. Even in the middle of winter you can sunbathe on top of a mountain, in awe that there is life at all and that you can experience it.

## Beinn an Dothaidh

17th December 2017

Martyn and I had been failing throughout the autumn to find mutual windows of opportunity to continue our adventures. He had made it plain that he was quite happy to accompany me whenever I wanted to bag the next Munros on my list, that he was up for revisiting any Munro, many of which he had climbed such a long time ago he had forgotten exactly what they looked like.

It was getting to be late in the year, but there would still be light enough in a day to get up the mountain next to **Ben Dorian**, the one we had failed to climb at the beginning of the year, *Beinn an Dothaidh* (pronounced Ben an Doe). At last we found a day that was forecast not to be too awful, with layering cloud, rising temperatures and light winds; it would be our last opportunity of the year and a fitting conclusion, finishing what we had started and moving on.

The weather looked good on the drive through Glen Dochart, with interesting temperature inversions and banks of cloud hanging at random altitudes. When we arrived at Bridge of Orchy however, cloud was engulfing the mountains all around. On the way up the path, just at the point where we first met, beside the same large boulder, we entered the gloom, and on the way back down, at the same boulder, we came out of it again. Only lingering sunlight, garnishing the tips of the Etive Hills in the distance, and the browns and dark ochres in Glen Orchy below offered any clue that the world was anything but monochrome.

From the boulder we followed a path rising steeply towards the bealach through thick melting snow. The ground was barely recognisable from our previous visit when the corrie was packed deep and this path buried beneath ice-solid drifts covered over with dry powder. From the bealach we turned left, following steps made by previous boots. Martyn kept an eye on his Garmin and I noted very carefully the changes in the contours of the land, making sure we remained within the bowl of the corrie and did not stray too far in the direction of the steep northern and western flanks of the mountain. Visibility was perhaps a hundred meters at best, but contrast was very poor with all this white. Protruding crags and obvious gradients kept us right, along with the footfalls of others in the snow and Martyn's Garmin. Coll bounced along happily snuffling through sludgy snow for interesting smells. We could feel as we rose that warmer air was on the way. The snow was turning more squishy and wet, very different from the drifts of dry stuff I had enjoyed on *An Socach* the previous week, and that we had experienced on *Ben Dorian* at the start of the year. It was a difficult slog through heavy snow, under perspective destroying gloom, always with the hope of sunlight breaking through, with intriguing glimpses of the Black Mount to the northwest. It was windy at the summit though, cold wet hill fog with a drizzle of soggy spindrift.

None of which contributed positively to my mood. For I was feeling morose, consumed by thoughts of death. In these societies that appear to know everything in advance, death is what we cannot know, and we fear it. Even though death is around us all day every day, an intimate component of the cycle of life, just one moment in everlasting processes of growth and decay, of development and regeneration, we hide it away, euphemise it and try to deny its effects. And consequently do not understand it properly.

The fear of death is a fundamental element of our social experience, it is built into theologies and rituals of religious observance, and it haunts the corridors of every institution of care and rehabilitation our societies maintain. Fear of death is the most difficult of emotional conditions, for it hammers home the inevitability of mortality, tells us that we are not in control and do not know everything, warning us that when our time comes, it will likely be painful and lonely.

Fear on its own is a rather complicated emotion too. It has an evolutionary function, anchored in the physiology of adrenaline by the mechanism of *fight or flight*. Fear is, in my opinion, one of the basic four emotions, along with rage, grief and joy. It is also one of the glues that holds society together, one of the reasons why damaged and broken relationships continue beyond their natural lifespan, it is the motivation behind subservience, the cue for bullies, the source of indifference, impotence, sectarian conflict and a lot more besides. It is both primeval and socially constructed, it is both a visceral and a learned response.

Of course, we are all going to die, but we expect this to happen once we reach the end of our lives, which we mostly expect to be after at least seventy years of being alive. We do not like to talk about death very much and we prefer to keep hidden anything that reminds us of it. Apart from highly sanitised memorial services and remembrance rituals, our cultures are very bad at dealing with death. We have learned to keep ourselves alive and looking young at all costs, we have learned to hide away the final stages of life, lest they remind us that we will all grow old. We have built societies that turn every stage in the process of being alive into a matter for medical intervention and we have come to believe, without the least bit of critical thought, that it is our right to have all our suffering and bodily imperfection taken away from us by doctors. We have learned to demand that everything that departs from a scientifically established image of health and vitality should be brought under the control of medicine and normalised with some sort of physical or pharmaceutical intervention, which will be provided either by social health care systems or insurers.

Despite our growing relationship I did not yet feel able completely to open up to Martyn about these feelings. It was obvious that he was a sensitive human being who, having brought up two children into successful careers would be perfectly able to talk through any difficult emotions I may have presented to him, but something was holding *me* back; despite him sometimes asking searching questions during the course of ordinary conversations, I was still not quite sure in my own mind how I felt, nor how I could put this into words, so I was perhaps a little evasive. Death. My own demise. My stubborn refusal to have anything to do with medical science carried along with it a certain bravado and my use of a substance in place of anything the medics could offer remained a source of insecurity, not only because of its legal status, but also because there was not much systematic knowledge that could guide or help me along the way.

I believed that I had come to terms with the "facts" of death, its consequences for the lives of those living under its shadow. In the wake of every death (even one that has yet to take place) those who experience this undergo four distinct emotional conditions; *denial, anger, grief* and *acceptance*. These do not however appear in stages; there is no serial progression from one state to the next, culminating in some enlarged serenity. Any or all of these emotions can crop up at any moment, for all sorts of reasons, combined with any or all of the others. At this moment I was simply feeling morose, a kind of elision of mild grief, subdued and not yet easy to articulate fury with a pinch of unhappy acceptance. I was sure that Martyn was aware of this, or at least that he realised there was something troubling me, but he was not yet able to dig it out; his experience of parenthood was however enabling him to be kind and gentle with whatever was going on as we continued to converse in our usual way, developing the basis of what would turn out to be a deep friendship that moved beyond the status of mountain buddies.

At the summit we found a very large cornice packed smoothly against the northern cliffs, which are much steeper than I realised. The cornice was fully integrated with the snow pack upon which we were standing with no clue about where the division was between snow covering the rock of the summit and probably unstable snow clinging over five hundred feet above the corrie below. None of the summit rocks crags or piles of stones was visible as more than a nose protruding through the surface, plastered with ice. We thought there might have been shelter somewhere near the summit, but everything was covered in snow and it was impossible to discern any features at all, so we ticked the box and took a bearing to descend in search of shelter. The way down went much the same as the way up. But we found no shelter and could only briefly huddle down in the gloom in the southern corrie of the mountain for soup and brief respite. It was cold, but necessary to rest our feet and ingest some energy.

The return route was easy to find. The thaw was evident as we crushed through slippery ice that in the morning we had to avoid. Behind us the cloud looked like it was dispersing, with a distinct tinge of blue behind cliffs dripping with icicles. Further down the path, looking back up, both peaks were now free of cloud and backed by clear blue sky, the exact opposite of the day we climbed **Ben Dorian**, when the cloud came down thick and we knew we had made the right decision to turn back rather than to make an attempt on ***Beinn an Dothaidh***.

We drove back to our rendezvous and I transferred my stuff into my own car. We agreed that we would be doing this sort of thing again in the future, that it was fine to have such companionship in the mountains, particularly in winter. We agreed to keep an eye open for windows of opportunity; I said that

I had my sights on a mountain near Braemar, **Carn Bhac**, that would contribute to the completion of the eastern Grampians, if he was up to it any time in the near future.

The turn of the year and its usual excesses took second place for both of us, to our base motivations to climb mountains. On all days when other stuff is not already arranged or becomes necessary, it is always possible, weather permitting, to head for the hills. We were both glad of the company and this developing friendship. It is not every day that a chance meeting on a mountainside leads in this direction. We both looked forward to our next outing, whenever that might happen to be. Although, neither of us was interested in the festive season as anything other than something that rather got in the way of ordinary life, he and his wife had made plans to be away from it all; Shona and I too were looking forward to visiting a cottage near Tomintoul.

We were not yet aware that we would become such good friends; though we knew we would always enjoy getting out together, that we were of a similar mind in the mountains and knew where our priorities lay. For the moment we said our farewells, which now included a vigorous man hug, and determined to meet up as soon as possible in the new year, weather permitting, probably nearby Braemar.

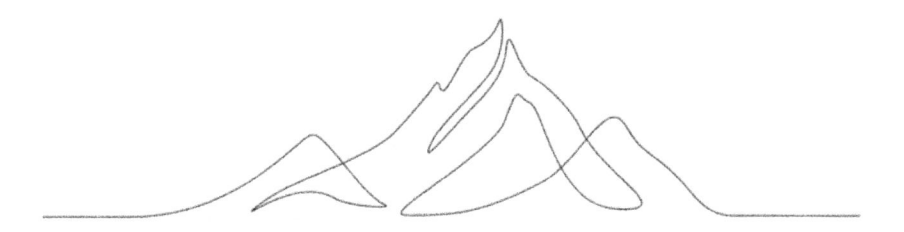

## The Bochel:
## New Year and the magic between-us

By all standards that I can think of, 2017 was the most remarkable and wonderful year of my life. Not only did I marry the love of my life and my best friend, I climbed fifty-four separate Munros while still diagnosed with a malignant cancer that was shaped in my mind by the first prognosis I received, according to which I should have died two years previously. I had thus taken my tally of Munros since said diagnosis to one hundred and thirty-six, only five short of halfway. It was humbling as much as exciting to know that in the coming months, I had a strong feeling that my body would be able to add many more to the list. By any standards, 2017 was indeed the most amazing and wonderful year of my life, and yet there seemed to be a lot more of this life waiting just around the corner.

Getting married is a commitment; to travel together into a shared future, without knowing what lies round the corner, but trusting each other to be able to deal with whatever comes to pass. It is a big risk, which is often dashed against the circumstances of unpredictable times, as both of us had already encountered. With each new shared experience, the depth and perspective of any new relationship can nevertheless develop and move on to encounter more new experiences and developments. Apart from being rather overawed that this happened to us when we were well into our fifties, we were happy and fortunate that it was for us a natural process, that because we had been good friends at school, we had a lot in common and shared deep cultural connections that made the risks less pungent.

Climbing fifty four separate new Munros in a year might seem like a remarkable achievement for anybody, but for me at this particular moment it seemed less of an achievement than the outcome of finding reason for getting out of bed in the morning, something to drive me away from the despondency of cancer and to take me to the place where fantasy and reality meet head on, where my childhood desire to be an intrepid explorer of wildernesses was carried along on an elderly Volvo V70 with well over quarter of a million on the clock. All of which massively widened my experience of the vast landscape that is hidden away in this country beyond the ends of roads and railway halts, or at the other side of mysterious lochs, far from municipal car parks and tourist attractions. At the beginning of the year I was unsure of the names or even the locations of the horizons I was surveying from summits; at the end I could name and pinpoint every bump and serration I saw, connecting to the country more profoundly than seemed possible.

This is a special kind of love, impossible to describe, of a land seeped so deeply in beauty and tragedy that to touch this, to glimpse it, even know of its existence is to understand *viscerally* exactly why it is shite being Scottish and to feel the intolerable pain of history. It is soaked into the denatured landscape, useful only to the privileged to consummate their bloodlust, to preserve outdated values of custodianship, and to sustain British state power; while a few responsible institutions and stalwart souls with visions of something else, tinker at the edges with regenerations and ecological projects of one sort of another, which they hope one day will create more natural habitats and a greater diversity of life. The rest of us meanwhile see grid references at the summits of mountains and routes towards these from places where we can park our cars, from which we cannot but avoid expanding our consciousness and through which we can begin to understand that values of simplicity, silence and slow contemplation are more important than arguing about what happened in the past. To have packed so much of this into one year was intense, to say the least.

It was a year of very high, high points. Clambering along the *Anoach Eagach* under the guidance of Martyn, inspired me to write one of the most oft read, and dare I add, powerful posts at my blog, which I called *Exposure* and which appears here unedited. My completion of the Loch Trieg circuit, despite being disappointed by no views from the *Easians*, took me on a wilderness adventure and offered a visceral experience of *the void* that will remain with me for as long as I breathe. Bagging the *High Laggans* with Chris in preparation for a retreat on the Holy Ilse was actually a great honour. Wandering along five of the South Cluanie Ridge, then bagging **Ciste Dhubh** and **Aonach Mheadhoid** the next day with Janine were very special journeys indeed along high ridges, which remain almost indescribable, apart from the great big silly smiles emblazoned on our faces for most of the two days. My three-hundred mile, seven-hour round trip to climb **Spidean Mialach** and **Gleouraich** during the rut was maybe a bit over the top, but it was a great day out that sorted out a lot of difficult stuff in my head. My discovery of the mighty **Ben Cruachan** with Chris, going up **Breariach** for the fifth time, camping out on the Great Moss in a blizzard, completing everything east of Glen Shee, not to mention driving to lots of lovely places in the campervan with Shona, in particular to the Uists and Barra. High points indeed!

My commitment to Buddhism was sealed when in May I attended public teachings given by His Holiness the Seventeenth Karmapa in London. Throughout the year I studied texts and visited Scottish Lamas for counsel, and in September spent a week on a meditation retreat with Lama Yeshe Rinpoche on the Holy Island at Lamlash Bay on Arran at his *Centre for World Peace and Health*. During the year, I also had a number of what might best be described as *spiritual* experiences in the mountains. I have always taken my journeys up mountains as opportunities for reflection and mind training, and I believe I learned much. In the wake of the retreat on Holy Island I was nevertheless confronted by my most unpleasant demons, my most inaccessible emotions and hateful resentments. This is, I discovered, in a very deep sense exactly what cancer is, what the gnawing of resentment does to a body, *kankeren*, and which

I may have put to rest, to a degree at least, upon writing it out in Dutch, sunbathing in the snow at the summit of the most accessible **_An Socach_**.

Before all this, during the first months of the year, I introduced an additional element to my diet. A plant extract with a reputation for miracle cures, which allegedly works by rebooting a body's immune system. At the start of the year I felt ill and I was in quite a dark place, I could discern something nasty in my chest, near where scans had identified an enlarged lymph node, I awoke every morning with a sickly feeling. Perhaps I was still working through the side effects of the medication I had decided no longer to take, but I was sure also I could feel the disease gnawing away inside. Kankeren. At the end of the year, all of these feelings were gone. I do not believe as some most certainly do, that this oil of hemp is a miracle cure for every ailment under the sun, but I do believe that it helped maintain the general health of my body in such a way that the spread of the disease was slowed down quite considerably.

In the midst of which my complicated ideas about medical science and how this was related to my relationship with my parents was being severely tested by real life, while being held in suspension by ordinary conversations and my refusal to know any of the knowledge supplied by medical science. My deliberate ignorance of blood values and scan results and so forth released me from a great deal of stress and freed up my mind for much else, making possible many different ways of thinking about almost everything. Most importantly perhaps, not giving the disease _solidity_.

Neither I nor any of my nearest and dearest knew what was going to happen next, my health appeared to be stable, there were no obvious signs on the outside that the cancer was spreading. So this was just another new year, with nothing expected to change much when the number of the year turned and January began.

As a wedding present we had been given use of a cottage over Christmas and New Year. Staying here was the perfect end to this most wonderful year; for reflecting upon previous turns of the year, and preparing for whatever was to come next. The cottage nestled near the Braes of Glen Livet, underneath a little hill called The Bochel, a variant of _Buachaille_ or shepherd; it is classified as a Marilyn, a hill with at least one hundred and fifty meters or five hundred feet drop on all sides. We climbed The Bochel from the south through a very old plantation as cattle surveyed us from a distance. It was cold and crystal clear. The northern fringes of the Cairngorms held my attention in the background with white shimmering light and cloud dissolving perspective. The Braes in the foreground, great shallow bowls where waters gather from springs high up on the moor, bubbling out of the ground, and destined to become one of several of the better whiskies in the land.

When we arrived at the cottage in my old Volvo, after an uneventful run over The Lecht, where there was less snow than expected, the world was crisp, the colours of autumn desiccated into the ground after a prolonged period without rain; watercourses and boggy places were now beginning to crunch with frost as temperatures dropped. Apart from our trip up The Bochel, we walked every day through an ancient birch forest alive with songbirds, dripping with lichens and mosses, concealing burrows and dens. The birches mixed with other species; rowans, oaks and alders along riverbanks and in boggy places among the trees. We found paths round the woods and up little hills, past fields of frisky heifers and along the edges of burns.

Around the third evening it began to snow, thick blizzards piling in from the northeast with a determination in their manner from the start, as if they already knew they were going be here for a while. We had no reason to go anywhere, as much food as we needed, a shed full of logs for the fire and the warmth of our love. During the next days, we walked through the woods during many varieties of snowfall as their character transformed and snow piled up to create great lumps of white held aloft by undergrowth. This was a magical experience. We had always managed from time to time to take ourselves away from the bustle of crowds and of others' desires and expectations, to celebrate our special relationship. But there was something extra special about this visit to The Bochel. More time away being together, somewhere peaceful, beautiful and interesting, with our secret intact, *that this love between us exists with such vigour; that we are actually here*. That I was still alive at all was always a bonus; that I was now feeling better than I did as the start of the year was miraculous. Our wanderings in the snow as it whipped past from the northeast to refill the Breas of Glenlivet were exhilarating, reinvigorating and enriching, marking the new year more deeply than any ritual. The sun disappears over the ridge of the hill at a different point each day until it reaches its most southerly point, after which it rises again every day slightly further north and the year begins once more.

We have not always actually been together at New Year though; the previous year Shona was in Canada meeting her latest grandson, while I pottered and vacillated at home, my only trip into the hills was a failed attempt on ***Stuc a' Chroin*** from Callander. The year before this we were on the Holy Isle on a meditation retreat, with again the year before, Shona in Canada visiting her son. A year earlier we were at Samye Ling monastery at Eskdalemuir, on a teaching retreat led by Ken Holmes, who was then the monastery's director of studies. Here we met Chris and Chantal for the first time, who along with Shona had long decided to follow the Dharma. Here was when I became so impressed by the discipline of the Dharma, and intrigued by how different this was from the traditional ways of thinking into which I had been schooled, that I decided to listen and learn; henceforth I was determined to do all that was necessary to follow a Buddhist path, to become part of the Sanga.

Since the first New Year after my return from abroad, the turn of the year had nevertheless always had an edge to it. For it was here when we most immediately learned what the anti-cancer, hormone suppressing medication actually does. It not only does the thing that makes oncologists happy, it produces side effects and creates collateral damage in a male sexed body, which cumulatively and quite inexorably change the body into something unnatural, almost monstrous, within which it becomes increasingly difficult to live any kind of ordinary existence, and in the company of which its responses become stilted, its motivations appear odd and its reactions often inappropriate. Before New Year 2014 we had no idea such a thing would happen to us, afterwards gradually, we began to develop coping strategies. This was why also always hereafter we were so reluctant to accept the Decapeptyl injection when the oncologists wanted to give it, why we always waited until the very last moment, even knowing that the medication would do its work, that the growth of the disease would be checked once more, while the pains and discomforts in my body declined and we would have to learn again to cope with its hideous side effects on our lives.

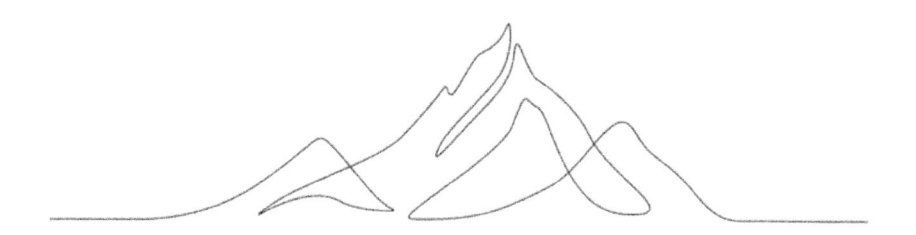

# Epilogue

The two young couples sitting at a table in the middle of the café remained self-absorbed, discussing in rather less than muted tones what they hoped from the future after their university studies were complete. At the centre table, a more elderly foursome, arguing the toss about anything and everything, thoroughly enjoying their own company, impervious to their surroundings, rather dominating proceedings, but not really getting up anybody's nose, glad of this enforced stop for soup and banter. At the far side of the room was a German couple, one of whom was pacing up and down, talking animatedly but very correctly on a mobile, trying to negotiate a later flight with *Lufthansa*. Not far off, relaxing on sofas, on the way home from a golfing trip to Machrihanish, half a dozen lads in their late twenties, several still rather the worse for wear and having given up pretending they were not asleep, were not bothered that service was a little slow, so they could catch up. It was warm and welcoming in the café. The proprietrix and her busy staff were making an effort; it was good craic. All present were utterly oblivious to the middle-aged couple in the corner giggling like teenagers and euphemistically talking about oral sex. Only a friendly border collie lying on the floor nearby felt any frisson of their wordplay; he certainly wanted to come over to say hello, but he was under the scrupulous control of a family conversing inaudibly, sitting round a low table beside the window with the best view of the watery conflagration beyond. Outside, the temperature was just above freezing, with lumpy rain hammering past horizontally on a south west storm. In this weather nobody was going anywhere in a hurry.

The café was situated on a slope at the west edge of Tarbert on the Mull of Kintyre. Just like all the rest, the middle-aged couple had stopped here because it was the first place they had come across that was open and offered hot food. After parking their car, they ran through piercing lumps of water, hoping to find warmth, because their car's heating system was not working very well. Actually, it was not working at all, so they had wrapped travel rugs and fleecy blankets around their legs as insulation, more in hope than expectation; they too sought information about how badly the storm was likely to impede their progress. Like many city dwellers, they were on their way home from celebrating New Year out of the city, which had become a jamboree for tourists from all over the world rather than a party enjoyed by residents as it had once been. They had instead enjoyed three nights on a farm just south of Campbeltown with views over the Clyde Sea to Arran and the Ayrshire Coast, and then a night in the honeymoon suite of an hotel a little further north, owned by an old friend of the man and closed to guests for the winter, looking over the boiling Atlantic to Jura, Islay and the north coast of Ireland. They had again lingered in bed that morning, experimenting, overcoming barriers, and had left rather later than they hoped, inventing euphemisms.

That morning was the third they had found it in themselves to *fall in love with cancer,* as they called it. This was becoming much more challenging though, not because the disease had suddenly flared up, but because they had decided about a month earlier and for the first time to take the medication prescribed to manage it, thereby curtailing what had hitherto been the most sustained period of passion either of them had ever known. They already lived with the possibility that maybe this would be the last new year the two of them would have together. But maybe not, they simply did not know. Despite cancer and being relatively hale and hearty at this particular moment, his recent experience had brought the man back to reality and to the bleak prognosis that had come with the diagnosis; that unless he took the medication immediately, he would only live a year further, and that even if he did, he would likely be dead in three. She was in a state of shock, completely dissociated from what seemed to be happening and yet joining in the fun, finding words to make light of their situation.

When they paid for their meal, the proprietrix said that they would be lucky if they were able to continue their journey, for she had just seen a film on the television of swans swimming along the main street in the town below. A storm surge had combined with the high spring tide and pushed the sea over the harbour wall. By the time they drove through the town though, high water had passed, the swans confined once again within the harbour. They were able to continue on their way in relatively good spirits, despite their broken heating system and deteriorating weather, along Loch Fyne to Lochgilphead and Inveraray, over the Rest and be Thankful, down Loch Lomond, through Glasgow and finally back east to Edinburgh where they lived.

During the journey home, while reflecting on the previous few days, just before their discovery of what the medication actually does, the woman recalled that the man had been able, earlier in the evening, to find the right words to review the previous year to his friends on Facebook. While the two of them had been sitting in front of a log fire, with the wind howling round the farm buildings waiting for the year to turn, he concentrated on writing out his story on social media. He described the previous year as one of the most difficult years of his life, but also the most beautiful. Despite selling his business, enduring the agony of divorce, saying farewell to his beloved cats and many good friends, giving up the best work he had ever had and moving away from a lovely little country where they join up their thinking and know how to organise stuff sensibly. At the same time, the cancer had let him experience directly the power of the international messenger community, from which he had received a huge amount of support from cities all over the world, while learning many lessons about love and friendship. But most importantly, he said, he had reconnected with his old friend, who he had met a year earlier at a messenger event in Edinburgh. Even after some thirty-five years, a spark had still been present and they had worked together during the latter part of this year to turn it into a roaring fire.

This had, he wrote, been the second year he believed he would not live to completion. He had gotten to the end of the previous year, he claimed, using sheer bloody-mindedness and determination; during this year he had learned finally to accept the help and support of many kind people. These people would, he said, know who they were, and he thanked them sincerely for supporting the beautiful journey he was now on, declaring that he did not know if he would make it to the end of the coming year, but then asking rhetorically whether anybody really did. He had cancer, yes, but he felt more alive now than ever before. Finally, he wished love and peace to all and signed off.

As he wrote, she had been wondering quietly why, tucked up in a solid stone building miles from anywhere with a howling gale outside, having eaten a tasty stew of organic lamb mince, polished off a bottle of good Burgundy, lounging in front of a roaring fire, in a room lit only by candles and in the company of the love of his life, he was making no moves, apparently untouched by her hints and desires, unaffected by the pheromones inevitably wafting his way, much more interested in getting his words in the right order. She knew that it was always important for him to write, particularly now with this cancer, and she tried always to respect his space, but this, she thought, was surely a special occasion, a time for romance and lovemaking.

Then later in bed, they discovered why. His penis would not work and his libido had vanished. Nothing would get it going, there were no feelings of passion, no stimuli that would coax them out. Only shame, fear, embarrassment and rage. Their anger was different; she was afraid that here was another man rejecting her just at the moment when she most wanted him. She had also known that sooner or later something like this was bound to happen, so she did not quite know what to do with her own desire. She did not want simply to put herself out there, worried that if she did, it would make things worse for him by reminding him of his impotence, that she would therefore feel guilty, not only for making him feel bad about himself, but also, like many women of her generation, for having any sexuality at all.

Their initial reaction was predominately confusion, unable to fathom why his penis was not doing what it had most successfully been doing only twenty-four hours earlier and continuously during their previous months together. He was absolutely terrified that this was the beginning of the end, afraid that he would never again feel the marvellous magic *between-them,* the inexorable pull of desire; the frisson of anticipation nor the building to consummation, genuinely scared that he would never again smell the juices flow, never again experience their beautiful congress, never feel her sex encapsulating his, pulling him inside her, feel her breathing rise, her heartbeat race and her body writhe beneath him as he kissed and thrust and caressed.

---

They had now discovered the practical meanings of the medical euphemisms, *erectile disfunction* and *reduced libido*. These were the most profound and debilitating side effects of the medication, which they had decided reluctantly a month earlier for the first time that the man should take. A three-monthly cycle of *Decapeptyl*, which would switch off the mechanisms in his brain that regulate the production of all hormones in his body. This would support and enhance a course of focused radiotherapy to his prostate that was due to begin in several months. The medics had it all worked out. Despite this cancer being aggressive and malignant, it would respond well and probably remain dormant for the time to come, although how long was not easy to predict. In the meantime, they had now to live together as partners but without his libido.

This had hit the man harder than he was prepared to admit; he was not finding the words to talk about it; she was often left alone to reflect upon what had happened. He hated this sudden inability to experience sexual attraction, while still feeling love and affection, and he was unable to talk about it with any clarity despite his capacity for language. And despite his generally sunny attitude to life, this was where he lied, pretending it was more manageable than it was. He detested the emotional condition he suffered because of this medication; he could not answer questions about how he felt, partly because it was just too bizarre, he could not comprehend that certain ideas should always have some attached *frisson* by virtue of chemistry alone, that all his feelings of lust were now gone, whatever words we use for them. For a long time, he was quite lonely, trying to remember *how to do* lust, *how to show* affection and, in many cases, *how to do* ordinary human interaction, which is often motivated by ordinary levels of testosterone. Sometimes his social responses were just inappropriate because he had forgotten how to do them properly.

They had been told by an oncologist only a few weeks before their experience at Campbelltown, quite precisely, that although he may not (rather surprisingly) have experienced any substantial loss of sexual function with the first drug he had taken against the disease, *Bicalutamide*, a female hormone analogue that slots into testosterone receptors thereby switching them off, once the *Decapeptyl* kicked in, he certainly would know what this meant, what the medication would do to his desires, penis and libido. He got it into his head too that this particularly salient departure from normality, was the first sign of the cancer escaping into the tissues surrounding his prostate, the first indication that he really was going to die.

More distressing though was the discovery that the only medical way of holding the disease at bay was worse than the disease itself. Managing prostate cancer means in the first instance the desexualisation of a male sexed body; shutting down its endocrine system and removing from it as much testosterone as possible, for without testosterone, prostate cancer will be held at bay, at least for a while. This is described in the medical literature as *chemical castration* and remains the goal of most prostate cancer management.

Whatever the reason these drugs are given to a body, their effects are not benign; it is a serious departure from the natural function of a male body to have its entire endocrine system shut down, to have its temperature regulation processes knocked completely off balance, to have muscle to fat ratios change radically, very similar to what happens to female sexed bodies during the menopause, to watch his body become desexed, desexualised, emasculated, his genitals atrophied, to become motivationally challenged, emotionally bereft, and after two years or so to expect to have minerals leech away from his bones, endangering osteoporosis, random fractures and spinal cord compression.

Their forays into euphemisms were just the start, only the beginning of their efforts to make light of the experience of this depletion of the endogenous chemicals that normally furnish a male body with its desires, emotions and motivations. The very start of the learning processes that would henceforth lead the man to the conclusion that his motivations could be created now only by the power of his mind, and that most of what he had regarded hitherto without the least critical doubt, as freely willed thought and activity was nothing but the effects of chemicals. This gave him deeper pause now to reflect than before the diagnosis; had his whole life been a series of chemical reactions? And if so, how could it be said that any of this was meaningful? What could meaning *actually be* when everything is a big complex chemical reaction?

Nobody reaches the age of fifty-something without accumulating baggage. During the days prior to their discovery, while his sex remained undamaged and as they walked in nearby fields and woods, they had talked through these things. Such conversations are never easy for anybody; as their relationship had developed, it had intermittently encountered similarities with relationships from the past. It seemed that they had both been through similar experiences with others, that they had created similar patterns in their emotional lives, come to terms with similar issues, similar, but at the same time very different, most significantly because the man had no children, while the woman had three, all of whom were now grown up with successful lives of their own.

In the past, both the man and the woman had been pulled into negative spirals of resentment and projection, but now each was genuinely more circumspect with relationships, mindful of any *other*, able to give each other space and time, so as just *to be with their own feelings* without threat, to be supportive and kind, to listen and talk honestly about everything, or to let it go, as and when it happened, while not taking things too seriously or projecting stuff from some strange past onto a wonderful present, endeavouring always to make light of life with optimism and balance.

Maybe it was the cancer, or more probably, the bleak prognosis, that encouraged them to be more careful in their attitudes towards each other, maybe it was just coincidence that their different past experiences had combined together to create such obvious opportunities for personal growth. There was however something else, which seemed very important. They had been good friends as teenagers, but had *never* consummated this. If they had realised then just how secure their friendship was, just how fiercely the spark could be ignited, just how rare and special such a feeling is, they would surely have found some way to consummate their passion before now, and would never have gone off to do with their lives what they had done, never allowed their adolescent egos and hormones to power them into difficult relationships with others with whom they would never have been able to learn how to develop mature emotional responses.

Hindsight of course provides the clearest view of everything, assuming of course it is applied with the appropriate intellectual rigour. Among many other principles and assumptions, the discipline of *history* has no choice but to look backwards. Literally, to engage in hindsight. But looking back can also create the most useless, the most painful, the most intellectually barren, the most psychologically stultifying and existentially stupid of all questions. What if things had been different? What if we had met again ten years previously? Or twenty? What if we had never got involved with so and so or such and such? What if we had never done this or that or the next thing? What if we could go back in time and do it all again without making the same mistakes? What if one of us had not gotten cancer at such a young an age? What if we were eighteen again? Fooling around on the way home from the pub, larking about, tentatively reaching out and giggling as we discovered where the physical border between us lay, where we could touch each other? Whether we could clasp hands? Feel the warmth and movement of the other's body, learn how the other reacts and responds? Maybe hug or embrace? Or even kiss? And then what?

What if we could live our lives again in such a way that we were not subjected to guilt nor consumed with regret, despite not actually regretting quite a lot of what we had in fact done with our lives? After all, what is there to regret about bringing up three beautiful, successful children? Or building bicycle wheels for a nation, speaking up when necessary on behalf of the international messenger community, and travelling all over the world to misbehave with your mates in cities on bikes? But seriously. *What if we really were able to return with knowledge that might enable us to avoid the pains of being alive*, to be free of *all this suffering*, and to know something of how to alleviate it for all? To know how to experience the beauty of love, the precious gift of human existence with clarity and without spoiling it with memories based on attachments to fictitious versions of ourselves and all the imagined others in the world around, who we always held out hope would surely recognise us for who we *really are*? What if we had been able to grow up without the tribulations of *ego* or *self* or *identity* or some other solidified form of being? Maybe we could have learned to live without these most difficult illusions? And been able to teach others?

In their wisest moments they were able to tell themselves that without their separate pasts, they would never have learned what was necessary for them to be able to come together again as they had. Although this was much more difficult for them to accept mentally, they had also to concede that if were it not for the cancer, they would probably not have come together at all, because cancer hammers home the precariousness of life in such a way as to encourage going for it, doing stuff while it is still possible. The man claimed repeatedly that he would be prepared to live his life over and over again, in every gruesome detail, watching the same spider in the same window at moonlight, *knowing that if he did so, it would culminate with this love*. He could happily clear his mind of all these *what if* questions because he knew that now, at this moment of his life, no matter how severe his condition, no matter how little time he had left, no matter what had happened in the past nor what the future might bring, he was in love with the most wonderful, the most beautiful woman in the world and was making passionate love with his best friend.

For what if they had got together earlier, without this cancer? Maybe none of this would have happened at all, maybe they would have spoiled the love with impatience, indifference or disrespect, allowed petty squabbles over stuff to destroy its compassion. Maybe one or other of them would have taken the other for granted, become lazy in their habits and bored the relationship into stagnation, or had affairs. But at the same time, they sometimes longed for that time machine to transport them back to the nineteen seventies with their middle-aged wisdom intact, where they might have dared do things differently as they fooled around on the way home from the pub. Because, after all, who knows, maybe if they had started younger, they would have learned to do things otherwise, more carefully, under very different circumstances, which they would have been more easily able clearly to perceive and understand? Maybe even he would never have come down with the disease? Active minds will of course never cease to ask such questions of active imaginations; the living, material, reality of the present is nevertheless where we must always, by absolute necessity, start on any journey anywhere.

They had come sincerely to believe that despite their residual adolescent consciousness, beneath their teenage insecurities and confusions, they trusted that one day their love would find a way to express itself, that even if their desires were taking them off in all sorts of directions, their bodies already knew each other and had agreed to wait until they were old enough *to know how to get it right*.

It was so obvious sometimes; *their bodies fitted together, always knowing this was going to happen, quite simply because they had been here before*. But what at that moment neither of them knew was that no matter how much they made silly remarks about special kisses, hoping that nobody in the vicinity would be remotely interested in what they were on about, that the destruction of his sexuality, the atrophy of his genitals and eventual damage to his ribcage and spine, would be responsible for so much more besides; that their dance could only work with both dancing. The magic of the *between-us* is such a fundamental binding force, the invisible unspoken power that holds together so much, both throughout society at large and in the minutiae of personal relations, that when one half is taken away, holding it together becomes such very, very hard work.

But they never gave up. Never. It simply did not occur to them. Not on their own love nor on love and compassion for everybody and anybody, an attitude which led them to become inspirational to many, which in turn inspired them to continue never giving up themselves, to celebrate in everything they did this precious gift of being alive and breathing. Sitting in that café in Tarbert, people watching and having fun, surrounded by the blessed ordinariness of life, by random travellers seeking refuge and lunch as a vicious Atlantic storm raged outside, they had not yet encountered their most profound ignorance, that from this moment forward, despite their linguistic tomfoolery, their relationship would never quite be the same again.

# Bibliography

Works influential, cited, referred to or described

Akong Tulku Rinpoche, (2005) Restoring the balance: Dzlalendara Publishing, Eskdalemuir.

Cisney, Vernon W. (2018), Deleuze and Derrida, Difference and the Power of the Negative: Edinburgh University Press, Edinburgh.

Deleuze, Gilles (1983) Nietzsche and Philosophy: The Athlone Press, London.

Gray, Muriel (1991) The First Fifty, Munro bagging without a beard: Mainstream publishing company, Edinburgh.

Gunn, Neil (1986) The Atom of Delight: Polygon, Edinburgh.

Irigaray, Luce (2013) In the beginning She Was: Bloomsbury, London and New York.

Irigaray, Luce (2017) To Be Born: Palgrave Macmillan, Cham, Switzerland.

Kalanithi, Paul (2016) When Breath Becomes Air: The Bodley Head, Penguin Random House, London.

The Karmapa, Ogyen Trinley Dorje (2017) Interconnected: Wisdom Publications, Somerville MA.

Mitchell, David (2010) The Thousand Autumns of Jacob de Zoet: Hodder & Stoughton, London.

Nietzsche, Friedrich (1968) Twilight of the idols and The Antichrist: Penguin, Harmondsworth.

Nietzsche, Friedrich (1974) The Gay Science: Vintage Books, New York.

Painting, Andrew (2021) Regeneration, the rescue of wild land: Birlinn, Edinburgh.

Scott, Bill (2011) The Buttercup: Leghorn Books Ltd, Alnwick.

Scottish Mountaineering Club (2013) The Munros, (3rd Edition 4th revision): Scottish Mountaineering Trust, Glasgow.

Shepherd, Nan (2011) The Living Mountain: Canongate Books, Edinburgh.

Shorto, Russell (2005) The Island at the Centre of the World: Vintage Books, New York.

Welsh, Irvine (1994) Trainspotting: Minerva Press, London.

Printed in Great Britain
by Amazon